Marketing Modernisms

The Architecture and Influence of Charles Reilly

PETER RICHMOND

LIVERPOOL UNIVERSITY PRESS

First published 2001 by
Liverpool University Press
4 Cambridge Street
Liverpool
L69 7ZU

British Library Cataloguing-in-Publication Data
A British Library CIP record is available.

ISBN 0-85323-756-5 cased
ISBN 0-85323-766-2 paperback

Typeset in Minion with Frutiger display by
Koinonia, Bury, Lancashire
Printed in Great Britain by
The Alden Press, Oxford

For my mother Jo
and in memory of my father and sister
George and Barbara

Contents

Illustrations

Acknowledgements

I would like to thank Professor Simon Pepper for his guidance and many suggestions throughout the course of my research, together with the late Professor David Thistlewood. My thanks also go to the following: Dr Stephen Bowe; Matthew Clough, University Art Gallery, Liverpool; Karen Howard, Maritime Archive and Library, Merseyside Maritime Museum; Sue McCann, Wirral News Group; Eileen Organ, Liverpool Record Office, Liverpool Libraries and Information Services; Joseph Sharples, National Museums and Galleries on Merseyside; Janice Taylor, Wirral Archives Service; Dr Maureen Watry, Head of Archives and Special Collections, University of Liverpool Library; the staff of the University of Liverpool's Sydney Jones and Harold Cohen Libraries, with particular thanks to the staff of the University Archive and Special Collections; and the Architectural Library of the University of Newcastle upon Tyne. I am also grateful to my editor, Rowan Davies, and Robin Bloxsidge and Andrew Kirk at Liverpool University Press.

Picture Acknowledgements

The publishers are grateful to the following for permission to reproduce copyright material:

Liverpool Record Office, Liverpool Libraries and Information Service for Figure 9; the RIBA Library Photographs Collection for Figure 27; Metropolitan Borough of Wirral, Archives Service for Figures 36–42; Birkenhead News and Wirral News for Figures 33–35; Board of Trustees of the National Museums and Galleries on Merseyside (Merseyside Maritime Museum/Stewart Bale Archive) for Figure 17; Liverpool University Archives for Figures 4, 6, 11, 43–45; Liverpool University Art Collection for Figures 1, 2, 12–14, 46.

Every effort has been made to trace copyright holders and obtain permission for reproduction. The publisher would be pleased to be notified of any omissions.

Preface

It was Sir John Betjeman who noted that 'History must not be written with bias, and both sides must be given, even if there is only one side.' Betjeman's wry comment on the problems facing the writers of history in their quest for objectivity has become further complicated by recent developments in how history is identified and reported. The old emphasis on a sequential history of facts and figures has been replaced by a Postmodernist interpretation in which history is seen as a series of discontinuous and fragmentary 'histories'. The Modernist view of historical analysis is founded upon 'the establishment of a discrete break or cut between a past (the time about which the historian writes) and a present (the time of writing)',[1] and it becomes something which may be constantly retranscribed. Previous histories are therefore up for reinterpretation, and whereas in the past writers of architectural history have looked to a canon of architects and master works as a means of ciphering events, the Postmodernist view denies all such certainties. The logical conclusion to such a theory may mean that we arrive at a stage at which if, as Charles Jencks puts it, 'meaning is not fixed once and for all it is therefore nonsensical or irrelevant (a reaction not unknown in the twentieth century), then we just remain uncomprehending.' Jencks goes on to put forward a case for an interpretation of history in which alternative histories 'point to a common centre of moral experience. This centre where meanings converge however, is not a place of mutual exclusion; no one set of meanings or myth is sufficient... or even final.'[2]

The changes wrought by Postmodernist theory in the means by which we write and view history have an impact upon the examination of a figure such as Charles Herbert Reilly (1874–1948), if only as a means of gauging why he has been marginalized by conventional writers of Modernist history. When such writers have considered him at all, they have compartmentalized him as an architectural educationalist, a founding father of town planning, a self-

1 B. Readings, *Introducing Lyotard: Art and Politics*, Routledge, London, 1991, p. 58
2 C. Jencks, 'History as Myth', in C. Jencks and G. Baird (eds), *Meaning in Architecture*, Barrie and Jenckins, London, 1970, p. 265.

publicist or a stylistic opportunist. The first draft of this book was written in 1996 and 1997 when I was a research student at Liverpool University, and was submitted as a doctoral thesis. The impetus for the research arose out of previous work I had undertaken for my Master's degree on one of Reilly's former students, Herbert Rowse, and his impact upon the interwar cityscape of Liverpool. The interconnected nature of Liverpool society and the relationship between Reilly and his students prompted me to look further into Reilly's role, both in the development of what came to be termed 'the Liverpool Manner' and in the establishment of the so-called 'Reilly Myth'.

In attempting to outline the aims and objectives of this book, it is perhaps wise to start by outlining what they are not. First, I am not attempting to provide a critical biography of Reilly; while I discuss a large proportion of his professional life in its various aspects, equally I omit whole areas – principally his early life and university days, together with his personal and family life – which would no doubt be crucial to any biography of the man. Second, I do not claim to provide a comprehensive survey of either Reilly's architectural work, which was relatively limited, nor his journalism, which was very extensive. In writing this book, I have aimed first to locate Reilly within the context of an established body of work by examining the development of architectural theory in the first half of this century, and second to investigate Reilly's role in the broader context of the national and international stylistic movements of the period and in the narrower confines of Liverpool's cultural and social life, a milieu that both informed Reilly's theories and illustrated their evolution.

The conventional Modernist histories have, as I have already mentioned, tended either to ignore or to marginalize figures such as Reilly. Pevsner, in books such as *Pioneers of Modern Design*,[3] completely overlooked developments in Britain during the period in which Reilly was starting to become active. Reilly does not fit neatly into Pevsner's general thesis that British design stagnated during the early decades of the century, only to be reawakened by the influx of European Modernist émigrés to the country during the 1930s. As David Thistlewood notes,

> Pevsner found little to celebrate in British architecture within the period which constituted Reilly's career: Reilly is thus identified with the supposed misinterpretation of the Arts and Crafts legacy and a number of other failings:

---

3 N. Pevsner, *Pioneers of Modern Design: From William Morris to Walter Gropius*, Penguin Books, Harmondsworth, 1975.

a failure to be alive to advanced European architectural thought, a failure to bridge the Atlantic, to internationalise, and to embrace the white cube.[4]

Where Reilly is acknowledged, he has generally been overplayed as the dominant figure in the development of architectural education, as in Robert Macleod's *Style and Society*. Here Reilly's skill in promoting the Liverpool School has led Macleod to produce a somewhat unbalanced account of the development of Beaux-Arts teaching in Britain, to the total exclusion of the Glasgow School. Alternatively, Reilly is viewed either as a peripheral figure in the Edwardian era, as in Alastair Service's *Edwardian Architecture*, or as a figure of no further consequence during the period of the development of Modernism beyond having acted as the head of a major school of architecture which produced a number of British Modernists, as in Anthony Jackson's *The Politics of Architecture*. It is in the histories of the development of town planning, such as Myles Wright's *Lord Leverhulme's Unknown Venture*, that Reilly has been most widely acknowledged and his relationship with William Lever, central to an understanding of so much of Reilly's early career, has been explored in some detail. On the whole, however, Reilly is generally not included, or is only scantly dealt with, in the major reviews of Modernism. The reasons for the relative lack of attention given to Reilly by conventional Modernist historians have been described thus by Thistlewood:

> because neither his own buildings nor the products of his School have exhibited requisite evidence of modernist consistency. There are occasional glimpses – in his work and that of his students – of a formalism recognisable as 'international modernist', but the intermittence has been a fact with which to condemn him.[5]

Reilly has received more attention from historians of American architecture. Leland Roth, in his account of the architectural firm McKim, Mead and White, acknowledges Reilly's links with the major east coast architectural firms and gives him much of the credit for the introduction of American Beaux-Arts theory into Britain. A more balanced account of the arrival of American Beaux-Arts is provided by Leonard Eaton in *American Architecture*

4 D. Thistlewood, 'The Liverpool School of Architecture under Charles Reilly', paper read to a study day attached to the exhibition 'Charles Reilly and the Liverpool School of Architecture 1904–1933', Walker Art Gallery, Liverpool, 9 November 1996.

5 Thistlewood, 'The Liverpool School of Architecture'. See also D. Thistlewood, 'Modernism with Ancestry', in 'Liverpool School of Architecture Centenary Supplement', *The Architects' Journal*, 11 May 1995, pp. 59–66.

Comes of Age, in which individuals such as Burnet and cities such as Glasgow and London are considered alongside Liverpool as important centres for the importation of American ideas. This reassessment of both Liverpool's and Reilly's roles in the promotion of Beaux-Arts in the context of other important British centres has been further developed by Alan Powers and Gavin Stamp.[6]

From a local perspective Reilly has unsurprisingly received a good deal more attention. Reilly's influence within the context of the University of Liverpool is dealt with by Thomas Kelly in *For Advancement of Learning*, in which his membership of groups such as the 'New Testament' is discussed. In accounts such as Quentin Hughes's *Seaport* and *Before the Bauhaus*, or Mary Bennett's *The Art Sheds 1894–1905*, Reilly is defined, upon his appointment to the Roscoe Chair in 1904, as representing a sea change in Liverpool's aesthetic history between the Arts-and-Crafts-dominated ideology of the late nineteenth century and the Beaux-Arts of the early twentieth century. Similarly, John Willett's *Art in a City* gives a good deal of emphasis to Reilly's pioneering role in this respect. From a more specialized perspective Roderick Bisson's history of the Sandon Studios group, *The Sandon Studios Society and the Arts*, provides an interesting, albeit largely anecdotal, account of Reilly's involvement in one of the most important cultural groupings in the city in the early years of the twentieth century. Similarly, W. S. MacCunn's *Bluecoat Chambers* looks at Reilly's involvement in the establishment of the country's first arts centre from a more critical perspective than most local history accounts. Other investigations into Reilly's cultural activities, such as Grace Goldie's *The Liverpool Repertory Theatre 1911–1934*, provide an insight into his ability to operate within the complex cultural web of the city.

Despite the above accounts, Reilly has remained, until relatively recently, untouched by any major critical reassessments. Alan Power's thesis on architectural education in Britain[7] has gone some way in placing Reilly's role as an architectural educationalist within the context of the rival schools in London and Glasgow, and has helped redress the balance within the orthodox view, largely established by Reilly's own accounts of his role in the promotion of Beaux-Arts ideology. It is the research undertaken by Christopher Crouch, which examines the design influences operating in Liverpool around the turn

6 G. Stamp. 'Glasgow, America and the Beaux-Arts', paper read to a study day attached to the exhibition 'Charles Reilly and the Liverpool School of Architecture 1904–1933', Walker Art Gallery, Liverpool, 9 November 1996.

7 A. Powers, 'Architectural Education in Britain 1880–1914', PhD thesis, Cambridge University, 1982.

of the century, that has done most to recontextualize Reilly's role.[8] Crouch, by establishing that Beaux-Arts theory had originated in Liverpool some ten years earlier than previous accounts had stated, has forced a reassessment of the orthodox belief that Reilly ushered the Beaux-Arts in to Liverpool following his appointment in 1904.

By examining the design initiatives in the city from the perspective of their illustration through cultural attitudes and processes, Crouch provides a break with many conventional approaches to architectural history, looking at the architectural systems operating within the city as opposed to concentrating simply upon architectural form. As Crouch himself puts it, 'It is the dialogue between architectural style and ideological motivation that interests me...'[9] It has been my intention in this book to take a similar approach to that of Crouch and, by so doing, to unearth Reilly's particular role in the cultural and architectural processes operating within Liverpool and beyond. As I have been working in an area closely related to that of Crouch, and have shared with him the same supervisor in Professor Simon Pepper, there has arisen what might be termed a community of ideas concerning developments in the School of Architecture and the city of Liverpool from the late nineteenth century to after the Second World War. This book therefore partly seeks to build on Crouch's post-1914 theories, and further attempts to trace the knock-on effect for an understanding of Reilly's subsequent career. In addition, I have sought to follow Reilly's cultural influences in Liverpool via his various acquaintances and alliances in order to disentangle a number of the local myths surrounding the establishment of the Bluecoat Society of Arts and the Liverpool Repertory Theatre (later the Liverpool Playhouse).

The exhibition 'Charles Reilly and the Liverpool School of Architecture 1904–1933' held at the Walker Art Gallery in Liverpool in 1996 went some way to realign our notion of Reilly's impact upon the architectural world. By examining the work of a number of Reilly's students – in the form of drawings, films and other ephemera – alongside his own work, we can trace some of the common threads in their respective careers. If Reilly has been largely forgotten in the period since his death, it is perhaps due to the very nature of his career, centred as it was upon teaching and journalism. These are largely ephemeral activities when weighed against the more enduring monuments of a large body of built work, something that Reilly did not achieve. While his students went to every corner of the world building in the Liverpool

8   C. Crouch, 'Design Initiatives in Liverpool 1881–1914', PhD thesis, University of Liverpool, 1992.
9   Crouch, 'Design Initiatives in Liverpool', p. 9.

Manner, they are now remembered in their own right rather than for their earlier connections with Reilly. Reilly's reputation rests largely, therefore, upon surviving articles, letters and books, together with the handful of buildings that he produced throughout the course of his career. The archive of his papers held at Liverpool University contains an account of his evolutionary (rather than revolutionary) impact on architectural theory in the first half of this century. Reilly's ability to negotiate and promote a complex range of stylistic theories and cultural developments, locally, nationally and internationally – in short, his marketing of modernisms – is the central theme of this book. I have attempted to explore the means by which he achieved this, together with some of the consequences of his initiatives (vis à vis an appreciation of his equally important skills in the manufacture of the Reilly Myth). For every layer I have peeled back, no doubt I have contributed another, for as Jencks notes, 'Architects make architecture, historians make history and what they both make is myth.'[10]

10   Jencks, 'History as Myth', p. 265.

1 Liverpool Circa 1900

Liverpool: a place which, of all cities and towns in the British Empire, is surpassed only by the metropolis in magnitude, wealth and importance: and which, in the quick yet solid growth of its commercial greatness, surpasses even the metropolis itself.[1]

The rise of Liverpool, from a small fishing village consisting of a few wattle and daub houses around a muddy creek on the north-west coast of England to the second city of the British Empire, began in 1207 when King John granted Liverpool its charter. His aim was to use Liverpool as part of his plans to conquer Ireland. Development was slow and Chester remained the principal port in the area up until the seventeenth century. However, with the combined effects of the silting up of the River Dee on which Chester stands, the onset of the Industrial Revolution, and the opening up of North America, Liverpool found itself in an important strategic position within the 'triangular trade' in slaves, sugar and cotton. In 1730 Liverpool employed 15 ships in the slave trade: in 1751 that number had increased to 53, in 1760 it was 74, in 1770 it was 96, and in 1792 it was 132.[2]

During the nineteenth century Liverpool consolidated its position as a major port and began to enjoy the spectacular growth which in 1804 led Dr James Currie to describe the town as 'busy, noisy, smoky, money-getting Liverpool'. Capitalizing upon the rapid developments brought about by the Industrial Revolution, Liverpool's merchants imported the raw materials that fed the newly developed industrial towns of the north and the midlands, and subsequently exported finished manufactured goods. Stephenson's opening of the Liverpool to Manchester railway in 1830 acted as a catalyst for even more spectacular growth, both geographically and commercially. As Paul Johnson notes, with

the grandiose project to link Liverpool, Britain's fastest expanding port, to Manchester, the textile-trade boomtown... with passengers drawn... between

1 *Illustrated London News*, Vol. XXV, No. 703, 23 September 1884.
2 K. Marx, *Capital* (first published as *Das Kapital* in 1867), Penguin, Harmondsworth, 1976, p. 924.

two of the world's fastest-growing cities at speeds of 20 miles per hour or more, there could be no doubt that the railway age had begun.[3]

In this symbiotic relationship, Liverpool's merchants grew even richer under the conditions granted in the charter of 1207, which allowed them to charge a tariff on goods moving through the port. This situation eventually moved the Manchester business community to develop the Manchester Ship Canal in the latter part of the nineteenth century, in an attempt to bypass the Port of Liverpool and its tariffs. Population growth was rapidly boosted by migration from nearby Lancashire and Cheshire, but as William Gould and Alan Hodgkiss note,

> the strongest and most distinctive migrant elements were from Ireland, Wales and Scotland. At mid-century barely half of Liverpool's population was Lancashire born: 22.3 per cent were Irish: 5.4 per cent Welsh and 3.7 per cent Scottish born. The potato famine brought some 580,000 Irish in 1846 and 1847, 236,000 of whom subsequently emigrated.[4]

In 1800 the town's population was 77,708, rising to 684,947 by 1899. Many of the immigrants had been driven from their original homes by extreme poverty caused by agricultural failures and the planned highland clearances; the consequence was that much of Liverpool's expanding population lived in wretched conditions. In 1847 the average life expectancy in Liverpool was just 20 years and 5 months. 'Behind the splendid architecture of the Victorian city there existed a continuing drama that involved the struggle for life itself. The Victorian city was, quite simply, a lethal place to live.'[5]

Many of the newcomers to the town were unskilled or had inappropriate skills for their adopted environment. The large pool of unskilled labour did, however, prove useful in the expanding activities of the port, although much of this employment was on a casual basis and provided little security for the employee. In contrast to the paternalistic relationship that existed in many of the mill towns of the same period, Liverpool's employer–employee relationships were brutal.[6] As William Trench and Charles Beard noted in 1871,

---

3   P. Johnson, *The Birth of the Modern: World Society 1815–1830*, Weidenfeld & Nicolson, London, 1991, pp. 582–83.
4   W. Gould and A. G. Hodgkiss (eds), *The Resources of Merseyside*, Liverpool University Press, Liverpool, 1982, p. 7.
5   A. Miller, *Poverty Deserved*, Liverpress, Liverpool, 1988, p. 1.
6   There were, of course, notable exceptions to both sides of this argument. With regard to philanthropic actions by Liverpool 'masters', Lever's worker village at Port Sunlight is a prime

In Liverpool... the intercourse between masters and men, between employers and employed, ceases on the payment of wages. This is a desolate condition of honest striving industry and bodes no good in the social system.[7]

Since much of Liverpool's economy depended upon this casual labour system, and upon the vagaries of weather, season or tide to bring goods to be unloaded, carted or processed, there were always at least two workers available for each job. The constant competition for work inevitably led to divisions within the labour force, which manifested themselves as racial and sectarian tensions. The uncertainty of employment and the constant pressure to find work instilled a strong independent streak in the working-class culture of the port, an independence that was commented upon by numerous visitors to the city. Nathaniel Hawthorne in 1854, on observing a labouring man publicly eating his midday meal on the ferry-boat, noted 'Here a man does not seem to consider what other people will think of his conduct, but whether it suits his convenience to do so and so.'[8]

If the city's poor had developed a sense of independence as a defence against the brutal realities of their lives, the wealthy displayed a similar spirit, but for very different reasons. As Liverpool grew and began to challenge London as a centre for trade and commerce, the merchants looked for symbols to mark their power and prosperity. Early examples can be seen in the squares and terraces they built for their private residences on the ridge above the town overlooking the river. The area that they vacated, by the old port core around the castle and town hall, was developed as a commercial centre.[9]

With the constant expansion of the town, the merchants looked further afield to build ever grander homes on both the Cheshire and Lancashire sides

example. See E. Hubbard and M. Shippobottom, *A Guide to Port Sunlight Village*, Liverpool University Press, Liverpool, 1988. An even earlier example, from 1717, is Bryan Blundell's Blue Coat School for orphans. For a history of the school see R. Hewitt-Jones, 'The Background, Origins and Development of the Blue Coat Schools of Liverpool and Chester, 1700–1834', MA thesis, Liverpool University, 1974.

7 C. Beard and W. Trench speaking in 1871, from *Liverpool Social and Economic Change*, Liverpool City Council Public Relations and Information Service, Liverpool, 1994, p. 2.

8 N. Hawthorne, *The English Notebooks*, New York, 1941. Quoted in T. Lane, *Liverpool: Gateway of Empire*, Lawrence & Wishart, London, 1987, p. 86.

9 For an early account of Liverpool's architectural development, see J. A. Picton, *Architectural History of Liverpool*, Liverpool, 1858; and *Views in Modern Liverpool*, Liverpool, 1864. For accounts of Liverpool's present architectural stock, see *The Buildings of Liverpool*, Liverpool Heritage Bureau, Liverpool, 1978; also P. Browning, *Liverpool Heritage Walks*, Liverpool Planning Department, Liverpool, 1989; and J. Quentin Hughes, *Liverpool: City of Architecture*, Bluecoat Press, Liverpool, 1999.

of the river. On the outer edges of the town quasi-country estates appeared, built by the heads of great shipping companies – men such as Thomas Ismay, whose White Star Line ships were noted for their opulence. His 390-acre estate, complete with a house designed by Norman Shaw – one of the most fashionable architects of the day – was massive in scale and built of the very finest materials. It cost £53,000 to build and was run by 22 indoor and 10 outdoor servants. For the slightly less wealthy, a number of private parks at Fulwood and Grassendale were built, together with Prince's Park. Prince's Park was originally conceived as private parkland for the use of the house owners whose properties fringed it, the sale of the building plots having helped defray the cost of its creation. A similar arrangement was employed for Sefton Park, the city's largest, when it was designed by the French landscape designer André and the Liverpool architect Hornblower between 1867 and 1872.[10] On the fringes of the parks, stretching away to the city, were row upon row of terraces descending in scale and grandeur, housing the chief clerks, clerks, bookkeepers and so on. These terraces wound through each level of the labyrinth of Victorian society, down to the 'two-up, two-down' dwellings of the artisans. For the very poorest in Liverpool, home was in one of the 'courts' or cellar dwellings clustered around the dock area.

As has been noted, much of the commercial development of the town took place around the town hall where the merchants had previously located their combined counting houses and private residences. From the mid-nineteenth century onwards the newly developed office building type began to spread with ever greater degrees of extravagance and in every conceivable style, although Classical was generally preferred. The city's merchants were largely conservative in their architectural taste, following the Neoclassical style of the period; however, there are notable deployments of pioneering techniques, such as Peter Ellis's Oriel Chambers of 1864, and 16 Cook Street of 1866, both of which combined glass and ironwork to startling effect. It is perhaps evidence of this conservatism that these are the only two buildings in the city that Ellis is known to have completed before ridicule and neglect forced him to abandon architecture for good. As the city's confidence grew, private and commercial displays of wealth turned to public philanthropic schemes, reaching high points in the St George's Hall competition of 1839 and the Liverpool Cathedral competition of 1902.

In cultural terms, Liverpool's founding father has often been identified

10   See Hughes, *Liverpool: City of Architecture*, pp. 67 and 93.

as William Roscoe (1753–1831), poet, antiquarian, lawyer, biographer and merchant banker, who played a significant role in the early years of the nineteenth century in establishing a cultural community in the city.[11] He was involved in the setting up of the Society for the Encouragement of Designing, Drawing and Painting in 1773.[12] This failed and was reformed in 1783 as the Society for Promoting the Arts in Liverpool, with the aim of appealing to as wide a public as possible. Out of these initiatives was finally established in 1810 what would eventually become known as the Liverpool Academy of Arts. This in turn was amalgamated into a wider literary, artistic and scientific body known as the Liverpool Royal Institution; Roscoe and his friend, the banker B. A. Heywood, were the prime movers. A constant theme that ran through all the early cultural societies of this time was expressed by Roscoe in a speech to mark the opening of the Royal Institution in 1817: 'the union of the pursuits of literature with the affairs of the world'.[13]

The affiliation of commerce and art was to remain at the forefront of Liverpool's cultural life throughout the century. Constant allusions were made to the merchant princes of Florence, Genoa and Venice in fifteenth-century Italy,[14] and the latter-day Liverpool merchant princes saw themselves as being the inheritors of their ideals. This had a profound effect upon both the intellectual and physical environment, as John Willett notes:

> It was one of the points of insistence of the leaders of the Liverpool Royal Institution, which dominated the city's artistic and intellectual life after the Napoleonic Wars, that a classical revival was the proper architectural expression for a booming mercantile community: and the building of St George's Hall in the 1840s meant that the formal core of the city, library, museum, art gallery, county sessions court... is in a grandly classical style... the buildings of central Liverpool seem, consciously or not, to reflect its early leaders' feeling that the Industrial Revolution was a second Renaissance.[15]

11 See G. Chandler, *William Roscoe of Liverpool, 1753–1831*, B. T. Batsford, London, 1953.
12 An earlier society had been established in 1769 at 30 John Street, just one year after the founding of the Royal Academy in London; an early example of Liverpool's desire to be independent of London in cultural as well as commercial terms.
13 W. Roscoe, 'On the Origin and Vicissitudes of Literature, Science and Art and their Influence Upon the Present State of Society', speech delivered at the opening of the Liverpool Royal Institution, 25 November 1817; printed by Harris & Co, London, 1817.
14 For an account of the cultural and philanthropic initiatives in Chicago, a city which displayed a number of cultural and developmental similarities to Liverpool, see H. Lefkowitz-Horowitz, *Culture and the City: Cultural Philanthropy in Chicago from the 1880s to 1917*, Chicago University Press, Chicago, 1976.
15 J. Willett, *Art in a City*, Methuen, London, 1967, p. 7.

Many of the leading figures of Liverpool's cultural community belonged to the numerous gentleman's clubs that were founded in the town in the early years of the nineteenth century. The Athenaeum (established in 1797), the Lyceum and the Palatine all contained fine libraries and were convenient meeting places for the transferral of ideas both intellectual and commercial. As the century progressed these private clubs were joined by public bodies such as the Liverpool Mechanics' Institution, founded in 1832–1833, which provided classes in landscape, mechanical drawing and architectural drawing for a wider public. Such democratic moves did not meet with unanimous approval and it was felt in some quarters that the enlightenment of the working classes was a dangerous move. The Mechanics' Institution ran into some financial difficulty in the 1840s, but in 1851 its art department was recognized on the South Kensington System of Art Education and was later to develop into the city's art college.

It was not until 1877 that Liverpool acquired a formal city art gallery following the announcement by Andrew Barclay Walker in 1872, after his election as mayor, that he would pay for its establishment. The gallery was seen as one more aspect of the extension of art and culture to the masses; by the turn of the nineteenth century the dignitaries of the city were congratulating themselves on being at the cutting edge of such developments. The reality of the matter was that the gallery under its first two curators acquired little work of outstanding merit; and for all its popularizing rhetoric, few members of the city's working class would have considered such an imposing institution to have been designed with them in mind.

The guiding cultural spirit of the second half of the century, just as Roscoe had been in the first, was Philip Rathbone. Part of the Rathbone dynasty and a member of the powerful Unitarian community in the city, he was behind many of the cultural and educational movements in Liverpool up until his death in 1895. Rathbone 'believed in strengthening corporate life and in quickening civic patriotism by appealing to men through their senses and in making the visible city a place to be proud of',[16] and was in that sense of a piece with Roscoe and the Royal Institution. It was Rathbone who persuaded many wealthy Liverpool merchants to endow chairs in the newly established university college.[17] In particular he was the chief promoter of the Roscoe

16   E. F. Rathbone, *William Rathbone: A Memoir*, Macmillan, London, 1905, pp. 460–61.
17   See T. Kelly, *For the Advancement of Learning: The University of Liverpool 1881–1981*, Liverpool University Press, Liverpool, 1981, for a full account of the establishment and development of Liverpool University.

Chair of Fine Art, which later changed its name to the Roscoe Chair of Architecture, the first university chair of architecture in the country. He was also a member of the committee for the Liverpool Art Congress held in 1888, a worthy but uninspiring event with the then-familiar theme of broadening the appeal of art and design to the general public.[18]

Liverpool in 1900 was a community secure in its position as the second city of the Empire. With a booming port, well-developed cultural institutions and a newly established university, it displayed all the self-satisfied confidence that would be the hallmark of the coming Edwardian period. It was a city at the height of its powers and as Tony Lane notes,

> London apart, Liverpool produced more wealthy families than any other English city. At its peak in the years 1890–1899, Liverpool produced as many millionaires as Greater Manchester, West Yorkshire, West Midlands, Tyneside and East Anglia combined.[19]

However, there were concerns about the security of the foundations of this prosperity, and the likely continuation of the remarkable growth the city had enjoyed throughout the previous 200 years. A contemporary commentator noted that: 'We are not great as a manufacturing centre. By the side of Manchester, Leeds, Birmingham, Bradford and many smaller places we have as manufacturers to hide our heads.'[20]

Yet few commentators could have foreseen the sharp decline that would follow, and for the time being at least dissenting voices were in the minority. Liverpool's rich lived as well as ever, while Liverpool's poor lived in conditions as desperate as any they had experienced throughout the nineteenth century, made more apparent by their very proximity to such extravagant displays of wealth. Private philanthropic efforts to relieve poverty had been directed for the most part to cultural activities and the public schemes that did exist – such as early council housing, public health works and so on – owed more to pragmatic responses to urgent need than enlightened local government.[21]

Liverpool was about to enter a new era in which, as a microcosm of wider British society, it would display all the weaknesses that had built up in

---

18 A series of congresses were staged: the first in Liverpool, the second in Edinburgh in 1889, and the third in Birmingham in 1890. A fourth was planned for Nottingham in 1891 but did not take place.

19 Lane, *Gateway of Empire*, pp. 54–55.

20 Lane, *Gateway of Empire*, p. 35.

21 For an account of Liverpool's political scene, see P. J. Waller, *Democracy and Sectarianism: A Political and Social History of Liverpool 1868–1939*, Liverpool University Press, Liverpool, 1981.

that system throughout the previous century. This was intensified by the particular social and economic problems the city would face following the decline of its core industries. It was into this complex, cosmopolitan, contra-dictory community that, in 1904, Charles Herbert Reilly was appointed the second Roscoe Professor of Architecture at the newly independent university.

2 Early Influences and Experience

It is important to trace the influences and relationships in Reilly's life in the years between his graduation from Cambridge and his acceptance of the Roscoe Chair at Liverpool University, as they would inform much of his early work in the Liverpool School. It was during this time that Reilly made a number of contacts with figures who would play an important role in his development of the school: figures such as Stanley Adshead, who would help him in one of the major projects of the early period of Reilly's university career – the establishment of the Department of Civic Design. In addition, Reilly's work within the architectural practices of John Belcher and Stanley Peach were to help inform the architectural philosophy that would drive his ideas following his Liverpool appointment.

In Britain, the period from the 1890s up until the outbreak of the First World War in 1914 was a time of prosperity and expansion, driven by an Empire that had reached the height of its powers and called for buildings, both private and public, to demonstrate its vitality. The proliferation of country houses, town halls, office buildings and hotels was evident in every major city in the country. As Stuart Gray notes,

> In Glasgow, Manchester, Liverpool, Leeds and Birmingham civic pride had found expression in proud city halls affording some relief from, and indeed some atonement for, the grim scenery of docks, warehouses, mills and workers' houses which had been imposed upon those towns and seaports.[1]

The advances in technology and public sanitation also required large civil engineering projects such as the Forth Bridge, the Severn Tunnel and the London Underground, as well as the development of totally new types of structures, such as electricity generating stations and exchange buildings, for the expanding network of the public telephone service.

The outcome of this prosperity was a multiplicity of building firms, speculative builders, architects and architectural styles. However, the two

---

1 A. Stuart Gray, *Edwardian Architecture: A Biographical Dictionary*, Duckworth, London, 1985, p. 11.

dominant styles of the last decade of the nineteenth century and the ensuing
Edwardian period were the Arts and Crafts movement and – its stylistic
antithesis – the revivalist style of English Baroque in the manner of Wren,
Vanbrugh and Hawksmoor. While the two might appear to have been
mutually exclusive, in fact there were a variety of hybrid styles connecting
them.[2] Commentators on the period have noted in this stylistic diversity a
deeper sense of loss of moral certainty, and a prefiguration of the identity
crises that would gradually come to symbolize the British condition throughout the twentieth century. Wilfred Mellers and Rupert Hildyard note that

> The Edwardian revival of architectural styles, for instance, with its markedly
> mannerist emphasis – Baroque, Byzantine, Wren, 'proconsular' – is hardly
> equivalent to the ethical quality with which mid-Victorian Gothic and neo-
> classical are imbued. This eclectic appropriation of styles, sometimes dignified
> as 'revivalism', would seem to be rather a case of identity being sought for
> identity's sake.[3]

Mellers and Hildyard's stance is particularly interesting when viewed in the
context of the battle of styles that raged over the Liverpool Cathedral scheme
of 1902, and its subsequent influence upon the architectural philosophy
within the city's architectural community.[4]

In London, the major architects of the 1890s were Alfred Waterhouse,
Thomas Collcutt, Norman Shaw, Aston Webb and John Belcher. Belcher was
the chief exponent of what became known as Free Classic, a style that was
acceptable for both public and private buildings. The eclecticism of the style
was epitomized by Belcher's Institute of Chartered Accountants building of
1889 in which, as Gray notes, 'the sculpture and the blocked or rusticated
columns and architraves… were to become part of the stock-in-trade of the
period, heralding the grand manner of Edwardian neo-Baroque'.[5]

---

2   See A. Service, *Edwardian Architecture: A Handbook to Building Design in Britain 1890–1914*,
    Thames & Hudson, London, 1977, for a full account of the variety of styles and building types
    during this period.
3   W. Mellers and R. Hildyard in B. Ford (ed.), *Early Twentieth Century Britain: The Cambridge
    Cultural History*, Vol. 8, Cambridge University Press, Cambridge, 1992, p. 9.
4   The debate which split the Classicists (Moderns) and Gothicists (Traditionalists) prompted
    Reginald Blomfield to write a letter to *The Times*, dated 15 October 1901: 'Either the spiritual
    thought and feeling of modern Liverpool are the same as those of the cathedral builders of the
    thirteenth century, or they are not. If they are the same, no doubt the language of the builders of
    Salisbury will precisely express the aspirations of the Liverpool merchant and mechanic of this
    century: if they are not the same that language becomes meaningless as an expression of modern
    thought, and to insist on its use is to reduce the work of architecture to a sham.'
5   Gray, *Edwardian Architecture*, p. 15.

John Belcher (1841–1913)

Belcher had been a founding member of the Art Workers' Guild, whose chief aim had been to stop the separation of the arts of architecture, sculpture and painting. While other members of the Guild had moved on to other stylistic concerns, Belcher remained fascinated by this central objective and saw in the Baroque style a means of achieving it. As Alastair Service notes,

> Thus the Belcher and Pite entry for the Accountant's competition was basically an Arts and Crafts design, including key motifs such as the sculptured frieze bands and the turret accent at the break of levels, but clad inside and out in luxuriantly Baroque raiment.[6]

The style had therefore been maturing for a number of years. It was known generally as English Renaissance (the term 'Baroque' being used pejoratively), and by 1897 it had gained enough support for the likes of Professor Simpson, Reilly's predecessor in the Roscoe Chair, to write:

> The movement towards a Classical revival has been steadily gaining ground for years. We see it in many of the public buildings erected lately and it is present in every competition. One of the best examples is Mr. Belcher's Chartered Accountants… it is one of the most interesting of modern buildings.[7]

It was in Belcher's offices, following a short unsatisfactory period working in his father's office, that Reilly obtained a junior position. According to Reilly, he obtained his place following the publication of a short piece written by the editor of *The Builder* concerning a competition entry Reilly had submitted for the town hall at Walsall. Reilly describes his entry as being of 'a plain stone building in no particular style, not unfortunately because I was an early modernist but because I did not know anything much about style'.[8] Whatever the actual degree of influence this short paragraph in *The Builder* had in Reilly's appointment as an 'improver at no salary but with no premiums to pay',[9] it meant he was now employed in one of the most prestigious architectural practices in London, with access to the current ideas on architectural style. The work being produced at the time of Reilly's arrival had changed in style somewhat from that of the Institute of Chartered Accountants building

6 A. Service, *Edwardian Architecture and its Origins*, The Architectural Press, London, 1975, p. 303.
7 F. Simpson, *Architectural Review*, Vol. 2, 1897, p. 90.
8 C. H. Reilly, *Scaffolding in the Sky*, Routledge, London, 1938, p. 47.
9 Reilly, *Scaffolding in the Sky*, p. 48.

design that had initially attracted him to apply for employment with Belcher. Reilly talks of the design for the South Kensington Museum and the Institute building – both of which he admired – as belonging to the previous Beresford Pite era, and his own time with the firm as belonging to the J. J. Joass era.[10] While the firm's house style may have changed, more importantly for Reilly's own architectural development, he notes that his time in Belcher's office allowed him, through 'the prestige of the office, gradually to get to know a number of the young men who were beginning to make names for themselves in the profession'.[11]

Stanley Davenport Adshead (1868–1946)

Chief among these young men was Stanley Adshead. Adshead's central role in the early years of the Chair of Civic Design at Liverpool University will be dealt with at greater length later. However, it is important to note here his talents with perspective, a skill that Reilly would make use of and later comment upon:

> These [perspective drawings] were lovely things. It is forgotten now that he [Adshead] is a famous man, a great town planner and an architect whose work always maintains its high standard of elegance, what a great draughtsman he was.[12]

He was also a reticent figure, unconcerned with self-promotion, and as such a perfect foil to Reilly. It was this degree of self-effacement that prompted Christian Barman to state of him: 'When one meets most famous men, it is with a certain degree of disappointment: they so frequently appear to be less than their work, but Adshead seems greater.'[13]

10 John James Joass (1868–1952), born in Scotland, worked as a junior for Burnet in Glasgow. In 1893 he went to London and in 1896 he joined the office of John Belcher shortly before Belcher's chief assistant, Arthur Beresford Pite, left. Joass became Belcher's partner in 1905 and remained so until Belcher's death in 1913.
11 Reilly, *Scaffolding in the Sky*, p. 50.
12 Reilly, *Scaffolding in the Sky*, p. 51.
13 Quoted in A. Powers, '"Architects I have known": The Architectural Career of S. D. Adshead', *Architectural History, Journal of the Society of Architectural Historians of Great Britain*, Vol. 24, October 1981, p. 103. Barman (1898–1980) graduated from the Liverpool school in 1918 and worked briefly with Sir Edwin Lutyens. He was the founder of *Architecture* (the journal of the Society of Architects) and was editor of both the *Architectural Review* and the *Architects' Journal*.

Reilly first met Adshead in 1900, and the unpublished opening chapter of an autobiography held in the archives of Liverpool University provides an insight into the interrelationships that existed within the architectural community in London at this time. It is particularly useful in assessing Adshead's friendships with E. A. Rickards – whose work was to have a profound effect on the whole course of Edwardian architecture – and the less well-documented figures of George Sherrin and William Flockhart.[14] By doing so it enables us to piece together the various strands of a number of Reilly's early architectural sources. Adshead was to produce some carefully executed perspective drawings for Reilly over the following years, most notably Reilly's entry for the Liverpool Cathedral competition,[15] and later – after Reilly's appointment to the Roscoe Chair – his entry for the London County Hall competition of 1907 (Fig. 4).[16] The two men appear to have shared opinions on current developments in architectural style, and when Ralph Knott's design was chosen for the County Hall competition, Adshead wrote of it as being 'unscholarly in conception, and commonplace in detail, in a style which is fast falling into disrepute',[17] while Reilly regarded it as 'a disaster to monumental architecture in England'.[18] Alan Powers notes that Adshead, during the course of working on the London County Hall design with Stanley Peach and Stanley Ramsey, became aware of contemporary American work: 'Ramsey introduced Adshead to the work of McKim, Mead and White and other American classical architects with which he was impressed.'[19] This was around the same time that Reilly was also shifting his architectural philosophy away from the neo-Grec he had flirted with in the early years of his appointment at Liverpool, and

14   As Powers notes, 'From Flockhart, Adshead learnt much of his skill as a perspective artist…', 'Architects I Have Known', p. 103.

15   An examination of Reilly's own attempts at draughtsmanship, as seen in his drawing of the cathedral design's main entrance – now held in the RIBA drawings collection – shows how great an asset Adshead's watercolour and pencil perspective drawings were in showing Reilly's designs off to their best advantage. See J. Lever (ed.), *Catalogue of the Drawings Collection of the Royal Institute of British Architects O–R*, RIBA Publications, London, 1976, p. 114.

16   Adshead also submitted a design in partnership with Stanley Peach (Reilly's former collaborator on various power station designs) and S. C. Ramsey (a former pupil of Reilly's during his time teaching at King's College, London). Ramsey described the result of their collaborations as looking like, 'the illegitimate offspring of the National Gallery and the Law Courts at Brussels'. Quoted in Powers, 'Architects I Have Known', p. 104.

17   S. D. Adshead, 'A New County Hall for London', quoted in Powers, 'Architects I Have Known', p. 104.

18   Reilly, quoted in *The Builder*, 21 February 1908, letter to the editor; Reilly Papers, Liverpool University Archives, Box D207/2/2/vi.

19   Powers, 'Architects I have Known', p. 104.

towards the full-blooded adoption of the Beaux-Arts (also via American sources). Reilly's account of his adoption of the Beaux-Arts is centred very much upon his own experience of the style during his travels in the US in the spring of 1909; he was to write of them in the RIBA journal.[20] However, it seems more than likely that Reilly was equally influenced in this matter by the enthusiasms expressed to his friend and colleague Adshead by his former student Stanley Ramsey. It is interesting to note here that other figures close to Reilly were also being influenced by American Beaux-Arts architecture at around the same time. We can therefore see that when, with the founding of the Chair of Civic Design, Reilly was given the task of finding a suitable candidate to head the new department, Adshead was an obvious choice given their common architectural background and the convergence of their philosophical and stylistic beliefs at that time.

Edwin Alfred Rickards (1872–1920)

It was also through Adshead that Reilly came to know E. A. Rickards.[21] Rickards shared with Adshead an ability as a draughtsman, but temperamentally he was a very different person: 'extraordinarily vigorous… never sank into the crowd, was never one of it, but remained, wherever he was, the individual'.[22] Rickards was a close friend of the author Arnold Bennett, who portrayed him in a number of his novels, most notably *The Roll Call*. Architecturally, Rickards occupied a central position in the establishment of the Edwardian Baroque. John Warren described him as

> more at the heart of the resurgence of 'free classic' architecture than any other English architect. He was that unusual thing in the English race – a natural designer in the Baroque… At the threshold of his career he plunged into the rising wave of sympathy for the Baroque or Free Classical Revival. His instincts were entirely in tune with it, and his youthful abilities carried him up to swim on the crest.[23]

20 'The Modern Renaissance in American Architecture', *RIBA Journal*, 25 June 1910, pp. 630–35.
21 In his autobiography Reilly describes how he met Rickards and Lanchester: 'Through Adshead… I got to know Rickards and his partner Lanchester… The chief meeting place was the Café Roche in Old Compton Street… There at the long table on the left on entering one was pretty sure to find someone of interest.' Reilly, *Scaffolding in the Sky*, pp. 51–52. This is an early example of Reilly's use of café and club life to establish and maintain a network of friends and contacts, something that he would develop into an art form during his time in Liverpool.
22 J. Warren, 'Edwin Alfred Rickards', in Service, *Edwardian Architecture and its Origins*, p. 341.
23 Warren, 'Edwin Alfred Rickards', p. 341.

While Reilly said of him 'He was the Augustus John of our profession, vigorous and disturbing...',[24] he acknowledged his debt to Rickards's influence when speaking of the design by Lanchester, Stewart and Rickards for the Cardiff City Hall and Law Courts of 1897, and the Deptford Town Hall design of 1902:

> Their great winning designs for Cardiff Town Hall and Law Courts seemed full of the glorious life we all wanted but could not yet afford. Rickards' tower to the town hall went to our heads, up and up from one glorious stage to another. Their little Deptford Town Hall, which seems with its projecting roof and carved balcony to overhang the High Street... is perhaps finer still and one of the best things the early part of the century produced. Like all his work it has bigness however small.[25]

Rickards was an early enthusiast for Beaux-Arts scholarship, and together with Bennett he was also an enthusiastic francophile. While Reilly and Adshead drew their inspiration from American sources, Rickards admired the French Free Classic style, founded as it was on the scholarly traditions of the Ecole des Beaux-Arts.

Rickards and Lanchester continued to occupy centre stage as the fashion for Baroque styling mounted in the early years of the century. Their submission for the London County Hall competition in 1907 displayed their wildest Baroque treatment to date. By contrast, Reilly's scheme incorporated elements of the more severe forms that were now coming into favour, and while he admired Rickards's baroque sensibility, he submitted a design that owed more to Belcher's influence than to Rickards. Knott's winning design was a clear indication of the coming mood and while Reilly disapproved of the choice, his own teaching at Liverpool would later take on many of the ideas encapsulated in the severity of the Classical design.[26] This mood shift was perceptible in the wider architectural community from as early as 1906, when

24 Reilly quoted in Gray, *Edwardian Architecture*, p. 311.
25 Reilly, *Scaffolding in the Sky*, p. 53.
26 Reilly was responding to the shift in taste of 1905–1906 away from Edwardian Classicism that favoured the Baroque – of which he had been an enthusiastic supporter – towards a purer Neoclassicism based on French models. Reilly was a little way behind the London leaders of the Beaux-Arts influence, such as Frank Verity, who was designing in the crisper and purer French style when Reilly was still wedded to the neo-Grec of his Students' Union, or the Baroque of the arts faculty building in Liverpool. Verity's Cleveland House of 1905 is a good example of this stylistic sea change. The 'Champs Elysées' style of Verity would be adopted a few years later by Reilly, via American sources, resulting in buildings such as Harold Dod's Athenaeum of 1924–1928.

the *Architectural Review* dismissed the Barocco of the Milan International Exhibition.[27] By 1911 the editor of *The Architects' and Builders' Journal* wrote of the St Marylebone Town Hall competition:

> We cannot help asking ourselves whether all these colossal columns, domes, towers, groups of sculpture and other imposing features are felt by their authors to be the only natural and inevitable expression of the necessities of the case and of the nature and purpose of building.[28]

The vast majority of the entries were indeed in the Baroque manner made popular by Rickards. Ironically, Rickards's own design for the competition was in a more restrained and imitative style; there is a perceptible shift in Rickards's later work to accommodate this sea change in taste. However, one of the fundamental principles of Rickards's work, as noted by Warren, is that it displays 'simplicity and severity of the basic masses when stripped of their ornament'.[29] It is perhaps this element that Reilly took from Rickards and used in his Monumental Classicism phase at Liverpool. This style would be adapted by Reilly and his students, and applied to every conceivable building type. This quality might explain Reilly's remark that 'all his [Rickards's] work… has bigness however small'.[30]

Reilly's own architectural tastes had, by 1908–1909, moved towards the purer Classicism promoted by people such as Sir Reginald Blomfield. A growing interest in Beaux-Arts styling also suited the plans he was developing during this time for the Liverpool School of Architecture. In Liverpool the taste for Edwardian Baroque had reached its zenith with the erection of the Mersey Docks and Harbour Board building in 1903–1907, designed by Arnold Thornley with Briggs and Wolstenholme (Fig. 3). Quentin Hughes notes that the design for the dome on the building was probably taken from Reilly's own design entry for the Liverpool Anglican Cathedral competition of 1901–1902.[31] This seems perfectly feasible given Reilly's documented contacts with the firm, but it is possible that the origin of the dome may be traced back still further to a design by Belcher for a competition entry of 1891 relating to the Victoria and Albert Museum. Reilly followed the lead of writers such as Blomfield during his first years in Liverpool, and based many of his methods

27   *Architectural Review*, Vol. 20, 1906, pp. 10, 94 and 139.
28   *The Architects' and Builders' Journal*, 1911.
29   Warren, 'Edwin Alfred Rickards', p. 341.
30   Reilly, *Scaffolding in the Sky*, p. 53.
31   J. Quentin Hughes, *Seaport: Architecture and Townscape in Liverpool*, Bluecoat Press, Liverpool, 1993, p. 74.

on them, stating that the Liverpool School's 'teaching at the beginning of the new century was largely based on Sir Reginald's. His books became textbooks for professors and students alike.'[32] The influence of Blomfield's writings such as *A History of Renaissance Architecture in England 1500–1800* (1897) and *Studies in Architecture* (1905) would be combined with the experience Reilly had gained as a part-time lecturer at King's College, London. Reilly would take each of these elements and adapt them to suit contemporary theories of architectural education and design philosophy.

Teaching Experience: King's College, London

Reilly's early teaching experience came about, according to his own account, by chance. He stated that he had no thought of teaching until he applied for the vacant chair at King's College, London:

> One day in Belcher's office, more for fun than for anything else, Joass pointed out to me an advertisement for the post of professor of architecture at King's College... rendered vacant by the death of Bannister Fletcher... Joass laughingly said I ought to go in for it and, more out of bravado than anything I said I would... To my great surprise I found myself on a short list of three.[33]

Just how light-heartedly Reilly entered upon this application is hard to say, but to apply for a post left vacant by such an illustrious figure as Sir Banister Fletcher, author of the influential *History of Architecture on the Comparative Method*, was certainly an ambitious step for a young man with little professional experience. The importance of this application to Reilly's future academic career lay not in his obtaining the chair – he did not – but in his being offered the post of lecturer under the successful applicant Elsey Smith. Smith would later introduce Reilly to Stanley Peach, with whom he produced a number of well-regarded designs for the expanding network of electricity generating stations around London.[34] The work produced in partnership with Peach is of interest in gauging the degree of influence exercised by the individuals above on Reilly's work at this time. As Powers notes,

32   C. H. Reilly, *Representative British Architects of the Present Day*, Batsford, London, 1931, p. 61.
33   Reilly, *Scaffolding in the Sky*, p. 54.
34   For example Ian Nairn, writing of the 'Lodge Road Power Station', notes: 'Adding art to industrial structures is usually a bad thing. But there's always an exception, and this is it... here the art was added by the young C. H. Reilly, later to become famous as a critic and the head of Liverpool School of Architecture. The classical dress is as noble as Behrens' turbine factory, and as logical: hefty pilasters marking the centre and sides, and coming down to the ground on great feet:

Reilly's designs, like the 'Italian Garden' sub-station in Mayfair, are typical of the 'Free Classic' of Shaw and Belcher, and the exterior of the cathedral [Liverpool] design shows his indebtedness to Rickards.[35]

The partnership with Peach allowed Reilly to conduct, on a part-time basis, some practical designs to inform his teaching work at King's, which was itself heavily studio-based. Indeed, Reilly's early teaching experience at King's appears to have set the pattern for his later work at the Liverpool School, where he placed a good deal of emphasis upon studio work as opposed to the formal criticism-and-lecture format. This latter method was, by Reilly's own account, the one that he had experienced during his time as a part-time evening student at the Architectural Association:

> At the Architectural Association we merely brought our designs in at some fixed date and did the work elsewhere. I soon found at King's, however, that I enjoyed going round the boards and sketching out one solution after another, exhausting as it is after the first half-dozen. It was through doing this and discussing the subjects with the men that I got more and more interested in teaching. Formal lectures, except perhaps critical and historical ones of old and new buildings, never interested me very much.[36]

As Powers notes of the evening classes at the Architectural Association,

> These were still running in the dual system inherited from the 1890s with the evening lectures and studio under W. G. B. Lewis... his classes... included a specialised study of sciography, and 'Time Sketch' design studies, both emulating French methods.[37]

Another Architectural Association student recalls that the teaching methods of Lewis set 'a stiff pace for his pupils, and... gave them a good grounding in the classical orders and a very heavy plateful of geometry'.[38] Reilly claimed 'I

swinging swags and garlands in between. Singing with the building too: plenty of plain yellow brick, all the ornament florid and flowing over, everything saying that this is a bloody great shed.' I. Nairn, *Nairn's London*, Penguin, Harmondsworth, 1988, p. 87. Reilly's recollections of his time with Peach, recorded in 1938 when he was inclined towards a Modernist sensibility, were that they consisted of 'nefarious business', and that Peach's efforts to design his generating stations meant 'he tried far too hard to dress up his engineering buildings, with their fine roofs and great chimneys, with "architecture" when they would have been much better left alone'. Reilly, *Scaffolding in the Sky*, p. 56. See also G. Stamp, *Temples of Power*, Cygnet Press, Burford, 1979.
35   A. Powers, 'Architectural Education in Britain 1880-1914', PhD thesis, Cambridge University, 1982, pp. 135–36.
36   Reilly, *Scaffolding in the Sky*, p. 55.
37   Powers, 'Architectural Education in Britain', p. 121.
38   F. R. Yerbury, 'Some AA Reminiscences', *The Builder*, Vol. CLXXIII, 1947, p. 697.

do not remember at the A A [that] we had any definite teacher,'[39] but since Lewis did not hand over his teaching at the AA to Frank T. Green until 1906, it seems probable that Reilly would have been taught by him. Reilly, therefore, apparently drew some of the elements he employed at Liverpool from his own evening class experience at the AA. Indeed he may well have been adapting the AA methods for his own teaching at King's, since he claims 'Although I was myself at the time attending a design class at the old Architectural Association evening school... I saw in that no reason again why I should not teach too.'[40]

Reilly continued in his partnership with Peach until his entry for the Liverpool Cathedral competition. At about this time he made his second application for a chair in architecture, this time at University College, London. This application, although once again unsuccessful, introduced Reilly to Professor Simpson, who would prove to be the last link in the chain that would finally lead to his appointment to the Roscoe Chair at Liverpool University. Simpson, Reilly's predecessor at Liverpool, was appointed to the University College chair, and as Reilly noted in his autobiography, 'Waiting for the interview we became friendly and he offered to do his best to help me at Liverpool if he were selected. He was and kept his promise.'[41]

Reilly's appointment to the chair at Liverpool at the age of 30 was a quite remarkable coup. His first class degree in engineering from Cambridge must have helped, considering that Liverpool University's existing professors included a number of other Cambridge men. Added to this was an impressive set of testimonials from John Belcher and Norman Shaw. Shaw, who had acted as an assessor on the Liverpool Cathedral competition, had been favourably impressed with Reilly's cathedral design. It is therefore important to examine the Liverpool Cathedral competition and Reilly's own entry in more detail, both as a way of gaining an understanding of Reilly's design philosophy at this stage in his career, and also as a means of obtaining an insight into a major design project in Liverpool. By investigating how it impacted upon the architectural community and beyond at an important time – immediately prior to Reilly winning the Liverpool chair – we can gain a better understanding of Reilly's future policy for the Liverpool School.

39   Reilly, *Scaffolding in the Sky*, p. 55.
40   *Scaffolding in the Sky*, p. 55. Reilly's ability to play the roles of student and teacher simultaneously had developed during his early years at Cambridge, where – due to lack of funds – he took on private pupils. As Reilly states, 'In my case, however, as they were taking the same Tripos as I was, it meant I had at least to keep ahead of them.' *Scaffolding in the Sky*, p. 8; see also pp. 39–40.
41   *Scaffolding in the Sky*, p. 64.

The Liverpool Cathedral Competition

The proposal to build a cathedral at Liverpool dated back to the grant of city status in 1880, and the establishment of a new bishopric independent of the ancient bishopric of Chester of which Liverpool had, until then, been a part. There were a number of abortive attempts to build on various sites within the city, most notably behind St George's Hall, which at that time was still developing its status as the cultural hub of the city. With the appointment of Bishop Chavasse in 1901, the scheme to build gained new impetus. The cathedral executive sub-committee decided on 8 March 1901 to approach Professor Simpson, then holder of the Roscoe Chair of Architecture, for advice on the choice of architect and to act as a consultant on matters of architectural style. Simpson's reply was that 'the question of style should be left open'.[42] A short time later the cathedral sub-committee approached Sir William Emerson, who had earlier put forward an unsuccessful cathedral design, for his opinion on the appropriate style for the new cathedral. Emerson stated that it should be Gothic, and in a letter from the secretary of the cathedral committee to Emerson it was stated that the committee had 'unanimously decided to adopt Gothic'.[43]

The debate surrounding the appropriate style for the new cathedral was widely covered, both in the national press and the professional journals. *The Builder* wrote of this decision as 'foolish and mischievous',[44] while *The Times* became the forum for a heated debate in its correspondence pages, initiated by the Liverpool architect Myddleton Shallcross who argued that the new cathedral's style should 'evidence for the future ages of thought, the science, the lives and environment, the pulse as it were, of the people of the period of its erection'.[45] Shallcross's letter provoked a flurry of correspondence between the chairman of the cathedral committee, Robert Gladstone, and Reginald Blomfield (among others), who expressed the opinion that

> Mr R. Gladstone finds his devotions quickened by the pointed arch, but surely this is rather a slender foundation on which to raise a law that this and no other is to be the only possible type of building under which future generations may devoutly worship.[46]

42   Liverpool Architectural Society's submission to the cathedral executive sub-committee, point 3(b), Liverpool Record Office, Liverpool Central Library.
43   Letter from J. Alderson Smith (Secretary, cathedral committee) to Sir William Emerson, dated 23 September 1901, Liverpool Record Office, Liverpool Central Library.
44   *The Builder*, 28 September 1901, p. 268.
45   T. Myddleton Shallcross, letter to *The Times*, 8 October 1901.
46   R. Blomfield, letter to *The Times*, 15 October 1901.

The debates in both the *The Builder* and *The Times* were brought to a close with concluding articles condemning the cathedral committee's decision. *The Builder* produced an article that argued for a new form of ecclesiastical architecture to be devised, free of imitation and appropriate to the conditions of the new century.[47] *The Times*'s leader column concluded that

> If architecture in the twentieth century is to be alive, it must, like the great architecture of the past, be spontaneous. Imitation is death, and life in any art is only found in the free play of the artist's intelligence.[48]

The decision as to whether the style of the new cathedral should be open or not was reached by a non-prescriptive demand by the cathedral committee reported in *The Times* on 29 October 1901. The adverse publicity both within the city and in the national press had, it seems, forced the committee to reverse its decision of 7 October that the cathedral should be Gothic in style. The result was that G. F. Bodley and R. Norman Shaw were appointed as judges for an open competition for the new cathedral. Both men were nearing the end of their careers. However, while Bodley was an apologist for the Gothic style and a veteran of the Gothic Revival, Shaw – as evidenced by his then current work in Liverpool and elsewhere[49] – was rather more open to the possibility of a range of styles and technologies being employed in the building.

Professor Simpson's own stylistic stance was further illuminated by a series of addresses he made to the Liverpool Architectural Society at the time of the cathedral debate. Simpson's first address, delivered in 1900, had examined the Gothic Revival in terms of its role in restoration, and the development of a period of experimentation. He highlighted the traditional craft skills of the Gothic Revival of the nineteenth century, and contrasted them with the then-fashionable Free Style: '[there is a] desire for architectural expression in all buildings, irrespective of the uses to which they were to be put...'[50] Simpson's second address, delivered on 7 October 1901, stated that the Gothic Revival 'stands out as the most remarkable feature in the architectural

47 'The Ideal of the Modern Cathedral', *The Builder*, 26 October 1901, pp. 350–51.
48 *The Times*, leader column, 23 November 1901.
49 Shaw had acted as assessor on Francis Doyle's Royal Insurance Building, North John Street, Liverpool (1897–1903). The building's design is described thus: 'Doyle, who had worked with Shaw on the White Star Building [also in Liverpool] was so heavily influenced by Shaw's style that he was able to refashion it, the gable being taken straight from the earlier building. It is however an extremely impressive building: the granite and Portland stone exterior conceals a steel frame of advanced design.' *Buildings of Liverpool*, Liverpool Heritage Bureau, Liverpool, 1978, p. 37.
50 F. M. Simpson, *Two Presidential Addresses*, The University Press of Liverpool, Liverpool, 1901. From Liverpool Record Office, Liverpool Central Library, Box H 720.6 SIM.

work of the last century'.[51] However, he qualified this point and went on to point out that the power of the Gothic style in the Middle Ages had rested upon the fact that

> The Gothic was the democratic style: whether democratic entirely or in part only is immaterial. The workmen had a much greater say in the development of a design than is now possible, and mouldings and carvings were left in a great measure, if not entirely, to the men who worked them.[52]

The significance of Simpson's acceptance of the impact of a changing cultural framework upon the appropriateness of the stylistic forms to be adopted for the new cathedral is commented upon by Christopher Crouch. Crouch states:

> It is this issue of cultural and stylistic significance that was so important to Simpson, and for those in Liverpool for whom he was acting as a mouthpiece. The Gothic Revival and the enthusiasm for Gothic was waning, architects were developing new approaches to design, and to insist that those architects who wished to design a new Cathedral should work within a style whose cultural significance had been eclipsed seemed a cultural absurdity to him.[53]

Simpson went on to call for an appropriate style to be adopted for the new cathedral, as Gothic had clearly ceased to hold the significance attributed to it by the likes of Gladstone and, as Crouch puts it, 'had been rendered impotent in the eyes of culturally progressive groups such as those in Liverpool who were centred around the School of Architecture and Applied Art...'[54] Simpson's stance has broader ramifications for a more complete understanding of the chronology of Beaux-Arts philosophy in the Liverpool School, and the part played by Reilly in the promotion of Beaux-Arts following his appointment as Roscoe Professor. It is therefore important to examine Reilly's own competition entry in the context of the debate within the city.

Reilly's Entry for the Liverpool Cathedral Competition

As stated above, at the time of the announcement of the cathedral competition Reilly was working in partnership with Stanley Peach. The design Reilly

51   Simpson, *Two Presidential Addresses*, p. 17.
52   Simpson, *Two Presidential Addresses*, p. 19.
53   C. Crouch, 'Design Initiatives in Liverpool 1881–1914', PhD thesis, Liverpool University, 1992, p. 42.
54   Crouch, 'Design Initiatives in Liverpool', p. 43.

submitted was classically inspired, drawing on Belcher's work from the 1890s – particularly in the design of the drum and dome – while also showing clear reference to Rickards in the exterior treatment of the building (Figs 1 and 2). Reilly claimed that his design was rejected for its unsuitability to the chosen site, a factor he had been unable to fully take into account as the plan had not been issued with the conditions of the competition:

> [I saw] St James's Mount, the site for the Cathedral, a plan of which had not been given with the conditions, and realised at once my vast classical design with a dome was no good. Nevertheless, it was the only classical design to be commended by the assessors, Norman Shaw and Bodley, so it may be said to have led the classical competitors who were nearly half the list.[55]

As Myles Wright points out in *Lord Leverhulme's Unknown Venture*, this has usually been regarded as one of Reilly's 'misrecollections', as it seems incredible that such an important document had not been available to prospective entrants. However, Vere E. Cotton in *The Book of Liverpool Cathedral*[56] points out that the site for the cathedral was still undecided at the time of the publication of the competition, and while St James's Mount was the slight favourite, it was by no means the unanimous choice.

Simpson, in his role as President of the Liverpool Architectural Society, was involved in a campaign within the architectural community to lobby for the cathedral to be sited on Monument Place at the top of London Road – an argument he outlined in an article in the *Architectural Review* from 1901.[57] Similarly, in an article in *The Builder* the Petitioning Committee's report on the site issue was discussed, and it was stated that the St James's Mount site was unsuitable, since it

> is not central: not readily accessible: not commandingly prominent: without vistas... That there is a vista extending for nearly half a mile, which would be terminated by the west end of the Cathedral, were Monument-place accepted: and the Cathedral would form the crowning feature of lines of streets, over a

55 Reilly, *Scaffolding in the Sky*, p. 65.
56 V. E. Cotton, *The Book of Liverpool Cathedral*, Liverpool University Press, Liverpool, 1964.
57 Simpson noted that 'Four sites have been generally mentioned as most suitable: (1) St Peter's Church; (2) St Luke's Church; (3) Monument Place; (4) St James's Mount. The first two may be rapidly dismissed; the last two possess stronger claims. The Monument Place site is unquestionably the better. This is admitted practically by everybody. Lord Derby, the chairman at the general meeting acknowledged as much; and, if money had been no object, this site would probably have been selected by the Committee.' Simpson, 'The New Cathedral for Liverpool: Its Site and Style', *Architectural Review*, Vol. X, October 1901, pp. 138–46.

mile in length, commencing at the landing stage and riverside station, and
passing the [city's civic buildings].[58]

The relevance of such statements can be seen in an increasing understanding
of what Crouch describes as the triumph of 'the municipal and symbolic
aspect of city life' over social aspects. This shift places Simpson and the
Petitioning Committee closer to the American Beaux-Arts concerns for civic
aggrandisement than to the social architectural philosophy of English
planners such as Ebenezer Howard (as outlined in Howard's book, *Tomorrow:
A Peaceful Path to Real Reform*). Reilly's design would, in the light of these
factors, have been ideally suited to the Monument Place proposal, linking well
with the Classical civic grouping around St George's Hall. However, the choice
of St James's Mount, consisting as it did of a long narrow site on the edge of a
cliff, rendered Reilly's Classical design totally unsuitable. Reilly noted that his
design, along with several others by men such as Charles Rennie Mackintosh,[59] received a good deal of individual attention, which – as Reilly stated –
'was certainly to help me to the Liverpool Chair'.[60] Of greater importance to
Reilly's appointment to Liverpool and his consequent development of the

58 *The Builder*, 'The Liverpool Cathedral Question', 21 December 1901, pp. 548–49.
59 Timothy Neat quotes from Mackintosh's Port Vendres letters, written to his wife in the 1920s.
Reilly is mentioned in a number of them and they display a deep sense of resentment of Reilly.
For example, Mackintosh states, 'I have written to say that I cannot write about present day
architecture in England because it does not exist – nor will there be any daylight until it is made
impossible for pompous bounders, like a well-known (at least a well-advertised) professor at
Liverpool, to have any say in architectural education... I have waited 20 years to get one back at
Reilly – and during 20 years I have not said one word about him to an outsider...' T. Neat, *Part
Seen: Part Imagined*, Canongate, Edinburgh, 1994, p. 130. Neat states that 'Reilly had years before
been involved with the MacNairs in Liverpool, and played some role in seeing that Mackintosh
did not win the competition to design the Anglican Cathedral there...' (p. 174). The explanation
Neat provides regarding Reilly's alleged role in Mackintosh's loss of the cathedral competition is
unlikely, given that Reilly was a young fellow competitor, and at that time a relatively unknown
architect, with little or no influence compared with Mackintosh, who was at the height of his
creative powers. Without documentary evidence to show otherwise, it seems more likely that the
seat of Mackintosh's resentment may be found in the perceived treatment of Mackintosh's
brother and sister-in-law, the MacNairs, and the loss of their teaching posts following the failed
attempt to set up an independent art school around the Sandon Terrace Group after the split of
the University School of Applied Art and Architecture and the establishment of the Municipal
School of Art. This chain of events coincided with Reilly's appointment to the Roscoe Chair at
Liverpool, but had been set in motion some time before Reilly's move to Liverpool. Mackintosh
appears to have credited Reilly with a greater influence than he actually had, and blamed him for
the failure of the MacNairs. See the chapter 'Cultural Enterprises' below for a fuller explanation
of the circumstances surrounding the Sandon Studios Group.
60 Reilly, *Scaffolding in the Sky*, p. 65.

School of Architecture was the fact that he was clearly identified through his Classical cathedral design as sympathetic to the objectives and style of the Monument Place supporters and their campaign for what Crouch describes as 'The debate over stylistic appearance…' which he claims

> demonstrates the significance of style and how it was read… The criticism of stylistic rigidity by opponents of the 'Gothic' decision by the Cathedral Building Committee went beyond appropriateness of style and examined the issue of methodology, putting the process of manufacture before its end result.[61]

We can therefore see that, rather than a clean break with the architectural philosophy of Simpson's Liverpool School following Reilly's appointment – as has been argued by various commentators and indeed by Reilly himself in his autobiography – there was in fact a strong continuity displayed during Reilly's early years in the school. Stylistic continuities included the theories formulated by Simpson, and other members of the city's architectural community, concerning planning philosophy and stylistic concerns along Beaux-Arts lines.[62] Simpson's role in the cathedral debate had shown him to be flexible and non-dogmatic in approach, willing to accommodate new ideas. His own aesthetic tastes found solid expression in the design for the Queen Victoria Monument in Derby Square, which he had produced in collaboration with Willink and Thicknesse in 1902–1906.[63] Reilly's appointment to the Roscoe Chair must therefore be re-examined. It owed more to the fact that he had been perceived as a man suited to the ideas and conditions already current in Liverpool around the turn of the century, than to any perception of him as a radical new broom sweeping in a new era. This, however, was to be the role in which he increasingly chose to be cast.

---

61   Crouch, 'Design Initiatives in Liverpool', p. 45.
62   F. M. Simpson, 'Old Architecture in Liverpool', paper read to the Warrington Literary and Philosophical Society, 16 March 1896. Among the topics discussed were Georgian housing in Liverpool, with an emphasis on the qualities of proportion. Simpson pointed out that prime examples of these qualities of design and detailing were the Strozzi Palace and the Palace of Antinori in Florence. As Crouch notes, 'This rather suggests that Simpson's awareness of the design philosophy underlying the Beaux-Arts was well-developed, if not before his residence in Liverpool, then certainly during the first couple of years of it…' Crouch, 'Design Initiatives in Liverpool', p. 118.
63   In 'Old Architecture in Liverpool', Simpson had outlined his interests in town planning through a discussion of the Town Hall–Custom House axis in Liverpool. His proposal that the removal of St George's Church would create a better vista between the two buildings was later achieved with his design for the Victoria Monument, which stands on the site of the demolished church.

3 Designs on Monumentalism

The credit for the introduction of the American Beaux-Arts educational and stylistic models to Liverpool and their adaptation by the Liverpool School of Architecture has traditionally been given to Charles Reilly. The theory, promoted by Reilly himself, goes that the demise of the integrated course in Architecture and Applied Art and the split of the Applied Art section from the School of Architecture coincided neatly with Reilly's appointment in 1904.[1] In Mary Bennett's *The Art Sheds 1894–1905*, in which a focus upon the production of the artifacts of the Applied Art section allows for a neater split to be represented than was actually the case, Bennett states

> The University itself entered a new phase with the appointment of Charles Reilly to the Roscoe Chair of Architecture in 1904, bringing with him a return to the classical tradition and an enormous advance in influence.[2]

The impression of a watershed having been reached at the time of Reilly's appointment is here promoted further. In the course of this, Reilly has been represented as a new broom sweeping through the Liverpool School, introducing much-needed new systems and methods. In his autobiography *Scaffolding in the Sky*, Reilly describes the School of Architecture on his arrival as 'the little Department of Architecture, not yet called a School and certainly not worthy of such a name...'[3] In this environment, Reilly recalls himself 'at once... putting away the Gothic casts and putting the Renaissance and classical ones into positions of greater prominence...'[4] Significantly, of his predecessor Professor Simpson little is said. One of the most striking comments about Simpson, which illustrates Reilly's intention to present himself as the successful promoter of the new ethos, can be seen in Reilly's

1 Reilly's appointment in 1904 gave him sole responsibility for the School of Architecture, although the Applied Art Section did not join the Municipal School of Art until 1905. The decision to split the two parts of the old integrated school had been taken a few years earlier.
2 Mary Bennett, *The Art Sheds 1894–1914*, introduction to exhibition catalogue, Walker Art Gallery, Liverpool, 1982.
3 C. H. Reilly, *Scaffolding in the Sky*, Routledge, London, 1938, p. 69.
4 Reilly, *Scaffolding in the Sky*, p. 71.

estimation of the architectural course during Simpson's term at University College, London. Reilly states, 'Under Professor Simpson it did not seem to make much headway.'[5] The idea that Reilly formulated a new philosophy on his appointment has also been put forward by John Willett in *Art in a City*, in which he states, 'The brief Art Nouveau movement seems to have fizzled out as soon as the Applied Art section parted company with the architects.'[6] Willett identifies Reilly with the maintenance of the Classical preference in civic art and architecture in Liverpool stretching back to the middle of the nineteenth century:

> the formal core of the city… is in a grandly classical style. Even later the dislike of Gothic persisted, most notably when the late Sir Charles Reilly came to be Professor of Architecture at the beginning of this century.[7]

Similarly Quentin Hughes gives credit to Reilly for the establishment of a new system within the school:

> With the appointment of Reilly, for better or for worse, the school became a school for architects, rather than a 'school for architecture'… It was to be tied firmly to the RIBA and, academically controlled by rigid examination, would soon receive exemption, first from the intermediate examination of the institute and later from its final examination.[8]

However, as Christopher Crouch argues, many of the initiatives credited to Reilly were actually put in place by Simpson. He notes,

> It is implied that Reilly's vision of architectural education was at odds with past practice at the School, and that he was responsible for the linking of the School with formal architectural structures… the Architectural Degree scheme was initiated in 1901, and it is this restructuring of the course, this formalizing of architectural education at the expense of the applied arts, that marks the end of the aesthetic and educational experiment every bit as much as the entry of the Applied Art section into the South Kensington system in 1902. By the time of Reilly's appointment, holders of the School's Certificate in Education had been exempt from the RIBA's Intermediate examination for two years… Reilly's importance to the development of the 'old' course was minimal, the structures that enabled him to create a flourishing Beaux-Arts school were already in place.[9]

5 Reilly, *Scaffolding in the Sky*, p. 114.
6 J. Willett, *Art in a City*, Methuen, London, 1967, p. 59.
7 Willett, *Art in a City*, p. 7.
8 J. Quentin Hughes, 'Before the Bauhaus', *Architectural History, Journal of the Society of Architectural Historians of Great Britain*, Vol. 25, 1982, p. 110,
9 C. Crouch, 'Design Initiatives in Liverpool 1881–1914', PhD thesis, Liverpool University, 1992, p. 111.

It is interesting to note here Reilly's use of the Classical motif current in the progressive elements of London architectural circles, and his subsequent adoption of Classical ideas in the environment he found in Liverpool.

Beaux-Arts and Architectural Training in Liverpool Pre-1904

Crouch examines Simpson's role (in concert with other important players such as Lever) in preparations for a Beaux-Arts-influenced school at Liverpool. The city was a significant entry point for American cultural ideals – ideals that impacted on all social levels. Liverpool relied heavily on trade with North America, as evidenced by publications such as the *American European Newsletter* of June 1895, which devoted an entire issue to a discussion of the links between Liverpudlian and American trade and social affairs. The Liverpool merchants looked to New York for their lead rather than to London, an attitude that pervaded Liverpudlian society. William Lever wrote a series of articles during 1892 for the *Birkenhead News*, in which he reported on American architecture and the vitality of American life and culture. In architectural circles, a paper had been read to the Liverpool Architectural Society by James Cook in 1893 entitled 'Three Years' Architectural Experience in America.' Other articles were in circulation within the tight-knit architectural community in Liverpool.

An examination of Simpson's position published in 1895 provides an insight into the theories that were current in the city in the latter years of the nineteenth century. In it, Simpson states,

> The greater part of the work done today [in France] is on the same lines as that done in the last century. They still have a vernacular style in which their architects and workmen are trained, and although it may not be a perfect one, it is surely better than 'the babel of tongues' which exists in England at the present time.[10]

Simpson admired both the French unity of art and architecture, and their unbroken tradition. He also paid tribute to the American system of architectural education, drawing heavily as it did on the French model. Simpson cited two American colleges as examples on which future developments at Liverpool might be based. These were Columbia College, New York, and the

---

10   F. M. Simpson, *The Scheme of Architectural Education*, Marples, Liverpool, 1895, p. 14.

University of Pennsylvania, both of which Simpson admired for their thoroughness. They also had the advantage of being based within the university system and were validated by the award of degrees, a plan Simpson favoured for the English system of architectural training. As Crouch notes,

> That Simpson ultimately planned a School of Architecture modelled upon the American is without doubt. His respect for the course at Columbia University is further reinforced through his acknowledgment of the receipt of 'much valuable information' from its Professor, William Ware.[11]

Simpson's thoughts on American architectural education were themselves built on a general interest in American educational affairs current in the Liverpool architectural community. A fellow member of the Liverpool Architectural Society, P. Waterhouse, had in the same year published an article in which he claimed that the culturally introverted RIBA 'may do worse than look to the Americans for an example of rational methods of education'.[12] The implication of this in any examination of Reilly's role in the implementation of a Beaux-Arts philosophy at the Liverpool School is, in Crouch's words, that

> it fundamentally alters the traditional perception of the evolution of Beaux-Arts training in Britain, placing its origins in Liverpool a decade earlier than has previously been thought. It also alters the ideological perception of the Beaux-Arts style as practised at Liverpool in the early twentieth century, because the style emerged from within the Arts and Crafts debate, and was not solely a reaction against its ideas.[13]

Since we can locate the origins of the Beaux-Arts in Liverpool during the time of Simpson's tenure as professor at Liverpool, Reilly's actions during his early years in the Chair of Architecture must be re-examined. Certainly Reilly's lack of acknowledgment of Simpson's work prior to his own appointment would seem to indicate a conscious decision on his part to disassociate himself from the Simpson era. The one tangible example of Simpson's allegiance to Beaux-Arts philosophy, the Queen Victoria Monument of 1902–1906 in Derby

---

11 Crouch, 'Design Initiatives in Liverpool', p. 91. Simpson said 'That this course of study is generally approved of in America may be gathered from the following extract from a paper read by Professor Ware of Columbia College – to whom I am indebted for much valuable information.' Simpson, *The Scheme of Architectural Education*, p. 13. The paper referred to by Simpson is W. Ware, 'Address Before the Alumni Association of Columbia College on the Twelfth of June 1888', New York, 1888.

12 P. Waterhouse, 'American Architecture', *RIBA Journal*, Vol. 3, Series 3, 1895.

13 Crouch, 'Design Initiatives in Liverpool', p. 80.

Square, Liverpool, was treated with derision by Reilly. Bisson recounts how the daughter of the artist C. J. Allen, who had collaborated on the monument, remembered Reilly as having been 'a perfect gadfly to my father about it'.[14] Certainly Reilly, with some justification, considered it an unsatisfactory, cramped composition; he described its dome, on a number of occasions, as appearing to be 'half on and half off its columns'. He thought that it was 'a pity that so much fine modelling has been expended on such a poorly placed and poorly conceived whole'.[15] While this is a minor example of Reilly's methods of disassociation from Simpson, he quickly developed other, higher-profile means of promoting the impression that he represented a new era at Liverpool.

Reilly and Architectural Education in Liverpool Post-1904

Reilly was to use the issue of architectural education to this end in his inaugural lecture 'Some Tendencies in Modern Architecture'. He indicated his allegiance to Classicism when he stated that the school under his direction would study late Georgian architecture in Liverpool 'in order to preserve a record of good taste'.[16] Shortly after his appointment he published a pamphlet entitled 'The Training of Architects', and in doing so gained considerable press coverage.[17] Reilly was not unique, either in Liverpool or the wider architectural scene, in identifying the current architectural debates concerning town planning and education as important indicators of the direction British architecture would take in the new century. As Alan Powers notes, 'There is no doubt that town planning was the subject which attracted the most discussion among architects between 1905 and 1914, second only to education, and often in connection with it.'[18] Reilly's adoption of town planning as a means of promoting and developing the Liverpool School's ethos will be examined in greater detail below.

   The timing of the publication of 'The Training of Architects' was fortunate, following as it did on a report by the RIBA Board of Architectural

14   R. Bisson, *The Sandon Studios Society and the Arts*, Parry Books, Liverpool, 1965, p. 24.
15   Reilly, 'Some Liverpool Streets and Buildings in 1921', *The Liverpool Daily Post and Mercury*, 1921, p. 32.
16   Reilly, 'Some Tendencies in Modern Architecture', *Building News*, 12 May 1905, pp. 673–74.
17   Reilly, 'The Training of Architects', July 1905, Reilly Papers, Liverpool University Archive, Box D207/8/1. See also Reilly Papers, Liverpool University Archive, Box S3215.
18   A. Powers, 'Architectural Education in Britain 1880–1914', PhD thesis, Cambridge University, 1982, p. 249.

Education published in February 1905, which examined ways in which the British architectural training system could be rationalized. It had in the course of its investigations approached all the interested bodies, including educational establishments; and its conclusions, read to the RIBA by Reginald Blomfield, contrasted sharply with the previous attempt to streamline the training system a decade earlier, which had resulted in the 'profession or art' controversy. The recommendations included proposals for a four-year course. This would consist of two years of study at a recognized school of architecture, combined with two years as an articled pupil in an architect's office. This scheme Reilly considered a 'very excellent compromise'.[19]

Throughout 'The Training of Architects', Reilly skilfully uses a language appropriate to the coming needs of the architectural profession. While the basic principles are very much in line with those espoused by Simpson and developed within the Liverpool School pre-1904, through a shift of emphasis Reilly was able to present them freshly. For example, he justified his enthusiasm for a university-based system of education by arguing that it allowed students access to the latest technological and scientific information available. This cannot be denied; however, by employing these arguments Reilly was also playing to his own strengths as a qualified engineer, as well as emphasizing his position at the forefront of the new technological ideology. In addition, this tactic helped to distance him from the pre-1904 Liverpool School, which was popularly believed to have been largely founded on Arts and Crafts ideology. Reilly also picked up on the acknowledged weaknesses of the French model of Beaux-Arts training, as outlined by Richard Phené Spiers who had in 1883–1884 noted that

> We find in France men who study, I will say, up to the age of 28 or 30, for the Grand Prix, and then go to Rome for 4 years, and come back at the age of 32 or 34, without, I may say, any practical knowledge or any knowledge of construction beyond its theory, and certainly without any economic knowledge of material.[20]

Reilly believed this problem could be overcome by his enthusiasm for the American Beaux-Arts model, with its emphasis on practical and technological training.

In his autobiography Reilly recalled the structure of the courses at the Liverpool School upon his appointment, noting that

19 Reilly, 'The Training of Architects', p. 247.
20 R. Phené Spiers in *RIBA Transactions*, 1883–1884, p. 116.

I did what I could with the help of the lecturer my predecessor had left me with the dozen or so students I had inherited. They were taking either a two year course for a certificate in architecture, or a three year course for a degree of BA in architecture… At the end both alike were allowed one year off their articles and the Intermediate Examination of the RIBA. That is to say they still paid premiums to architects… No wonder the architects of the town mildly supported the School of those days, or rather 'Department' as I found it called though I soon changed that… I began to alter the courses and lengthen them out…[21]

Reilly's claims for his own marked effect on the school's curriculum are not entirely supported by the available figures. While there is no information to enable us to compare the structure of the new course with the old integrated system, the changes referred to by Reilly were the introduction of a degree of Bachelor of Architecture[22] (gained through two years of study after the BA had been achieved, in addition to office practice), plus a new diploma course. Of the students affected by Reilly's 1906 changes, there appears to have been only a small increase in the number of students taking the original certificate course. The first diploma was not awarded until 1908, and the first Bachelor of Architecture was not awarded until as late as 1915.[23] However, Reilly did succeed in gaining press coverage for his course changes. *The Builder*, in an article on the school, talked of 'various changes' to the curriculum; Reilly had promoted these changes from as early as 1906,[24] while an open letter to the *Daily Courier* of 12 October 1907 was addressed to the parents of prospective students and extolled the virtues of the Liverpool curriculum. Simpson's contributions have not been, and indeed were not then, entirely overlooked,[25] but as Crouch notes, 'Reilly's skill… lay in his amplification and elaboration of these practices, rather than their instigation.'[26]

21 Reilly, *Scaffolding in the Sky*, pp. 81–82.
22 Reilly publicized the new course in the professional press, saying 'It is felt that the difficulty of maintaining a standard and of examining in the art of architectural design, as apart from knowledge of the methods of construction, is largely eliminated when for the final test the whole of a student's drawings and designs, made over a sufficient length of time to show progressive capacity for his art, can be collected and weighed. This is the reason why the University of Liverpool has now decided to give a substantive degree in a fine art rather than continue to include architecture, as it has till now, in common with the universities of Manchester and London, as one of the subjects for a BA degree.' Letter from Reilly to *Builders' Report*, 4 December 1907.
23 For student figures see L. B. Budden (ed.), *The Book of the Liverpool School of Architecture*, Liverpool University Press, Liverpool, 1932, p. 59.
24 'Architectural Education at the University of Liverpool', *The Builder*, Vol. XCV, October 1908, p. 341.
25 'Architect's Pupils and Our Technical Schools', letter from J. H. McGovern to *Daily Courier*, 18 October 1907.
26 Crouch, 'Design Initiatives in Liverpool', p. 132.

The model Reilly chose in 'The Training of Architects' as his ideal university system was American, and more specifically that offered by Harvard, where students undertook a liberal arts course before moving on to specialized study. Reilly noted that

> If the example of Harvard is to be followed, a student reading for a degree in architecture would, in general, be required to graduate with BA degree first. This is no doubt the best of all plans.[27]

This, in fact, echoes the calls made by Simpson in his 1895 paper, and was in line with the system already employed at Liverpool at the time of Reilly's pamphlet. However, the most substantial indication of future policy in Reilly's 1905 paper was the enthusiastic adoption of the American Beaux-Arts as the preferred style for the Liverpool School. The introduction to Liverpool of American models on Beaux-Arts lines has a documented history that predates Reilly's appointment by several years. Indeed Simpson had made similar calls for just such a system. However, Reilly went further and made his admiration of the American model, in particular, more explicit, stating that

> in America… large architectural schools doing good work are to be found attached to most of the universities, the good influence of which is to be seen in much of the best recent American building.[28]

For Reilly, the Beaux-Arts training methodology, in which emphasis was placed on consistency of style, allowed for a greater sense of autonomy and control for the institution that administered it; hence the desire on his part to keep the power of educational training in the hands of the universities. By calling for university architectural education along Beaux-Arts lines, Reilly could clearly strengthen his own position, particularly given the history of Beaux-Arts influences that Liverpool had, stretching back to the 1890s. Reilly was, however, well aware of the dangers inherent in advocating a national system of education, even one within a university system, and he commented in his autobiography that

> The danger I saw was the establishment of a sort of South Kensington system, with the great architects in London dictating what the schools everywhere should do and what they should not do, but without the experience as actual teachers which the similar leading architects in France, with their ateliers allied to the Ecole des Beaux-Arts, always possessed.[29]

27 Reilly, 'The Training of Architects', p. 254.
28 Reilly, 'The Training of Architects', p. 253.
29 Reilly, *Scaffolding in the Sky*, p. 116.

In order to secure his chosen vision, Reilly sought to gain the support of members of the Board of Architectural Education. When Reginald Blomfield visited the school in 1907,[30] he reported that

> very satisfactory progress is being made here under Professor Reilly... The students are trained to set up their designs in Isometrical projection, and this appears to us to be a practice that might with advantage be followed generally in schools, in order to give the students a better grasp of construction and of the meaning of his design.[31]

Reilly was, as Powers notes, 'clever to emphasise to these architects of the older generation how the school's work was both traditional and national'.[32] In doing so he gained their qualified support – and from one of the board members, Mervyn Macartney, useful publicity in the *Architectural Review*. The outcome, according to Reilly's own account, was that

> They finally invited me to join their Board. Lethaby and I were the only teachers on it. I was... glad to serve so that, from the start, the body setting out to control architectural education in the country should include at least one practising teacher of architecture.[33]

The battle over the appointment by RIBA of external examiners to oversee and regulate the standards of the university schools illustrates Reilly's fears, and the justifiable desire on his part to keep as much control within the university system as possible. This ties in with his stated position that he did not wish to see the new universities, such as Liverpool, becoming mere 'secondary schools'[34] through the influence either of the lay members who sat on its council, or of external bodies such as RIBA. In a letter to Reginald

---

30 This followed an earlier visit shortly after Reilly's appointment in 1905. Reilly noted that 'it did surprise me... to receive one day a visit from such eminent architects as Reginald Blomfield, Mervyn Macartney... Ernest Newton and John Slater... The object of their visit was to discuss the training of architects...' Reilly, *Scaffolding in the Sky*, p. 115. The visitors reported that there were weaknesses in the design policy of the school.

31 R. Blomfield, *Liverpool School of Architecture: Report of the Board of Architectural Education*, 15 March 1907. Vice-Chancellor's Papers, Liverpool University Archive, Box P6B/3/3.

32 Powers, 'Architectural Education in Britain', p. 139.

33 Reilly, *Scaffolding in the Sky*, p. 116.

34 Reilly, *Scaffolding in the Sky*, p. 168. The matter of the location of academic power was of concern to the New Testament group, of which Reilly was a member in the years before the First World War. His aim in preventing the lay members of the University Council from appointing academic members of staff lay in 'preventing the new university being managed like a secondary school, and consequently sinking to the level of one...'

Blomfield, Reilly requested that the university have a representative on RIBA's Board of Architectural Education, in the same way that it did on the Central Medical Council. Mindful of the leading position Liverpool occupied in terms of university architectural schools, he asked whether the board could not 'Differentiate between universities on the one hand giving degrees under statutes and characters of their own and on the other hand bodies without such authority?'[35] At this date (1910) Reilly was referring to a handful of departments within the university system, and he would certainly have placed Liverpool at the very top of these. He went on to argue for a further differentiation within this small group, presumably to help strengthen his own status within the university and to further Liverpool's case externally:

> Would it not be possible to distinguish among the universities themselves, between the university which devotes a fully endowed chair on a life basis to architecture, and one that does not? This would raise architecture to parity with other subjects such as law, history and medicine.[36]

The outcome was a restructuring of the Board of Architectural Education and a recommendation that

> The universities should agree to the board drawing up a list of persons suitable for the posts of external examiners in architecture, that the university should instruct the external examiner to make an annual report to the board on efficiency of schools where examined.[37]

Reilly's desire for absolute autonomy for the university schools would appear to have been thwarted. However, he did manage to retain a certain degree of control through a compromise in which, as Reilly stated, 'I eventually consented that I would choose the man I recommended to the Liverpool Senate from an agreed panel.'[38] The first appointee was Ernest Newton in 1911. In 1912, Reilly set out in an interview his vision of an English School of Architecture and the problems in design set for the final examination for RIBA. In the course of the discussion he touched on a number of points that would come to dominate the ethos of the Liverpool School. When asked,

---

35 Letter from Reilly to Blomfield, 5 July 1910, Vice-Chancellor's Papers, Liverpool University Archive, Box P6B/3/3.
36 Letter from Reilly to Blomfield, 5 July 1910.
37 Letter from Blomfield to the Vice-Chancellor, 24 November 1910, Vice-Chancellor's Papers, Liverpool University Archive, Box P6B/3/3.
38 Reilly, *Scaffolding in the Sky*, p. 117.

Is it not a fact that there is a danger of overlooking the necessities and actualities of everyday practice… when attention is so largely devoted to problems of design in 'the grand manner?'

he replied:

Whatever manner we work in, 'grand' or otherwise, becomes an affectation if it is not consistently applied… I maintain that the architect trained in what is called 'the grand manner' is more likely to build a really good cottage than the man who has only considered cottages… There is no reason to my mind therefore, why in the pursuit of a more monumental and more worthy architecture for our public buildings, all classes of buildings should not profit.[39]

The question of consistency is further dealt with by Reilly in relation to the application of the neo-Georgian, and the teaching methods employed at the Liverpool School. When asked,

would you like to see the neo-Grec movement an established thing in this country to the practical exclusion of other styles; that is to say, so that the general body of practising architects might be counted on to produce buildings of good average merit?

Reilly replied:

Yes that is the condition of things I should like to see if you interpret the term 'neo-Grec' sufficiently widely. Schools of design have this great advantage, that while they do not hamper the genius from giving individual expression to his work, they prevent the average man from falling below a certain level.[40]

Reilly was therefore prepared to allow for a certain bland consistency in his adoption of a Monumental Classicism within the university, at the expense of the office system that allowed, in his view, excellent and poor training to coexist. While the partial victory over the process of examination was a vindication of the method and style adopted by the Liverpool School up to that date, Reilly continued to promote the system adopted by the Liverpool

---

39 Reilly, 'On the Need for an English School of Architecture', *The Architects' and Builders' Journal*, 31 January 1912, pp. 115–17.

40 Reilly, 'On the Need for an English School of Architecture', p. 117. Simpson replied to the points raised by Reilly in this article the following month by quoting the view he had expressed as early as 1890: 'I do not think I am at all singular in holding that it is impossible to examine a man in architecture. By examination you can find out, perhaps, what practical knowledge he has, what his acquaintance is with the history of architecture, but that is all. It is only in his designs that he can show whether or not he is a good architect.' Simpson, 'On the Need for an English School of Architecture', *The Architects' and Builders' Journal*, 21 February 1912.

School up to and beyond his retirement in 1933. In articles such as 'The Training of Architects in the Liverpool School' of 1927, and 'Architecture as a Profession for Men and Women' of 1931, both published in *The Journal of Careers*, he provided what were in effect recruitment articles extolling the virtues of the Liverpool system.

Reilly employed a number of other devices to help further these aims. His conception of a Monumental Classical house style for the school was helped further by his travels, at William Lever's expense, in North America in 1909. This was to be the first of a series of transatlantic links between the school and many American architectural practices. The North American experience would also help to inform the ethos of the Department of Civic Design; American Monumental models held sway in the early years of its development. The transatlantic links also had an effect on the physical appearance of Liverpool itself, principally through the work of the Liverpool graduate Herbert Rowse in the 1920s–30s. While Reilly made much of his pioneering work in forging links with the United States, it is important to note that this work was echoed – and some might argue predated – by initiatives in Glasgow and London. Indeed, the Beaux-Arts, much vaunted by Reilly as *the* Liverpool style, had been introduced to the Glasgow School by the French architect Eugene Bourdon, who had trained at the Ecole des Beaux-Arts. He was building upon what might be argued to be a stronger and less sporadic commitment to Classicism in that city.[41] Similarly, the AA in London was producing Beaux-Arts- and Classically inspired student work, albeit of a less eye-catching nature than that produced at Liverpool.[42] That commentators and historians have, until recently, overlooked this fact is a testament to Reilly's public relations skills in the intervening years.

41 This thesis was outlined by Gavin Stamp in a paper read to a study day attached to an exhibition at the Walker Art Gallery in Liverpool, 9 November 1996 (see J. Sharples, *Charles Reilly and the Liverpool School of Architecture 1904–1933*, Liverpool University Press, Liverpool, 1996). The paper was entitled 'Glasgow, America and the Beaux-Arts'. Stamp argued that Glasgow, from 'Greek' Thompson through Burnet, had remained faithful to the Classical style. The recent attention given to Charles Rennie Mackintosh's work has masked the fact that Glasgow's appearance and feel owes more to Classicism and American influence, and that in fact a dual approach to architectural design existed in the city at the turn of the century.

42 Reilly wrote to Bourdon, in a very dismissive manner, with regard to what might be described as the low-key Classicism being produced at the AA around 1910: 'this cottage idea of architecture which to my mind is the bane of English work at present. I'm afraid the Architectural Association with its glorification of the primitive farmhouse is responsible for a good deal of it.' Letter from Reilly to Bourdon, 19 October 1910, Reilly Papers, Liverpool University Archive, Box D207/2/3.

Transatlantic Links: American Monumental Classicism

Despite Reilly's commitment, from as early as 1905, to American models of architectural education, it was not until 1909 that he had the opportunity to experience American architecture at first hand. Reilly's enthusiasm for the American Beaux-Arts came via his friend Stanley Adshead and a former student, Stanley Ramsey. In 1932 Ramsey generously credited Reilly with the American model's introduction to Britain, reinforcing the impression (long held in Liverpool's architectural and educational circles, particularly among the 'New Testament' group)[43] that the city represented a new Athens at the hub of a vast mercantile empire:

> The reaction from the French standard to a more national style set the pioneers adventuring in America. Liverpool, as the chief port for Americans advertising in this country, was particularly susceptible to American influence and Reilly was, architecturally speaking, one of the first to cross the Herring Pond… 15 to 20 years ago I can remember the intense excitement that the publication of the American work caused: it seemed to have all the breadth of the French with the refinement of the Italian, and yet somehow was wonderfully Anglo-Saxon. Comparisons were made between the reaction of America on this country, and the influence that the Colonial Greek architecture exerted on Athens.[44]

Following his return from America, Reilly sought to promote his American enthusiasms, which had been reinforced by first-hand experience of the work. He wrote to Reginald Blomfield enthusing: 'I am back from America with a new scale for life…'[45] A major outlet for this newly fired enthusiasm would be the Department of Civic Design; another would be the various writings on American architecture he produced after his return. In his article in 1910, Reilly noted that

> the ordinary American man or woman whom I there met knew not only the names of the architects in their own towns and their chief buildings, but also where in the States I should find, say, the latest work of Messrs McKim, Mead

43   This name was given to a powerful, semi-secret caucus within the Arts Faculty at Liverpool University, founded and led by Professor John Macdonald Mackay (1856–1931), Rathbone Professor of History from 1884–1914. Reilly was invited to join the group shortly after his appointment in 1904. An oil painting by Albert Lipczinski, in the University's Art Collection, shows Mackay addressing fellow members of the group, including Reilly.

44   S. C. Ramsey, 'Charles Herbert Reilly', in Budden (ed.), *The Book of the Liverpool School of Architecture*, p. 27.

45   Letter from Reilly to Blomfield, 3 May 1909, Reilly Papers, Liverpool University Archive, Box S3205.

and White, or of Messrs Carrere Hastings. This interest by the general public, which the rest of my visit confirmed, is very striking. New buildings... are objects of intense public curiosity: the daily papers not only illustrate them profusely, but give the careers of their designers, treating them as public benefactors, or the reverse, with highly salutary frankness: while papers like the *Architectural Record* exist and flourish with the express object of feeding and stimulating this interest among the public at large.[46]

The lessons concerning popular journalism learned in the United States would be put into practice, with remarkable success, in regular contributions to the non-professional press such as the *Liverpool Daily Post*, the *Manchester Guardian*, *The Listener* and the *Evening Standard* in the subsequent years. The most immediate effect of his visit, however, was the annual placement of six students in various American offices[47] Another effect came via the large assortment of American publications he had accumulated and brought back from his trip, which would be used to aid the teaching of American Beaux-Arts methods in the school.[48]

While Reilly made a good deal of his visit to the United States, he was by no means alone in fostering transatlantic links. Glasgow had a strong tradition of ties with America, while within Liverpool itself around 1909 other architects – such as the recently qualified Herbert Rowse – were also making visits to North America and developing experience of American styles and working methods. Such experience was to have a major effect upon the Liverpool cityscape during the 1920s and 1930s, in work such as India Buildings in Water Street of 1924–1932, and Martins Bank in Water Street of 1932 (Fig. 20).[49]

46   Reilly, 'The Modern Renaissance in American Architecture', *RIBA Journal*, 25 June 1910, pp. 630–35.

47   The placement of students would continue throughout the 1920s, until it was ended by the Wall Street Crash of 1929. For accounts of student work undertaken during these placements see E. M. Fry, *Autobiographical Sketches*, Elek, New York, 1975, pp. 95–98; G. Stephenson and C. Demarco, *On a Human Scale*, Freemantle Arts Centre Press, 1992, pp. 21–22; and J. Sharples, 'Reilly and his Students', in Sharples (ed.), *Charles Reilly and the Liverpool School of Architecture*, pp. 28–29.

48   Reilly noted in a letter to Sir Aston Webb that he had 'collected two packing cases full of material...'; 12 May 1909. See also letter of 15 June 1909, Reilly Papers, Liverpool University Archive, Box S3205.

49   Rowse was visiting the US at about the same time as Reilly, but he stayed for a much longer period, and unlike Reilly he actually worked within American architectural offices. P. Richmond, 'Rebuilding the Temple: The Inter-War Architecture of Herbert Rowse', MDes thesis, Liverpool University, 1992. As Gavin Stamp has noted, subsequent commentators have generally failed to acknowledge other centres of American cultural transference, for example Glasgow, or other sources within Liverpool, for example Rowse, in their assessments of the period. Stamp, 'Glasgow, America and the Beaux-Arts', paper read to a study day attached to the exhibition 'Charles Reilly and the Liverpool School of Architecture'.

Leonard Eaton, while citing the work of Burnet and the influence of Glasgow in Anglo-American cultural transference, nevertheless largely credits Reilly with the importation of American Neoclassicism into Britain when he notes that

> Charles Herbert Reilly made no less than six trips across the Atlantic and possibly had a larger acquaintance in the American architectural profession than any of the others [Eaton cites Ferdinand Boberg and Adolf Loos, among others, as examples of other architects looking to the United States at this time]. He, however, was the only one for whom the neoclassicism of McKim, Mead and White had any great appeal.[50]

Reilly had made contact with the firm of McKim, Mead and White prior to his first American trip, when he wrote to them requesting photographs for use by his students.[51] Reviews of student work at the school during 1909 reveal the growing influence of American work on Reilly's teaching.[52] A reviewer from *The Builders' Journal* noted on 10 July 1912 that

> It is, in fact, evident that the United States furnishes either the model or the inspiration for the composition, and even detail, of nearly every essay in design... the manners of... Charles Follen McKim, Hornbostle, Cass Gilbert and Van Buren Magonigle are the chief favourites.

The firm's work exemplified for Reilly all that was good about modern American architecture, with its Classical styling allied to technological ingenuity. He described the American Beaux-Arts as representing 'the finest aspirations of a great people at a great epoch'.[53] Ramsey was also an admirer of the firm and wrote an article in 1917 for the *RIBA Journal* on the subject.[54] Despite Reilly's appreciation, it would not be until 1924 that he would produce a slim volume, edited by Ramsey, extolling their work.[55] The book is interesting as an examination of Reilly's earlier motivations in adopting the American Beaux-Arts model; Reilly describes the work of McKim, Mead and White as displaying 'a universal spirit such as our present-day civilization should do even if it does

50   L. Eaton, *American Architecture Comes of Age*, MIT Press, Cambridge, MA, 1972, p. 234.
51   Reilly to McKim, Mead and White, 25 May 1909, Reilly Papers, Liverpool University Archive, Box S3205.
52   *RIBA Journal*, 28 August 1909, pp. 693–94.
53   Reilly, *McKim, Mead and White*, Ernest Benn, London, 1924, p. 24.
54   S. C. Ramsey, 'The Work of McKim, Mead and White', *RIBA Journal*, Vol. 25, 5 December 1917, pp. 25–29.
55   Reilly, *McKim, Mead and White*.

not'. He also discussed the eclectic nature of Beaux-Arts styling, which for Reilly logically led to an inevitable and welcome move away from the individual 'master architect' to a more anonymous form of creation. This issue, of a universal and less personal style, would be repeatedly echoed in the Modernist rhetoric of the 1920s and 1930s. The universal nature of the McKim, Mead and White style was well suited to Reilly's own vision of an urban culture that was rooted not in the parochial concerns of nationalism or a national style – a preoccupation that had dogged British architecture for so long – but rather represented, as Crouch puts it, 'a fitting symbol representing a universalised metropolitanism'.[56]

The notion of a universalized metropolitanism had developed in the United States following the World's Columbian Exposition, in Chicago in 1893. This had, in turn, stimulated a nascent interest in Beaux-Arts in America. In an article in the *Architectural Record* from early 1894, Montgomery Schuyler outlined the points which made Beaux-Arts *the* American style. These included issues of coherence in design, leading to uniformity of expression:

> In the first place the success is first of all a success of unity, a triumph of ensemble. The whole is better than any of its parts and greater than any of its parts, and its effect is one and indivisible.[57]

This led, according to Schuyler, to a feeling of cultural neutrality, allowing Beaux-Arts to be used as 'a decorative envelope of any construction… without exciting in most observers any sense of incongruity, much less any sense of meanness'. Applied to this was a sense of 'magnitude', which meant not simply bigness, but rather 'artistic manipulation of scale'. The combination of these factors meant that, as Crouch puts it,

> What Beaux-Arts styling was able to do, in the eyes of its adherents, was to enable the construction of large buildings whose subsequent proportions were familiar enough culturally for them to be accessible, and so to become monumental in appearance, rather than incoherently large.[58]

Given Reilly's own concerns and interests in Liverpool, the adoption of a style that was both linked with the past through its Classical language, and yet was also able to appear culturally neutral, allowed him to play devil's advocate

---

56 Crouch, 'Design Initiatives in Liverpool', p. 124.
57 M. Schuyler, 'Last Words about the World's Fair', *Architectural Record*, January–March 1894, p. 293.
58 Crouch, 'Design Initiatives in Liverpool', p. 122.

in the national style debate still raging in Britain. The Classical envelope could be argued to be quintessentially British because of the traditionalists' belief that Georgian Classicism represented the essence of British identity, while the Beaux-Arts's adaptation of Neoclassical imagery gave a transnational dimension to the work – which strongly appealed to Reilly's own political and architectural ideology.[59] The adoption of the American Beaux-Arts model also solved a number of other problems for Reilly. His rejection of the strict adherence to Classicism (advocated by the likes of Blomfield in books such as *The Mistress Art* and *A History of Renaissance Architecture in England 1500– 1800*) gave him the freedom to develop and promote his theories on architectural education, free from the baggage of the national style and historicism debates that had preoccupied and stifled architectural development in Britain since the end of the nineteenth century. With his trip to the United States in 1909, the growing interest in American Beaux-Arts evident in his writings and teaching to date gained new impetus. Building on the Beaux-Arts influences established before his arrival in Liverpool, Reilly continued to look for new channels through which he could promote his enthusiasms still further. Most prominent among these initiatives would be the in-house publications produced by the school from 1904 onwards.

Early Promotional Publications

Reilly's commitment to his students' study of Liverpool's Georgian architecture, as set out in his 1905 lecture *Some Tendencies in Modern Architecture*, was allied to a decision to publish the results of their study. For Reilly, the publication of the work was both an affirmation of the direction he wished the school to take, and also a means of publicizing that aim. Although not unprecedented,[60] this was also yet another indicator of Reilly's desire to distance himself from the Simpson era, and thus establish a sense of his own development of a new direction in Liverpudlian policy. Reilly recalled that the publication of the *Portfolio of Measured Drawings* – as the earlier books were called – was 'The obvious thing to do then… I really think the measured

---

59 Reilly's socialism, although not always strict or consistent, has largely been ignored by commentators on his life and work.

60 For example, from 1867 the Architectural Association had published an annual *Sketchbook*, which contained measured drawings, while Gilbert Scott's office published the *Spring Gardens Sketchbook*.

drawings we published of St George's Hall were the beginning of the dispropor-
tionate influence of the little Liverpool School.'[61] The first edition appeared in
1906, followed by a second in 1908; both attracted a good deal of mixed
publicity in the local, national and professional press.[62] One commentator
considered it 'a very handsome volume, which does great credit to the
editor...';[63] but the *Athenaeum*, reviewing the second volume, noted that 'we
drew attention to the need for greater accuracy and fuller information, in
order to render the drawings of value... we regret to see that similar defects
are again apparent in the present issue.'[64] Reilly replied, 'your reviewer does
not appreciate the main object these drawings serve. "The sole reason for
publication" as he inaccurately quotes... is not "to form a permanent
historical record of notable works of art." This is distinctly stated in the
volume... as a secondary objective.'[65] Reilly went on to point out that the
volume was intended as an architectural record rather than as an archeo-
logical one, displaying as it did 'the actual architectural forms, details, and
mouldings used by the masters'.[66] It was essential for Reilly to place an
unambigious emphasis on the publication's principal intention – the application of Classical form and detail to student work – in order to prevent
allegations of historicism being levelled at the school's teaching programme.
By aligning Classical teaching methods with progressive architectural
thought, Reilly was placing himself in the vanguard of architectural theory.
The *Portfolios* produced in 1906 and 1908 largely achieved their intended
objective of establishing the Liverpudlian ethos that remained unexpressed in
building – an option that would not be available to either Reilly, or his
students, for several years.

In addition to marketing the school to the professional press, Reilly
recognized the importance of establishing contact with prospective students.
The prime means of attracting a broad range of applications to the school was
its prospectus;[67] inspired by some he had seen and brought back from his

61   Reilly, *Scaffolding in the Sky*, p. 119.
62   Reilly sought to increase the school's international profile by attempting to distribute copies of
     the portfolio in the US. See Reilly Papers, Liverpool University Archive, Box D207/2/1.
63   Reilly Papers, Liverpool University Archive, Box S3214, p. 47.
64   The *Athenaeum*, 8 August 1908.
65   Letter from Reilly to the *Athenaeum*, 10 August 1908.
66   Letter from Reilly to the *Athenaeum*, 10 August 1908.
67   In a letter to a prospective student, Reilly emphasizes the autonomy of the school to distinguish
     it from 'crammers' for RIBA exams, and mentions the advantages of the school's RIBA exemp-
     tions. Letter from Reilly, 4 January 1910, Reilly Papers, Liverpool University Archive, Box S3205.

American travels in 1909, Reilly sought to improve and expand on the publications already being produced by the school. In justifying this move, Reilly
reveals the lesson he had learned from the Americans about the power of the
image in selling the message of the school's house style to prospective
students. In a letter to the Registrar in May 1909, Reilly stated that

> since visiting America and making a collection of the prospectuses of the
> American Schools of Architecture I have come to the conclusion that it would
> be well to somewhat alter the form of our own prospectus. The alteration I
> wish to make is the omission of the detailed regulations governing the various
> courses… and the inclusion in their place of illustrations of the actual work of
> the students in each year. These illustrations will explain at a glance the
> character of work done and be more convincing to architects than any number
> of printed pages. So strongly do the American schools feel this that they all
> issue a separate pamphlet of illustrations…This they distribute gratuitously.
> The head of the big school at Cornell told me that an issue of their illustrations
> increased the school numbers from under 50 to over 100 at one entry.[68]

The introduction of colour printing was decided on later that year, and the
impact of the new-style prospectus was increased further by its distribution to
the national and professional press.[69] A year later, in a letter to the Vice-
Chancellor, Reilly commented that

> You will remember perhaps that the finance committee last year allowed me to
> issue my annual prospectus in an enlarged form costing the university £20… I
> consider, if I may be allowed to say so, this enlarged prospectus has been a very
> good investment and I think a large proportion of our increase in students,
> during this last year when our profession has been suffering… can be traced to
> it… For instance the prospectus itself was reviewed in some of the technical
> papers including the *Journal of the Royal Institute of British Architects*, a
> treatment of our prospectus which has not occurred before.[70]

The effect of this increased publicity was that Liverpool started to attract
increasing numbers of able students from both Britain and the Empire.[71] The
consequence of this was that the Liverpool School, which had from 1909

---

68   Letter from Reilly to the Registrar, 21 May 1909, Reilly Papers, Liverpool University Archive, Box
S3205.
69   Reilly Papers, Box D207/2/3.
70   Letter from Reilly to the Vice-Chancellor, 8 June 1910, Vice-Chancellor's Papers, Liverpool
University Archive, Box P6B/3/5.
71   William Holford, a former student, recalled that reading the school's prospectus gave him 'the
enthusiastic conviction that Liverpool was the architectural Mecca'. W. Holford, 'Sir Charles
Reilly: An Appreciation', *The Listener*, 15 July 1948, pp. 93–94.

onwards become increasingly associated with Monumental Classicism, began to re-export a variant of Beaux-Arts styling around the Empire as Reilly's overseas students returned home to practice.[72]

Reilly's other publication venture of the period was the first in a series entitled *The Liverpool Architectural Sketch Book*. Editions were produced in 1910, 1911, 1913 and 1920 (by which time it had become *The Liverpool University Architectural Sketch Book*) and they are a useful chronicle of the school's stylistic principles during the middle period of Reilly's tenure at Liverpool. In the introduction to the first edition, Reilly clearly sets out the school's stylistic position as being Monumental Classicism:

> Is it possible for a School of Architecture, which is largely and necessarily a training ground in building technique for fledgling architects, to attempt the wider sphere of a school of architectural thought?... Without making claim in any way to have accomplished the answer to our initial question, in Liverpool we have at any rate made our choice. We have determined that Monumental architecture shall be the basis of our system.[73]

The illustrations in the first *Sketch Book* continue in the manner of the *Portfolios* but on a larger scale, with measured drawings of Liverpool's Classical architecture – including Elmes's St George's Hall and Cockerell's Bank of England – alongside other buildings in Liverpool and Manchester, and designs by students. An examination of the student work from the period reveals the strengths and weaknesses of the course. For example, Ernest Prestwich's *Design for a Casino* is, in Powers's words, 'a design of unrelieved dullness, while the *Design for an Art Gallery* by L. B. Budden, is perhaps trying to achieve too many things at once...' (Fig. 7)[74] Of the finer examples, the *Design for an Art Gallery* by H. A. Dod from the 1911 edition shows the school's technique at its best. Dod went on to design a number of buildings in the school's mature Beaux-Arts style, most notably the Liverpool Athenaeum Club (1924–1928, Fig. 19), which Leonard Eaton described as being polished and elegant in proportion: '[it] bears a strong relationship to similar buildings in New York, such as the Metropolitan Club... by McKim, Mead and White.'[75]

By 1912 Reilly, when writing to Percy Hastings of the *Architectural Review*, was proud enough of the *Sketch Books* to comment that 'I imagine in

72 For examples see Budden, *The Book of the Liverpool School of Architecture*.
73 Reilly, 'Introduction', *The Liverpool Architectural Sketch Book*, 1910, pp. 11–12.
74 Powers, 'Architectural Education in Britain', p. 147.
75 Eaton, *American Architecture Comes of Age*, p. 31.

my more optimistic moments posterity judging the revival of Classical Architecture in the twentieth century, by the *Sketch Book*.'[76] However, the designs in the 1913 edition highlight the inherent weaknesses of the Liverpudlian philosophy. The *Design for an Art Gallery* (a now-familiar theme) by T. T. Jenkins, with its colonnaded frontage, relies on a Mannerist enlargement of design to gain effect; when compared with H. C. Bradshaw's design on the same subject, it illustrates how the developing Liverpudlian Monumental style could to be taken to extremes. Bradshaw had been one of Reilly's earliest protegés; Reilly had helped him gain a scholarship to the school. Bradshaw subsequently justified Reilly's faith in him by taking the Rome Prize when it was first introduced in 1912.

The downside of this emphasis on stylistic consistency was a lack of originality in approach; but for Reilly, this was a price worth paying. He believed that the technical abilities of students trained in his system would triumph over the vagaries of quality and style displayed by office-trained architects. As Crouch notes, 'At its most rudimentary, Reilly's idea was not to encourage genius, but to make mediocrity as respectable and sober in architecture as it generally manages to be elsewhere.'[77] The consistent design philosophy and highly directed compositional drawing style gave Liverpool an advantage over other schools of architecture in competitions such as the Rome Prize. This was to be reflected in the number of Liverpool students who won the prize after its inception in 1912.

The Rome Prize

Britain's growing awareness of its relative weakness, and its late adoption of formalized architectural education compared with major competitors such as France and the United States, led to the establishment of a Faculty of Architecture at the recently established British School at Rome. Sir Rennell Rodd, British Ambassador to Italy, was one of the prime movers behind this extension of the school; he saw it as 'a training ground for the humanists of a new Renaissance'.[78] The weakness in the British system had been highlighted in 1884 by Phené Spiers, who commented that

76 Letter from Reilly to P. Hastings, 15 June 1912, Reilly Papers, Liverpool University Archive, Box S3210.
77 Crouch, 'Design Initiatives in Liverpool', p. 130.
78 'Sir Rennell Rodd on the British School at Rome', *RIBA Journal*, 26 November 1910, p. 61.

The first great failing in England is that the student coming straight from school is not prepared to make that use of the practical training to be had in the office which is universally assumed. He has little or no knowledge of either freehand or geometrical drawing, of physics, mechanics, or of any of the elements of architectural style... He has picked up an idea here and there in the office... but he finds himself unable to grasp the composition of a building... He has in fact taken from three to five years to learn imperfectly what might have been learned in one or two if his mind had been previously trained to receive it.[79]

In 1909, Reginald Blomfield advocated an advanced school of architecture along Beaux-Arts lines; the same views were behind Reilly's own efforts at Liverpool. However, the system that had long esteemed the private architect over the publicly employed one would continue to have an effect on the Rome Prize and the course of architectural education in Britain. The judging process for the prize was intended to be at least as rigorous as its French equivalent, yet it also needed to avoid the closed nature of the French system; French winners rarely went on to build anything after their time in Rome. As Louise Campbell notes,

> The faculty wished to influence the teaching of architecture, although less directly than in France, where the jury which awarded the Prix de Rome consisted of eight architects, who were elected life members of the Académie des Beaux-Arts... The prize frequently went to students from an atélier directed by a member of the jury. In England, with a less centralized system of architectural education and an academy which had effectively relinquished control over standard of architecture training to RIBA, it was hoped to administer the prize more fairly.[80]

The faculty consisted mainly of educationalists, and indeed a number of the winners of the British Prize returned from Rome to teaching posts; the consequence was that the British system took on many of the characteristics of the French. During its early life the competition underwent almost continuous change, particularly concerning the methods by which the candidates' talents were judged. By 1921 it was considered that the first stage of the competition had 'resulted in a wholly unnecessary elaboration of drawing... the competition has become one of architectural draughtsmanship rather

79 R. Phené Spiers, 'The French Diplome d'Architecture and the German System of Architectural Education', *RIBA Transactions*, XXXIV, 1884, p. 124.
80 L. Campbell, 'A Call to Order: The Rome Prize and Early Twentieth Century British Architecture', *Architectural History, Journal of the Society of Architectural Historians of Great Britain*, Vol. 32, 1989, p. 136.

than one of design.'[81] This led to a conference in 1922 attended by 13 heads of architectural schools, including Reilly. Given that the system suited the students of the Liverpool School so well, Reilly was naturally unhappy about the major changes proposed by men such as Beresford Pite of the Royal College of Art, who called for 'designs really expressive of modern constructions and materials irrespective of historical style...'[82] that were based on working drawings. Reilly took a centrist position, backed by Addison of the Leeds School, that drawings should be 'constructible', as opposed to purely working drawings. As a result, changes were made to the competition rules concerning the length of time allowed for the production of drawings.

Throughout the 1920s, the links between the university schools of architecture and the Rome scholarship were strengthened. In 1921 the competition was restricted to 'students whose credentials of previous training have been approved'[83] – that is, those who had attended one of the approved schools of architecture. This allowed the Liverpool School to play an increasingly important role in the Rome project. It was a prestigious, high-profile competition run on lines that were well-suited to his own design philosophy, and it assisted him in attracting both publicity and students. Reilly recalled that 'the winning of the Rome Scholarship seemed to some to indicate that the Liverpool School had become a force in the outside world...'[84]

Campbell points out that the faculty's insistence on 'approved schools' restricted the availability of the Rome Prize to those 'able to pay fees and, if necessary, maintain themselves while attending courses away from home'.[85] This must be viewed in the context of the almost total absence of maintenance grants (ex-servicemen were the exception) until 1927, when they were introduced by RIBA. While an element of elitism cannot be denied, Reilly did help to find funding for a number of able students who might otherwise not have had the chance of university education; as noted above, the first Rome winner Chalton Bradshaw benefited in this way.[86]

The standards being achieved by the competitors varied a good deal from year to year; in 1924, 1928 and 1935, the standard was considered too

81 The Faculty of Architecture, the British School at Rome; report dated 21 March 1921.
82 Conference of the Faculty of Architecture, the British School at Rome, 2 May 1922.
83 Meeting of the Faculty of Architecture, the British School at Rome, 31 May 1921.
84 Reilly, *Scaffolding in the Sky*, pp. 137–38.
85 Campbell, 'A Call to Order', p. 138.
86 Bradshaw had entered the School of Architecture as a 'lantern and studio boy' in 1908 and enrolled as a student following Reilly's help finding funding in 1911. Reilly, *Scaffolding in the Sky*, p. 137.

low for the prize to be awarded. In the early 1920s, conditions at the school itself had deteriorated, leading to the appointment in 1925 of Bernard Ashmole as Director; he instigated a number of changes, including the provision of married quarters for students. The faculty was critical of the standards of work being sent back by the Rome scholars, particularly the measured drawings of Classical and Renaissance buildings. In general, we can perceive an overall decline, despite efforts by the faculty to instigate changes to the rules to help rectify problems. Other factors were starting to impinge on the effectiveness of Blomfield's model for the atélier at Rome, particularly the development of Modernism as expressed in the English publication of Le Corbusier's *Towards a New Architecture* (1927) and Bruno Taut's *Modern Architecture* (1929). Blomfield was part of an older generation and the apparent rejection of Classical models led him to take an extreme stance against what he saw as a wholly foreign threat to British culture – a view he articulated in his 1934 book *Modernismus*.

The Rome Prize provides an interesting chronicle to this transitional period in British architecture and illustrates the differing ways in which it was perceived. When the 1926 Rome scholar Amyas Connell returned to England, some months before the end of his scholarship, to work on a commission for Bernard Ashmole, the threat seemed (at least to Blomfield) uncomfortably close to home. The published reviews of the house, named 'High and Over', embodied the polarized positions of British architecture in the starkest terms. Other houses by George Checkley and Marshall Sissons followed quickly, and while these architects went to some length to identify the links between Classical and Modernist architecture in order to counter Blomfield's claims of wilful disregard for tradition, the conservatives remained unconvinced.

By the time of Reilly's retirement in 1933, the Rome Prize was no longer as prestigious as it had been intended to be; and while it had provided another useful strand in Reilly's promotion of his conception of a Monumental Classical house style for Liverpool, it had as Campbell notes 'lost its status as the apex of progressive architectural education and by the 1930s came to be regarded as highly reactionary'.[87] In his autobiography of 1938, Reilly concentrates on the early years of the scholarship, having by that time firmly aligned himself with the Modernist school. From 1933 onwards, Reilly's successor Lionel Budden instigated changes in the ethos of the school, particularly in competition and research. Rejecting Reilly's emphasis on the Rome

87   Campbell, 'A Call to Order', p. 131.

School's Monumental scale, he preferred a system in which groups of students worked on modern housing and public building projects. He outlined this stance in his 'Theory of Architecture' lecture course.

By the time of the outbreak of the First World War in 1914, the suitability of Neoclassicism for modern architecture was well established. Reilly, while not alone in championing the Neoclassical, was certainly in the vanguard of those commentators who recognized the cultural and ideological implications of the Classical model when applied to the urban environment. The publication of A. E. Richardson's *Monumental Classic Architecture in Great Britain and Ireland during the Eighteenth and Nineteenth Centuries* in 1914 helped to affirm Reilly's move towards a Monumental Classicism. The importance Reilly placed on the use of Classical forms, and their appropriate application to a suitable building type, was articulated in his examination of the Monumental Beaux-Arts of the Selfridges department store (1907–1909 and 1928), in which he noted 'You would think from looking at its vast colonnade that shop keeping was really the height of our ideals.'[88] This view is interesting when contrasted with his review of Herbert Rowse's rather more modest Lloyd's Bank on Church Street in Liverpool, of which Reilly said 'Because of its delightful design, this brick bank has more dignity than the emporia of lingerie for which massive Greek columns have previously been the accepted architectural expression.'[89]

For Reilly therefore, the more important the cultural symbolism of a building, the greater architectural emphasis should be placed upon it. Classical form should be applied according to a distinct hierarchy, with publicly prestigious buildings at its apex and commercial buildings much lower down the scale. To mix architectural form was, for Reilly, to debase the whole system. Sigfried Giedion, in his book *Mechanization Takes Command*, would call this the 'devaluation of symbols'; Tim Benton has commented on an environment in which 'banks dressed up as temples, department stores as palaces'.[90] This clearly tied in with Reilly's views on the uniformity of expression and architectural 'good manners', which he believed were naturally produced through the appropriate application of Classical models:

> In the eighteenth century most people lived in terraces of houses, in which externally each individual house did not differ materially from its neighbours.

88 Reilly, *Some Architectural Problems of Today*, Liverpool University Press, Liverpool, 1924, p. 3.
89 Reilly, 'Lloyds Bank, Church Street, Liverpool', *The Architects' Journal*, 19 October 1932, p. 497.
90 T. Benton, 'The Myth of Function', in P. Greenhalgh (ed.), *Modernism in Design*, Reaktion Books, London, 1990, p. 45.

This was a fine sign of urbanity, a tribute to the community... Any excessive expression of individuality or of personal importance in a building was considered bad manners.[91]

This had been Reilly's position from as early as 1905, when he argued for 'The value of the Classical style, modified by English taste, in domestic as well as public architecture.'[92] Reilly was to expand on this generalized view of Classical style with his adoption of the American model. The link between stylistic stance and cultural significance was already clearly acknowledged by other sources; Geoffrey Scott's *The Architecture of Humanism* (1914) was an examination of this relationship and an attempt to put the Neoclassical revival into some sort of context. He sought to

trace the natural history of our opinions, to discover how far upon their own premises they are true or false, and to explain why, when false, they have yet remained plausible, powerful, and, to many minds, convincing.[93]

In attempting to explode the ideological fallacies of what he termed the Romantic, the Mechanical, the Ethical and the Biological, he concluded that 'For the material of architecture, no system of accepted meaning has been organized'[94] and that architectural values of mass and space relied as much on learned response as any physical or material reality. For Scott, style and taste were the deciding factors:

Style, through coherence, subordinates beauty to the pattern of the mind, and so selects what it presents so that all, at one sole act of thought, is found intelligible, and every part re-echoes, explains, and reinforces the beauty of the whole... of all the styles that have yet been created, the forms of Greece and Rome, with those of the Renaissance after them, were in this point the most exact and strict... They are... the fittest instruments for giving clarity to sharp ideas... of function and of scale... first we must discard a century of misplaced logic...[95]

Scott articulated the ideological framework by which men such as Reilly were able to imbue the Neoclassical style with cultural significance in the early years of the century. For some commentators the significance of Scott's

91   Reilly, *Some Architectural Problems of Today*, p. 6.
92   Reilly, 'Some Tendencies in Modern Architecture', *Building News*, 12 May 1905.
93   G. Scott, *The Architecture of Humanism*, The Architectural Press, London, 1980 (1914).
94   Scott, *The Architecture of Humanism*, p. 61.
95   Scott, *The Architecture of Humanism*, p. 238.

book goes even further. In the introduction to the 1980 edition of the book, David Watkin quotes Clough Williams-Ellis in arguing that Scott provided a new intellectual justification for Classicism:

> The *Architecture of Humanism* was, of course, published at a singularly unpropitious moment in the summer of 1914, and but for the war would undoubtedly have been even more of a bible to architects anxious to bring about a Classical renaissance in English architecture similar to that which had swept America after the World's Fair at Chicago in 1893.[96]

Such a claim, however, ignores the Classical and Beaux-Arts experiments that took place in Liverpool, and elsewhere, from the 1890s onwards. Other commentators have seen Scott's significance in even broader terms. Robert Macleod in *Style and Society* claims,

> not only did Scott confirm the existing trend towards Classicism in architectural teaching and practice, he created a climate of opinion, and a set of values, which made the Modern Movement in its International Style guise entirely acceptable on its importation from Germany a decade later.[97]

If, as Macleod puts it, Scott's book confirmed the 'trend towards Classicism in architectural teaching', by 1914 the Liverpool School's adoption of American Monumental Classicism was equally in evidence. The ideological framework that Scott's book sought to articulate was parallel to Reilly's in many respects. The success of the development of the Liverpool School style, and Reilly's promotion of it, can be gauged by the fact that in 1915, the architectural critic Randall Phillips wrote to Reilly to tell him that of all the entries in the competition for the new town hall at Stepney '80 per cent of the designs were in the Liverpool manner'.[98] Crouch describes this as 'a rationalised classical one, large in scale and restrained in detail'.[99] The Liverpool School had, justifiably or not, managed to eclipse its rival institutions in the minds of many architectural professionals, and establish itself as *the* architectural school in Britain.[100]

96 D. Watkin, foreword to Scott. *The Architecture of Humanism*, p. xxiii.
97 R. Macleod, *Style and Society: Architectural Ideology in Britain 1835–1914*, RIBA Publications, London, 1971, p. 134.
98 Reilly, *Scaffolding in the Sky*, p. 121.
99 Crouch, 'Design Initiatives in Liverpool', p. 127.
100 'Apart from the RA and a scrappy course at King's College later transferred to University College (and the AA?) I thought all architectural education was by apprenticeship till Reilly got going.' M. Wright, quoted in Powers, 'Architectural Education in Britain', p. 119.

The evolution of the Liverpudlian Monumental style, and its accommodation throughout the late 1920s and early 1930s with Modernism, in many ways mirrors the reform of the Edwardian schools of architecture 30 years earlier. For some commentators however, the very basis of Reilly's teaching was flawed. As Powers notes,

> Following the lead of the American classicists, Reilly and other British admirers of the École des Beaux-Arts in Paris misinterpreted what they saw as being a system based on classicism, rather than a rationalist system whose principal manifestations were classical. The difference may seem subtle, but is nonetheless crucial, for as the Liverpool School developed under Reilly the specific style he liked to call 'Monumental Classic' became an end in itself rather than the means to the abstract end that it had been at the outset.[101]

The differing ways in which figures such as Richardson, Reilly and Blomfield reacted to Modernism can be accounted for by the differences in their original conception of the role Classicism should play in the development of architectural education. For Blomfield it was part of a liberal arts education tradition, with all the attendant enduring qualities that that suggests, which as Campbell puts it 'could confer a rich store of ideas and images encouraging a mature and well informed approach to design problems'.[102] While Reilly broadly shared these values, the difference lay in the fact that he, in the words of Powers, 'had never seen Classicism as anything but a stage on the way to an as-yet unrealized future style'.[103] Powers suggests that it failed to develop and evolve in the 1920s, and I shall be examining this point in greater detail at a later stage. By adopting a pragmatic stylistic stance, Reilly was able to adjust his ideas throughout the 1930s and 1940s, and to accommodate Modernist theories without seeming to renege on his original principles.

101 Powers, 'Liverpool and Architectural Education', in Sharples (ed.), *Charles Reilly and the Liverpool School of Architecture 1904–1933*, p. 9.
102 Campbell, 'A Call to Order', pp. 143–44.
103 Powers, 'Architectural Education in Britain', p. 269.

4 Cultural Enterprises

In many respects, the cultural circumstances that would dominate Liverpool's artistic community in the early decades of the twentieth century were already in place by the time of Reilly's arrival in Liverpool in 1904. A number of institutions, such as the Liverpool Academy, had sprung into life at sporadic intervals for over 100 years. Newer institutions, such as the Walker Art Gallery, were the civic face of artistic ambition. The Walker, however, proved rather inadequate under its chairman John Lea, who is described by his biographer as 'slow to push out into new depths... he had certain spiritual and intellectual limitations.'[1] The decision to separate the Applied Art Section from the School of Architecture had been made by the university before Reilly's appointment; it would lead to the formation of the Sandon Studios Society, a breakaway art school in competition with the Corporation's School of Design. The Sandon Group gave the artistic community fresh impetus to to develop alternatives to such 'official' bodies as the Walker. Examples of such alternatives are exhibitions such as the New English Art Club show organized by Gerald Chowne at the Royal Institution building in 1905, the Sandon Society's spring exhibition of 1908, and the two Post-Impressionist shows of 1911 and 1913. John Willett summarizes the position: 'the irreconcilable gap was no longer between the art-lovers and the Corporation, as it had been at the time of the St George's Hall panels, but between the official bodies and the unofficial one'.[2]

Reilly's position in this cultural web is, in many ways, ambiguous. On the one hand, he was associated – via his university appointment – with the artistic establishment. Shortly after taking up the Roscoe Chair he was appointed a governor of the Corporation Art School; yet he used the appointment to encourage Gerald Chowne – a member of the New English Art Club who would later play a leading role in the Sandon Society – to come to Liverpool. Reilly's association with the leading families in the city – people such as the Rathbones and the Holts, who had connections with official cultural groups – was combined with close affiliations with Gerald Chowne,

---

1   F. Elias, *John Lea, Citizen and Art Lover*, Philip, Son and Nephew, Liverpool, 1928, p. 25.
2   J. Willett, *Art in a City*, Methuen, London, 1967, p. 61.

Augustus John and Herbert MacNair, who chose to remain outside the cultural establishment. Reilly, therefore, seems to have attempted (with varying degrees of success) to keep a foothold in both camps. On many occasions Reilly mediated between the two groups, but his main skill was his ability to synthesize and adapt ideas from both sides of the divide, and present them in ways that could appeal to both.

The Art Chair that Failed

In 1909, tensions between the Sandon Group and the Municipal Art Gallery led the Sandon to publish a pamphlet entitled *The Sport of Civic Life, or Art and the Municipality*.[3] Along with items lampooning the Liverpool Academy and the Walker's chairman John Lea, the main item was an essay by William Rothenstein in which he wrote

> I would say, first, let the Corporation pay one or two men of tried character and attainment sufficient to induce them to settle in your city: let them have it for their duty to advise and organise the collective efforts of gallery, museum and theatre, under their present directors, and to assist the local school to direct its talents and energies towards the fulfilment of whatever work of building or decoration these or other municipal institutions have it in their power to supply. Thus might be founded as it were a University of the Arts...[4]

Willett describes Reilly's invitation to Rothenstein to become a lecturer at the School of Architecture, an offer that Rothenstein refused. Willett suggests that this was part of a larger plan, outlined by Reilly in *Scaffolding in the Sky*, to create a powerful grouping within the university centred on the Faculty of Arts. Reilly describes the scheme thus:

> a complete Faculty of Fine Arts, the first in any English university if not anywhere in the world. The curatorship of the Walker Art Gallery was vacant. D. S. MacColl, who was then at the Wallace Gallery, was to be tempted to apply for it by the offer, at the same time, of a Chair of Aesthetics at the university. The Chair and others of painting, sculpture and music, Lord Leverhulme was to found. Augustus John was to be brought back to Liverpool... and appointments

3 C. W. Sharpe (ed.), *The Sport of Civic Life, or Art and the Municipality*, Sandon Studios Society, Liverpool, 1909. Copy held in Liverpool Record Office, Liverpool Central Library, Box H 709 SHA.
4 W. Rothenstein in Sharpe (ed.), *The Sport of Civic Life*, p. 8.

like Epstein and Elgar were to be made to the other chairs. Architecture already in existence, was of course to be part of it… everything seemed to be going swimmingly… unfortunately the Corporation got to hear of it too soon. They actually sent a deputation of the Governors of their School of Art to Port Sunlight to try and stop it… Painting and sculpture, they said, were their preserve by the arrangement whereby architecture was left in the university…[5]

The scheme failed; but while Willett notes that it owes a good deal of its inspiration to Rothenstein, there is evidence of an earlier plan from 1905–1906, initiated by Reilly, to persuade Lever to fund a chair in art as part of a broader arts faculty scheme. The minutes of the committee set up to discuss the matter record that it was proposed that 'a Professorship of Art be then established, to deal with the history, principles and criticism of Art'.[6] Lever eventually withdrew his offer after having reservations about encroaching on the art school's territory.[7] Nevertheless, this plan contained the nucleus of the scheme put forward in 1909. It seems that Reilly was attempting to synthesize his earlier scheme with Rothenstein's plan in order to create a powerful arts faculty – with Reilly at the centre – in the university. He saw it as 'A Faculty of Fine Arts with all the independence a university like Liverpool gives to its professors with their life appointments to endowed Chairs, and with men like MacColl, John and Epstein leading it!'[8] We can only speculate that Reilly wished to see his own name added to that list. There is little doubt that to have been associated with such illustrious company would have strengthened his own position within the university, and helped enormously in his plans to promote and develop the School of Architecture.

Willett writes that 'something of the plan seems to have filtered into the 1914 project for a Lancashire Society of Arts centred on the Blue Coat School'.[9] How far this is true is debatable. Nevertheless, the Blue Coat scheme – which was developed by the Sandon Studios Society – provides another example of Reilly's ability to operate within a number of cultural groupings simultaneously.

5 C. H. Reilly, *Scaffolding in the Sky*, Routledge, London, 1938, pp. 124–25.
6 Minutes of the committee, 24 October 1905, Liverpool University Archive, Vice-Chancellor's Papers, Box P/5/12.
7 Letter from W. Lever to A. W. W. Dale, 30 May 1906, Liverpool University Archive, Vice-Chancellor's Papers, Box P/5/12.
8 Reilly, *Scaffolding in the Sky*, p. 125.
9 Willett, *Art in a City*, pp. 64–65.

The Sandon Studios Society

In the early years of the new century a number of seemingly unrelated events were to have far-reaching effects on the cultural and educational life of the city. In 1906 the Liverpool Blue Coat School moved to its new premises in Wavertree, leaving the early-eighteenth-century building in School Lane that had been its original city-centre home. The school trustees were, it seems, unconcerned about the fate of the old building and prepared to sell it for redevelopment. At more or less the same time Sandon Terrace, which had become the home of the breakaway art school following the split within the university school, was bought by Alfred Holt. He offered it to the Liverpool Institute, of which he was a governor. The terrace would be demolished to provide playground space for the boys' school, leaving the Sandon Group without a home.[10]

The problem was solved through the contacts of a leading member of the Sandon Studios, Miss Lister, whose father James Lister was a trustee of the Blue Coat. In a letter from J. E. Tinne, Treasurer of the Blue Coat School, to Miss Lister, he states

> The Sandon Studios (and Miss Lister in particular) are welcome to use part of the old Blue Coat at £30 per year, subject to three months' notice. I fear however that up to the end of September the Palestine Committee want the premises and the Head Master, Mr Mercer, is away on his holidays until the 20th September.[11]

It is clear from this that the building was already part-let and that the Sandon Studios would have to share the premises from the outset. However, the group wanted to expand their activities and they moved into other parts of the building in the course of the following year. Financial difficulties followed, and Herbert MacNair and Gerard Chowne – who had been acting as instructors – ceased to be formally employed. They remained for a short time on an informal basis, but by 1908, according to a circular sent by Miss Lister to members of the Sandon Studios,

10   The prospectus of the Sandon Terrace Studios stated that 'The students of the late university "School of Applied Art" have organised studios on the continental system in Liverpool.' The prospectus had been in the papers of Reilly who comments that the group refused to join the new School of Art established by the Corporation. Liverpool Record Office, Liverpool Central Library, Box HQ 360.
11   R. Bisson, *The Sandon Studios Society and the Arts*, Parry Books, Liverpool, 1965, p. 41.

members of Sandon Studios wish to thank most gratefully those ladies and gentlemen who by their subscriptions for the last three years have enabled them to pay salaries to two masters Mr Chowne and Mr MacNair. The two masters have now left Liverpool and the members of the Sandon Studios have resolved not to ask for a continuance of the subscription at present to engage new masters but to attempt to run the school without outside help.[12]

The financial difficulties continued to mount and the only solution was to expand the activities of the studios to encompass the mounting of exhibitions. In so doing the name was changed to the 'Sandon Society of Artists'. The first tangible result of this move was an exhibition of modern art at the Blue Coat School in May 1908.[13] It consisted mostly of work by society members, together with contributions by Frances MacNair, Charles Bonnier, M. G. Lightfoot, and Claude Monet, who had received a special invitation. This would be the first time Monet had exhibited in Liverpool, and it would be another 50 years before the Walker Art Gallery bought one of his paintings for the city collection. This exhibition appears to have resulted in an increase in membership, but the precarious nature of the tenancy of the building remained unresolved.

The members of the society were not alone in their interest in the Blue Coat building. Reilly had suggested, in January 1906, that the building should be saved, and later that year proposed that it be used as a museum.[14] Reilly and Lascelles Abercrombie drew up a circular for an appeal to help raise the £32,000 needed to save the building. W. S. MacCunn states that the circular was perhaps not drawn up before Lever rented the building in 1909[15] and may well never have been issued, but a copy survives in the university archives, along with covering letters to the Vice-Chancellor discussing the distribution. The appeal stated that

Liverpool, though a city of great artistic tradition, may lose through mere inaction that building which, of all her achievements, is in some ways the most considerable – the old Blue Coat Hospital... Its central position, combined

12   Bisson, *The Sandon Studios Society*, p. 43.
13   Sandon Society of Artists' Exhibition of Modern Art at the Old Blue Coat School, School Lane, Liverpool, 2–30 May 1908. On the list of honorary members of the Sandon were Augustus John, Charles Rennie Mackintosh, John Lavery, Wilson Steer and Henry Tonks. Catalogue held in Liverpool Record Office, Liverpool Central Library, Box H 706 5 CAT.
14   Letters from Reilly to *Daily Post and Mercury*, 'A Beautiful Liverpool', 29 January 1906, and 21 May 1906; Reilly Papers, Liverpool University Archive, Box S 3214.
15   W. S. MacCunn, *Bluecoat Chambers*, Liverpool University Press, Liverpool, 1956, p. 3.

with the quiet seclusion of its courtyard, would make it an admirable centre for any educational activity.[16]

Reilly took the opportunity to further a scheme he had been nurturing for some time, that of finding a new home for the School of Architecture. He suggested that the building's

> unique character and charm… point to some use in furtherance of the arts, and particularly of the art of architecture itself. For the university School of Architecture, at present most unsuitably and inadequately housed far away from the architects of the town, no more fitting home could be imagined than the Chapel block, together with two or three adjoining rooms… The rest of the building… could be very well let out as studios for painters, sculptors and other artists… Thus a community of practising artists and craftsmen centred on the School of Architecture would be formed, the influence of which might be very far reaching.[17]

The circular is interesting in that Reilly puts into words for the first time the notion of using the building as an arts centre. He effectively places the School of Architecture, and himself, at the hub of this new cultural centre, while failing to mention that the community of artists and craftsmen he talks of already existed in the form of the current tenants, the Sandon Studios Society.

The appeal for funds was unsuccessful and the future of the building remained uncertain well into 1909. Reilly said that it was the Chownes who brought him the news that the Blue Coat trustees were putting the school up for auction as a building site. Reilly turned to the one person he knew who had both the money and the inclination to help him achieve a new home for the School of Architecture:

> What was to be done? Clearly the one hope was Lord Leverhulme. No one but he would put down £40,000 or some such sum to save an old Queen Anne building. It seemed hopeless but nevertheless I persuaded him to come over to Liverpool to look at the buildings… Soon he had secured an option on it and the auction was called off… Then he offered the building at no rent at all to me, that is to say to the university for the School of Architecture. It had all happened again within a week.[18]

16 Printed appeal and covering letters to the Vice-Chancellor, 28 April and 18 May 1908. Vice-Chancellor's Papers, Liverpool University Archive, Box P/4A/3/4.
17 Printed appeal and covering letters to the Vice-Chancellor, 28 April and 18 May 1908.
18 Reilly, *Scaffolding in the Sky*, pp. 132–33.

This was a fortunate outcome for Reilly, who had been battling with unsuitable premises for the school since taking up his appointment in 1904.

Reilly, Lever and the Liverpool School of Architecture

Following Lever's interest in the Blue Coat, he wrote a letter to Reilly regarding the terms of the university's tenancy of the building:

> A lease to be given of the building to the Liverpool University for five years with option of purchase during the five years at a price to be fixed. The rental I would suggest would be £750 a year, and the purchase price £20,000 to £22,000. This option of course would only be available for the Liverpool University, and therefore the property purchased would become an adjunct to the Liverpool University... I think it most important that the Liverpool University should have in the centre of the town a building of this nature, and I know of none that would so admirably suit the purpose as the Blue Coat School.[19]

The university had managed to secure exclusive rights on an option to buy the building. This had important implications for Reilly's future dealings with the Sandon Studios Society. The terms for the university's move into the building seem to have been agreed by early August in 1909; Lever agreed to pay for any necessary repairs to the building.[20] Mrs Calder – formerly Miss Lister and now the wife of a local solicitor Hamel Calder – and the Sandon Studios Society were left in a precarious position. Bisson quotes from a letter from Tinne to Mrs Calder in which he states that the university would be willing to keep them on as tenants. However, a month later Tinne wrote again to Mrs Calder stating that 'I now have the unpleasing task of giving you formal notice of three months... to vacate your tenancy.' Bisson suggests that 'Reilly in his characteristic way, had been trying to rush things...'[21] However, it would seem that it was Lever who was anxious to move the university into the building as quickly as possible. Writing to Reilly on 19 August 1909, he says,

> I must say that I feel very great disappointment that the weeks are slipping over and we are rapidly approaching October, and apparently we are as far off as we

19 Letter from W. H. Lever to Reilly, 4 February 1909, Liverpool University Archive, Vice-Chancellor's Papers, Box P/4A/3/4.
20 Letter from Lever to Reilly, 5 August 1909, Liverpool University Archive, Vice-Chancellor's Papers, Box P/4A/3/4.
21 Bisson, *The Sandon Studios Society*, p. 53.

were some weeks ago in getting the matter settled… I cannot finally give up all hope of the intention of opening the new buildings in October being accomplished. I still feel that although time has been lost it is not yet hopeless, but unless prompt action is taken within the next few days it certainly will be impossible.[22]

Reilly and the school moved in during October, apparently causing some discord with Tinne because it was in advance of the agreed date.

Reilly's move into the Blue Coat caused the Sandon Studios Society to rethink their whole ethos. They considered whether they should remain an independent art school, or broaden their appeal and become a looser art society with an open membership run on a subscription basis. Reilly promised to support a scheme in which those who were not necessarily artists might have use of a club room. A provisional committee, of which Reilly was a member, met on 4 December 1909 and produced a manifesto that included the proposal for a club room 'which all members can use freely and where meetings can be held for discussion and for social and artistic purposes'.[23] Reilly had gained a useful addition to his school – a meeting place for his staff and students as well as the artistically minded members of the city. The nucleus of the arts centre he had written about in 1906 had been formed.

The Sandon Society secured rooms on the ground floor of the west wing of the building, and agreement was reached with the university on rent and rates. Reilly remained a member of the committee, together with other prominent members of the university such as Professor Adshead and Professor Mackay. By and large this seems to have been a period of consolidation, both for the School of Architecture and for the Sandon Society. A quarterly newsletter entitled *The Bulletin* was initiated, providing a forum for discussion and argument for the society's members.[24] Reilly helped with the second major

22 Letter from Lever to Reilly, 19 August 1909, Liverpool University Archive, Vice-Chancellor's Papers, Box P/4A/3/4.
23 Bisson, *The Sandon Studios Society*, p. 56.
24 *The Bulletin*'s satirical articles provide an interesting barometer of the members' attitudes towards Riley *et al*. They include a skit on *Alice in Wonderland* entitled 'Alice in Sandon Land':

> 'BLABBER–MOCKY'
> 'Twas sillig and the Riley coves
> Did spire and fimble in the Blabe,
> All Czinsky were the Ogusjoans
> And the Rathbones outrabe.
>
> Beware the Abercrock, my son!
> With centripetal claws that clatch!
> Beware the Club–club Bird and shun
> The Bohemious Hanker–Batch…

exhibition of paintings held in April 1911, which included contributions by
Anning Bell, David Muirhead and Herbert MacNair, together with 46 French
Post-Impressionist paintings that had not previously been shown in
Liverpool.[25] The relationship between Reilly and the society, however, did not
always run smoothly. In a letter to the Vice-Chancellor, Reilly asks 'can you
arrange for the Sandon Society to have its own telephone… My private room
is becoming a public telephone box and my work is almost stopped…'[26] The
year before Reilly had written to Dr Londini at the university complaining
that

> There are two men – artists – who occupy a room here without paying any rent
> – Messrs Preston and Capstick. They paid Mrs Calder no rent but in return
> gave their services as instructors in her classes. As these are now at an end I
> think they ought now to pay a small rent to the university. They stay very late
> and necessitate light being kept on for them. I think also they have been getting
> coal free. They use the building too a great deal on Sundays when no one is
> about.[27]

Such minor irritations seem to have been indicative of a broader discontent in
the relationship between the university and the Sandon Society, despite the
public declarations of common purpose.

During this period the Sandon – of which Reilly was a committee
member – formulated two closely interwoven aims for the future of the

---

'That's enough to begin with,' said Humpty, 'there are plenty of hard words there. "Sillig" is the
time when everyone is much more themselves than usual. "Riley" is an adjective denoting
touchiness in matters relating to Town Planning. One may be called "riley" when one is so
provoked with modern "style" so as to "rail" (Cockney pronunciation). The word may have more
"Es," "Is," and "Ls" in it according to taste. A "Cove" is an architectural term for a hollow member.'
'I see it now,' said Alice, thoughtfully. 'And I suppose "to spire" is to rise high, at any rate in one's
own imagination.' 'Yes,' said Humpty, 'and to make one's remarks to the point.' 'And what is
"fimble?"' asked Alice. 'To fimble,' said Humpty, 'is not exactly to fumble.' 'And the "Blabe" is
where the Riley coves spire and fimble,' Alice remarks, delighted with her understanding. 'Yes,
"Blabe" is short for Blue-Coat-School-now-called-Liverpool-University-School-of-Architecture-
and-Civic-Design-Liberty-Buildings-School-Lane…' Carrolus, *The Bulletin of the Sandon
Studios Society*, No. 4, January 1913, Liverpool Record Office, Liverpool Central Library, Box H
708 6 BUL.

25 *Catalogue of Sandon Studios Society Exhibition of Modern Art Including Works by the Post
    Impressions at Liberty Buildings*, Liverpool Record Office, Liverpool Central Library, Box H 706 5
    CAT.

26 Letter from Reilly to the Vice-Chancellor, 27 June 1911, Reilly Papers, Liverpool University
    Archive, Box S3206.

27 Letter from Reilly to Londini, 5 January 1910, Reilly Papers, Liverpool University Archive, Box
    S3205.

society and the building. These were set out thus: '(i) to persuade Lever to buy the building and recondition it: and (ii) to hand it over to a body of Trustees to be used as a centre for the arts.'[28] The first definite steps regarding this proposal – according to MacCunn – took place on 4 July 1913, when committee member Clifford Muspratt and Reilly attended a meeting with Lever regarding the future of the building. According to MacCunn the July meeting resulted in an expression of interest by Lever. He requested that an architectural scheme be drawn up for the alteration of the interior. Muspratt then suggested to Mrs Calder that E. L. Bower and W. Naseby Adams be appointed as architects. MacCunn quotes a letter from Reilly to Mrs Calder expressing very qualified support for this scheme:

> We have talked over the suggestion that both Mr Abercrombie and Mr Budden should be asked to join our small pioneer committee and that Mr Adams should be asked with Mr Bower to prepare first drawings to show Mr Lever... I am quite sure from knowing him that Sir William, if he provides the money, will want to have the final word in the appointment of the architect... What will probably happen will be that Sir William will say that the scheme as a whole is a good one but that the architects are unknown young men, very likely good artists... but that he would sooner someone more experienced and with more knowledge of architectural detail... should be joined to them as consultant... Both [Adams and Bower] are keen people and enthusiastic members of the club. Mr Adams is quite a good man, well above the average young Liverpool architect. Of course neither he nor Mr Bower are as good or know as much as Mr Budden or Mr Abercrombie and none of them compare in knowledge, capacity for work, or taste to Professor Adshead.[29]

According to MacCunn, Mrs Calder then wrote to Lever laying out the Sandon Society's position and asking for clarification on Lever's intentions regarding the building's future:

> You will no doubt remember that when some of us laid before you a short time ago a scheme for the preservation of Liberty Buildings and their use as an Art Centre for Liverpool, you very kindly said that you would be willing to give a substantial sum towards the purchase of the site... on condition firstly that we could show you a really fine scheme, and secondly that we raised a sufficient sum in Liverpool to show that a genuine interest was taken in it by the

28 MacCunn, *Bluecoat Chambers*, p. 4.
29 MacCunn, *Bluecoat Chambers*, pp. 4–5. It is interesting to note Reilly's partisan approach to the possible allocation of work. Bower (Cert. Arch. 1901) had been a former pupil of his predecessor, Professor Simpson, and Adams (Cert. Arch. 1906) had graduated under the system initiated by Simpson, while Budden, Abercrombie and Adshead were all what might be termed 'Reilly's Men'.

citizens… We are confident of being able to obtain considerable support among Liverpool citizens, and have no doubt that many hundreds will gladly give to the scheme according to their means… It is with great regret that we trouble you again with the matter now, but knowing the interest you take in Liberty Buildings, and as you asked to be kept informed of any fresh developments, we think you would have cause to reproach us, if we let it be destroyed without giving you the opportunity of saving it… I am speaking for a provisional committee… They are: Mrs James Calder, Mr Heywood Melly, Professor Reilly, Mr Patrick Abercrombie, Mr Lionel Budden and Mr J. G. Legge, the Director of Education.[30]

Lever replied affirming his interest in the building, but he considered the Adams–Bower scheme too modest, and said 'we must either do the thing well or leave it alone'. He put forward a proposal that 'a competition could be instituted giving my ideas as guides only, and not as binding obligations'.[31]

MacCunn suggests that Reilly had been nursing the hope of being entrusted with the reconditioning and reconstruction work:

Lever's suggestion of a competition destroyed this hope and at this juncture he [Reilly] appears to have dissociated himself from the committee. His behaviour was certainly equivocal and both Mrs Calder and Muspratt were convinced that behind their backs he was working against the committee and putting forward a scheme of his own. At one point Lever seems to have been perceptibly less cordial in his relations with the committee and they believed this was due to Reilly's influence.[32]

MacCunn then goes on to quote a series of letters between Mrs Calder, Legge and Muspratt that clearly indicate their mistrust of Reilly. In a letter from Muspratt to Mrs Calder, headed 'Liberty Buildings – Confidential', he said,

I am obliged for your letters and wire. I have also heard from Professor Reilly who states that he will not press any claim to compete in any competition in connection with the above building. The point however I should like cleared up is the actual position of the committee in reference to Sir William and also Reilly's relation to it. Taking the latter point first: is Professor Reilly a member of the committee? If not is he going to become a member?… The important thing is however to find out our status in reference to Lever: and Reilly's relation to both Lever and us.[33]

---

30   MacCunn, *Bluecoat Chambers*, pp. 6–8. The reference to Liberty Buildings reflects Lever's change of the Blue Coat's name after he won a libel action in 1909.
31   MacCunn, *Bluecoat Chambers*, pp. 8–9.
32   MacCunn, *Bluecoat Chambers*, pp. 9–10.
33   MacCunn, *Bluecoat Chambers*, pp. 69–70.

The following day, Mrs Calder wrote to Legge explaining her suspicions about Reilly's agenda:

> From things I have heard lately it was evident that Professor Reilly was trying to shake the committee off. He told me at the City Guild Meeting and has told others that the negotiations had 'gone back to where they were four years ago', which means between Sir W. L. and himself. When I told him last week that Sir W. had sent plans (his own) and a draft scheme to Clifford, I could see that he was frightfully upset. Then when I saw him two days ago and he had received the plans and letter from Clifford, he began by saying to me that he believed he had written to me once saying he hoped his claims would not be overlooked in choosing an architect, but that he had now decided to stand aside entirely as he felt he could help us with Sir William more as a disinterested adviser. When he gave me the papers to read I saw the reason for the change of front: Sir W. L. wishes to have a competition among young architects. Obviously he couldn't compete with his own students!... I am wondering if it would be good policy to put Reilly formally on to the Committee so as to curb his independent action a little. Of course he is most nice to talk to about it... My own opinion is that he knows everyone despises the way he ratted about the building last winter, deserted us completely and evidently would not have cared if it were lost so long as he had a new one to do, and he wants to work this now so as to retrieve his position by making it appear that he has done everything in saving it.[34]

The fact of Reilly having 'ratted' during the winter of 1913–1914 is given as the explanation for his allegedly duplicitous dealings with the general committee. MacCunn describes it in the following terms:

> The committee's plan for using the building as an art centre seems to have included the provision of accommodation for the School of Architecture. Apparently at some time in the winter of 1913–1914, at Professor Reilly's suggestion, Sir William Lever offered the university, as an alternative, a sum of money for the erection of a new building to house the school. Reilly can hardly be blamed for preferring this offer, in the interests of the school, altogether apart from any personal wish to have the opportunity of designing a new building. At the same time this diversion of Lever's interest must have come as a severe shock to the rest of the committee, when it came to their knowledge, and Mrs Calder's outspoken indignation (in, it must be remembered, a confidential letter) is understandable.[35]

This seems to be a plausible explanation given the evidence provided by MacCunn. However, an examination of material in the university archives

34 MacCunn, *Bluecoat Chambers*, pp. 70–71.
35 MacCunn, *Bluecoat Chambers*, p. 71, footnote 1.

reveals that Lever, in a Deed of Gift dated 1910, gave the university a range of options regarding the Blue Coat. The Deed would provide for the

> Lease by the university of land and buildings called the 'Blue Coat Hospital' for four years from 1 January, 1910, at a rent of £450... The lease further gives the following options of purchase of the freehold of the premises to the university... In case the university does not exercise either option to purchase to pay £24,195 to the university to be applied in or towards the purchase of a site and the erection and maintenance of buildings or the erection and maintenance of buildings alone to be used for the School of Architecture [including the Department of Town Planning and Civic Design] or for other university purposes.[36]

The offer to the university of a new building therefore dates not from 1913–1914, as MacCunn suggests, but from 1910.

With regard to the School of Architecture's commitment to the tenancy of the Blue Coat, Mrs Calder's accusations of ambivalence on Reilly's part seem equally ill-founded. In a series of letters between Reilly and the Vice-Chancellor dating from 1911 and 1913, Reilly is consistent in his desire to remain in the Blue Coat, despite the standing offer of a new building from Lever. In July 1911, Reilly stated,

> I have very carefully considered (as you requested me to do) the question of the university either buying this building for the use of the School of Architecture and the Department of Civic Design or using the £25,000 available for the purchase of a site and for the erection of a new building nearer to the main university buildings to take its place. The opportunity of erecting a special building for a School of Architecture – the first for such a purpose in England – is not to be lightly discarded and it is only on consideration of the great advantages of the present building that I am led to consider this inadvisable. And in this connection it must be borne in mind that the new building would not provide, by a very considerable extent, the accommodation of Liberty Buildings, which though larger than at present required might easily become fully occupied at a future date. The advantages of remaining in the present building may be enumerated as follows...[37]

Reilly went on to list six merits claimed by Liberty Buildings over a new building. Principal among them were the superior accommodation, proximity

36 *Deed of Gift: 1910: Short Abstract of Provisions Affecting the Tenure of Liberty Buildings,* Liverpool University Archive, Vice-Chancellor's Papers, Box P/4/1/23.
37 Letter from Reilly to the Vice-Chancellor, 8 July 1911, Liverpool University Archive, Vice-Chancellor's Papers, Box P/4/1/23 and P/4A/3/5.

to the city's architectural offices, and the quality of the architecture. In addition to this we can speculate that Reilly must have enjoyed the sense of autonomy afforded by not being part of the main campus, and his awareness that the building was becoming an important cultural centre in the heart of the city. Reilly seems to have maintained this position for the next few years. In a letter to the Vice-Chancellor he states,

> A year's further residence here has not materially altered the opinion... I should now sum up the matter as follows. If the advantage to the School of Architecture alone is considered it would be wiser to build. No department of a university would profit so much by a good building, which was at the same time adequate to its work... Only one such building exists – the School of Architecture at Harvard and it is typical of all that is best at the present moment in American Architecture for which in a sense it stands. If on the other hand the larger outlook of the university and the... growth of allied departments is taken as the determining factor it would be far wiser to stay here.[38]

Reilly's preferences were conveyed to the committee appointed by the university council, and their decision is recorded in a report issued on 12 February 1913:

> 1) The Committee-appointed Council have inspected the accommodation afforded by Liberty Buildings, and have carefully considered the question of tenure in its relation to the interests of the School of Architecture and the university.
> 2) The Committee have not failed to give due weight to the natural desire that the association of the university with an historical and a beautiful building should be preserved. They also recognise that for students in evening classes Liberty Buildings is more convenient than a school in the immediate neighbourhood of the university.
> 3) They have arrived, however, at the conclusion to recommend to Council not to exercise the option to purchase Liberty Buildings, but to accept the sum of £24,195 offered by Sir William Lever for the provision of a new building.[39]

It is clear from this that despite Mrs Calder's and Muspratt's suspicions, Reilly's reason for distancing himself from the Sandon committee was not the desire to obtain a commission for a new building. Mrs Calder's opinion that

38 Letter from Reilly to the Vice-Chancellor, 21 January 1913, Liverpool University Archive, Vice-Chancellor's Papers, Box P/4/1/23.
39 *Report of the Committee on the Tenure of Liberty Buildings*, The University of Liverpool, Liverpool University Archive, Vice-Chancellor's Papers, Box P/4/1/23.

Reilly 'would not have cared if it [the Blue Coat] were lost so long as he had a new one to do...' appears to be far off the mark. It is questionable how public the university committee's decision to withdraw from the building was. It may have been the case that Mrs Calder and her committee knew of the university council's decision, but not Reilly's personal thoughts on the matter, and so jumped to the conclusion that Reilly had recommended withdrawal. Whatever the case, it seems most probable that Reilly's decision to remain at arm's length from the Sandon committee was due in part to finding himself in a potentially compromising position. When the university elected to take up Lever's cash offer, Reilly may have felt that to associate with any committee dedicated to extracting further money from Lever (in this case, to help save the Blue Coat building) might test Lever's generosity too far. Reilly was therefore committed to the university line, leaving him with no option but to withdraw from the Sandon committee scheme.

There is no documentary evidence to suggest how matters developed in the period between the university's decision to waive the option to buy, taken in February 1913, and the letters quoted by MacCunn from early 1914. However, in Reilly's letter books there exist copies of letters to Mrs Calder and Lever, outlining his reasons for remaining outside the committee. To Mrs Calder, he wrote:

> I am honoured by your committee wanting me to become a member of it again but I really think I am in a better position to advise Sir William if I stay away. He was here yesterday and asked me to send him as soon as possible my own ideas as to the constitution of the new institution and the services it could render to art. This I shall do very shortly. While I am and have always been very sympathetic to the aims of the Sandon Society, I do not feel I have been closely enough associated with it in the past to identify myself with it now. I think I can take a possibly broader and certainly a more independent view if I remain away from the committee. I have no doubt that the two schemes prepared independently will have more effect on Sir William than one joint one. He will form his own views in any case and act upon them.[40]

Reilly's stated position here seems broadly consistent with the speculative reasons I have outlined above for Reilly having distanced himself from the Sandon Society. The Sandon committee, however, was not satisfied with Reilly's

---

40   Letter from Reilly to Mrs Calder, 16 March 1914, Liverpool University Archive, Reilly Papers, Box S3212, p. 184. See also letter dated 6 March 1914. Reilly wrote to Lever of his decision stating that 'I have no desire to be employed in this matter professionally. I am too interested in the success of the idea...' Letter from Reilly to Lever, 10 March 1914.

decision, and Muspratt and Mrs Calder sought to force a clarification from him as to where he stood. Reilly wrote to Muspratt in March 1914 saying,

> I enclose copies of my last two letters to Sir William and the draft scheme I prepared at his request... I have not made any drawings for Sir W. and do not propose to do so... When you have read the enclosed documents you will realise I hope that my attitude all through has been an entirely friendly one to the Sandon Studios Society. I feel that by giving Sir William the general advice I have done on independent, but I think acceptable lines, I have done the best I could to help the aim we both have in view...[41]

Muspratt seems not to have been satisfied with Reilly's explanation of his position, and recommended to Mrs Calder that Reilly should not be invited on to the committee. In a letter to Mrs Calder of March 1914, he says,

> I should not on any account take him [Reilly] back on the committee... if he [Sir William] asks us to take Reilly back of course we would agree. Speaking personally I do not care to be on a committee with no status at all...[42]

Mrs Calder and Legge drafted a letter to Lever, signed by Muspratt, in which they set out the Sandon Society's aims and asked for clarification of Lever's position with regard to Liberty Buildings in general and the Sandon Society in particular:

> Professor Reilly writes that he does not propose to remain a member of our committee as he considers that he can be of more service to us from outside. We have strongly urged him not to withdraw but he has since written to Mrs Calder not only that he thinks it better to do so, but that he is submitting a scheme of his own to you. We have always understood that our ideas and wishes for the future of Liberty Buildings and those of Professor Reilly are completely sympathetic if not absolutely identical and feel that there is no real division in aim... we are most willing to place our services at your disposal, or, if you prefer it, we are willing to dissolve our committee and to leave the future of the buildings with you and Professor Reilly.[43]

The outcome of this request appears to have been a maintenance of the status quo. Greater events were to overtake the decision on Liberty Buildings' future with the outbreak of the First World War in August 1914.

---

41 Letter from Reilly to Muspratt, 23 March 1914, quoted in MacCunn, *Bluecoat Chambers*, pp. 74–75.
42 Letter from Muspratt to Mrs Calder, 27 March 1914, quoted in MacCunn, *Bluecoat Chambers*, p. 75.
43 Letter from Muspratt to Lever, no date but thought to have been sent in early April 1914, quoted in MacCunn, *Bluecoat Chambers*, pp. 76–77.

The School of Architecture continued to occupy the building through-out the war. Reilly handed responsibility over to his deputy Lionel Budden, and took up an appointment as an Area Inspector of Munitions, occupying an office in the Blue Coat buildings.[44] The Sandon Society also remained in the building, but their feelings of resentment towards the university did not diminish. Mrs Calder, when writing to Lever concerning wartime difficulties, commented,

> As you are now the owner of Liberty Buildings, I am going to venture to write to you about the business side of the tenancy of the Sandon Studios Society... Now, however, I suppose that the university is no longer in the position of being our landlord but is itself your tenant, and owing to your kindness is allowed to occupy the premises rent free... I wonder whether you would consider the question of treating the Sandon Studios Society on the same footing as the university... When I think of how the university practically dissociated themselves from the old building and its future by their decision of that year [1913], I feel it rather an anomaly that they should be making money out of its use from the little society which has made such efforts to save it...[45]

Mrs Calder's version of events seems somewhat one-sided given the evidence above. The plea was met with a typically businesslike reply from Lever, which is interesting in gauging Lever's changing attitude to the project during this largely undocumented period:

> the rents that used to be paid to the Liverpool University are now paid to myself... these rents must continue to be paid otherwise Liberty Buildings would be, as I pointed out to you in my letter, without income from any source.

44   See Reilly, *Scaffolding in the Sky*, pp. 181–202, for his account of his wartime activities. He talks of his organizing role as an Inspector of Munitions and his instituting a system of worker participation, albeit a qualified one. This is interesting in the light of Reilly's stated commitment to socialist ideals and was certainly, for its time, an uncommon attitude to shop floor workers. He states that his scheme took the following form: 'I got together the women working on a bench and asked them to tell me frankly who, in their opinion, was the most careful and conscientious worker... the bench-leader, by putting a mark on the shells or fuses or whatever it was they were examining, represented the work of the bench as a whole. After meeting by themselves for a little while and talking it over they would suggest to me so and so, and in every case it was a good suggestion. I then got the bench-leaders together and asked them in turn which should be made overlooker for the room and so on. Although the actual appointments were in my hands, and I had my foremen to check them, it was a system of organisation from the bottom upwards and it worked excellently... If in peace time some similar motive, to correspond to the desire to help their friends at the front, could be added to factory wages, a large part of the industrial problem would, I think, be solved. A share in the management, however small, for that is what my scheme amounted to, abolishes at a stroke all feelings of slavery.' *Scaffolding in the Sky*, pp. 193-94.

45   Letter from Mrs Calder to Lever, no date, quoted in Bisson, *The Sandon Studios Society*, pp. 103–04.

I cannot say that I regret being unable to accede to your request, although I am very anxious to assist you, but I feel that assistance in this way would be unsound and disastrous.[46]

When the war ended, Lord Leverhulme – as Sir William was now known, having been raised to the peerage in 1917 – was approached by Mrs Calder who reminded him of the pre-war scheme to found an arts centre, which she described as 'a project so splendid and so important to the higher side of education'.[47] Leverhulme's reply was to have a profound effect on the development of both the Sandon Studios Society and the School of Architecture:

I am not now disposed to carry out the scheme as originally proposed, but I shall carry out a scheme of some nature that would be for the public interest, but not the scheme originally proposed four or five years ago.[48]

MacCunn states that 'no explanation of this complete *volte face* has ever been forthcoming'.[49] Edward Morris believes that Leverhulme's growing business empire was drawing him away from Liverpool to London, where he may have felt that such a scheme was better placed.[50] Bisson speculates that the reason behind Leverhulme's decision was that

He [Leverhulme] was particularly interested in the School of Tropical Medicine and he greatly admired Sir Ronald Ross... When he [Ross] left the university in 1917 he was not granted a pension and Leverhulme was indignant... It is thought that he [Leverhulme] made amends himself and it appears he decided to teach the university a lesson.[51]

While Bisson does not provide any documentary evidence to support his speculation, letters between Reilly and Hugh Rathbone in January 1922 partly confirm his theory:

It was absolutely inevitable that some friction would arise with Lord Leverhulme when the university had to refuse to comply with his request to

46 Letter from Lever to Mrs Calder quoted in Bisson, *The Sandon Studios Society*, p. 104.
47 Letter from Mrs Calder to Lord Leverhulme, 6 November 1918, quoted in MacCunn, *Bluecoat Chambers*, p. 11.
48 Letter from Leverhulme to Mrs Calder, 7 November 1918, quoted in MacCunn, *Bluecoat Chambers*, pp. 11–12.
49 MacCunn, *Bluecoat Chambers*, p. 12.
50 E. Morris, 'Painting and Sculpture', in *Lord Leverhulme*, exhibition catalogue, Royal Academy, London, 1980, pp. 26–27.
51 Bisson, *The Sandon Studios Society*, p. 105.

endow one of our professors who left us to better himself long before his pension age – left us, I must add, to our great regret. To have contributed as Lord Leverhulme asked on that occasion would have set a precedent which would have made it very difficult to have refused other similar applications...[52]

Reilly's reply is more specific:

I feel myself that the university could not have taken any other line than it did at the time over the pension difficulty at the Tropical School. But the net result is that the School of Architecture is suffering very seriously from the ill-advised actions of Sir Ronald Ross.[53]

A combination of all these factors was probably behind Leverhulme's actions. The net result was that the School of Architecture moved out of their rooms in the Blue Coat buildings and into much less salubrious premises on the main university campus. Myles Wright describes the new accommodation as

part of the former Lock hospital in Ashton Street, which comprised a two or three storey central block in gimcrack classical style with single-storey wards on either side. The latter became 'Reilly's cowsheds', first so called in mockery and later with pride.[54]

Reilly found himself back in much the same position as 1908, occupying makeshift premises on the main university site.

Reilly and the Bluecoat Society of Arts, 1919–1948

Reilly continued to maintain contact with the Sandon Studios Society (which changed its name to the Bluecoat Society of Arts in 1927), using the club room and exhibiting in various annual exhibitions, as well as participating in the annual Architects' Ball.[55] The building served as a means for him to remain in touch with Liverpool's cultural community, and throughout the period

---

52 Letter from Rathbone to Reilly, 24 January 1922, Liverpool University Archive, Vice-Chancellor's Papers, Box P/4A/3/5.

53 Letter from Reilly to Rathbone, 27 January 1922, Liverpool University Archive, Vice-Chancellor's Papers, Box P/4A/3/5.

54 M. Wright, *Lord Leverhulme's Unknown Venture*, Hutchinson Banham, London, 1982, p. 62.

55 Wright notes that 'The Annual Architects' Ball at the Blue Coat School was one of the biggest events of the year for the School of Architecture...' Reilly, typically, took a starring role: 'the architectural students put on a floor-show in which Reilly quite frequently appeared as an emperor or in some similar such role' (Fig. 11). Wright, *Lord Leverhulme's Unknown Venture*, p. 65.

between the wars the society was a cultural interchange between the artistically inclined members of Liverpool's establishment and its bohemians.[56] It might be argued that the challenging, modern aspects of the society's ethos were being adapted and were declining under the influence of the more conventional members. A commentator in 1951 noted that 'In the years between the wars the Sandon Society became an accepted – even respected – part of the cultural life of Liverpool.'[57] Reilly seems to have accommodated himself to the changing climate of the Sandon, having always kept a foot in both camps. Maxwell Fry, a student at the School of Architecture during this period and also a member of the Sandon, recalled that, to Reilly, 'The Studio Club was a privileged extension to the school. Reilly wafted in and out of it as opportunity allowed, for he was a professor first and a bohemian later, and kept too many balls balancing to devote more than the breathless moment to a society that took its ease as this did.'[58]

Financial difficulties continued to plague the Bluecoat Society, despite new tenants such as the Liverpool Architectural Society and the Liverpool Philharmonic Society. To relieve the growing financial crises, a special appeals committee was established to source works of art, furniture and so on to be sold by public auction. MacCunn notes that Reilly was chosen to chair the committee, for

> His acute sense of publicity values and his power of interesting and persuasive writing were invaluable and he entered on the campaign, in the late autumn of 1929, with characteristic gusto.[59]

Reilly managed to raise around £4,000, including a donation from Lord Leverhulme, but by early 1930 he and the committee had done as much as they could. One of the last large enterprises Reilly embarked on before his retirement was the organization of the exhibition of Jacob Epstein's *Genesis*. This was held in 1931 and staged by the Sandon in support of the Bluecoat Society of Arts Building Fund. The choice of exhibit had been proposed by Reilly and H. Hinchcliffe Davies, and was typical of Reilly's flair for publicity

56 Bisson outlines the members of the Sandon Studios Society during this period in detail. Bisson, *The Sandon Studios Society*, p. 159.
57 N. Martin Bell, *Fifty Years of Merseyside Art*, catalogue to the exhibition held at Bluecoat Chambers 22 July–12 August 1951. Liverpool Record Office, Liverpool Central Library, Box H 708 8 SAN.
58 E. Maxwell Fry, *Autobiographical Sketches*, Elek, London, 1975, p. 94.
59 MacCunn, *Bluecoat Chambers*, p. 30. For a full account of the financial situation faced by the society see MacCunn, *Bluecoat Chambers*, pp. 25–40.

in that it is a controversial Modernist work, chosen in order to maximize press coverage and so increase attendance figures. Bisson states that

> During the month 49,687 people paid sixpence each to gaze at her, some, the newspapers reported, to froth at the mouth, others to be baffled and some, it was said, with reverence. Sermons were preached all over the city on the theme. There was excited correspondence in the press, one writer protesting that the fund should go to the Maternity Hospital.[60]

Whatever the actual reasoning behind the choice, the outcome was highly successful and caused a sensation.

The Bluecoat Society's annual report for the year ending March 1932 acknowledged the contribution made by the exhibition to the balance of accounts, and thanked Reilly for his efforts.[61] Reilly remained a member of the executive committee, but within a year he had been forced to retire from the Roscoe Chair and leave Liverpool for Brighton on the grounds of ill-health. A farewell supper was held for him at the Bluecoat in May of 1933. While Reilly's major involvement with the building was now at an end, he continued to maintain an interest in Liverpool matters. As Bisson notes, he would 'return to Liverpool and the Sandon with sudden bursts of energy until his death in 1948'.[62]

The Liverpool Repertory Theatre

The second major cultural enterprise in which Reilly played a leading role was the founding of the Liverpool Repertory Theatre. In many ways this is intimately tied up with the events surrounding the Sandon Studios Society and the Bluecoat, involving as it did a number of people who were closely associated with both schemes. Liverpool had a distinguished theatrical history,[63] but by the time Reilly arrived in the city, the standard had slipped a good deal. In *Scaffolding in the Sky*, Reilly notes that

---

60 Bisson, *The Sandon Studios Society*, p. 174.
61 Bluecoat Society of Arts Report for the year ending 31 March 1932, Liverpool Record Office, Liverpool Central Library, Box HQ 360.
62 Bisson, *The Sandon Studios Society*, p. 179.
63 See R. J. Broadbent, *The Annals of the Liverpool Stage*, Edward Howell, Liverpool, 1908. For an anecdotal account of the Liverpool Repertory Theatre (Liverpool Playhouse), from its inception up until its closure in 1998, see P. McMahon and P. Brooks, *An Actor's Place*, Bluecoat Press, Liverpool, 2000.

We had seen enough, anyhow, to make us discontented with the sort of plays we found in four or five Liverpool theatres, 'mere booths', as Ramsey Muir called them, for travelling companies. In them mainly were to be seen the plays approved by the London suburbs, otherwise they would not have been sent on the road, sentimental and musical comedies and melodrama.[64]

Reilly recalls that in response to the poor quality available, he organized a meeting at the university club to discuss the possibility of forming a repertory theatre along the lines of the Abbey Theatre, Dublin, and the Gaiety in Manchester.[65] To this meeting, which took place in May 1910, he invited Mrs Horniman, founder of the Gaiety Theatre, Nigel Playfair and Granville Barker. Also in attendance were the great and the good of Liverpool society, among them prominent members of Liverpool's press, such as Robert Hield (editor of *The Daily Courier*), Sir Edward Russell (editor of the *Daily Post*) and Ronald Jeans (son of the managing director of the *Daily Post*). The meeting does not seem to have been a success, and talk of financial losses and suspicions that the theatre would only be for the benefit of 'intellectuals who would probably want to stage… strange and unwholesome foreign plays'[66] meant that it broke up without any firm proposals being reached. Reilly's recollection of the meeting was that

> The elite and wealthy departed murmuring something ought to be done, but did nothing. A little group at the back, however, consisting of a chemist's assistant, Oscar Waddington, the owner of a small hardware shop, Richard Mason, a young man in the coal trade named Sharman and James Coulton, an insurance clerk, all of whom I had somehow got to know and invited, stayed behind. They suggested the formation of a Playgoers' Club, not of the usual provincial kind, organised to entertain visiting celebrities, but one designed to educate the public and to back good plays… I agreed and we formed ourselves into a committee. We asked Robert Hield to be president, and when he refused I was pressed into the job.[67]

This seems to be another example of Reilly's misrecollections. The group he named were already members of a playgoers' society that had been formed in 1901 to campaign for better-quality theatre in Liverpool.[68] The fact that they

64 Reilly, *Scaffolding in the Sky*, p. 140.
65 The Gaiety Theatre, Manchester had been opened in 1906 by Miss Horniman. G. W. Goldie, *The Liverpool Repertory Theatre 1911–1934*, Liverpool University Press, Liverpool, 1935, p. 21.
66 Goldie, *The Liverpool Repertory Theatre*, p. 33.
67 Reilly, *Scaffolding in the Sky*, p. 141.
68 'The Liverpool Playgoers' Club', *The Liverpolitan*, Vol. 10, No. 5, May 1945, p. 16.

were already a coherent group prior to the university club meeting accounts for Reilly's vague recollection of how he came to know and invite them. Bisson in *The Sandon Studios Society and the Arts* makes this clear:

> Afterwards a small group in the audience, Oscar Waddington, James Coulton, Richard Mason and George Sharman, those who had founded the Liverpool Playgoers' Society, which now met at the Yemen Cafe in Bold Street, spoke to Reilly and, together, over the next twelve months they greatly increased the membership and influence of the Society.[69]

Reilly's main contribution over the following months was to use his contacts with the rich and powerful members of Liverpool's social, media and intellectual circle[70] and introduce them to the young and enthusiastic members of the Playgoers' Society, increasing its membership and influence. As George Sharman, one of the founding members, recalled,

> When the Repertory Theatre was discussed the Playgoers were enthusiastic and promised all support, apart from money, of which we had none. But we were the nucleus of an audience, which was of equal value.[71]

Grace Wyndham Goldie makes the same mistake as Reilly, by referring to the fact that 'a Playgoers' Club had been started. Professor Reilly was invited to become its chairman. This linked up with the "university section" of the "repertorists"...'[72] Sharman points this error out in an article he wrote for *The Liverpolitan*:

> The Liverpool Playgoers' Club... is not the body referred to by Mrs Grace Wyndham Goldie in her admirable book on the Repertory Theatre. Mrs Wyndham Goldie has been led astray in this matter: it was the old Playgoers' Society of those brave days and not this club to which so many mistaken references are made in her history of the Playhouse. Although the club was not then in existence it is important to note that its founders were among the active minority in the Playgoers' Society, whose enthusiasm resulted in the memorable meetings and traffickings out of which the Liverpool Repertory Theatre later emerged.[73]

69   Bisson, *The Sandon Studios Society*, p. 70.
70   Goldie lists the names of the prominent members of Liverpool society. Many of them are familiar from the Sandon Society, including the Muspratts and Mrs Challoner Dowdall; others, such as the Rathbones, had Liverpool University connections.
71   Quoted in Bisson, *The Sandon Studios Society*, p. 70.
72   Goldie, *The Liverpool Repertory Theatre*, p. 34.
73   G. O. Sharman, 'A Unique Liverpool Institution', *The Liverpolitan*, January 1936, p. 29.

Reilly's chairmanship bore fruit in 1911 when Alfred Wareing of the Glasgow Repertory Company offered to bring his company to Liverpool for an experimental six-week season. With financial backing from Sir Alexander Jeans of the *Daily Post*, guarantees from the Playgoers' Society, and the collaboration of a young producer by the name of Basil Dean, a season was arranged in Kelly's Theatre at the corner of School Lane and Paradise Street in Liverpool city centre. When the plan was called off after Wareing fell ill and withdrew his offer, the project seemed doomed. As Dean recalled,

> Our chances of success seemed flimsy indeed. We knew no one in the city. All we had to go on was the suggestion... that we should get in touch with Professor Reilly. I was told to see the editor of the Liverpool *Daily Post*. Alan [Jeans] passed me on to his younger brother, Ronald... who proved to be the vital link in a chain of interest stretching from the enthusiastic Playgoers' Society and the lively professors at the university, right up to the editorial chair of the newspaper.[74]

Dean had been a member of the company at the Gaiety Theatre for the previous four years and was still only 22. His drive and enthusiasm impressed both Ronald and Sir Alexander Jeans and it was decided to go ahead with the booked season at Kelly's Theatre with Dean as producer. The season proved a success, making £1,600 profit, and consequently Reilly and the committee decided to capitalize upon the mood of optimism and press ahead with plans to establish a permanent repertory theatre in the city. One thousand shares were offered to the public who responded with enthusiasm. Bisson provides an amusing anecdotal account of the daughter of Charles J. Allen, the Liverpool artist, going along with her mother to buy shares. 'Professor Reilly was himself selling them and telling everyone that even his cook had bought some!'[75] It was then decided by Clifford Muspratt and Reilly to take out an option on the Star Theatre on Williamson Square, as it was in financial difficulties. The list for the prospectus was opened in May 1911, and consisted of 23,000 shares at £1 each. In the prospectus it was stated that

> Hitherto Liverpool has had to depend mainly for its dramatic entertainment on touring companies from London. It is now proposed to organise and maintain a Repertory Theatre with a resident company of actors and actresses,

---

74   B. Dean, *Seven Ages*, Hutchinson, London, 1970, p. 74.
75   Quoted in Bisson, *The Sandon Studios Society*, p. 71.

and to produce plays which will give to Liverpool playgoers the opportunity of witnessing the best classical and modern drama of every type.[76]

To ensure as broad an appeal for uptake of the offer, the 'Repertory System' was recommended in glowing terms for

> It is believed that the spread of popular education has created a public desire amongst all classes for the best plays, and that such desire can most readily be met by the Repertory Theatre System… One feature of the repertory system is that the expense of production of any one play is relatively small and the shortness of its run prevents any serious loss being incurred. The financial risk ordinarily incidental to theatrical enterprises is therefore to a large extent avoided.[77]

A list of the names of the directors of the new theatre was included in the prospectus together with their occupations. They included, along with Reilly, prominent members of Liverpool's business, media and academic communities.[78] Reilly noted the importance of his decision to involve the press in the project from the outset, and their part in the theatre's success, when he stated,

> When the Liverpool Theatre started there were two sets of each [morning and evening papers] in opposition to one another. I received a good deal of chaff and covert criticism for inducing the editors of both of the morning papers to sit on the board. People on opening their papers were reputed to say, 'Let us see what the Repertory has to say about itself this morning', and there was a certain amount of force in the remark. On the other hand, it meant from the start both papers treated the Playhouse as something the town owned and was interested in…[79]

The enterprise soon attracted the title of 'Citizen's Theatre', and the issue of £1 shares was promoted as evidence of this broad appeal. It is doubtful, however, just how broad this appeal could have been. While it might have allowed for enthusiastic junior clerks to take up a few shares, it is unlikely that

76 *The Liverpool Repertory Theatre Limited Prospectus, 1911*, p. 4. Copy in Liverpool Record Office, Liverpool Central Library, Box HQ 792 1 PLA.
77 *The Liverpool Repertory Theatre Limited Prospectus, 1911*, p. 4.
78 The full list read as follows: Godfrey Edwards, Merchant: Robert Hield, editor of the *Liverpool Courier*; Ronald Jeans, stockbroker's clerk; Ramsey Muir, professor, Liverpool University; Clifford Muspratt, company director; George Rathbone, metal merchant; Alec Lionel Rea, shipowner; Charles Herbert Reilly, professor, Liverpool University; Sir Edward Russell, editor of *Liverpool Daily Post and Mercury*; John Joseph Shute, cotton broker. Quoted in *The Liverpool Repertory Theatre Limited Prospectus, 1911*, p. 3.
79 Reilly, *Scaffolding in the Sky*, pp. 157–58.

the majority of Liverpool's working-class population would have had either the means, or the inclination, to take part in the scheme. Nevertheless Reilly's vision of a broadly based theatre – albeit a somewhat qualified one – prefigures the work of bodies such as the Arts Council of Great Britain after the Second World War, with their aim to bring theatre to as wide an audience as possible. The share issue seems to have been only a partial success, as Dean noted:

> In a last rallying call for victory Sir Edward Russell was induced to write yet another signed article for the *Daily Post*. Only in the nick of time, as it were, was sufficient money raised – £13,000 out of the £23,000 asked for in the prospectus – to justify the directors in proceeding to allotment.[80]

With the decision to proceed taken, the reconstruction work for the theatre was undertaken by Stanley Adshead (Fig. 10). Bisson notes that the ceiling 'was painted with the Loves of Jupiter, by the Sandon artists at thirty shillings per Jovian amour'.[81] Reilly's own theories concerning theatre design were discussed in a paper he wrote sometime in the 1930s entitled 'The English Contribution to Theatre Design Since the 19th Century'. In it he states,

> The quality of the architecture in which an object is housed is a very good criterion of the value set upon that object and the kind of reverence paid to it... Judged by such standards our English theatres, mostly built during the last century, must rank somewhere between the Victorian hotel and the Victorian public house, both pretentious and neither good of their kind. There was a certain amount of solid comfort in both and there is that to be found in the auditoriums of the theatres with their plush seats and draft-proof stuffiness.[82]

He then goes on to criticize the over-ornate nature of Victorian theatre interiors, and posits the work done on the Liverpool Repertory Theatre as a model of its kind:

> The theatre was an old music hall of the three tier type... The decoration of the interior, one could hardly call it architecture, might be called in the seraglio style, with a number of little boxes on either side, useless for seeing the performances on the stage... Professor Adshead, the architect employed, converted the auditorium largely by abolishing the numerous side boxes and in

80 Dean, *Seven Ages*, p. 84.
81 Bisson, *The Sandon Studios Society*, p. 71.
82 Reilly, 'The English Contribution to Theatre Design Since the 19th Century', p. 1. Reilly Papers, Liverpool University Archive, Box D207/12/1.

their place substituting a single monumental one with plenty of plain wall round it from its vicious Victorian ugliness into a simple and elegant one, rather of the Empire type. The intimate coziness of the interior remained but it was no longer vulgar. The immense beer cellar of the old days… was converted into a foyer with a grille through which the orchestra, now placed under the stage, could be heard.[83]

With the establishment of the new theatre, tensions were soon developing between the main players in the scheme. An uneasy relationship seems to have existed between Reilly, Dean and Muspratt in relation to the future ethos of the new theatre. Reilly wished to emphasize the social appeal of the theatre. In the supplement produced in 1961 to celebrate its golden jubilee, Dean recalls how he struggled to prevent too much money being spent on the auditorium at the expense of the stage. 'Meanwhile, Reilly, waving a silver cigarette case in his hand – a favourite gesture – was insisting upon a foyer where people could circulate and discuss the play in the interval.'[84] Dean acknowledges that this was an idea in advance of its time. C. E. Montague, drama critic of the *Manchester Guardian*, commenting on the uniqueness of such a feature in 'legitimate theatre', said,

> the Playhouse directors deserve infinite honour for all the gumption shown in their use of its foyer, their provision for coffee and so forth. Simple matter maybe, and yet in most 'legitimate' theatres does it not seem to be a sacred principle that any care for the play-goer's physical well-being is as the mark of the beast and ought to be rigidly left to the music-halls? To practise this 'abstract and frailry humour' in the service of any Muse is a severe handicap for her business. The Playhouse has chosen the better part in treating man not wholly and solely as a spirit.[85]

Reilly was fully aware of the importance of attracting the socialite element of Liverpool's society if the theatre was to be a financial success. The need to provide them with a space to meet, to see and be seen, was therefore paramount. A writer for the *Liverpool Courier*, commenting on the opening night of the theatre, said,

> Society, wearing its prettiest frocks, occupied boxes and stalls and circles. Muspratts, Forwoods, Holts, Batesons, Willinks were there. The two boxes were

83   Reilly, 'The English Contribution to Theatre Design Since the 19th Century', pp. 5–6.
84   Dean, quoted in 'Playhouse Golden Jubilee Supplement', *Daily Post*, 4 November 1961, p. 2. Liverpool Record Office, Liverpool Central Library, Box HF 792 1 PLA.
85   C. E. Montague, 'A City That Has a Theatre', *Manchester Guardian*, 18 September 1922.

occupied – on the one side by Rathbones and on the other by Bowrings…
Professor Reilly was the hero of the evening.

Dean notes that the piece read like 'a description of an eighteenth-century rout'.[86]

This apparent financial astuteness was allied to a desire on Reilly's part to present challenging and experimental drama, which was at odds with his other more commercial impulses. For the opening night a compromise was reached with the decision to stage a production of J. M. Barrie's *The Admirable Crichton*, a work that would be guaranteed to appeal to a broad audience. Although Reilly was known to have detested Barrie's work, he was mollified by the stated future objective for the theatre, which was to produce plays as adventurously as possible.

The Playgoers' Society continued to function and served as both a critical and an encouraging arm to the project. A journal was established as a forum for discussion, entitled *The Liverpool Playgoers' Society*. In an issue from March 1913 the function of the Playgoers' Society was discussed. It was stressed that the group should not lose sight of its critical function now that the establishment of a repertory theatre had been achieved:

> The repertory theatre, though coming as a boon to the playgoer, is often a source of danger. He, the playgoer, having got his Repertory Theatre, is apt to think 'the King can do no wrong.' The only way to counteract this is by preserving a strict independence, and saying what has got to be said whenever the King makes a slip… One stumbling block in the way of such public criticism is the fact that repertory theatres generally are financed by local men, and where local newspaper men have a financial interest in the theatre, it may be difficult to use the newspaper columns.[87]

This was what Reilly referred to as the 'good deal of chaff and covert criticism' he had received from various quarters for inviting members of the local press onto the board of directors. He countered these criticisms by stressing his standard line about the importance of publicity to fledgling enterprises such as the theatre, and placed the onus with organizations such as the playgoers themselves:

> It did not mean, at any rate after the first year or so, a less exacting standard of criticism: indeed, in the end it meant the reverse. It meant a peculiar interest in

---

86   Quoted in Dean, *Seven Ages*, pp. 86–87.
87   H. Duggan, 'The Function of a Playgoers' Society', *The Playgoers' Society*, No. 5, March 1913. Liverpool Record Office, Liverpool Central Library, Box HQ 792.1 PLA.

everything connected with the theatre... How a repertory theatre is to establish itself in a town with no daily paper of its own is a very difficult question. I really think it should, in that case, start some kind of journal or news-sheet.[88]

A similar question of public versus private finance for the theatre was discussed in a critical article in *The Bulletin of the Sandon Studios Society* from August of the same year. Reviewing the second season of the theatre, the writer comments,

> The second repertory theatre season came to an end with a series of comedies which brought grist to a mill which is beginning to creak, but little of that renown which the New Playgoer looked for when he became a shareholder... We cannot lay the blame of the apparent failure of the repertory theatre on the board of directors, which is composed of energetic and businesslike gentlemen. No. On the great City of Liverpool, that has inherited the commerce of Caesarea, the wealth of Venice and the affluence of Antwerp, lies the stigma. To her lasting shame she has allowed the repertory theatre to struggle in absolute penury for two years... she will be guilty if she lends not a helping hand to the repertory theatre, and raise it in importance beyond the plane of Goodison Park and Anfield Football Fields.[89]

The article was accompanied by a satirical cartoon of Basil Dean entitled *Basil Dean Trying to Fit His Repertory Boot on The City of Liverpool* (Fig. 9).

Nevertheless, the tensions regarding finance and programming continued to mount, and a rift appeared between Dean and the board of directors. Goldie states that 'The first two years of the theatre's existence were full of hard work, enthusiasm, excitement, difficulty...' and that the 'programme of plays was ambitious'.[90] It was finally a production of Hauptmann's *Hannele* that led to Dean's dismissal, and to Reilly standing down as chairman. Dean recalled that 'the chairman [Reilly] thought I had outwitted him over *Hannele*, which was true enough. He also bitterly resented my failure to secure Stanley Houghton's *Hindle Wakes* for the theatre.'[91]

Reilly's vision for the theatre underwent a major change over the following years. John Shute took over the chairmanship, and with his superior contacts among the financiers of the city, he was able temporarily to put the

---

88   Reilly, *Scaffolding in the Sky*, p. 158.
89   *The Bulletin of the Sandon Studios Society*, No. 6, August 1913. Liverpool Record Office, Liverpool Central Library, Box H 708 6 BUL
90   Goldie, *The Liverpool Repertory Theatre*, p. 68.
91   Dean, *Seven Ages*, p. 101. Reilly's main objection to this loss was financial, while Dean rejected it, according to his own account, on artistic grounds.

theatre on a better financial footing. With the outbreak of war, Alec Rea took over from Shute and it was a condition of his advance of £600 that the theatre change its name to 'The Playhouse'. Reilly felt that 'to give it so colourless a name as "The Playhouse", seemed to me almost like throwing up the sponge'.[92] Reilly nevertheless continued to occupy a seat on the board. Disputes continued with the various producers and directors who worked for the theatre, among them William Armstrong who had started as a young actor in the theatre. Armstrong was asked in 1922 to take over as producer following a period of financial difficulty. The familiar arguments regarding the balance between commercial and experimental theatre re-emerged, and Armstrong was criticized for taking too popularist an approach. Reilly was a persistent critic of Armstrong's philosophy. Bisson relates a conversation with Armstrong in which he complained,

> Professor Reilly would be quite happy if the stage was in darkness and only vague moanings could be heard and if the auditorium contained only two persons – Professor Reilly and the Official Receiver.[93]

Reilly, despite his misgivings, was generous enough to credit Armstrong with having made the theatre 'a school of acting second to none in the kingdom'.[94]

The original vision shared by Reilly and the founding members of the Playgoers' Society of an experimental citizen's theatre had been translated into a somewhat different institution. The reputation established by Armstrong did much to position the theatre in the minds of the Liverpool playgoing public and beyond. When, in November 1936, the theatre celebrated its silver jubilee, the *Manchester Guardian* paid tribute to both Armstrong and Reilly:

> every speaker had much to say in praise of Professor Reilly whose inspiration and irresistible blandishment had counted for so much in the 25 years of the playhouse's history.[95]

However, it was necessary for Reilly, and the others involved in the early days of the repertory movement, to maintain their dream of a theatre for all. The pull of finance over art was always, without substantial private or public backing, going to lead to greater commercialization. Reilly, while not entirely

---

92 Reilly, *Scaffolding in the Sky*, p. 155.
93 Quoted in Bisson. *The Sandon Studios Society*, p. 123.
94 Reilly, *Scaffolding in the Sky*, p. 152.
95 *Manchester Guardian*, 24 November 1936.

consistent in his actions, maintained plans for a challenging role for the theatre's future into his retirement. He wrote that it

> must take no narrow view of its duty. All worthy dramas past and present from every country should be its field, just as the municipal picture gallery should cover the whole field of the graphic arts. In order to do this it must have a second small auditorium and second producer.[96]

Writing in 1938, in the days before the golden age of public sponsorship of the arts of the 1950s and 60s, Reilly had devised a plan in which his shareholding in the theatre could be transferred to the university.

> The plan depended upon a clause that had been arranged at the time of the theatre's foundation. Reilly states: 'In the original Articles of Association I persuaded the lawyers, much against their will, as they could find no precedent for it, to introduce a clause that for voting purposes, after the first 100 shares in one name, each successive 100 counted for 10. The holder of a 1,000 shares therefore has only 190 votes. This was to prevent the speculator buying up the shares as they fell in value. I think it has done so. Comparatively few transfers are put forward... The result is that the number of shareholders is shrinking and will, I hope, go on doing so.[97]

Reilly envisaged a future in which

> the university, as a body that does not die, may possibly find itself, years hence, owning the majority of the shares and therefore in control. What a position! The university of a great town owning the only theatre in it! How good, too, for the university to possess such a great social and educational instrument.[98]

Reilly finally stepped down from the board in 1944, by which time the theatre was making a modest but healthy profit.[99] Reilly's vision of a theatrical monopoly run by the university might seem in hindsight too extreme a position. Nevertheless, had his scheme come to fruition, the university would have gained a valuable cultural and educational asset.

It would be wrong to place too much emphasis upon the various roles Reilly played in the establishment of both the Bluecoat Society of Arts and the Playhouse Theatre, and by so doing suggest that he was in some way alone in

96 Reilly, *Scaffolding in the Sky*, p. 159.
97 Reilly, *Scaffolding in the Sky*, p. 160.
98 Reilly, *Scaffolding in the Sky*, pp. 160–61.
99 'Liverpool Repertory Theatre Report for Year Ended June 30 1944', *Liverpool Evening Express*, 17 October 1944.

his cultural endeavours. It cannot be denied, however, that he was instrumental in initiating debate and action at a number of crucial points in the history of both organizations. Reilly worked in a complex web of interlocking relationships. He acted according to the circumstances that prevailed in that community, and there are many instances of failure. In many respects he was fortunate in his acquaintances and friendships, most notably that of Lever, without whose money and influence Reilly could have achieved very little in concrete terms.

5 The Chair of Civic Design

Arguably the most important initiative in which Reilly was involved in the years leading up to the First World War was the founding of the Chair of Civic Design at Liverpool University, the first in the world. As with many of the schemes involving the educational and cultural life of Liverpool, William Lever was central to the establishment of the department, providing not only the financial means but also a good deal of the driving power behind the project. Reilly's own recollection of the founding of the department, as outlined in his autobiography, is characteristic in concentrating upon his own central role. Reilly recalled that

> I was walking down Brownlow Hill. I turned into the University Club and wrote to Lever. I pointed out the need for connecting the words 'town planning' with architecture in the public mind. I think I said it was in the main an advanced form of architecture as it is or rather should be. I have no doubt I reminded him how he had practised it himself at Port Sunlight. I wound up my letter with a suggestion of an endowment for a Chair, for a lectureship and for a Journal in the subject. By return of post I had an encouraging letter asking me to come and see him. The deed was done in a few days.[1]

It is hard to ascertain exactly what the circumstances surrounding the initial idea for the chair were. As Myles Wright points out, it is unlikely that the scheme was set up with the speed Reilly relates. What is certain is that Reilly was responding to contemporary debates that had taken place over a number of years prior to the establishment of the department, calling for the development of a greater sense of public planning in the expanding towns and cities. The debates concerned the fundamental means by which cities should present themselves, and developed out of the conflict between the Gothic/Arts and Crafts axis, and the Neoclassicist/Beaux-Arts enthusiasts.

Throughout the nineteenth century the growing complexity involved in the development and running of urban areas called for increasing intervention by local government, leading to a system that provided for a range of

---

1   C. H. Reilly, *Scaffolding in the Sky*, Routledge, London, 1938, p. 126.

local amenities.[2] By the end of the century many of the larger towns and cities were encountering problems with the rapid, largely unplanned growth they had experienced during the preceding 100 years. The Liberal government elected in 1906 had promised to introduce a bill for the alleviation of over-crowding and unplanned development, and it was a speech made by John Burns, President of the Local Government Board, that prompted Reilly to approach Lever concerning the establishment of the department.

At a local level there had been a number of initiatives that pre-dated Burns's speech. The planning of urban spaces in Liverpool can be traced back to the efforts of John Foster, the city surveyor who had been responsible for laying out the formal squares and streets around Abercromby and Falkner Squares at the start of the nineteenth century.[3] By the start of the new century, the debate over the siting of the new Liverpool Cathedral had raised issues regarding the formulation of a planned environment along Beaux-Arts lines. This debate had culminated in a 'City Beautiful Conference' held in 1907.

The City Beautiful Movement

The City Beautiful movement had been popularized by Charles Mulford Robinson in his 1901 book *The Improvement of Towns and Cities.* While it lacked any coherent philosophy (Sutcliffe claims that 'consistency of thought and clarity of expression were not his strongest points')[4] the importance of the book with regard to the establishment of the department is that it was acquired by the library of the department in 1909. The term 'City Beautiful' may have been coined during the American debate over civic planning, and had appeared regularly in the New York journal *Municipal Affairs* around 1899.[5] There are also recorded examples of the phrase being used in Liverpool as early as 1895.[6] A number of other initiatives occurred in Liverpool early in 1906: T. T. Rees delivered a speech to the Liverpool Architectural Association on the 'Beauty and Dignity of Liverpool', which Reilly attended, in which he

2   For a full discussion of the development of public intervention policy throughout the nineteenth century see A. Sutcliffe, *Towards the Planned City*, Basil Blackwell, London, 1981.
3   See J. Quentin Hughes, *Seaport*, Bluecoat Press, Liverpool, 1993, pp. 107–19.
4   Sutcliffe, *Towards the Planned City*, p. 104.
5   Sutcliffe, *Towards the Planned City*, p. 103.
6   'New Liverpool', *Sphinx*, Vol. 2, 1894–1895, p. 124.

discussed issues of 'civic planning'.[7] In response to the speech Reilly wrote a letter to the *Daily Post and Mercury*, in which he called for greater unity in town planning.[8] In March 1906, Philip Rathbone delivered a lecture at the Liverpool Royal Institute entitled 'The City Beautiful', subsequently reported in the *Liverpool Post*, to which Reilly sent a letter regretting his inability to attend.[9] By late 1906, reports had appeared in the Liverpool press[10] concerning the proposed formation of a society to promote the aims of the City Beautiful movement. Within a short time the movement had become known as the 'City Beautiful Society'[11] and Reilly was voted on to the executive committee. The society quickly joined forces with the other interested local bodies such as the Trees Preservation and Open Spaces Association and the Kyrle Society[12] to form the Liverpool City Guild under the chairmanship of the Marquis of Salisbury.

When the City Beautiful conference was staged in June 1907 the Guild had, as Crouch puts it, 'done its job in sufficiently motivating the local intelligentsia to back what was substantially Reilly's City Beautiful Conference'.[13] Indeed Reilly displayed his developing promotional talents by writing to the editors of the *Architectural Review*, *The Building News* and *The Builder* offering each exclusive use of the pre-conference material.[14] Reilly only succeeded in gaining coverage in *The Builder*, but it was his paper on 'Urban and Suburban Planning' that received all the press attention.[15] This provided national reinforcement of the impression – one that Reilly had already developed locally – that Reilly was the prime mover on the Liverpool scene. The extent to which Reilly was influenced by French models of urban planning is indicated by the fact that he consulted his colleague Charles Bonnier, a lecturer in French at Liverpool University whose brother was a practising architect in France, over the writing of his speech for the conference. Reilly enquires after the methods employed by the French in designing their urban spaces:

7   T. T. Rees, 'Beauty and Dignity of Liverpool', speech given to the Liverpool Architectural Association, reported in *Daily Post and Mercury*, 23 January 1906.
8   Reilly, letter to *Daily Post and Mercury*, 29 January 1906, Reilly Papers, Liverpool University Archive, Box S3214.
9   P. Rathbone, 'The City Beautiful', lecture given at the Royal Institute, 23 March 1906, reported in *Liverpool Post*, 24 March 1906.
10 *Liverpool Post*, 16 November 1906.
11 *The Building News*, 30 November 1906.
12 The Kyrle societies were philanthropic associations aiming to promote environmental awareness. C. Robinson, *The Improvement of Towns and Cities*, Putman, London, 1901, p. 196.
13 C. Crouch, 'Design Initiatives in Liverpool 1881–1914', PhD thesis, Liverpool University, 1992, p. 141.
14 Letters dated 18 May 1907, Reilly Papers, Liverpool University Archive, Box D207/2/2.
15 Reilly, 'Urban and Suburban Planning', *The Builder*, 6 July 1907

What I want to get at from your brother if possible is the vast superiority of the street architecture and the general layout of the streets of any considerable French town to any corresponding English one. I think this cannot be entirely due to the superior work of the average French architect, though with his fine training I should be the first to admit to the pull he has over his English colleague. Who makes these general schemes and how are the rights of private owners of property reconciled? In England the corporations of our towns have no artists or architects of any sort to advise them only surveyors and drain men to say how the sewers are going to go. Then going into details what control has the town if any over the design of each new block of buildings? Here we only control its construction for the safety of the public. Can the height of buildings be limited in Paris and the main lines of roof and cornice be kept level in one street?... How does Paris so often achieve the balancing of buildings on opposite sides of a street? This cannot always be the case of one owner. I cannot help thinking that besides a general artistic consensus which we haven't had in England since the 18th century Paris today has some very extensive powers of control over the individual builders. Do you think your brother could tell me what they are and perhaps send me a copy of these bye laws?[16]

The conference agenda was in two parts: 'Town and Suburban Planning' and 'Garden Cities'.[17] This split represented the two approaches to urban planning that Crouch notes:

It is clear that apart from the desire for rational planning which united the two approaches, what separated them was the conception of the city as a domestic environment, in opposition to the city as an expression of a collective civic culture. Initially it might seem incongruous that two such seemingly different approaches to architectural style, and planning principles, should be sharing the same platform provided at the Liverpool City Beautiful Conference. However that division between the two – put crudely, between the Gothic romantics and the rational Neoclassicists – was not as closely defined as it has become in retrospect, and was to become within the next few years.[18]

It was the contributions made by other speakers such as T. C. Horsfall – a prominent Christian Socialist and expert on German town planning who also

16 Letter from Reilly to C. Bonnier, 29 May 1907, Reilly Papers, Liverpool University Archive, Box D207/2/2.
17 George Rose, Chairman of the Liverpool Garden City Association, read a paper in which he stressed the non-utopian nature of the Garden City Association's ethos, perhaps in response to the growing rationalist argument put forward by Reilly *et al.* G. Rose, 'Garden City Ideals', paper read at the City Beautiful conference, Liverpool Town Hall, 28 June 1907; Liverpool Record Office, Liverpool Central Library, Box H 711582 ROS.
18 Crouch, 'Design Initiatives in Liverpool', p. 143.

spoke on the issue of town and suburban planning – and Sybella Gurney[19] that would have an immediate impact on commentators on the conference; but Reilly's involvement was significant, since as Crouch notes,

> Reilly's contribution combined the wider national and international issues of city planning and made it pertinent to Liverpool, thus at the same time increasing the city's importance through the nature of his comparisons. Essentially, Reilly demanded the rational planning of cities modelled on the paradigm of Wren, the Woods (thus creating an historical importance for Liverpool) and nineteenth century Paris.[20]

It would be wrong to suggest that Reilly was alone in his appreciation of the importance of civic design. While he wanted to stake a claim for architects to occupy a central, coordinating role in the rapidly developing discipline, other architects were also active in the area: H. V. Lanchester worked on the layout of New Delhi, while Inigo Triggs moved, like Thomas Mawson, from landscape design to town planning. However, as Powers notes, 'It was this urban approach to town planning which Reilly wished to boost.'[21] With the establishment of the department at Liverpool University, he had stolen a march on his contemporaries and major competitors in the field.

Combined with the historical perspective,[22] what Reilly sought to bring to the City Beautiful debate was an awareness of the need for attention to be given to the aesthetic qualities of town planning, and the material wellbeing this could bring to a city, above and beyond the basic amenities provided by local government legislation. By identifying the philosophy espoused by the Ecole des Beaux-Arts, with its emphasis on 'balanced, symmetrical, dignified buildings',[23] Reilly demanded a logical uniformity in the way cities presented themselves, and by so doing rejected the individualism which had character-ized British architecture throughout the nineteenth century. Reilly was able to formulate a design philosophy allying architecture and town planning, and so

---

19 Gurney was the Secretary of the Co-partnership Tenants Housing Council. She provided a model for Liverpool as a radically planned city using a parkway system, as a model for other city development. H. V. Lanchester quoted her contribution in his essay 'Park Systems for Great Cities'.
20 Crouch, 'Design Initiatives in Liverpool', pp. 141–42.
21 A. Powers, 'Architectural Education in Britain 1880–1914', PhD thesis, Cambridge University, 1982, p. 256.
22 'It was possible less than ten years ago for Nash's fine architectural scheme in Regent Street to be broken up by two odd and ugly domes erected to advertise certain shops. It is still possible in Liverpool to introduce a yellow terra-cotta dressed building into the quiet dignity and repose of Rodney Street.' Reilly, 'Urban and Suburban Planning', p. 11.
23 Reilly, 'Urban and Suburban Planning', The Builder, 6 July 1907.

provide an innovative stance from which the Liverpool School of Architecture could operate. His vision of the city was one in which it celebrated its urbanity, in contrast to (as he saw it) the garden-city enthusiasts who sought to create an environment in which town, suburb and countryside mixed with little or no definition. It was a policy Reilly would continue to promote, with minor adjustments to accommodate the changing social climate, up until his death. More importantly it would be the policy that would shape and inform the foundation of the Department of Civic Design.

Background to the Department of Civic Design

Of all the projects in which Lever and Reilly worked in partnership, it was the founding of the Department of Civic Design that combined their talents to best effect, and to the greatest mutual benefit. Lever, by the time Reilly came to know him in 1904, was already a sophisticated patron of the arts.[24] Reilly notes in his autobiography that Lever 'kindly said I was at liberty to suggest any such way of using up his surplus money provided he was equally free to refuse'.[25] Reilly's association with Lever provided him with the money and clout to extend his sphere of influence within architectural and cultural circles, both in Liverpool and beyond. In Reilly, Lever gained an enthusiastic source of new ideas. Reilly and the School of Architecture had, from as early as 1905, been involved with Lever's Port Sunlight project.[26] Reilly had designed a quadrant of cottages with a distinct Regency flavour for the village in 1906, somewhat at odds with the work produced by Lever's main architects for the village, William and Segar Owen. The cottages were not considered a success, and there were plans to demolish them.[27] Surprisingly, given their other close collaborations, they remained Reilly's only major architectural work for Lever.

Shortly after the school's move into the Blue Coat building in 1908, plans were drawn up to establish the Department of Civic Design. In contrast

24 Reilly wrote to Lever shortly after his appointment to the Roscoe Chair in 1904 requesting to look at the church and one of the houses in Port Sunlight. Reilly to W. H. Lever, 23 April 1904, Reilly Papers, Liverpool University Archive, Box D207/2/1.
25 Reilly, *Scaffolding in the Sky*, p. 123.
26 See P. Richmond, 'Rebuilding the Temple: The Inter-War Architecture of Herbert J. Rowse', MDes thesis, University of Liverpool, 1992.
27 M. Shippobottom, 'Reilly and the First Lord Leverhulme', in J. Sharples (ed.), *Charles Reilly and the Liverpool School of Architecture*, catalogue to exhibition at Walker Art Gallery, Liverpool, October 1996–February 1997, Liverpool University Press, Liverpool, p. 45.

to Reilly's account of the whirlwind development of the idea for the department, it is interesting to note Lever's more cautious, businesslike approach to the scheme, as a means of gauging the balance of the relationship between the two men. In a letter to the Vice-Chancellor from Lever concerning the establishment of the department, Lever notes,

> in view of the fact that we have no data to go on with reference to the success such a departure might meet with, probably the lesser of the two evils is to work on the lines of limited time period rather than to commit for a longer period to find when too late that there was not sufficient scope for a town planning scheme in connection with the Liverpool University.[28]

The formal decision to set up the department had been made at a meeting of the Senate in February 1909, at which it was agreed to offer both day and evening classes in a department in which the professor's role would be to undertake research into the problems of the design and development of towns.[29] It seems that it was Reilly's suggestion that the term 'Civic Design' be adopted, to which Lever responded,

> I feel that the title of 'Town Planning and Landscape Architecture' is cumbersome, and that we ought to get a better title. What I want, seeing that this is an entirely new idea, is that there shall be no misconception as to the field to be covered. I will think over the name you suggest, which has the great merit of shortness.[30]

In addition to the points made by Lever with regard to the superiority of Reilly's suggestion, the importance of Reilly's victory in securing his preferred title of Civic Design lay mostly in disassociating the new department from any 'landscape architecture' or 'garden suburb' connotation. This set the tone for the work to be undertaken by the department.

Stanley Adshead: First Lever Professor of Civic Design

The choice of professor in the new department had been made a short time before the Senate decision, with Reilly's friend Stanley Adshead being

28 Letter from Lever to Vice-Chancellor Dale, 17 March 1909, Vice-Chancellor's Papers, Liverpool University Archive, Box P/5/4.
29 Liverpool University Senate Papers, Vol. 3/23, 22 February 1909, Liverpool University Archive.
30 Letter from Lever to Reilly, 20 November 1908, Vice-Chancellor's Papers, Liverpool University Archive, Box P4/1/26.

approached. For Adshead, whose fortunes were undergoing a difficult phase, it was a lucky offer, and one that would radically alter the course of his career. In an unfinished manuscript in which Adshead describes aspects of his early life, together with the establishment of the Department of Civic Design, he notes that

> I did fourteen competitions without success. I seemed to fail in everything and was reduced to running my office with one boy and busying myself with reading papers on architecture before societies... one day through the instrumentality of my friend Professor Reilly, I received an invitation to occupy the newly funded Chair of Civic Design at the Liverpool University.[31]

From this account Adshead would hardly have seemed the ideal choice. For Reilly, however, he provided the opportunity to build around him a group of like-minded colleagues who would help in the promotion and development of both the School of Architecture and the new Department of Civic Design. Reilly had already invited Patrick Abercrombie, the brother of his friend and colleague from the Department of English Lascelles Abercrombie, to join the School of Architecture as lecturer and studio master. Abercrombie had for some time been interested in town planning, and while he had expressed a strong desire to join the new department, it seems probable that Reilly considered him too junior to take the position of professor at that stage. He was joined by a group of part-time lecturers: H. Chaloner Dowdall,[32] John Brodie, and Thomas Mawson, all of whom brought specialisms with them.[33] With the choice of Adshead, Reilly's position at the centre of a growing empire within the university was further strengthened, and as Powers notes, 'It was more important to Reilly to have a man who represented the right architectural creed than one, such as Raymond Unwin, who had practical experience in town planning.'[34] In addition, Adshead was acceptable to

---

31 S. Adshead, *Architects I Have Known*, unpublished manuscript, Adshead Papers, Liverpool University Archive, Box D247/1. See also A. Powers, '"Architects I have known": The Architectural Career of S. D. Adshead', *Architectural History, Journal of the Society of Architectural Historians of Great Britain*, October 1981.

32 Dowdall was a barrister who lectured on civic law in the department. See R. Bisson, *The Sandon Studios Society and the Arts*, Parry Books, Liverpool, 1965, for full details.

33 Mawson had done some work for Lever on landscape: 'Mawson tended to introduce formality and architectural treatment into landscaping, and in civic design shared Lever's admiration for grand and broad classicism, affined to the American City Beautiful Movement.' E. Hubbard and M. Shippobottom, *A Guide to Port Sunlight Village*, Liverpool University Press, Liverpool, 1988, p. 68.

34 Powers, 'Architectural Education in Britain', p. 255.

Lever,[35] as well as the then-powerful New Testament group within the Faculty of Arts, of which Reilly was a member.[36] It would be wrong, however, to suggest that Adshead himself saw the department, and indeed himself, as a mere appendage to Reilly and the School of Architecture. In a number of letters he wrote to Reilly early in 1909, he sets down his own very clear views of how the new department should operate:

> Since seeing you I have had time to consider more fully the many points at issue in connection with the formation of your School of Town Planning. In the first place I may say that I regard a School of Town Planning as one which in its curriculum would embrace rather than be a branch of a school of architecture. It is impossible to consider town planning without reference to architecture: but architecture does not necessarily cognate town planning.
> (1) I therefore feel that whoever may be entrusted with the organising and carrying on of this new departure should be in the first place an architect, in the best sense of the word. His outlook must be a broad one, he must have order and system in his methods of design. His work must not be the expression of fads and fancies. It must be scholarly and academic. He must not be a pedant, and he must not live entirely in the past. He must be abreast of the times and alive to all the possibilities of the future.[37]

He goes on to outline his preference for architectural composition, architectural character, and colour in the curriculum for the school, and concludes by saying:

> America and the Continent must be reassessed, but let the school start on a few well chosen examples of town planning... Then again being a school with an absolutely philanthropic object, it must be made to extend as wide an influence as possible... it must spend much of its energy in the issuing of publications and must intimately concern itself in the making of books.[38]

35 'I have been very glad to read the letter from Mr Adshead which I return herewith, and also Mr Adshead's paper published in the RIBA journal, which I also return. Mr Adshead impressed me most favourably at our interview on Saturday.' Letter from Lever to Reilly, 15 March 1909, Vice-Chancellor's Papers, Liverpool University Archive, Box P/5/4.

36 See Reilly, *Scaffolding in the Sky*, p. 127. 'The University accepted the, to them, unknown Adshead on my recommendation. Adshead came down and Mackay and everyone liked the frank, honest way in which he expressed his views and enjoyed his sense of fun and humour.'

37 Letter from Adshead to Reilly, 11 January 1909, Vice-Chancellor's Papers, Liverpool University Archive, Box P/5/4.

38 Letter from Adshead to Reilly, 11 January 1909.

Adshead was initially appointed Associate Professor of Civic Design in March 1909, for a period of three years.[39] Abercrombie was his assistant and editor of the *Town Planning Review*, the quarterly journal set up as part of the new department. *The Municipal Journal* noted on his appointment that

> we shall come to look on our towns as organic unities, which ought so to be built: they will become eventually, not congeries of buildings, but 'landscape architecture' – a phrase which seems well fitted to express the right idea of a town.[40]

To what degree either Reilly or Adshead would have described their vision of civic design as 'landscape architecture' is, however, doubtful.

In his inaugural lecture, Adshead called for a suppression of the individualism that had marked architecture in the previous century:

> In the well organised city individual expression is subordinate to the civic expression of the city as a whole... people are the reflection of the city in whose environment they have lived and... so ought not to be left entirely to individual control.[41]

By stating this he was obviously drawing on the sociological aspects of town planning outlined by the likes of Patrick Geddes from as early as 1892. In addition, Adshead made a number of prophetic statements of his own, calling for the establishment of smokeless zones, the setting up of comparative museums to examine industrial and civic design, and the need for a 'moral force' in public planning. For Adshead this meant the integration of agencies such as the church, local government and public utilities to provide a coherent civic policy. The latter point would be largely neglected by subsequent planners and indeed is only now finding new resonance in the 'community build' schemes currently in vogue. Adshead further outlined this idea, which he termed 'social civics':

> I therefore foresaw that town planning if separated into different aspects would need to make social civics the chief of them. Other aspects were landscape art,

39   The position became full professorship in 1912 with the creation of the Lever Chair of Civic Design, following a progress report submitted to Senate in March of that year in which it was decided that the department had proved itself a success.

40   'Civic Design: The Appointment by The University of Liverpool', *Municipal Journal*, 20 April 1909.

41   Adshead, 'Civic Design', inaugural lecture delivered at the University of Liverpool, 8 October 1909.

engineering, law, town furnishing and the aesthetics of towns. These then give the subjects of my six lecture courses. The first, Social Civics, is treated of under the heading of 'Outlines of Town Planning' and is covered with 20 lectures which deal with the functional requirements of a town, its intellectual, administrative, residential and recreative requirements...[42]

He went on to call for the creation of an ideal city:

What we need is the controlling influence of the Greek... All great cities are either white or grey. That which is a golden red harmonising with the rich green verdure of the surrounding land will ever suggest ease of existence, simplicity and primitive life. Such harmony can never suggest solidity of existence as does grey, nor vivacity as does white or cream. The characteristics of a city expressed in its colour, its texture, and its form, reflect on the citizen himself.[43]

At this time Adshead and Reilly seem to have been in total agreement as to both the vision and the means by which this ideal city might be achieved.

As part of the establishment of the department Lever also provided funding for Reilly and Adshead to undertake overseas research. Reilly, with typical boldness, notes,

It was decided that he and I should divide the world between us at his lordship's expense. Adshead was to travel through Europe collecting information as to what was being done in town planning in Germany, Austria and elsewhere, and I was to go to the eastern states of America and do the same.[44]

Reilly returned from his trip fired with enthusiasm for the monumental American Beaux-Arts architecture he had experienced there. Writing to Sir Aston Webb, Reilly notes that he had 'collected two packing cases full of material'.[45] It was during this trip in the spring of 1909 that Reilly gained his own first-hand experience of the American work that Adshead and Ramsey had drawn to his attention some years earlier (it seems he had not at that time been totally convinced). Writing in the *RIBA Journal* the following year, Reilly stated that

---

42   Adshead, 'The School of Civic Design at the Liverpool University', p. 3, Adshead Papers, Liverpool University Archive, Box D247/2.
43   Adshead, 'The School of Civic Design at the Liverpool University'.
44   Reilly, *Scaffolding in the Sky*, p. 127.
45   Letter from Reilly to Sir A. Webb, 12 May 1909, Reilly Papers, Liverpool University Archive, Box S3205.

Before I visited the University Club at New York, by Messrs McKim, Mead and White, I was not a little amused to be told by an unemotional Scotch architect practising in New York that I should find in this club a palace worthy to rank with the Farnese, the Massimi, or any of the great Italian palazzi, but after I had visited it I was very much of the same opinion myself.[46]

Reilly's enthusiasms were to be tempered by the reactions of his colleagues, and it is possible to detect the early signs of a rift developing between the philosophical stances of Reilly and Adshead. As Abercrombie recalled, Adshead

perplexed Reilly, who had returned from his American tour gathering material for the new department's library full of fire for Monumentality: the grand manner of the Renaissance to be revived in Europe as a reflection of the civic centres and vistas being planned by Burnham and others in the States. Adshead appreciated and welcomed these great schemes right enough: he too thought big and could design big... his first reaction to the Reilly stimulus was to prepare some fine bold architectural schemes for Liverpool... These schemes were critically examined by a colleague, the historian Ramsey Muir. Adshead I know was impressed by these criticisms: to Reilly they were merely curbs upon the exuberance of monumental planning.[47]

It is interesting to speculate what the outcome might have been had Adshead been given full control of the Department of Civic Design's policy – a hybrid of American and European influences perhaps? As it turned out, Reilly's penchant for Monumentalism along the American Beaux-Arts lines won the day and became the house style for the Liverpool School. Powers notes that the department was to act 'more as a centre for research and propaganda than as a teaching institution'.[48] The first of the major organs for the transmission of the ideas generated within the School of Architecture and the Department of Civic Design was the *Town Planning Review*, under the editorship of Abercrombie. The second consisted of a series of Lever Prizes awarded to senior students within the school.

---

46   Reilly, 'The Modern Renaissance in American Architecture', *RIBA Journal*, 25 June 1910, pp. 630–35.

47   Abercrombie, *Adshead at Liverpool University 1946–47*, quoted in Powers, 'Architectural Education in Britain', pp. 257–58.

48   Powers, 'Architectural Education in Britain', p. 258.

The *Town Planning Review*

In the report on the department's first three years of existence submitted to the Senate in March 1912, Reilly noted that

> It is not too much to say that the *Town Planning Review* has raised the whole subject of town planning in England from the purely utilitarian point of view from which it was at first regarded, and has therefore justified the inclusion of the subject in the work of the School of Architecture.[49]

The *Town Planning Review* set out, from its inception in 1910, to be a forum for national and international debate on planning issues; and moreover, as Crouch notes, 'the *Town Planning Review* was as much a mouthpiece for the Liverpool School as it was an objective journal examining the nature of town planning'.[50] Abercrombie wrote a good deal of the early articles, 16 under his own name, and plenty of other, anonymous, items. From the outset he used the sum set aside for travel to the full, and produced articles on the planning of Brussels, Ghent and Berlin, as well as commenting on the Birley Griffin plan for Canberra and the new city at Delhi. Just how successful the journal was as a mouthpiece for the school can be judged by an examination of the debate about the broader issues of town planning.

Added to the strong international angle of the journal's editorial, the city of Liverpool also figured heavily in the early editions in articles such as Adshead's 'A Suggestion for the Reconstruction of St John's Gardens, St George's Hall, Liverpool',[51] or 'Liverpool: A Preliminary Survey with Some Suggestions for Remodelling its Central Area'.[52] Many of the projects illustrated tended to rely on the illustrative impact of the plans rather than the practical implementation of the schemes. This concern with the local issues of planning, informed by an understanding of the wider cosmopolitan context of the debate, tied in neatly with the general policy Reilly had employed at Liverpool since his appointment regarding the promotion of Classicism. Reilly's enthusiasm for an internationalist approach to planning issues, with a strong preference for French and American Beaux-Arts models, was in part informed by his own socialist sympathies. However, such leanings were not

49   The University of Liverpool, Faculty of Arts, Chair of Civic Design, Report to Senate, 20 March 1912, Vice-Chancellor's Papers, Liverpool University Archive, Box 6B/3/7.
50   Crouch, 'Design Initiatives in Liverpool', p. 149.
51   Adshead, *Town Planning Review*, Vol. 1/1.
52   Adshead, *Town Planning Review*, Vol. 1/2.

universally popular in the British architectural press, and many of the criticisms levelled at Reilly's methods were centred on the internationalist aspects of the Liverpool School's style. As one commentator noted, 'Modern architecture (of which the Liverpool School is held to be important) has in reality no more foundation, no more stability, than so much stage scenery.'[53] Much of the criticism, it has to be said, lacked any real intellectual rigour when compared with the stance that had been developed by Adshead and Abercrombie, and promoted by Reilly.[54] The unfavourable comparison between the two approaches only added weight to the Liverpool argument, and provided the *Town Planning Review* with the opportunity to seize the initiative in the developing planning debate.

Moves towards an international debate were made in the pages of the *Town Planning Review* from 1910 onwards, and with Reilly's trip to the United States new impetus was added in the form of articles such as 'Town Planning Schemes in America'. Reilly continued to contrast the American model of a civic centre as representing the public face of the city, its ethos and aspirations, with the English position, in which 'the idea of the garden suburb is the little imitation village on the edge of the town – and as yet [has] hardly got beyond it'.[55] Reilly argued for stylistic coherence and used the burgeoning suburbs as examples of all that was stylistically incoherent, and as such in opposition to the Liverpool philosophy. As early as July 1910, Reilly's strategy gained some national support when *The Builder* stated that

> the Liverpool School seems to be quite considerable enough to take a stand of itself, and perhaps even to suggest a style to others. We feel acutely the value of a strong common speech among a body of men... preferable to a Babel of polyglot talk.[56]

The theme of the cosmopolitan city was further reinforced in an article by Adshead in the third issue of the *Town Planning Review*[57] in which he called for an erosion of national distinction, and the need for a unifying design

53 L. March Phillips, 'Liverpool and its Architecture', *Morning Post*, 9 June 1913.
54 For example, *The British Architect* stated, 'we must be cosmopolitan in many ways, no doubt, but the cosmopolitan art which effaces nationality and individuality, which loses the unpersonal in the general, will bring about a culture at the cost of much that makes architecture worth the while'. 'Cosmopolitan Art', 20 June 1913. Such indecisive argument allowed the relative clarity of the Liverpool argument to gain the upper hand.
55 Reilly, 'Town Planning Schemes in America', *Town Planning Review*, Vol. 1/1, 1910, p. 54.
56 'The Liverpool School of Architecture', *The Builder*, 16 July 1910, p. 64.
57 Adshead, 'City Improvement', *Town Planning Review*, Vol. 1/3, 1910.

philosophy modelled on the American system as promoted by the likes of McKim. The final triumph in the debate between Reilly's American model and the English garden suburb style can be traced in a series of articles by Arthur Trystan Edwards in which he condemns the movement for its 'perfect hatred of design'[58] – that is to say, its lack of uniformity. Edwards had been a protegé of Reilly's; in 1913 Reilly suggested to his friend and colleague at the *Architects' and Builders' Journal*, Randall Phillips, that Edwards be employed as a leader writer – presumably to help promote the Liverpool message on a national level. Reilly described him to Phillips as having taken a 'First Class in Maths at Oxford. His hobby is architecture and philosophy. He has spent two years in the school here in Adshead's department and has sat for his final RIBA.'[59] Edwards was the perfect advocate for the Liverpool style in the national press, having – as Powers notes – 'the right intellectual training to establish the Liverpool doctrine on a philosophical basis'. This dimension had been largely missing up until that time.[60]

The Lever Prize Competition

The prize initiated by Lever in 1909 – which by 1912 had acquired the title Lever Prize – provided another mutually beneficial arrangement for Lever and Reilly. For Reilly it allowed one more avenue for the promotion and dissemination of the Liverpool School ethos; while for Lever, it provided a source of ideas for projects he was planning to implement, or fresh ideas for possible future implementation.[61] The theme for the first was a redesign of the central area of Port Sunlight, and was won by Ernest Prestwich (Fig. 8). The prize is also interesting as a barometer of the extent to which the ideas promoted by Reilly had started to influence important philanthropic figures such as Lever. The design by Prestwich was a grand formal axial plan consisting of a series of intersecting boulevards to create bold vistas in the then-undeveloped

---

58   A. T. Edwards, 'A Criticism of the Garden City Movement', *Town Planning Review*, Vol. 4/2. See also Edwards, 'A Further Criticism of the Garden City Movement', *Town Planning Review*, Vol. 4/4.

59   Letter from Reilly to Randall Phillips, 23 April 1913, Reilly Papers, Liverpool University Archive, Box S3211.

60   See Powers, 'Architectural Education in Britain', pp. 272–73.

61   For example, the first two schemes for 'Port Sunlight Central Area' and a 'Block of Cottages' gave Lever valuable ideas at a relatively modest outlay of £5, £10 and £20, plus a £100 fee on the adoption of the winning scheme.

internal space of the village, with a grouping of civic buildings: art gallery, museum and baths. The work was largely carried out according to Prestwich's original plan, with the exception of the omission of the civic grouping. The art gallery was completed at the end of a main axial boulevard in 1913 by William and Segar Owen, in a Beaux-Arts style at Lever's own suggestion. Hubbard and Shippobottom have suggested that 'the work of Professor Reilly and the Liverpool School of Architecture must have played a part in influencing him [Lever]'.[62] Shippobottom confirms this tentative theory when he states,

> The school and Reilly's own tastes clearly influenced Lever, and not just by way of the prizes. The promotion, for example, of the neo-Georgian mansion by the Liverpool School as the most appropriate model for post-war housing, coupled with consideration of industrialised building methods, was taken up in Lever's own speeches advocating standardisation and the use of concrete, and its influence may be seen in the later houses erected by him at Leverburgh on the Scottish island of Lewis, and not least in the hints of classicism creeping into Port Sunlight cottage design from 1919 onwards.[63]

The winners of the 1912, 1913 and 1914 prizes, unlike Prestwich, did not see their designs implemented. They all display what Crouch terms 'a coherence that stems from the teaching programme of the school'.[64] Certainly the hand of Reilly and his Beaux-Arts enthusiasm is clearly seen in the schemes for the 1912 competition involving the redesigning of Brownlow Hill, Liverpool, which would 'be reconstructed as an example of monumental town planning'.[65] Reilly, however, did not consider this to be just an exercise, and he told the Vice-Chancellor that 'it would be a wonderful but not a quite impossible thing if Sir William took up seriously a scheme for this land'.[66] Despite Reilly's obvious ambitions for this and the other schemes from the pre-war period, they were to remain unbuilt. A competition was held in 1914 for the redesign of St John's Gardens,[67] but it is the 1913 designs that come closest to Reilly's vision of the ideal city.[68] The prizes, despite their relative lack of success in concrete terms,

62 Hubbard and Shippobottom, *A Guide to Port Sunlight Village*, p. 40.
63 Shippobottom, 'Reilly and the First Lord Leverhulme', in Sharples (ed.), *Charles Reilly and the Liverpool School of Architecture*, p. 56.
64 Crouch, 'Design Initiatives in Liverpool', p. 166.
65 *Town Planning Review*, Vol. 3/1, 1912, pp. 80–81.
66 Letter from Reilly to the Vice-Chancellor, 8 January 1912, Vice-Chancellor's Papers, Liverpool University Archive, Box P4A/3/5.
67 *Town Planning Review*, Vol. 5/1.
68 Reilly's vision had been outlined in articles such as 'The City of the Future', *Town Planning Review*, Vol. 1/3, 1910, pp. 191–97

did provide useful public relations material in furtherance of the school's ambitions to be seen as the pace setter in the developing ideological debate.

The Duchy of Cornwall Estate

By the outbreak of the First World War, the 'Liverpool Manner' – as it was coming to be known – was well established. One of the major projects from this period, and one which would come to exemplify the Liverpool style, was undertaken by Adshead and Ramsey on the Duchy of Cornwall estates at Kennington in London. This followed a meeting in 1909 between the Secretary of the Duchy of Cornwall estates, Sir Walter Peacock, and Adshead, during a housing tour of Germany. Adshead was subsequently asked to examine and report on the condition of the rundown Kennington Estate, and published his report in 1911.[69] Ironically, given the Liverpool School's established working methods, and Adshead's own considerable talents as a perspectivist, there were, as Powers notes,

> no grand preliminary perspective drawings of the estate, and no preconceived axial vistas. Instead the new blocks were worked into the existing street pattern in the sensitive and delicate way advocated by Geddes in his Edinburgh tenement improvements.[70]

What made the scheme so successful was the appropriateness of the application of the Liverpool Classical style, and its sensitive integration with the existing property. In the case of Courtenay Square, this produced what Ian Nairn has described as 'the best Georgian square in London'.[71] The estate was illustrated in the *Architects' and Builders' Journal*,[72] accompanied by an article written by the 'Liverpool Man', Arthur Trystan Edwards, and was also reviewed in *Country Life*.[73] Ramsey commented on the evolution of the style for the estate by stating that

> From the outset Adshead insisted that it was to be a *Royal* Estate and it was he who laid down the broad principles of development. There remained, and do

---

69   Adshead, *The Duchy of Cornwall Estate in London*, HMSO, London, 1911.
70   Powers, 'Architectural Education in Britain', p. 261.
71   I. Nairn, *Nairn's London*, Penguin, Harmondsworth, 1988, p. 116.
72   A. T. Edwards, 'The Duchy of Cornwall Estate', *Architects' and Builders' Journal*, 1914, p. 151.
73   L. Weaver, *Country Life*, June 1915, pp. 2–8.

remain to this day, many fine examples of late eighteenth century and Regency buildings in the neighbourhood, and we decided that the architectural expression for the new buildings should be a modern transcript of these styles. From the outset Adshead favoured the Regency, whilst I was more enamoured of the late eighteenth century prototypes and the work we did together reflects these two, not necessarily conflicting phases.[74]

Reilly's impression of Adshead's approach was that 'His architectural style may be described in general terms as an adaptation of classical modes to modern needs, with special attention to significant details in windows, mouldings, cornices, and so forth.'[75] This pragmatic approach to the adoption of Classical forms was also a part of Reilly's own philosophy, which saw Classicism as a means to help promote the school, rather than as an end in itself. As Powers notes, 'Reilly had never seen Classicism as anything but a stage on the way to an as yet unrealized future style.'[76]

However, despite the apparent similarities in the two men's approaches, they continued to drift apart in their interpretation of how town planning might be used in the transformation of the urban environment. Reilly veered towards a Monumental Classicism that was at odds with Adshead's quieter, more site-specific approach. This may well have contributed to Adshead's decision to return to London in 1915, although Wright cites a number of other factors in this decision, including his disappointment at not being given the New Delhi planning commission.[77] Adshead accepted an offer from Professor Simpson – Reilly's predecessor at Liverpool and the Professor of Architecture at University College London – to set up a Department of Town Planning there. Simpson may well have recognized that Adshead shared the same planning philosophy as himself, and was also aware that through publications such as the *Liverpool Sketchbooks* and the *Town Planning Review*, Liverpool was perceived by many commentators to have built up a lead in planning issues in the preceding ten years. This position he no doubt wished to redress.

74 S. C. Ramsey, *Our Work Together*, quoted in Powers, 'Architects I Have Known', p. 123.
75 Quoted in M. Wright, *Lord Leverhulme's Unknown Venture*, Hutchinson Banham, London, 1982, p. 94.
76 Powers, 'Architectural Education in Britain', p. 269.
77 Wright, *Lord Leverhulme's Unknown Venture*, pp. 94–96.

Patrick Abercrombie: Second Lever Professor of Civic Design

When Adshead departed, the Department of Civic Design went through a short period of uncertainty.[78] When it was decided to continue with the provision of a civic design element at Liverpool, Abercrombie – who had been Adshead's assistant, editor and the co-author of the *Town Planning Review* for the past five years – was appointed second Lever Professor.[79] Abercrombie had the backing of Lever,[80] together with an impressive range of sponsors including Patrick Geddes, H. V. Lanchester, Raymond Unwin and Thomas Adams, as well as strong support from Adshead himself. In a letter to Reilly, Lever stated that 'I do not think it was probable that a more experienced man would be found available.'[81]

Abercrombie was, from an early stage, engaged on a number of projects, most notably *Dublin of the Future: The New Town Plan*, which he published in 1922.[82] It was important for him to bring current planning problems to his teaching; without them he considered that 'teaching (in planning and architecture) would gradually be etiolated into a pallid enunciation of theory based on second-hand information.'[83] The work Abercrombie produced both built on and extended the legacy of his predecessor. In the many schemes in which he was involved until his departure from Liverpool in 1935, such as the plan for Doncaster of 1920 and the plan for Sheffield of 1920–1924, he greatly enhanced the reputation of the Department of Civic Design. It was after 1920, when increasing amounts of consultancy work coincided with a decline in the number of full-time students, that his reputation started to grow. In terms of the development and promotion of the Liverpool School, the timing of Abercrombie's appointment was fortunate, in that throughout the 1920s Abercrombie was at his creative peak and therefore most able to add to the growing impression of Liverpool's position as the pace-setter in planning education. As Wright notes, 'one has the impression that he came to his full

78 See the papers of Professor F. E. Hyde, Liverpool University Archive, Boxes D116/2, D116/3 for letters between Reilly, Lever and Abercrombie concerning the future funding of the department.

79 For a general account of Abercrombie's life and career see G. Dix, 'Patrick Abercrombie 1879–1957', in G. E. Cherry (ed.), *Pioneers in British Planning*, The Architectural Press, London, 1981, pp. 103–30.

80 Letter from Lever to the Vice-Chancellor, 12 August 1914, Vice-Chancellor's Papers, Liverpool University Archive.

81 Letter from Lever to Reilly, 16 June 1915, Hyde Papers, Liverpool University Archive, Box D116.

82 P. Abercrombie, A. Kelly and S. Kelly, *Dublin of the Future: The New Town Plan*, Liverpool University Press and Hodder & Stoughton, London, 1922.

83 Quoted in G. Dix, 'Little Plans and Noble Diagrams', *Town Planning Review*, Vol. 49, 1978, p. 331.

powers in the 1920s (aged 41 to 51): that in the 1930s he applied his great knowledge and experience rather than added to them and his final flowering came in the two London plans, published when he was 64 and 66'.[84]

The establishment of the Department of Civic Design illustrates perfectly the symbiotic relationship that existed between Reilly and Lever. The 'designs on monumentality' pursued by the two men – catalogued in the shifting nature of their relationship and manifested in the work they produced and commissioned – allow us to chart the development of the Liverpool School's architectural ethos. Lever's acknowledgment of the part Reilly played in the foundation of the Department of Civic Design is documented in a letter he wrote to the Vice-Chancellor in 1908, in which he states, 'I can only say that Professor Reilly by his enthusiasm in the cause of town planning has been the influence that has brought this matter to a definite stage earlier than would otherwise have been the case...'[85] Similarly, recounting the impact the department had had on town planning issues, Reilly noted,

> More important is the fact that the whole outlook towards town planning on a large scale in the meantime has altered. Who can say how much of that alteration is not due to the step which, with Lord Leverhulme's help, the University of Liverpool took in 1909 when it founded the first Chair and teaching in the subject?[86]

84 Wright, *Lord Leverhulme's Unknown Venture*, pp. 136–37.
85 Letter from Lever to Vice-Chancellor Dale, 25 November 1908, Vice-Chancellor's Papers, Liverpool University Archive, Box P4/1/26.
86 Reilly, *Scaffolding in the Sky*, p. 130.

6 Early Architectural Work: 1904–1914

Reilly was appointed to the Roscoe Chair of Architecture in 1904 at the age of 30, quite shortly after he had become an associate of RIBA in 1898, leaving him little time in which to build substantially. His partnership with Peach had given him a limited amount of practical experience, but apart from this Reilly's major works (such as the Liverpool Cathedral design) were all on paper, and were destined to remain so. What little work Reilly had in progress at the time of his appointment consisted of a scheme for a generating station, laundry and associated buildings for Lord Newton, at Lyme Park, Cheshire in 1904–1905, which it seems he had brought with him from his partnership with Peach. The designs are firmly within the Arts and Crafts tradition, and as it is well-evidenced that this was not to Reilly's taste, we can assume he was following the specific requirements of his patron, Lord Newton. The scheme figures heavily in Reilly's early correspondence books.[1] In a letter to the Vice-Chancellor of Liverpool in the early months of his appointment, Reilly astutely makes the most of his meagre practical work and mentions the scheme as a good example to his students of 'real work in the course of execution'.[2] He thought it important for the students to see such work undertaken by their professor.

Other schemes from around this time include plans for a new building to house the Faculty of Arts and Fine Arts. This was intended to form part of the plan, devised by Reilly and other members of the New Testament group, to found a number of chairs in fine art, music and so on, which major practitioners would be invited to take up. The faculty buildings planned by Reilly were sited, well away from the main university campus, in the Haymarket district near to the city's museum, library and art gallery. He wrote that he had envisaged that the library would become part of the university, along with the art collection and museum, forming part of its learning resource.[3] The scheme

---

1 See Reilly Papers, Liverpool University Archive, Box D207/2/1.
2 Letter from Reilly to the Vice-Chancellor, 8 November 1904, Vice-Chancellor's Papers, Liverpool University Archive, Box P6B/3/5.
3 C. H. Reilly, *Scaffolding in the Sky*, Routledge, London, 1938, pp. 123–25.

came to nothing; following consideration by the City Council, in an education committee report of 1904 it was felt that it would provide too much competition to the newly formed and expanded School of Art. The designs produced by Reilly for the faculty, however, were illustrated in *The Builder's Journal and Architectural Record*[4] in 1905, and illustrate that he was still heavily indebted to his friend and former colleague, Alfred Rickards. So close was the referencing to Rickards's style that Reilly was obliged to write a letter to *The Builder* in May 1905, by which time the designs had been exhibited at the Royal Academy, to apologize for any unintentional plagiarism. Many of the designs Reilly produced in the early years of the century, including those for the Liverpool Cathedral competition of 1902 and his London County Hall design of 1907, show what a strong influence Rickards had on him.

In 1906 Reilly produced a block of cottages for William Lever at Port Sunlight (Fig. 5). The style was distinct from that generally used in the village; the design consisted of a crescent plan with Neoclassical, quasi-Regency detailing, particularly in the trellis work on the cottage fronts. This was very much in line with Reilly's general approach in the early years of his appointment. However, the design seems neither to have satisfied his client nor Reilly himself, who felt that 'I wish my cottages could be further from the road but there is no escape from that. They look as if they ought to have a village green in front of them.'[5] This is an interesting observation given Reilly's adaptation some 40 years later of a 'village green' plan for his 'Reilly Green' communities. The cottages were later criticized, on a purely practical basis, by W. L. George, who felt that the verandah excluded sunshine from the cottages' interiors: 'This is the one and only instance of such a mistake…'[6] The cottages were Reilly's only architectural commission for Lever, although he worked closely with him on a number of university and cultural projects up until Lever's death in 1925.

A number of other small-scale projects were undertaken by Reilly at this time. He acted as consultant architect in the remodelling of Belmont, near

---

4 *The Builders' Journal and Architectural Record*, Vol. 22, 18 October 1905, p. 225. As Michael Shippobottom notes, 'His dramatically inflated design for this [arts faculty building] was shown at the 1905 Royal Academy Exhibition, but it could hardly have been considered a serious project, though in its use of the twin Greenwich Hospital domes it nicely anticipates his more mature London County Hall design of 1907.' M. Shippobottom, 'Reilly and the First Lord Leverhulme', in J. Sharples (ed.), *Charles Reilly and the Liverpool School of Architecture 1904–1933*, Liverpool University Press, Liverpool, 1996, p. 44.

5 Letter from Reilly to W. Lever, 27 November 1905, Reilly Papers, Liverpool University Archive, Box D207/2/1.

6 W. L. George, *Labour and Housing at Port Sunlight*, 1909, p. 69.

Chesterfield, for C. B. Ward, and during the design of gardens for Louis Cappel at 5 Ullet Road, Liverpool, and Mr and Mrs J. Reynolds at Dove Park, Woolton (Fig. 6).[7] However, it was not until 1909 that he was able to undertake his first major architectural commissions. The year 1909 was a significant one in many respects, marking as it did the foundation of the Department of Civic Design, as well as Reilly's first trip to the United States. The first major commission – the students' union building for Liverpool University – can be traced back to an earlier design of 1906–1907, which he had produced for a different site within the university precinct. The union building is a useful indicator of Reilly's architectural style at this point in his career, and it also highlights a number of tensions that were developing between Reilly and the university authorities over the allocation of architectural commissions.

Liverpool University's Building Programme 1904–1914

The University of Liverpool underwent a large-scale, if somewhat intermittent, building programme that had begun in the university college days and con-tinued up until 1914. As Thomas Kelly notes in his history of the university, *For Advancement of Learning: The University of Liverpool 1881–1981*,

> The great building boom which had begun in the college years came to an end with the opening of the Muspratt Laboratory… in 1906… It was not until 1910 [that]… building works… resumed, a start being made with the first phase of the Students' Union… The Harrison Hughes Mechanical Engineering Labora-tories were officially opened in 1912; the second phase of the students' union in 1913; the long awaited New Arts building in 1914; and a new building for the School of Tropical Medicine in 1915. In the summer of 1914 the old asylum building was demolished, and the layout of the quadrangle was at last completed.[8]

Reilly's main involvement lay in his work on the new union building. However, he appears also to have been involved with the selection of the scheme for the new arts faculty building in Ashton Street (next to Waterhouse's Victoria Building). Reilly was involved in the building committee that had was set up in 1906, and which ran until 1914 to oversee progress. He seems to have run

---

7 Correspondence on these projects is listed in Reilly Papers, Liverpool University Archive, Box D207/2/2.
8 T. Kelly, *For Advancement of Learning: The University of Liverpool 1881–1981*, Liverpool University Press, Liverpool, 1981, pp. 138–39.

up against difficulties within the committee, presumably over the proposed style for the new faculty, although this is not stated in the minutes. As Adrian Allan and Sheila Turner note in their article 'Si Monumentum Requiris Circumspice: A Note on the Older Plans in the Custody of the Chief Engineer', Reilly was called in to

> advise on the draft conditions for the competition. Professor Reilly submitted conditions, but resigned from the Committee for reasons which are not stated in the minutes, and shortly afterwards there was further disagreement in the Committee, a move to include a certain number of architects not practising in Liverpool being defeated.[9]

The choice of architects for the university projects had been a source of annoyance to Reilly since shortly after his appointment. In a letter to Vice-Chancellor Dale in February 1906, he complains that

> The thing I am anxious to get recognised is the principle that as Professor of Architecture I am not unworthy of being consulted professionally by the university. If I am I have no business to be professor and had better go back to town... Everyone must see I think the awkward position I am placed in professionally, at the Royal Institute for instance, on the Council of the Architectural Society, if my own institution has not faith in me... It is not even as if the university employed the recognised heads of the profession, they are content with local men and it is among them that I have to take up a proper position if the School of Architecture is to flourish.[10]

Reilly drafted a list of points, which would appear to date from around this time, entitled 'Some Reasons Why the Professor of Architecture Should be Professionally Employed by the University'. In it he reiterated the points made to Dale, adding that without such employment 'the Professor cannot be an efficient teacher if he is not actively engaged in the practice of his art. This is recognized in the conditions of his appointment.'[11]

It seems that the first outcome of these complaints was Reilly's involvement in the new arts faculty building – which was to prove a more realistic

9 A. Allan and S. Turner, 'Si Monumentum Requiris Circumspice: A Note on the Older Plans in the Custody of the Chief Engineer', *The University of Liverpool Recorder*, No. 81, 1979, pp. 162–67.
10 Letter from Reilly to Vice-Chancellor Dale, 25 February 1906, Vice-Chancellor's Papers, Liverpool University Archive, Box P4A/3/5.
11 'Some Reasons Why the Professor of Architecture Should be Professionally Employed by the University', no date, presumably circa 1906, Vice-Chancellor's Papers, Liverpool University Archive, Box P4A/3/5.

plan than his own 1905 scheme – and the commission for the students' union which, although not a university-funded project, was a high-profile scheme of the kind Reilly wanted to be designed in-house. An anonymous review in the *Liverpool Courier* from July 1909, which Allan and Turner suggest may have been written by Reilly, recommends the designs for the arts building to the reader, describing both as 'thorough Classic'. In 1911, after a number of internal disputes, a Classical style for the building was settled upon, in line with Reilly's preference and those of the chosen architects Briggs, Wolstenholme and Thornley. Reilly later admitted that the change of style was at least partly obtained by 'making myself obnoxious… I secured I think the change in style…'[12] The building was formally opened in June 1914 and marked the end of the early phase of university building.

The second commission Reilly won as a consequence of his pleas to the university council and Lever was for the new School of Architecture building. The school had been occupying the Bluecoat building in the centre of the city along with the Sandon Studios Society, in a somewhat uneasy relationship. The design of a new building was a contentious question both for the members of the Sandon Studios Society and for Reilly himself. Reilly was in favour of remaining in the Bluecoat despite the standing offer of a commission to design a new building. Nevertheless he did produce designs for a building in 1914, with perspective drawings produced by the rising star of the school, Harold Chalton Bradshaw (Fig. 12). The commission was finally offered jointly to Reilly and Stanley Adshead, but Adshead declined. In a letter to the Vice-Chancellor in March 1914, he stated his reasons:

> I am honoured exceedingly by this appointment, but regret that I will be unable to accept it for the following reasons:
> 1) Though by training an architect my associations with the university are only in reference to the allied subject of town planning and with a Professor of Architecture in the university I hardly feel justified in accepting the position of equality in his subject which as joint architect I should assume.
> 2) Professor Reilly's interests in the new building are greater than mine. My school is smaller in point of numbers: my session shorter and my appointment compared with his a comparatively recent one.[13]

---

12   Letter from Reilly to Jones, 12 December 1919, Vice-Chancellor's Papers, Liverpool University Archive, Box P/3/30.
13   Letter from Adshead to the Vice-Chancellor, 12 March 1914, Vice-Chancellor's Papers, Liverpool University Archive, Box P4A/3/5.

1 Liverpool Anglican Cathedral competition design – exterior, C. H. Reilly, 1902. Reilly's entry was the only Classical design to be commended by the assessors, Norman Shaw and G. F. Bodley. Adshead provided impressive perspective drawings for the exterior and interior. Reilly claimed in his autobiography that no plans for St James's Mount, the proposed site for the cathedral, were provided to entrants and that when he visited the site he immediately realized his 'vast classical design with a dome was no good' (*Scaffolding in the Sky*, p. 63). The drawings were exhibited at the Royal Academy in 1903 and the St Louis exhibition in 1904.

2 Liverpool Anglican Cathedral competition design – interior, C. H. Reilly, 1902.

3 Mersey Docks and Harbour Board building, Sir Arnold Thornley with Briggs and Wolstenholme, completed 1907. The first of the three buildings which form the Pier Head group on the Liverpool waterfront that have come to symbolize the mercantile power of the city in the early years of the 20th century. The design combines a Renaissance palace with the dome of a giant Classical church, and it has been suggested that the inspiration for the dome came from Reilly's Liverpool Cathedral design.

4 London County Hall competition design, C. H. Reilly, 1907. This rough sketch by Reilly was worked up into a perspective drawing by Stanley Adshead, although perspective drawings were not allowed under the competition rules. Reilly's entry was featured in *Building News*, 15 November 1907. Ralph Knott (1878–1929) was the competition winner, a decision Reilly considered 'a disaster for monumental architecture in England'.

5 Cottages, 15–27 Lower Road, Port Sunlight, 1905–06, C.H. Reilly. The cottages represent Reilly's only executed commission for the soap entrepreneur Viscount Leverhulme – although the two men collaborated on other projects including the establishment of the Department of Civic Design at Liverpool University. In contrast with the designs for other cottages in the village influenced by the Old English manner of Shaw and Nesfield, Reilly employed a Regency style with an ironwork verandah.

6 Garden at Dove Park, Woolton, C. H. Reilly, 1907. This was one of a number of small commissions Reilly undertook in the early years of his appointment to the Liverpool chair.

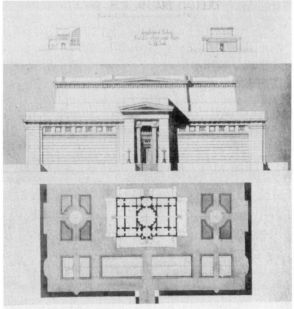

7 Design for an Art Gallery, L. B. Budden. In 1911 the first of the series of publications entitled *The Liverpool Architectural Sketch Book* was published containing reproductions of measured drawings of major Classical buildings together with the work of Reilly's students. The aim was to promote Classicism, the Liverpool School of Architecture, and Reilly himself – although not necessarily in that order! Lionel Bailey Budden (1887–1956) was one of Reilly's earliest students, entering the school in 1905. He taught in the school from 1911 and eventually succeeded Reilly to the Roscoe Chair in 1933.

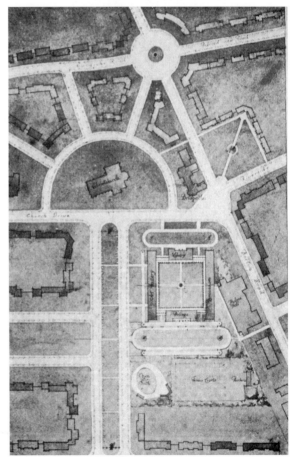

8 Scheme for the laying out of the central portion of Port Sunlight Village, Ernest Prestwich, 1909. Ernest Prestwich (1889–1977) was the first winner of an annual prize set up by William Lever, open to senior students of the School of Architecture, as part of the establishment of the Department of Civic Design. The first place prize money was £20 and an additional fee of £100 was to be paid if the chosen scheme was finally implemented. Prestwich's design – a grandly formal axial plan on Beaux-Arts lines – was finally modified and extended by James Lomax Simpson and T. H. Mawson. Prestwich was to recall, many years later, that on winning the prize he felt like a 'millionaire' and headed for Aintree racecourse, where he was 'discovered' by Reilly, who upbraided him for wasting his money!

9 *Basil Dean Trying to Fit His Repertory Boot on the City of Liverpool...*, illustration by George Harris, 1913. Basil Dean had been appointed as the Liverpool Repertory Theatre's first producer in 1911. However, lack of financial support and pressure from members of the board such as Reilly who wished the theatre to stage avant-garde but unprofitable productions made his position increasingly untenable. This satirical illustration accompanied an article in *The Bulletin of the Sandon Studios Society,* which criticized the wealthy and prominent figures in the city for their underfunding of the fledgling theatre.

BASIL DEAN TRYING TO FIT
HIS REPERTORY BOOT ON
THE CITY OF LIVERPOOL..

Geo. W. Harris, del.

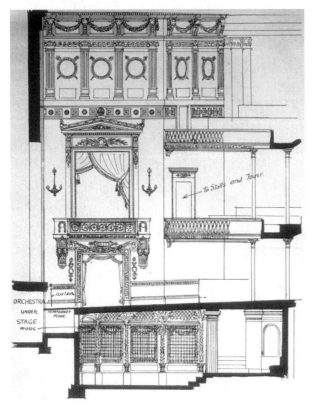

10 Section through the Liverpool Repertory Theatre, Williamson Square, Liverpool, design by Stanley Adshead, 1910–11. The task of remodelling the old Star Theatre was given to Reilly's friend and colleague Stanley Adshead, who added 10ft (3m) to the stage and replaced the original twelve boxes with two large ones. The style used is neo-Grec which was enjoying a revival in the city, due in part to Reilly's efforts. The old beer cellar under the auditorium was cleverly converted by Adshead into a foyer where refreshments were served – something of an innovation for the time in the so-called 'legitimate' theatre.

11 Reilly with colleagues and students in fancy dress, *circa* 1930. Reilly had from his earliest days in Liverpool been an enthusiastic member of clubs in the city. The School of Architecture held its own annual Architects' Ball in which staff and students would dress up according to an agreed theme: Imperial Rome, Arabian, Oriental, etc. The photograph shows Reilly (centre) seated on his Imperial throne dressed as Caesar.

12　Design for a new School of Architecture, Liverpool University, design by C. H. Reilly, perspective drawing by Harold Chalton Bradshaw, 1914. The design – much influenced by the 1904 Harvard University building by McKim, Mead and White – was proposed for a site on Bedford Street. Sir William Lever had promised to provide money for a purpose-built School of Architecture for the university, but with the outbreak of war and a change of heart on Lever's part the plans were put on hold, and the design was to remain unbuilt.

13 Design for Students' Union, Ashton Street, Liverpool University, C. H. Reilly, perspective drawing Stanley Adshead, 1907. This scheme, which was never built, underwent a series of changes, the original design being in a straightforward vernacular Georgian, while this slightly later version shows more of the neo-Grec influence in the addition of pediments and Greek masks.

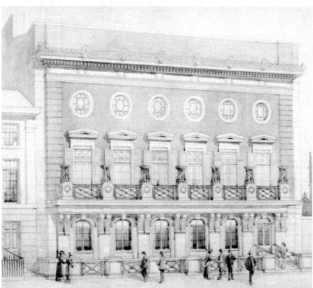

14 Design for Students' Union, Bedford Street façade, Liverpool University, C. H. Reilly, perspective drawing Stanley Adshead, 1909–14. Reilly redesigned his 1907 scheme for a site on Bedford Street with an entrance on Mount Pleasant. The first design for this site shows Reilly's original intention was to have treated both elevations in Greek doric. However, the building was finally constructed in two halves, with a heavier Greek doric treatment on the Mount Pleasant façade and a lighter French-influenced Classicism for Bedford Street.

15 Students' Union building, Brownlow Hill façade, Liverpool University, C. H. Reilly, 1909–14. The third façade to Reilly's Union building faced onto a cutting leading into one of Liverpool's main railway terminals, Lime Street. The sparcity of windows and plain massing of brick was as much a pragmatic response to the problems of the site – pollution from the coal-fired railway engines – as any aesthetic statement. However, now that the cutting has been covered over, we can fully appreciate the boldness of the façade and see stylistic links with Reilly's St Barnabas church design of 1910.

16 Church of St Barnabas, Shacklewell Lane, Dalston, London, C. H. Reilly, 1909–10.
This church was built to serve the Merchant Taylors' School Mission in the East End of
London. The site – tucked away behind a collection of factories – was unpromising and
Reilly cleverly chose to echo the industrial aesthetic in the interior, using brick and
reinforced concrete with little decoration. The design is certainly presciently modern,
and Reilly – near the end of his life, when he had become an enthusiastic exponent of
Modernism – stated that this was the building by which he would wish to be
remembered.

17 Crypt of the Metropolitan Cathedral of Christ the King, Liverpool, Sir Edwin Lutyens (1869–1944), 1932–40. Sir Edwin Lutyens's design for Liverpool's Catholic Cathedral fused Romanesque, Renaissance Classicism and Byzantine influences into a highly individual conception on a truly monumental scale. Only the crypt was built to Lutyens's design before the outbreak of war and lack of money meant the design had to be abandoned. Reilly travelled with Lutyens to India in 1927–28 and greatly admired his work.

18 Devonshire House, Piccadilly, London, Thomas Hastings with C. H. Reilly, 1924–27. Reilly was invited to propose an American architect to design an apartment block to replace the old Devonshire House. Reilly suggested his friend Thomas Hastings (1860–1929) and was appointed joint architect with him. The design was modified mid-way through, the original scheme being too large, but it remains a fine example of American Beaux-Arts Classicism in London.

19 The Athenaeum Club, Church Alley, Liverpool, Harold Dod, 1928. Harold Dod (1890–1965) was one of Reilly's early students in the Liverpool School. He joined the firm of Willink and Thicknesse and worked on the Cunard Building in the city. Dod's design is heavily influenced by the work of McKim, Mead and White and is a perfect example of the American Beaux-Arts which Reilly had helped to promote through his teaching and writing from 1909 onwards.

20 Martin's Bank headquarters (now Barclays Bank), Water Street, Liverpool, Herbert J. Rowse, 1927–32. Herbert Rowse (1887–1963) was another of Reilly's early students in Liverpool, graduating with a Cert.Arch. in 1907. Rowse worked and travelled widely in North America after graduation, experiencing at first hand American ideas which he put to use in projects such as India Buildings, Liverpool (1924–32) and the Martin's Bank headquarters building. Rowse was unquestionably the most influential Liverpool architect of the inter-war years – his later work such as the (Royal) Liverpool Philharmonic Hall moved towards a variation of Modernism along the lines of Dudok.

21 Egyptian State Telegraph building, Cairo, Maurice Lyon, 1927. Maurice Lyon (BA 1906) was one of the students whom Reilly 'inherited' from his predecessor, Professor Simpson, on his appointment to the Liverpool chair in 1904. Lyon's design was exhibited at the Royal Academy in 1927 and is a typical example of the monumental Classicism for which the Liverpool School of Architecture became famous in the inter-war years. Graduates of the school exported the style to all corners of the British Empire and beyond.

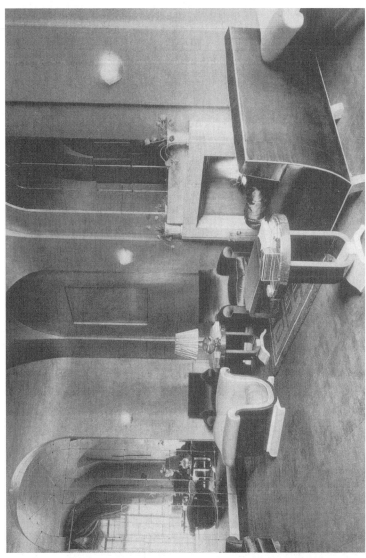

22 Sitting room for Mrs Payne-Thompson, 20 Belgrave Square, London, Wellesley and Wills. Trenwith Lovering Wills (1891–1972), a graduate of the Liverpool School, worked in the offices of Detmar Blow and Fernand Billerey from 1910 to 1920, where he met Gerald Wellesley. Together they designed numerous country houses including Sherfield Court, Hampshire, Inverchapel Lodge, Argyllshire and Naldridge Manor, Buckinghamshire. They also designed premises for Heinemann the publishers at Kingswood, Surrey, as well as smaller 'society' commissions such as this interior.

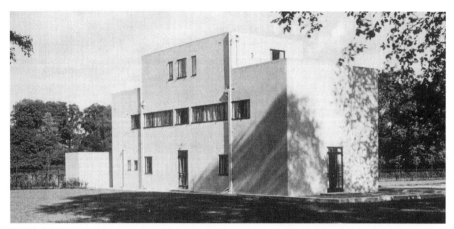

23 House at Conduit Head Road, Cambridge, George Checkley, 1930–32. George Checkley (1893–1960) was a New Zealander who attended the Liverpool School from 1919–22 on an ex-serviceman's grant. After graduation he taught at Cambridge University School of Architecture and designed a cluster of Modernist houses for himself and other Cambridge dons around Conduit Head Road in the early 1930s.

24 Veterinary Hospital, Liverpool University, C. H. Reilly, L.B. Budden & J. E. Marshall, 1929. The first in a trio of buildings Reilly, Budden and Marshall designed for Liverpool University in a stripped Classicism/Modernist hybrid style.

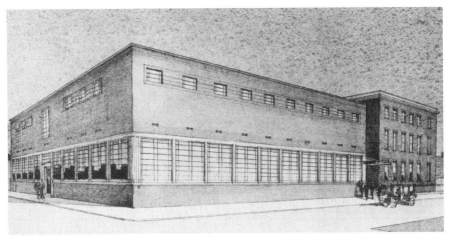

25 Drawing of the 'Leverhulme Building', new School of Architecture, Liverpool University, Reilly, Budden and Marshall, 1933. The purpose-built school that Lever had promised the university before the war was finally realized by his son the second Viscount Leverhulme in 1933 – ironically the year that Reilly retired. The building forms an extension to one of the Georgian houses on Abercromby Square, and while recognizably Modernist in intention, Reilly *et al.* have paid close attention to achieving harmony between the new and the old.

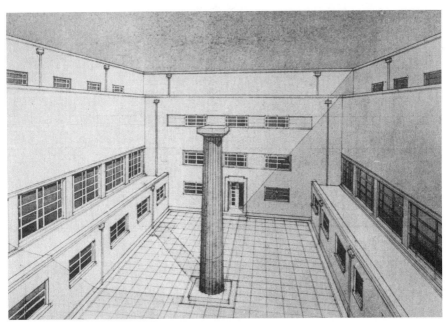

26 Drawing of the courtyard of the 'Leverhulme Building', Reilly, Budden and Marshall. The intention was to include a doric column to be taken from the demolished chapel of the Liverpool School for the Blind 'as a symbol of architecture and of permanent architectural values'.

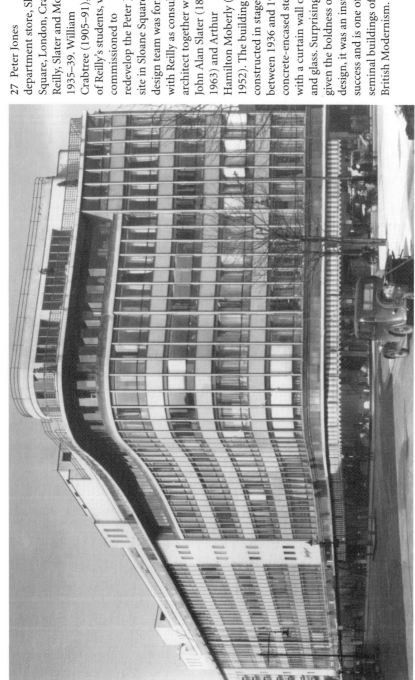

27 Peter Jones department store, Sloane Square, London, Crabtree, Reilly, Slater and Moberly, 1935–39. William Crabtree (1905–91), one of Reilly's students, was commissioned to redevelop the Peter Jones site in Sloane Square. A design team was formed with Reilly as consultant architect together with John Alan Slater (1885–1963) and Arthur Hamilton Moberly (1885–1952). The building was constructed in stages between 1936 and 1939 in concrete-encased steel with a curtain wall of steel and glass. Surprisingly, given the boldness of its design, it was an instant success and is one of the seminal buildings of early British Modernism.

28 Plan of the 'Reilly Greens', from *The Reilly Plan*, Lawrence Wolfe, 1945. The Reilly Greens concept sought to arrange two-thirds of houses in any planning scheme around an open green space and combine educational and social amenities such as a community centre, swimming pool, nursery and allotments. It owed much to the ideas pioneered in the 19th-century workers' villages, such as Port Sunlight and Bournville.

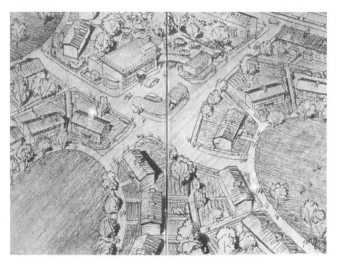

29 Illustration from *The Reilly Plan*, Lawrence Wolfe, 1945. The Reilly Greens concept was expanded upon in a book by Lawrence Wolfe, *The Reilly Plan*, in which the communal aspects of Reilly's scheme are expanded upon from a sociological point of view and suggested as the model upon which post-war Britain should be developed. The book contained several perspective drawings of the Reilly Greens showing the open-plan gardens in the American style facing onto the communal greens where people promenaded and played cricket, evoking the feeling of a village-green idyll in an urban setting.

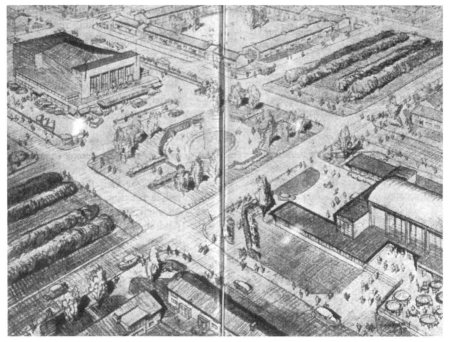

30 Illustration from *The Reilly Plan*, Lawrence Wolfe, 1945.

31 Illustration from *The Reilly Plan*, Lawrence Wolfe, 1945.

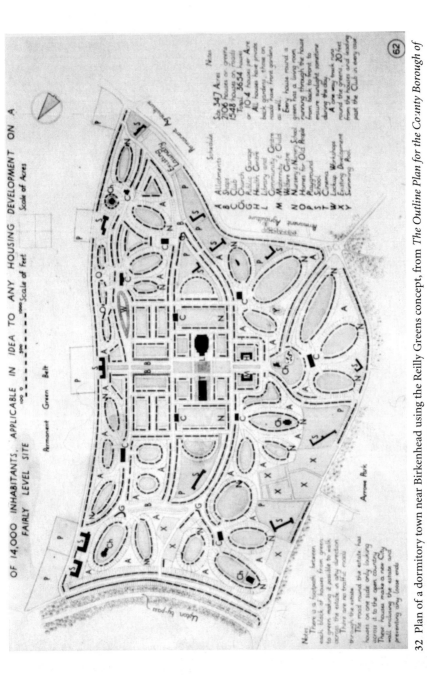

32 Plan of a dormitory town near Birkenhead using the Reilly Greens concept, from *The Outline Plan for the County Borough of Birkenhead*, C. H. Reilly and Naim Aslam, 1947.

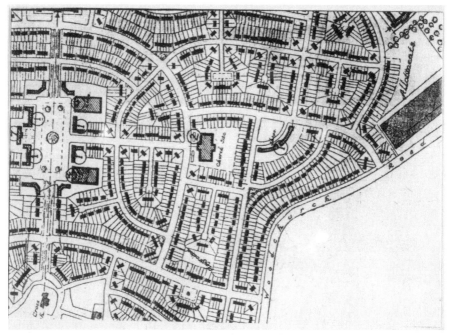

33 'The Robinson Plan' as drawn up for the Woodchurch Estate, Birkenhead, 1944.

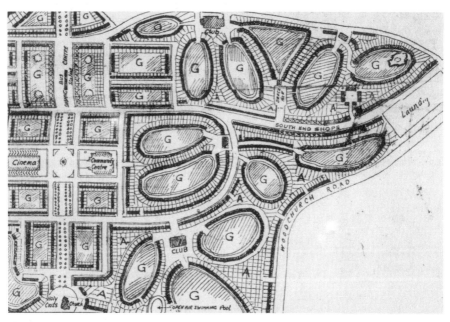

34 'The Reilly Plan' as drawn up for the Woodchurch Estate. Birkenhead, 1944.

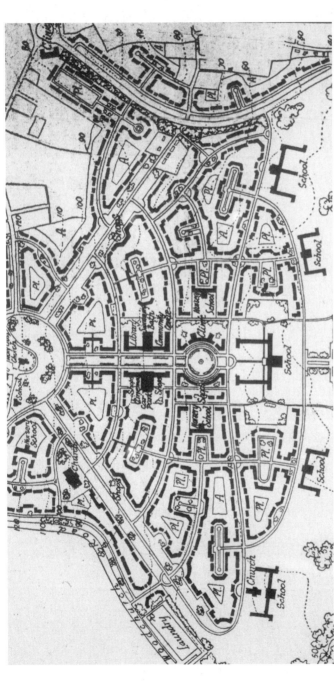

35 'The Rowse Plan' as drawn up for the Woodchurch Estate, Birkenhead, 1945. When it was proposed that a satellite town be built on the edge of Birkenhead, Reilly put forward a version of his Reilly Greens concept challenging an existing proposal by the Borough Engineer and Surveyor, B. Robinson. The two plans split the Borough Council along party political lines with the Conservative group supporting Robinson and the Labour group, Reilly. A fierce debate raged in the local press and the council delayed a decision during which time a third plan prepared by the Liverpool architect – and Reilly's former student – Herbert J. Rowse was submitted. The Conservative group switched their preference from Robinson's proposal to Rowse's and it was his plan which was finally built. Rowse combines elements from both Robinson's and Reilly's plans, with a formal Beaux-Arts avenue containing the central core of civic amenities in the manner of Reilly, but with housing layouts closer in spirit to Robinson's proposal.

36 Argyle Street bypass, from *The Outline Plan for the County Borough of Birkenhead*,
C. H. Reilly and Naim Aslan, 1947. Reilly was commissioned to work on the plan for the
redevelopment of Birkenhead and adapted his 'Reilly Greens' proposal. The plan – written in
collaboration with a former Liverpool student Naim Aslan – was published in book form in
1947 and contains perspective drawings of the housing schemes showing two- and three-
storey blocks consisting of a mix of houses and flats arranged around a more formal
hexagonal 'Reilly Green'. The plan also contained proposals for a high-rise hotel and a 'Crystal
Palace' entertainment complex with a casino overlooking the riverfront. Interestingly, Reilly
envisaged Birkenhead as 'Wirral City', the Western-most terminal of a European railway
system, following the construction of a channel tunnel.

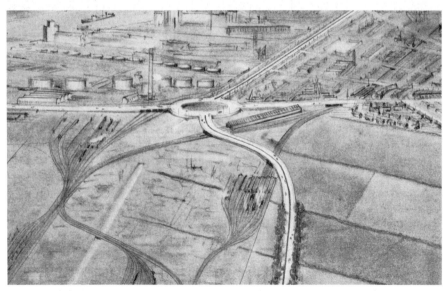

37 Bidston bypass, from *The Outline Plan for the County Borough of Birkenhead*, C. H. Reilly
and Naim Aslan, 1947.

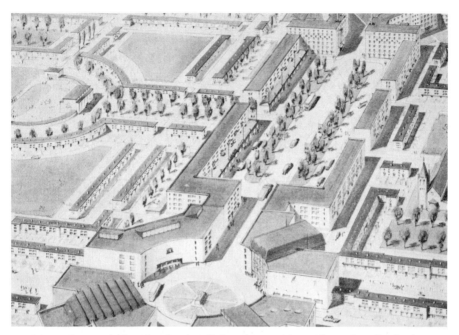

38 Conway Street neighbourhood unit and shopping area, from *The Outline Plan for the County Borough of Birkenhead*, C. H. Reilly and Naim Aslan, 1947.

39 Crystal Palace to include a casino, from *The Outline Plan for the County Borough of Birkenhead*, C. H. Reilly and Naim Aslan, 1947.

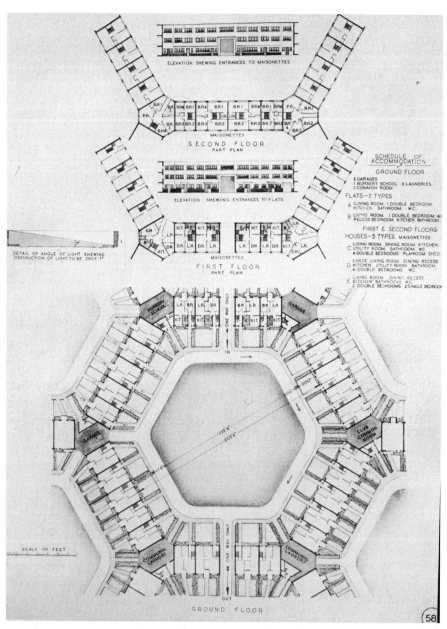

40 Unit of the hexagonal layout for housing, from *The Outline Plan for the County Borough of Birkenhead*, C. H. Reilly and Naim Aslan, 1947.

41 A new Woodside Hotel, from *The Outline Plan for the County Borough of Birkenhead*, C. H. Reilly and Naim Aslan, 1947.

42 Perspective drawing of the hexagonal housing unit, from *The Outline Plan for the County Borough of Birkenhead*, C. H. Reilly and Naim Aslan, 1947.

Easy lies the Birkenhead
By the hands of Reilly fed;
Who to three score years & ten,
Joins Youth, & Hope, & Acumen.

43 Caricature of Charles Reilly standing in front of his polygonal 'Reilly Green' plan for Birkenhead, Marjorie Holford, 1944. Marjorie Holford, wife of Reilly's former student William Graham (Lord) Holford (1907–1975), drew this caricature of Reilly walking towards his plan for Birkenhead as a 70th birthday card.

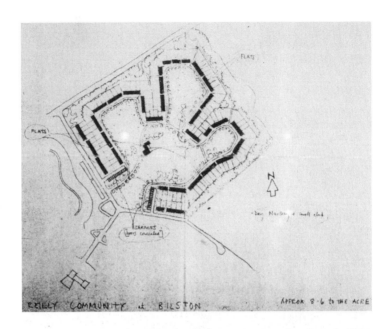

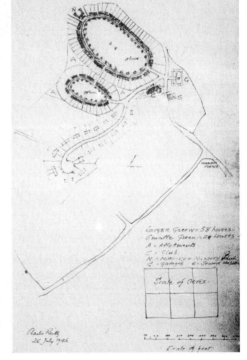

44 & 45 Sketch for a 'Reilly Green' community at Bilston, Staffordshire; sketch for a 'Reilly Green' community for the Miles Aircraft Company, Reading, Berkshire, July 1946. Reilly's plans for Woodchurch and Birkenhead were not implemented. However, his 'Reilly Greens' plan was taken up by the towns of Bilston, Staffordshire, Dudley, Worcestershire and the Miles Aircraft Company, Berkshire.

46 Portrait of Charles Reilly, Augustus John, 1931. Augustus John (1878–1961) was teaching in Liverpool at the time of Reilly's appointment to the Roscoe Chair and they remained friends after John's departure from the city. John had painted a number of portraits of the leading professors at Liverpool University and so when the university decided to commission a commemorative portrait of Reilly, John was Reilly's obvious choice. Reilly later wrote in his autobiography that during the course of sitting for John 'He seemed to look into my soul in such a searching way that I wilted under it...' (*Scaffolding in the Sky*, p. 319).

Adshead, perhaps sensing that his refusal might be interpreted as the sign of a rift between himself and Reilly, wrote a further letter in which he said that, having discussed the matter further, he wished to suggest that he might instead be appointed consultant architect with Reilly 'at a fee to be arranged between the two of us and payable out of his [Reilly's] commission'.[14] Whatever the actual reasons behind Adshead's refusal, the outcome was that Reilly produced a design that drew heavily on his enthusiasm for American Beaux-Arts. The design paid particular reference to McKim, Mead and White's Harvard University School of Architecture. When the designs were published in *Building News*, the reviewer noted that, of the names of the eminent architects that were to be inscribed on tablets sited below the windows,

> Elmes alone serves to represent the nineteenth century in England, no gothicist being so much as named or worthy. The outlook of such a school must be narrow, judged by this choice, though Le Duc is included.[15]

A fair description, I would suggest, of Reilly's stylistic stance at that point in time.

Reilly's resentments about the university's commissioning policy continued. In a series of letters to the Vice-Chancellor from May 1915,[16] he complains that the university council have no confidence in him. By 1919 Reilly's relationship with the university authorities appears to have reached a very low ebb indeed. Despite this, Reilly still manages to maintain his unshakable belief in himself and the school. In a letter to Sydney Jones dated 12 December 1919, Reilly lays out his resentments in the light of what he sees as his success in building up the School of Architecture:

> It is a very difficult position for me as Professor of Architecture in the university to find time after time when any large architectural schemes are being considered by the university that neither my advice nor the advice of any member of the School of Architecture is sought in any way. It happened over the Dendal [sic] School, the Tropical Medicine School, the engineering building, and now according to Baly, the university is about to spend £250,000 on new chemical buildings, and again those representing architecture in the university will have nothing to say to the project. It is not the monetary side of

14 Letter from Adshead to the Vice-Chancellor, 18 March 1914, Vice-Chancellor's Papers, Liverpool University Archive, Box P4A/3/5.
15 *Building News*, 30 April 1915, p. 486.
16 Letter from Reilly to the Vice-Chancellor, Vice-Chancellor's Papers, Liverpool University Archive, Box P4A/3/5.

the matter, please believe me, which is the most hurtful, though in building up the School of Architecture to the position it occupies… I have sacrificed the possibility of creating the practice I had a right to expect. It is the slight which is put on me and the school generally which stings. It is a treatment of the Professor of Architecture which does not occur at London, Cambridge, Manchester, McGill or any other university where such a professor exists and yet there is no doubt the Liverpool School of Architecture ranks above any of those mentioned.[17]

The situation improved somewhat with the new School of Architecture building, and in the long term a number of Reilly's former pupils, most notably Dod and Maxwell Fry, were to produce work for the university. Nevertheless, the School of Architecture in general, and Reilly in particular, remained largely under-utilized by the university authorities.

The Liverpool Students' Union Building

The students' union project can be divided into two separate schemes. They were stylistically connected in that a number of the features included in Reilly's first designs were re-used in his later proposals. Reilly was commissioned in 1906 to design a union building close to the main university Victoria Building. The *Sphinx*, the magazine of the student body, noted that

> Considerably over a year has passed since the union committee was constituted, and many, especially among the impetuous and, perhaps, unthinking students, are beginning to ask why there are, as yet, no outward and visible signs of its work… We are glad, however, to be able to report of the extremely satisfactory state of the movement… The architect is, as has been announced, Professor Reilly, and of his qualifications to solve what promises to be not the easiest of architectural problems, there can not be the slightest question.[18]

The article went on to list the subscribers to the scheme, which was to be financed solely from private subscription without any university funding. Reilly is listed as having contributed £10 to the fund. Among the other contributors are the usual names from Liverpool's business and cultural

17   Letter from Reilly to Jones, 12 December 1919, Vice-Chancellor's Papers, Liverpool University Archive, Box P/3/30.
18   *Sphinx*, 16 July 1906, Vol. XIII, No. 16, pp. 259–61.

communities: Sir John Brunner gave £1000; Miss Holt, £500; Sir W. H. Tate, £250; Hugh Rathbone, £250; and Professor Ramsey Muir, £50.

Reilly produced a booklet of sketches of interior and exterior views for a building of five floors (Fig. 13). The Ashton Street elevations consisted of three bays separated by broad pilasters, each bay containing three windows at each floor. The fourth-floor windows were ovoid, finished with a Mansard roof, and punctuated with a series of dormer windows topped by a cupola. The 1907 design was featured in *Building News* in September 1907. The earliest designs were largely in the Free Classical manner, mixing vernacular Georgian with Arts and Crafts details. As the designs progressed, they became more definite in their Classical detailing – for example, pediments were added to the central windows of the ground floor. Internally the building was arranged to give separate quarters to male and female students, with communal debating and library areas. The Ashton Street elevation shows the separate entrances for men and women at either end of the building, while the separation of the sexes is carried through into every detail. As Adrian Allan and Sheila Turner note,

> Reilly's impression of the women students' dining hall contrasts with that of the men's dining hall in its suggested furnishings, oval tables and Windsor chairs creating a more intimate and urbane feel than the men's dining hall, which is provided with rectangular tables and upright ladder back chairs.[19]

This early design was eventually shelved due to objections by the nearby Royal Infirmary, who felt that the erection of the building would interfere with the right of light of its nurses' home. The revised plan, drawn up by Reilly in 1909, was for the site on Bedford Street on which the union now stands (Fig. 14). This consisted of entrances on Bedford Street for male students and Mount Pleasant for female students. A number of features of the second scheme can be traced from the 1907 plan, although the Bedford Street/Mount Pleasant site provided its own advantages and disadvantages. Reilly was able to expand the stylistic treatments used to differentiate between the sexes beyond the earlier interior decorations of 1907 to the whole of the two elevations. The building was reported in *Building News* in October 1909 and July 1910, demonstrating the evolution of its stylistic details. While the vernacular Georgian of the 1907 design had been replaced by a stricter Classicism – reflecting Reilly's own retreat from the influences of his London

19   Allen and Turner, 'Si Monumentum Requiris Circumspice', pp. 164–65.

days to a stance given impetus by his growing enthusiasm for American Classicism – the designs were still in the process of development during the 1909–1910 period. For example, the Bedford Street façade illustrated in *Building News* of 1909 shows a relatively simple design with little use of detailing. There is a balcony running the full length of the building, supported by a series of doric columns, while the first-floor windows have simple headers. The Mansard roof and cupola of the 1907 design have been replaced by a simplified roof line and Classical dentil cornice. By 1910, the design had been dressed up further with the doric columns to the ground floor replaced by scrolled brackets to support the balcony, which in turn had heavier detailing. These neo-Grec details were carried through to the interior of the building and particularly used in the Gilmour Hall, the central debating chamber. The first-floor windows each had pediments added, while the cornice was also further embellished.

By contrast, the Mount Pleasant façade as built in 1914 appears to have remained largely unaltered from the 1909 design, with a large bowed balcony supported by fluted doric columns. The building was erected in two parts: the Bedford Street section first, and then the women's half on Mount Pleasant in 1914. The Gilmour Hall was placed between the two. In the interim period, as *Building News* noted, 'Bedford Street... is temporarily to be used for both men and women... the latter entering for the moment through the service entrance.'[20] In 1910 they describe the building as being of

> Portland stone and small wire-cut bricks. The enriched portion of the main cornice is in grey terracotta, and is being modelled by Miss Ethel Martin, sculptor, an old student of the School of Architecture. Miss Martin is also modelling relief figures for some of the internal decoration.[21]

The adoption of the neo-Grec style for the building's detailing has been criticized by recent commentators. A. Stuart Gray considers that 'the most that can be said of this building for the Students' Union, Liverpool, is that it would have been done better in the same style a century earlier'.[22] This seems to be unduly harsh; while far from a perfect example of Greek Revival work, the building does have a number of redeeming features. One such feature ironically arose out of what, at the time, was perceived as the major

20 *Building News*, 29 October 1909, p. 641.
21 *Building News*, 8 July 1910, p. 47.
22 A. Stuart Gray, *Edwardian Architecture: A Biographical Dictionary*, Duckworth, London, 1985, p. 302.

disadvantage of the Bedford Street site, namely, that it abutted a railway cutting, requiring Reilly to treat the third elevation with a strikingly different approach. The modern observer, now that the cutting has been covered over, can fully appreciate the building in the round. This is by far the most successful treatment of the three façades, consisting as it does of a bold expanse of brick and a simple massing of forms, with few windows (Fig. 15). In the adoption of a simplified Classicism, lack of ornamentation and functional use of materials, it shares a number of qualities found in Reilly's other major commission from 1909: the Church of St Barnabas, Dalston, London.

Church of St Barnabas, Dalston, London

The commission for the church appears to have arisen – as with so many of Reilly's projects – out of contacts he had made in other contexts. In this case, Reilly had been a student at the Merchant Taylors' School, and the church was to serve the Merchant Taylors' School Mission. The site is, to say the least, unprepossessing, being tucked away behind factories in the north-east of London. However, as with the students' union site, Reilly managed to make a virtue of the poor location, and in this case concentrated his efforts on the interior of the church (Fig. 16). The foundation stone was laid on 3 July 1909, and the building was completed the following year. A commentator in the *Architectural Review* noted that

> this is a very interesting piece of work, both constructionally and from the standpoint of architectural design. Economy being a ruling factor, and exterior effect being impossible owing to the situation of the church, the architect concentrated his attention on the interior.[23]

The interior is indeed particularly striking for its almost total lack of decoration and reliance on the effect of the materials (brick and reinforced concrete). What decoration there is was provided by the Liverpool sculptor Herbert Tyson Smith later on,[24] and consists of a rood screen and candlesticks. The candlesticks were illustrated in *The Studio* in 1923, which stated that 'Mr H. Tyson Smith is one of the few sculptors present Liverpool can boast. His work is grave and dignified, with a well balanced mixture of early classic and

23 *Architectural Review*, September 1910, p. 124.
24 For a full account of Herbert Tyson Smith's work see S. Poole, 'A Critical Analysis of the Work of Herbert Tyson Smith, Sculptor and Designer', PhD thesis, Liverpool University, 1994.

modernist feeling.'[25] The delay in decoration was, as Roderick Bisson points out, largely due to lack of funds at the time of building.[26] However, it is unlikely, even given more funds, that Reilly's intention was to use more decoration than we see today.

The functional and economic use of materials is commented on in the *Architectural Review*, where it is noted that they consist of

> stock bricks, and the roof and vault, which are in one, are of concrete reinforced with expanded metal and asphalted over. This form of construction has resulted in an economical yet substantial building.[27]

This concentration on the functional use of material has been commented on by subsequent writers. Gavin Stamp has noted that Reilly 'is determined to show that rational classical monumentality can be achieved by the simplest means – as with a good warehouse'.[28] Ian Nairn places Reilly's achievement at the very heart of the proto-Modernist wave in Britain, saying,

> the outside is just a big plain stock-brick warehouse. The inside is the best church of its date in London, sure in its domed and barrel-vaulted spaces, incredibly fresh in its detail, concrete and exposed yellow brick. England could so easily have stepped across to modern architecture from here, instead of relapsing into an eclectic fog. This is the kind of quintessential classical composition Lutyens tried for and never had the integrity to achieve. Only the big gaudy Adamesque screen jars: everything else is pure space: or rather, something better – pure space charged with feeling.[29]

The comparison with Sir Edwin Lutyens is interesting in that it is possible to detect echoes of St Barnabas in the crypt Lutyens designed for Liverpool's Metropolitan Cathedral of Christ the King in 1932 – the only part of the design that was actually built (Fig. 17). In particular, the bold brick vaulting and stripped Classicism is suggestive of Reilly's work some 20 years earlier. Reilly's own inspiration for St Barnabas is unclear, but the monumental brick massing of the Liverpool dock system warehouses, such as Jesse Hartley's Albert Dock of 1839–1845, may well have affected his handling of the bricks and simplified Classical detailing of the 1909 church.

25   *The Studio*, Vol. 86, 1923, p. 112.
26   See R. Bisson, *The Sandon Studios Society and the Arts*, Parry Books, Liverpool, 1965, p. 84.
27   *Architectural Review*, September 1910, p. 124.
28   G. Stamp, *London 1900*, Academy Editions, London, 1978, p. 381.
29   I. Nairn, *Nairn's London*, Penguin, Harmondsworth, 1988, p. 150.

Nairn's assertion that Britain should have proceeded with the kind of work Reilly had produced at St Barnabas is tempered by Alan Powers. While acknowledging the power of the building, Powers notes,

> the church... is like a miniature, tougher version of Westminster Cathedral, and... is remarkable for its use of exposed concrete, while the uninterrupted vault is a synthesis of many styles. It is unique among Reilly's buildings and there is little to compare to it in the work of his students.[30]

What might have been, had Reilly followed through with this work rather than pursuing the American Beaux-Arts path, we can only speculate on. Certainly it could have placed the Liverpool School at the forefront of British Modernism and established Reilly's reputation as a leading innovator on an international level. The type of work Reilly was capable of producing around 1909–1910 – when restrained from his wilder neo-Grec impulses and constrained by factors such as the site – shows a robustness that bears comparison with Charles Jeanneret's Free Classicism. This can be traced in work such as the Villa Schwob of 1916, designed in the period just before Jeanneret became Le Corbusier. The railway elevation of Reilly's students' union building shares some of the qualities of Villa Schwob, of which Charles Jencks has written that it consists of 'architectural details... almost Neoclassical in their robust, simplified geometry: blank, flat rectangles, punched into by oval voids... set off against half cylinders'.[31]

Reilly did not pursue this simplified Classicism to its logical conclusion for his next two commissions, but instead tempered it according to rather more provincial tastes by dressing his later church designs in the neo-Grec garb of the students' union's less impressive elevations. For Powers, the contrast between St Barnabas and the students' union building illustrates that Reilly misunderstood the whole Ecole des Beaux-Arts system. By contrasting 'St Barnabas... which effectively exemplifies the doctrine of abstract form derived from classicism, [with] the... Student Union in which abstract form is overlaid with excessive ornament of uncertain quality',[32] Powers notes that Reilly and his fellow admirers of the Ecole saw it as 'a system based on classicism, rather than a rationalist system whose principal manifestations were classical'. The

---

30 A. Powers, 'Architectural Education in Britain 1880–1914', PhD thesis, Cambridge University, 1982, p. 142.
31 C. Jencks, *Le Corbusier and the Tragic View of Architecture*, Penguin, Harmondsworth, 1987, p. 44.
32 Powers, 'Liverpool and Architectural Education', in Sharples (ed.), *Charles Reilly and the Liverpool School of Architecture*, p. 9.

consequence was that, instead of taking the route of logical Modernism, Reilly chose to follow the Monumental Classic, which became the hallmark of the Liverpool Manner. As Powers puts it, this 'became an end in itself rather than the means to the abstract end that it had been at the outset'.[33]

In 1909, Reilly was invited by his friend Mr Mitchell, the incumbent of Holy Trinity Wavertree, to submit plans for a remodelling of the church.[34] The work involved removing the old side galleries and slotting a new chancel in, by extending the building eastwards.[35] The detailing is elegantly handled and when the new chancel was consecrated in December 1911, the *Manchester Guardian* review noted 'the colour scheme of red and drab, with the pews and woodwork black, entirely justifies itself. The expense has been large – over £5,000.'[36] Reilly manages to pull off a unified design that has dignity, without seeming to have been imposed on the old church. As Quentin Hughes notes,

> with its beautiful and delicate Greek Revival detailing and its Renaissance organization of space... Even the old tower is buttressed to give it an obelisk effect... the work shows Reilly at his best.[37]

While I don't agree it is Reilly at his best – I feel we need to look to St Barnabas for that – together with his students' union, it is certainly a more than competent handling of the neo-Grec.

Of the handful of buildings Reilly designed pre-1914, St Barnabas was, according to him, 'the building I should like to be remembered by... the old School Mission in North-East London.'[38] Presumably the church had, by then, come to represent those Modernist qualities Reilly had moved towards. The ideas developed in the St Barnabas scheme were re-used by Reilly in another project, the design for a Church of Humanity, Liverpool, in 1911. The design was commissioned by Edmund Rathbone, a member of the leading Liverpool merchant family and a follower of the Positivist Church which expounded the teachings of Auguste Comte.[39] The design consists of the basic plan used at St

33   Powers, 'Liverpool and Architectural Education', p. 9.
34   A plan of Reilly's scheme is held in the Liverpool Record Office, Liverpool Central Library, Box 283 DIO 251/117.
35   J. Schroeder, *The Life and Times of Wavertree Parish Church of the Holy Trinity 1794–1994*, 1994.
36   *Manchester Guardian*, 15 December 1911.
37   J. Quentin Hughes, *Liverpool: City of Architecture*, Bluecoat Press, Liverpool, 1999, p. 28.
38   Reilly, *Scaffolding in the Sky*, p. 113.
39   The Rathbones were part of the Liverpool 'aristocracy' of merchant families who were very active in various cultural and educational philanthropic activities. A number of family members were practising artists and had links with Reilly through groups such as the Sandon Studios Society

Barnabas, but with the addition of elaborate Greek Revival detailing. The proposals for the church were published in the *Architectural Review* of March 1911, which illustrated the statue of Humanity represented by a mother and child that was to have formed the focal point of the church. Rathbone wrote the accompanying article in which he states that

> the writer was attracted by some photographs of... the church of St Barnabas... by Professor Reilly, and thought that the feeling of cultivated peaceful religious repose suggested by that interior would exactly suit the sentiments of the members of the Liverpool Church of Humanity.[40]

The church was not built to Reilly's design, and the Positivists finally obtained a church in Upper Parliament Street, Liverpool in 1914, designed by W. H. Ansell. However, the design serves as an indicator of Reilly's retreat from the simplicity of his St Barnabas church towards a heavier neo-Grec, and as one more thread of the part Reilly played in the interwoven nature of Liverpool's cultural life.

The body of architectural work Reilly produced in this period illustrates his stylistic development: from the free style of his formative London years, through a neo-Grec interpretation, and into his more familiar American Beaux-Arts style. The case of St Barnabas – although it can be read as part of his developing Classical vocabulary – remains a tantalizing glimpse of what might have been.

---

and the Liverpool Repertory Theatre, as well as being active in University affairs. The Church for Humanity was part of a number of similar groupings which existed in the city during this period based on religious or quasi-religious lines.

40   E. Rathbone, 'Current Architecture: The Church of Humanity, Liverpool', *Architectural Review*, March 1911, pp. 148–50.

7 Journalism and Other Writing

Reilly's writing career, which took the form of articles for the local, national and professional press together with a handful of books, and his work as a major figure in the field of architectural education were intimately inter-woven. His approach to writing had the aim of promoting architecture in general, and the Liverpool School and its students in particular. While the genres ranged from travel writing[1] through book reviewing to cultural criti-cism, they had a common theme: the impact of architecture and the urban environment on people's lives. However, as Reilly noted of his journalism, 'People laughed... because they said whatever subject was started I ended up with the Liverpool School of Architecture.'[2] The publications to which he contributed ranged from *Country Life* to *Tribune*. In addition to prestigious journals such as these, Reilly was not averse to contributing to publications that some might have thought too low-brow for a university don. As Reilly noted, 'I have often noticed the lower the brow of the paper, the higher the fee.'[3] However, it was not until the early 1920s that Reilly's journalistic career started in earnest. It was also at this time that he published his first volume on the work of McKim, Mead and White. Prior to this, Reilly's writing output was modest and specifically targeted to raise his own profile and that of the Liverpool School of Architecture.

Early Writing 1904–1921

Reilly's writing began with various small items in the local press on matters relating to such things as the saving of the Blue Coat Hospital building and the development of the architectural teaching programme at the School of

---

1 Reilly wrote numerous travel articles for the *Liverpool Post*, *Quebec Telegraph*, *Manchester Guardian* and *Tribune*. See Reilly Papers, Liverpool University Archive, Box D207/28/1. See also J. Sharples, 'Reilly and his Students', in J. Sharples (ed.), *Charles Reilly and the Liverpool School of Architecture 1904-1933*, Liverpool University Press, Liverpool, 1996, pp. 38–39.
2 C. H. Reilly, *Scaffolding in the Sky*, Routledge, London, 1938, p. 238.
3 Reilly, *Scaffolding in the Sky*, p. 245.

Architecture. The items were generally designed to generate interest in schemes that Reilly was either involved with or hoping to become involved with. Following Reilly's appointment in Liverpool, his first major piece was *The Training of Architects*, published in 1905, in which he outlined his conception of architectural training as belonging firmly within the university system.[4] The paper acted as a means of consolidating his position in one of the few university schools of architecture then in existence, as well as providing ideas for the expansion of its sphere of influence. The local press was used at every opportunity to remind the citizens of Liverpool, and in particular prospective students, that the School of Architecture was at the forefront of modern architectural training and was in effect the only rational way forward.[5] The *Portfolio* series produced by the school in 1906 and 1908 enabled Reilly to keep the school in the press and thus create the impression of a large, highly productive department – which was quite at odds with the reality. Reilly also took every opportunity to ensure that developments within the school – whether it was the establishment of a Bachelor of Architecture degree,[6] the publication of a new prospectus, or the establishment of a travelling scholarship – were designed to gain the maximum press coverage.

Events within the broader community of Liverpool enabled Reilly to raise his profile during these early years. The campaign to save the Blue Coat school not only provided ample opportunity to advance his own pet project for the building, but also enabled him to get better acquainted with members of Liverpool society, including prominent figures from the local press. Similarly, his involvement in the establishment of the Liverpool Repertory Theatre provided extensive local and national coverage. As Bisson outlines in *The Sandon Studios Society and the Arts*, such cultural campaigns provided a focal point for the city's social elite as well as a meeting place for the artistic community. This relatively small and close-knit community, centred around the Club Room at the Blue Coat or the bar at the repertory theatre, provided a forum for the exchange of ideas. Reilly had managed in the space of a few short years to place both himself, and eventually the entire School of Architecture, at the very centre of this cultural network.

4 Reilly, *The Training of Architects*, Sherrat and Hughes, London, 1905. Reviewed in a variety of papers and journals, local and national, including *Liverpool Post*, 15 July 1905; *The Architect*, 21 July 1905; *The Builder*, 25 July 1905. It was also published in New York.
5 'The University Teaching of Architecture', letter addressed to parents of prospective students outlining the advantages of the new university system, signed by Reilly and Ramsey, *Daily Courier*, 12 October 1907, Reilly Papers, Liverpool University Archive, Box S3214.
6 *Builders' Reporter*, 4 December 1907, Reilly Papers, Liverpool University Archive, Box S3214.

Reilly's writing remained relatively modest, despite his growing connections and friendships with leading figures in Liverpool's media circles. However, in 1913 he was appointed Consultant Editor at the *Builders' Journal*, after turning down the editorship of *The Builder*,[7] and it was through this appointment that his journalistic career took off after the war. Reilly was also producing a number of more scholarly papers at this time, which he read to local societies. Examples include 'The Grand Manner in Architecture', read to the Manchester Society of Architects on 11 February 1908 and reported in *Building News* on 13 October, as well as a paper entitled 'Criticisms of Drawings Submitted for the Institute Prizes and Studentships 1910–1911' presented to RIBA, in which Reilly promoted his by now well-advertised theories on the future of architectural training. Reilly stated that

> Facility in design, like facility in draughtsmanship, comes with constant practice… This may seem a digression from my main subject tonight, but it leads to this suggestion, that the institute which has now taken in hand the training as well as the examining of students should make training in design the keystone of its system. History, mathematics, construction, materials, everything else, should be subsidiary to what after all is our main excuse for existence.[8]

Reilly adopted a similar theme in an essay he contributed to *A Miscellany Presented to J. M. Mackay*,[9] in which he continued to stress the importance of the Liverpool School modelling itself along Beaux-Arts lines. Published in 1914, the *Miscellany* was one of the last pieces of published work Reilly produced before the outbreak of war. Prior to this he contributed to the newly founded *Town Planning Review* a series of articles exploring the adoption, both in Britain and in the United States, of Monumental Beaux-Arts planning schemes.[10]

Reilly spent the war as a munitions inspector. His time was fully occupied by this work and he appears to have written little during this period with the exception of a contribution to the *Town Planning Review* discussing

---

7   See Reilly, *Scaffolding in the Sky*, pp. 119–20.
8   Reilly, 'Criticism of Drawings Submitted for the Institute Prizes and Studentships 1910–11', *Journal of the Royal Institute of British Architects*, 4 February 1911, pp. 220–21.
9   *A Miscellany. Presented to John Macdonald Mackay*, Liverpool University Press, Liverpool, 1914. Reilly's paper was entitled, 'Architecture as an Academic Subject'.
10 Reilly, 'Town Planning Schemes in America', *Town Planning Review*, Vol. 1/1. Also Reilly, 'The City of the Future', *Town Planning Review*, Vol. 1/3.

post-war housing.[11] The coming of peace saw Reilly's journalistic career step up a gear. From 1921 onwards, up until his death in 1948, he produced by far the largest proportion of his literary output.

Journalism 1921–1933

In terms of his philosophy of architecture, the years after the war represented a gradual move away from the Monumental Beaux-Arts towards an appreciation of the Modernist theories which were becoming increasingly dominant from the late 1920s. This move was naturally paralleled in his writing, culminating in 1938 with the publication of his autobiography *Scaffolding in the Sky*, in which he clearly attempts to identify himself with Modernism. Reilly noted that

> By 1921… I appear to have become a thorough-going journalist. Everything I saw in Canada and the States… was an excuse for an article… Most of the stuff I wrote in those days appeared in the *Liverpool Daily Post*, and I dare say had an added piquancy to Liverpool folk in coming from a professor at the university.[12]

The contacts Reilly had made in media circles in Liverpool before the war now enabled him to develop his journalistic and academic careers to mutual benefit. He noted that

> By 1921 the editor [of the *Liverpool Daily Post*] had given me a commission to write a column and a half once a week about some important street in the town and its buildings. These articles, afterwards published in book form, caused some interest. It was the first time, one might almost say, that the ordinary everyday buildings of a town, which no one looked at particularly and all took for granted, were discussed critically as with a new eye.[13]

Reilly had taken a format normally reserved for scholarly papers, and adapted it to appeal to the broader audience that formed the readership of a typical provincial daily newspaper. The series of articles published in the *Liverpool Post* were eventually collected into a book, *Some Liverpool Streets and*

11 During his time as an inspector of munitions Reilly was, of course, in the same organization (albeit in a different role) as many of those involved in the war-time housing schemes and the post-war housing programme. See Chapter 8 for a more detailed discussion on this point.
12 Reilly, *Scaffolding in the Sky*, pp. 237–38.
13 Reilly, *Scaffolding in the Sky*, p. 238.

Buildings in 1921. This was a practice Reilly was to use for a number of his subsequent publications. The book was introduced with what Reilly called 'a chapter on Character in Modern Architecture, which formed... a more serious lecture... to the Liverpool Architectural Society...'[14] It consisted of a series of chapters on Bold Street, Rodney Street, Castle Street, and so on. In his discussions on Bold Street, then regarded as the most fashionable shopping street in the city, still able to boast the title of 'The Bond Street of the North of England', Reilly states

> What is it that makes Bold Street the pleasantest street in Liverpool? Why, in most moods, would one sooner walk there than anywhere else? Why in order to get, say, from the Adelphi or the University Club to St Luke's Church, does one instinctively avoid the direct route of Renshaw Street... I think it is that the one street is in essence vulgar and noisy, and the other civilised and intimate... it commences well... The Lyceum Club on the left hand, Greek yet gracious, is followed closely by the Palatine, Italian, reserved and rather noble... one regrets that so soon one comes, on the left hand side, upon a great store, with plate glass windows running through two storeys. The windows seem out of scale with the street. There is a rococo front, too, with glazed tile interior on the opposite side... which also transgresses the character of the street, bringing to it the very air and manners of Church Street. These things seem a pity, but for some reason one does not resent in the same way the great height of Messrs Cripps' shop front. The scheme in black and gold has a certain dignity and reserve.[15]

Having thus established himself in the local press, Reilly was approached by the editor of the *Manchester Guardian* to write a similar series of articles on the architecture of Manchester. This started in March 1923 and was eventually brought together as *Some Manchester Streets and their Buildings*. With both the Liverpool and Manchester street reviews, Reilly anticipated the work of subsequent writers such as Pevsner, Clifton-Taylor and Nairn, in providing a systematic account of a town or city's architectural stock. If Reilly's descriptions lack the scholarship of Pevsner, they nevertheless provide for the historian interesting pen portraits of streets in both cities – the characters of which have since radically altered. In 1923 Reilly also published a short

14 Reilly, 'Some Liverpool Streets and Buildings in 1921', *The Liverpool Daily Post and Mercury*, Liverpool, 1921, p. 3.
15 Reilly, 'Some Liverpool Streets and Buildings in 1921', pp. 19–20. The shop frontage to Cripps department store is, in fact, an example of the early use of iron work in shop frontages in Liverpool dating from the previous century. Bold Street had a number of other examples now unfortunately destroyed; however, the Cripps' frontage has remained largely intact.

monograph on the work of McKim, Mead and White, which provided further evidence of his continued commitment to American Beaux-Arts in the early 1920s.[16] The journalism he produced quickly led to his being approached by the *Westminster Gazette* to write a series of articles on 'Architectural Problems of the Day', which Reilly – in now characteristic fashion – collected together as a volume entitled *Some Architectural Problems of Today*.[17]

Reilly was approached by *Country Life* to contribute a series of articles of his own choosing. The magazine had been founded in 1895–1896 by Edward Hudson and George Riddell, and had been conceived as 'a weekly illustrated paper of the highest quality…'[18] It had subsequently come to epitomize the very essence of English upper class life. John Cornforth, in his history of the magazine, noted that Reilly's

> first article in *Country Life* was a review of the Modern American Architecture exhibition at RIBA on November 26 1921: and on February 18 1922 he wrote about 'The City of Washington and American Architecture.' However most of the articles were about public architecture and public buildings in Britain, starting with a series on 'London Streets and Their Recent Buildings,' which began on May 22 1922.[19]

Reilly said that Riddell felt that

> I could provide that paper with ideas and I was appointed nominally Architectural Editor. I did provide ideas, or thought I did, in large numbers but it was not till I left the paper that I began to see some of them, like an interest in Modern design and in what the theatre was doing, creeping in.[20]

His association with the magazine was short-lived, and after nine articles he was dropped. According to his own account this was due to the fact that 'The editor did not like my remarks about the building of one of his chief advertisers.'[21] The description to which Reilly refers was most probably of the

16   The book appears not to have been published in America, as Roth notes: 'Reilly's… small but sensitive study… came as a complete surprise to the younger partners; Lawrence White, who chanced to see a copy in London, greatly appreciated Reilly's praise.' M. L. Roth, *McKim, Mead & White Architects*, Thames and Hudson, London, 1984, p. 349.

17   Reilly, *Some Architectural Problems of Today*, Hodder and Stoughton, London, 1924. For a review of Reilly's book see 'Architecture Furniture and Music', *Manchester Guardian*, 24 December 1924.

18   B. Darwin, *Fifty Years of Country Life*, 1947, quoted in J. Cornforth, *The Search for a Style: Country Life and Architecture 1897–1935*, Norton, London, 1988, p. 13.

19   Cornforth, *The Search for a Style*, p. 66.

20   Reilly, *Scaffolding in the Sky*, p. 259.

21   Reilly, *Scaffolding in the Sky*, p. 239.

Royal Insurance Building, Lombard Street, discussed by Reilly in his 1924 article 'London Streets':

> a race of City architects has grown up largely separated from the rest of the profession… Knowing of the immense value of the property they are dealing with, they think, perhaps, more seriously of a right of light than the right compositions for their buildings. They are likely to sacrifice broad effects for some small gain in floor space. Yet, when they do let themselves go with their façades, having, perhaps, spent some much of their time over legal points, they cannot bring to their proper work the severely critical and trained mind of the complete architect… There is, for instance, in that narrow lane called Lombard Street, where only concerns of highest financial standing can afford to exist, the luscious over-modelled building of the Royal Insurance Company. Now, obviously, in a very narrow street, a flat façade is what is required, for it is the only kind that can be properly seen. Not only is the façade of this building of the most ornate and extravagant description, but a great group of coarse and colossal women lean out a considerable distance across the pavement from the pediment over the main entrance. There is no feeling here for delicacy, refinement or restraint – the qualities one hopes of the highest finance. If one did not know the financial standing of the Royal Insurance Company one might, from its habitation, think it some bucket shop concern.[22]

If, as it would seem, Reilly was unwilling to accommodate his critical stance to the commercial requirements of running a magazine, it is more than likely that he would not have remained long with *Country Life* in any case. Reilly's taste for all things urban and his increasing moves towards Modernist architecture in the late 1920s and 1930s was out of step with the Picturesque[23] and 'Moderne' taste in architecture favoured by the likes of Christopher Hussey, who had arrived on the magazine in 1921.[24]

There were advantages to be gained from his association with the magazine, principally the commission to work on the Devonshire House project, which was received via a proposed article. As Reilly put it,

---

22   Reilly, 'London Streets and Their Recent Buildings X', *Country Life*, 13 December 1924, pp. 942–43. The description was probably even more insulting to the company given that it came from the Professor of Architecture at Liverpool University, the city in which the company had been founded and in which it had its headquarters.

23   See C. Hussey, *The Picturesque: Studies in a Point of View*, Frank Cass, London, 1967 [1927]; also J. Cornforth, 'The Husseys and the Picturesque', *Country Life*, 10 May and 17 May 1979.

24   See J. Holder, 'Promoting Modernism in Britain', in P. Greenhalgh (ed.), *Modernism in Design*, Reaktion Books, London, 1990, p. 134. See also J. Cornforth, 'Christopher Hussey and Modern Architecture', *Country Life*, 22 October and 29 October 1981.

> I had for that one day in London a 50 per cent addition to my university salary and, what was almost better… a first class season ticket to London. It was the sense of freedom it gave me and the illusion that I had London at my mercy…[25]

He used this freedom to secure further journalistic work, and established a friendship with Brendan Bracken[26] leading to work on the *Banker*[27] magazine as well as numerous other publications such as *John O'London's Weekly*,[28] and *Strand Magazine*. Reilly spent a good deal of his time away from the university, leaving Budden in the role of 'caretaker director' of the school.

In addition to his London journalism, Reilly maintained a healthy output in Liverpool. He contributed sporadic articles to local journals such as *Cox's Merseyside Annual*[29] on architectural and university themes, as well as items for publications such as *Merseyside: A Handbook to Liverpool*,[30] produced to accompany the meeting of the British Association for the Advancement of Science held in the city in 1923. Much of the material used in articles such as these was repeated in a slightly different form elsewhere. For example, the articles Reilly wrote in the late 1920s and early 1930s for *The Liverpool Diocesan Review* consisted of a mixture of reviews of new work in Liverpool – usually by former students[31] – and broader articles under the general title 'Mainly About Liverpool'.[32] Here he explored old and familiar themes, such as the Blue Coat, the university, the cathedrals, and town planning issues. Work also came from former colleagues at the university. In 1923 Ramsey Muir invited Reilly to contribute to a new publication, *The Weekly Westminster*, which according to Muir was aimed at 'intelligent people, but not an

25 Reilly, *Scaffolding in the Sky*, p. 259.
26 Reilly continued his friendship with Bracken when he was a Member of Parliament and a confidante of Winston Churchill's during the war. See Reilly Papers, Liverpool University Archive, Boxes D207/38/1–8, and D207/40/1–136.
27 For copies of *Banker* articles from 1926–1937, see Reilly Papers, Liverpool University Archive, Box D207/42/1–2.
28 See Reilly Papers, Liverpool University Archive, Box D207/28/1–4.
29 Reilly, 'The University of Liverpool', in *Cox's Liverpool Annual and Year Book 1922*, pp. 105–13; also Reilly, 'A New Liverpool', in *Cox's Merseyside Annual 1929*, pp. 85–89.
30 Reilly, 'A Note on the Architecture of Liverpool', in *Merseyside: A Handbook to Liverpool*, Liverpool University Press and Hodder & Stoughton, London, 1923, pp. 48–56.
31 For example, Reilly, 'St Christopher's Church, Norris Green', *Liverpool Diocesan Review*, Vol. 7, 1932, pp. 360–62. Liverpool Record Office, Liverpool Central Library, Box H283.05 LIV. This was a review of a church by Bernard Miller (Cert. Arch. 1914, B.Arch. 1928), a member of the School of Architecture staff from 1919 onwards.
32 For example, Reilly, 'Mainly About Liverpool – A Causerie VII', *Liverpool Diocesan Review*, Vol. 4, 1929, pp. 244–46. Liverpool Record Office, Liverpool Central Library, Box H283.05 LIV.

esoteric clique'.[33] Reilly produced a number of articles for the paper between 1923 and 1925.[34] An element of his impish humour can be seen when he noted that

> Once he [Lord Riddell] asked me to provide him with a list of writers who had not yet appeared in print in his papers. For fun I gave him the names of Oliver Elton, Sir Alfred Dale, Professor Mackay and the more serious members of the Senate who were all shortly afterwards invited to contribute, much to their surprise, to the *News of the World*, the *Humorist, Tit-Bits...* of which latter it appeared his Lordship was also the head. Whatever the others may have done I did not flinch: I wrote about 'Modern Architecture' in the *Strand Magazine* and was highly paid for it.[35]

In the early 1930s, just prior to his retirement, Reilly produced two more books. *Representative British Architects of the Present Day*[36] developed out of a series of articles he wrote for *Building*. The choice of architects for inclusion demonstrates that Reilly was still rather conservative in his architectural viewpoint, and while the articles included relatively 'progressive' architects such as Oliver Hill, Gray Warnum and Joseph Emberton, they were not included in the book. Instead, Reilly included a mixture of traditionalists such as Reginald Blomfield and Arthur Davis, friends and colleagues such as Stanley Adshead and Clough Williams-Ellis, and former mentors such as H. V. Lanchester and Sir Edwin Lutyens. The following year Reilly published *The Theory and Practice of Architecture*,[37] combining a historical overview with his evolving theories on the developments in modern architecture in both the United States and Europe. Both books come from Reilly's transitional period, in which he was attempting to assimilate the theories associated with the Modernist developments coming out of Europe. Reilly's developing views on Modernism were to be more explicitly outlined in his autobiography, in which he sought to distance himself from former allies such as Blomfield, and place himself within the Modernist camp.

33   Letter from R. Muir to Reilly, 25 August 1923, Reilly Papers, Liverpool University Archive, Box D207/28/2.
34   For copies of articles written by Reilly, see Reilly Papers, Liverpool University Archive, Box D207/28/2.
35   Reilly, *Scaffolding in the Sky*, p. 245.
36   Reilly, *Representative British Architects of the Present Day*, Batsford, London, 1931.
37   Reilly, *The Theory and Practice of Architecture*, Victor Gollancz, London, 1932.

Scaffolding in the Sky: Autobiography and Myth

Although Reilly's autobiography was not published until 1938, it had appeared in a limited serialized form in the *Liverpool Daily Post* between 1928 and 1933. The book was obviously embellished by the time of its publication in 1938, with a heavier emphasis placed on Reilly's by then strong commitment to Modernism. The dust cover featured a photograph of the Peter Jones department store as if to emphasize the point, while the contents mixed anecdotal reminiscences and historical details with varying degrees of accuracy. The book played a central role in consolidating Reilly's reputation as a modernizer and a radical force, although as I have already stated, he was often tempted to rewrite the facts to suit his current architectural stance.

Maxwell Fry contributed an enthusiastic review, written from the standpoint of a former student who had himself undergone something of a stylistic conversion:

> This review is something in the nature of an itemised thanksgiving, but it serves to show that our experience at Liverpool, whatever you may have to say of the stuff we produced, was lively and direct, and centred always upon this man, who gave so easily and with no condescension the overplus of his vital existence.[38]

The *Journal of the Royal Institute of British Architects* devoted two pages to a review of the book, and while it was generally favourable it did note that 'One only wishes that his information was as reliable as his descriptions interesting.'[39] A footnote to the review concerning Reilly's account of his part in the *Architects' Registration Act* of 1931 gives some indication of the extent of Reilly's 'artistic license' with the facts. It states,

> We are, of course, very grateful to Professor Reilly for the help which he gave so readily and so enthusiastically in the campaign... But in the interests of historical accuracy I am bound to warn readers that the account of the proceedings in the House of Commons which appears on pages 299 to 302 has very little relation to the facts.[40]

---

38   E. Maxwell Fry, *Focus*, Winter 1938.

39   *Journal of the Royal Institute of British Architects*, 5 December 1938, pp. 144–45.

40   'Professor Reilly and the Registration Act', *Journal of the Royal Institute of British Architects*, 5 December 1938, p. 145. Reilly wrote a letter, dated 19 December 1938, to the *Journal* protesting at the implication of inaccuracy in his book. See Reilly Papers, Liverpool University Archive, Box D207/7/1.

Others were less polite in their estimation of the validity of Reilly's accounts. Maud Budden, the wife of Reilly's second-in-command at the Liverpool School, wrote a skit for the Sandon Society reviewing Reilly's Liverpool life, in which the figure of 'Truth' appears to Reilly: 'TRUTH [played by a beautiful girl] coming forward. "Professor Reilly. I am TRUTH, and we have never met."'[41] Budden himself is said to have regarded *Scaffolding in the Sky* as 'An amusing work of light fiction.'[42] Maurice Webb, son of Sir Aston Webb, wrote to Reilly saying 'You're indeed an honest crook...' and he included a short rhyme written by a mutual friend in the Arts Club that reads 'Professor Reilly, notes architects highly, but that means it must be confessed, he considers Professor Reilly's the best.'[43]

Reilly was eager to use his autobiography to confirm his position as a pioneer in developments within the University of Liverpool, and in the broader architectural scene. His treatment of his predecessor Simpson and his almost total disregard for initiatives made during the period prior to his own appointment would seem to confirm this. Nevertheless, despite its short-comings, Reilly's autobiography has come to represent, as Turner and Allan have noted,

> one of the major sources for portraying the feel of the university in the first three decades of this century. Inaccurate in parts, and 'gossipy'... it stands out as a brilliant pen portrait of the university and those personalities who played a major role in its early development.[44]

Journalism 1933–1948

The period between Reilly's retirement from the Roscoe Chair in 1933 and his death in 1948 is characterized by an increasing absorption with the twin concerns of Modernism and the problems associated with post-war town planning. Reilly had been invited in 1929 to write an annual review of the year's work for *The Architects' Journal*. An examination of the selections he

41   Reilly Papers, Liverpool University Archive, Box D207/7/1. A programme of the *Review* is dated 21 December 1938. This box contains numerous letters, reviews and other matters relating to the publication of Reilly's autobiography.
42   Quoted in A. Powers, 'Architectural Education in Britain 1880–1914', PhD thesis, Cambridge University, 1982, p. 8.
43   Letter from M. Webb to Reilly, Reilly Papers, Liverpool University Archive, Box D207/7/1.
44   S. Turner and A. Allan, 'The Papers of Sir Charles Reilly: A Recent Accession to the University Archives', *The University of Liverpool Recorder*, No. 81, 1979, pp. 159–62.

made up until the outbreak of war in 1939 shows his increasing awareness and appreciation of the Modernist work being produced both at home and abroad. The articles act as a catalogue of the progression of Modernism in Britain throughout the 1930s. Reilly was able to state in his review for 1938 that

> Of recent years it has been my practice, in reviewing some of the buildings in the great pile of illustrations the editor sends me towards the close of each year, to divide the buildings into 'modern' and 'traditional' ones. This has been a convenient enough arrangement if not a very scientific one. This year, however, the division seems less appropriate. The traditionalists must either be retiring at a great rate to the South Coast, or to another world, or becoming converted... This... does not mean that other traditionalists of a baser sort have not been more actively at work... Such things of course do not reach respectable papers like *The Architect's Journal* or the *Architectural Review* and are not therefore in my pile.[45]

An additional means by which Reilly was able to keep in touch with the latest developments in architectural thinking was his extensive work as a book reviewer. He was able to review most of the seminal works on architectural theory in the inter-war years, including Blomfield's *Modernismus,*[46] F. R. S. Yorke's *The Modern House,*[47] Raymond McGrath's *Twentieth Century Houses,*[48] and Gropius's *The New Architecture and the Bauhaus.*[49] The reviews, mainly written for the *Manchester Guardian,* were indicative of Reilly's growing moves towards a Modernist standpoint, which culminated in the early 1940s in articles and broadcasts such as 'Modern Movements in Architecture' for *The Listener.*[50] Reilly's use of the plural in the title of the article might be construed as being indicative of his pragmatic approach to Modernism in which he neither abandoned the historical precedents he recognized as being evident in the movement, nor embraced the notion that Modernism consisted of one 'true' style; a central tenet in Modernist ideology. Having said that, Reilly does state in his article

> these buildings [Modern architecture]... are no longer decked out in the fancy dress of long past styles... If this is everywhere as I think it is, the general characteristic of true modern buildings... it would be more correct to speak of

45   Reilly, 'The Year's Work at Home', *The Architects' Journal,* 19 January 1939, pp. 133–46.
46   Reilly, 'The Moderns as Target', *Manchester Guardian,* 12 March 1934.
47   Reilly, 'The Little New House', *Manchester Guardian,* 26 July 1934.
48   Reilly, 'Modern Houses', *Manchester Guardian,* 26 June 1935.
49   Reilly, 'Professor Gropius', *Manchester Guardian,* 1 August 1935.
50   Reilly, 'Modern Movements in Architecture', *The Listener,* 20 March 1941, pp. 399–401.

the modern movement in the singular and not of modern movements in the plural…

Despite this assertion Reilly nevertheless chose to use the plural in the title, and also illustrated his article with examples of historical styles of which he claimed, although they were not relevant as styles to be implemented, 'Their meticulous rules of proportion and composition are an excellent foundation for taste. I would not however teach them today as part of an art to be practised…'

The contradictory nature of his statements tells us about Reilly's inability to reconcile the hardline Modernist philosophy (which insisted upon a single stylistic approach) with his own experience in attempting a similar approach with Classicism some 20 years earlier. Reilly would, up until his death, be unable to square the circle, and instead formulated a pluralistic approach to Modernism that accommodated some of his earlier theories. This would, in part, be why he was largely ignored by writers of Modernist history, who felt that he and others like him were not sufficiently sincere or committed to Modernism.

By the late 1930s Reilly was an elder statesman of architecture, and was increasingly invited to contribute articles in which he cast an eye over the general architectural scene.[51] One such series was for *The Architects' Journal*, and was entitled 'Professor Reilly Speaking'. In the editorial note introducing the first of Reilly's contributions it was stated that

> Since he retired from Liverpool, Professor Reilly has been inclined to cultivate the affectation of being old, but as no more vital men are to be found amongst architects of any age, and since his views are invariably significant as well as diverting, we have ventured to goad him into fresh activity, of which this column is an outcome.[52]

The column caused a good deal of heated debate[53] due to Reilly's often un-guarded comments on contentious issues, admittedly encouraged by Hubert de Cronin Hastings, the paper's editor. Having encouraged Reilly to write

51   The editor of the *Architectural Review* notes in a letter to Reilly that 'We have closed with your offer as keen hawk-nosed business men who feel that "Professor Reilly's column" (or title to that effect) once a month, will bring new records in circulation, conducted as it will be with that kindly venom of which you alone, in the architectural world, are master… As regards the other papers. It would be advisable don't you think, to stop doing the same kind of thing for them. Any other kind of article, but not your "poissonal notes".' Letter from H. de C. Hastings to Reilly, 6 July 1937, Reilly Papers, Liverpool University Archive, Box D207/3/8.
52   'Editor's Note', *The Architects' Journal*, 21 October 1937, p. 609.
53   See the exchanges between Harold Falkner and Reilly in *The Architects' Journal*: 28 April 1938, pp. xxix–xxxi; 26 May 1938, pp. 893–94; 23 June 1938, pp. 1035–36.

contentious copy to help increase circulation, Hastings began to get cold feet when Reilly strayed into broader territory. In a letter to Reilly he states,

> In your last article on official architects which I think is absolutely magnificent, you mention at the end that the subject why architects ought to vote socialist or fight for the Spanish Government might make a possible future article. I hope you will not misunderstand me if I ask you whether you think it wise to write on such a theme. The question is not whether architects should have strong political convictions but whether they should discuss them in their own professional paper whose proper sphere is the techniques of architecture and not the politics of architecture. We all know of course that such water-tight divisions are artificial, but they serve a useful purpose.[54]

Reilly was finally encouraged by his editor to temper his political outbursts in the column and produce a less contentious copy – at least in relative terms – dealing with architectural personalities of the day. Hastings wrote to Reilly, saying,

> We have been considering our New Year policy and the question of 'Professor Reilly Speaking' has come up for discussion. To stop you [sic] mouth ie to prevent you starting a new world war in the *Architect's Journal* it looks as though we have got to try and pin you down to some subject that you can get your architectural teeth into… The tempting morsel I have to offer… devote your monthly commentary to an architectural personality… dealing with him somewhat in the manner you dealt with Goodhart-Rendel, only perhaps including your own assessment of his contribution to the architectural scene… Everyone will enjoy reading it immensely, and the more pungent it is, the more they will enjoy it.[55]

Reilly replied,

> I… can see your point of view very clearly. As long as I write about general topics I shall probably drift into the one topic which is filling all our minds or become purely banal and dull. I think your idea… is a very good one provided he is not one of those established old buffers of whom we are all tired. I should like to deal with the good, younger men… The sort of people I have in mind are: Velarde, Cachemaille-Day, Chermayeff, Armstrong, Maxwell-Fry and I might even include the winners of the Rome…[56]

---

54 Letter from Hastings to Reilly, 19 January 1938, Reilly Papers, Liverpool University Archive, Box D207/3/8.

55 Letter from Hastings to Reilly, 7 December 1938, Reilly Papers, Liverpool University Archive, Box D207/3/8.

56 Letter from Reilly to Hastings, 9 December 1938, Reilly Papers, Liverpool University Archive, Box D207/3/8.

Reilly's later writing increasingly concerned itself with matters of town planning in general and post-war rebuilding in particular. In articles such as 'Architecture after the War'[57] and 'Building the Britain of Tomorrow',[58] he outlined his vision of the society that would take shape after the war, and the suitable architectural expression for this brave new world. He wrote in a variety of publications on a similar theme, as well as providing comments on various planning debates for inclusion in other journalists' articles. With the publication in numerous newspapers and journals of the ideas expressed in his 'Reilly Greens', and Lawrence Wolfe's book on the Reilly Plan, Reilly brought a number of these theories together in a short pamphlet entitled *Architecture as a Communal Art.* A reviewer noted that

> Sir Charles Reilly shows quite simply how the great periods of Greek, Gothic, and to a lesser extent Roman, architecture were inspired by the same communal spirit, and then asks whether there is any likelihood of our achieving it again. Sir Charles thinks that any hope of this rests on two things: the discovery and development of new building materials, and 'some new social need or needs of a similar universal character'... Although he recognised that steel and ferro-concrete 'are not so easy to play with as stone and wood', he believes that they will eventually establish their own conventions... but whether we can share his confidence in the invigorating influence of 'the big co-operative enterprises of whole towns and the great undertakings of the State' is more open to question.[59]

Reilly's concern with the historical precedents to his theories on communality as a solution to the problems of modern urban living can also be seen in the various articles he contributed to books published in the final years of his life. His article on 'The Heritage of the Town' examined the historical development of Britain's towns and cities. It concluded by noting that the modern developments in town planning then underway would result in urban environments that were 'not only places of historical interest but, as towns should be but so rarely are, examples of the finest works of man'.[60] To *The Architects' Yearbook*,[61] for which Reilly was on the editorial board, he contributed an article on the 'Best Buildings of the Year'. Similarly a short article for the *Official Architect* on 'Wooden Houses'[62] mixed historical

57   Reilly, 'Architecture After the War', *Manchester Guardian*, 18 October 1940.
58   Reilly, 'Building the Britain of Tomorrow', *Telegraph and Independent*, 16 December 1940.
59   J. H. B., 'Art', *Journal of Education*, June 1945.
60   Reilly, 'The Heritage of the Town', in M. Lightman (ed.), *The British Heritage*, Odhams Press, London, 1948, pp. 209–45.
61   J. Drew (ed.), *The Architects' Yearbook*, Paul Elek, London, 1945.
62   Reilly, 'Wooden Houses', *Official Architect*, February 1946, pp. 80–82.

overview and contemporary post-war concerns with fast economical erection and standardization techniques. Pieces such as these characterized the last articles Reilly completed before his death. His journalism had long been regarded as integral to his general architectural and academic career, and following his death in February 1948, in one of the many tributes that were paid remarking upon his skills as a writer, *The Observer* noted that

> Sir Charles Reilly... made architecture vivid to pupils and readers in a unique way. To call him the School-Master-builder is to honour him for his great work at Liverpool University as well as in journalism. Architecture can be very dull in print. Reilly could turn a column of prose into a pillar of steel and stone that met the mind's eye with a gleam...[63]

Subsequent commentators have been less enamoured with Reilly's journalistic efforts and while acknowledging the importance of his writing in the context of his career, they have detected other motivations. Powers notes that

> Reilly's journalism at the time continually harps on the new cult of youth, and he seems to have been prepared to turn it in any direction in order to remain in the stream of contemporary affairs.[64]

This seems too harsh a judgment on Reilly, and suggests an insincerity that is at odds with the evidence I have outlined above. While his writing does demonstrate obvious moves towards the Modernist perspective throughout the 1920s and 1930s, often inconsistent and sometimes illogical, Reilly was not the stylistic opportunist Powers suggests. Perhaps a better insight into the contradictory nature of Reilly's writing can be seen in Budden's interpretation. Mediating between the hyperbole of the obituarist and the notion of Reilly as a careerist, Budden addresses the personality behind the writing and acknowledges the attendant shortcomings:

> As a journalist he had an initial advantage which few writers and still fewer architects possess: he actually enjoyed writing. The volume of his output was astonishing and what he wrote was almost invariably readable. He, at least, belied the saying that easy writing makes hard reading. His articles might be – indeed usually were – dashed off at enormous speed, sometimes with a fine disregard for the nicer points of grammar and syntax, but they were so lively, so amusing and so provocative that their appeal was immediate and general... He had the rare gift of making architecture comprehensible and interesting to

63 'Comment', *The Observer*, 8 February 1948.
64 Powers, 'Architectural Education in Britain', p. 269.

laymen: and in exploiting that gift he performed a great educational service...
Although he could on occasion pay tribute to architectural scholarship, he was
not himself greatly interested in historical research: nor did he as a rule over-
value factual accuracy. On most issues, political as well as aesthetic, he preferred
to be the warm and generous-hearted partisan rather than the objective judge.
Often he seemed to reach his conclusions through his emotions rather than his
intellect: and in architecture certainly his emotions served him well.[65]

In an assessment of Reilly's journalism it is possible to identify aspects of
his writing that illustrate facets of his professional and personal life. From the
early 1920s, when Reilly's journalistic career began to take off, broad themes
emerge, such as his identification of the need to stimulate architecture's connection with the general public, something which he understood could best be
communicated in publications not necessarily associated with architectural
criticism. In journals such as *John O'London's Weekly* and the *Liverpool Post*, he
discussed important local and national architectural themes with which his
readership could identify. That is not to say that Reilly was content to write for
the lowest common denominator; his journalism was often controversial in
its content but written with sufficient enthusiasm for its subject matter that
his criticisms were always entertaining and engaging. Combined with this,
Reilly mixed discussions of his numerous foreign trips that brought an
international dimension to the pages of provincial newspapers reflecting his
own interests in the universal nature of architecture – a point of view that
often set him at odds with his contemporaries. His foreign trips took him to
many of the major centres of European Modernism, as well as to North
America, North Africa and India, and while his pieces contained discussions
of the architectural aspects of the town or city visited, they combined this with
a broader cultural debate of the societies that were generating these new ideas.
In this Reilly was instinctively aware that it is often in the inconsequential
details that we can best understand and identify with another culture.[66]

Another common theme that ran throughout his journalistic career was
an interest in the decorative aspects of architecture, and he continued to
pursue this even when he became a convert to Modernism. In articles such as
'The Tunnel Entrance',[67] 'Colour in Concrete Buildings'[68] and 'Painting

65 L. B. Budden, 'Charles Reilly: An Appreciation', *RIBA Journal*, Vol. 55, No. 5, March 1948, pp.
    212–13.
66 Among the places Reilly visited were North America, France, Germany, Holland, Belgium, Italy,
    Austria, Switzerland, Spain, Scandinavia, North Africa and India.
67 *Liverpool Post*, 8 August 1934.
68 *Manchester Guardian*, 16 June 1935.

Architectural Stonework',[69] Reilly discussed the use and misuse of decoration in architectural schemes. Reilly's political views were often explicitly expressed in many of his articles, and his correspondence with Hubert de Cronin Hastings is testament to how this could lead to difficulty. If Reilly's attempts at overt political posturing were curtailed, we can detect implicit political references in articles such as 'The Epstein Statues'[70] in which his defence of the work of the emigré American Jewish sculptor Jacob Epstein – whose work and radical views had so disquieted the British art establishment – reaffirms his political sympathies. While Reilly wrote for a variety of journals throughout the 1930s and 1940s spanning the political spectrum, he was also a regular contributor to publications such as *Tribune* and *New Statesman and Nation*, in which he wrote on a variety of social and planning issues. He seemed able to maintain a dialogue with a wide variety of audiences, through his journalism, at a time when the political scene was particularly fractured.[71]

While the honours Reilly received towards the end of his life were ostensibly awarded for his contributions to architectural education, it is more than likely that the large body of articles he produced throughout his career played a considerable part in their conferment. Why it was Reilly, among all the other provincial architects, who was able to carve out a niche for himself and become a much respected figure to a number of the key members of the national and professional press was perhaps due as much to good luck as any natural ability to communicate in the written word. Reilly, as in other aspects of his career, was fortunate in making the acquaintance of influential people in the London journalistic world, impressing them by virtue of his natural charisma, enthusiasm and writing ability; but in that respect it is unlikely he was unique. Certainly his campaigns with regard to the Architectural Board of Education and early writing and publishing activities marked him out as opinionated and willing to speak out against the prevailing orthodoxies – all of which must have impressed editors and proprietors looking for entertaining copy.

It is interesting to speculate about what might have happened had Reilly been born 20 or 30 years later than he was. While he made a brief foray into

69 *Liverpool Post*, 6 August 1938.
70 *Manchester Guardian*, 5 June 1935.
71 The political scene during this period was as ever prone to cliques and sub-groups, not least on the left. As Valentine Cunningham notes, 'If we think of the 30s as a seamless political whole we are grossly distorting them. Even on the Left there was great disunity… for thinking and creative Leftist people, the same mixed shades and ragged divisions obtained.' V. Cunningham, *British Writers of the Thirties*, Oxford University Press, Oxford, 1989, p. 33.

the world of broadcast journalism in the late 1920s with a series of talks for the BBC, he largely confined himself to the written word. Given what we can gather of Reilly's extrovert personality, had he been born at the turn of the century perhaps his journalistic career might have led him more into the developing fields of radio and television. On the other hand had Reilly been born into a later era he may well have become part of the London celebrity lecture circuit centred around RIBA, and perhaps by doing so he would have lost touch with those skills as a writer that enabled him to successfully communicate with professional and non-professional readerships. As it is, the body of journalism Reilly left provides a fascinating insight into the 'personal Reilly', together with a valuable series of snapshots of the evolving local, national and international architectural and cultural scene in the first half of the twentieth century.

8 Moves Towards Modernism

The development of Modernism in Britain has been presented, depending on the writer's outlook, as either constituting the importation of an alien European style, inappropriate for the true national style, or as the rehabilitating and revitalizing element of a decadent British design philosophy. Writers such as Nikolaus Pevsner in *Pioneers of Modern Design*, first published in 1936, and *The Sources of Modern Architecture and Design* of 1968, suggested that Britain's influence in the development of twentieth-century architecture lay primarily in the work of William Morris and the proto-Modernist phase pre-1900. It then became dormant from the turn of the century until the arrival of European emigrés in the early 1930s. Pevsner claimed that

> England's activity in the preparation of the Modern Movement came to an end immediately after Morris's death. The initiative now passed to the Continent and the United States, and, after a short intermediate period, Germany became the centre of progress. English writers have not failed to acknowledge this fact: but hardly anybody has tried to explain it. One reason may be this: so long as the new style had been a matter which in practice concerned only the wealthier class, England could foot the bill. As soon as the problem began to embrace the people as a whole, other nations took the lead...[1]

Pevsner goes on to construct a theory which suggests that the work of Gropius, Morris and Ruskin forms a neat historical unit. Outside this unit, whole design philosophies such as Art Nouveau, as well as the developments of entire countries such as England, could be discounted. For Pevsner,

> Gropius regards himself as a follower of Ruskin and Morris, of van de Velde and of the Werkbund. So our circle is complete. The history of artistic theory between 1890 and the First World War proves the assertion... that the phase between Morris and Gropius is an historical unit. Morris laid the foundation of the modern style: with Gropius its character was ultimately determined.[2]

---

1 N. Pevsner, *Pioneers of Modern Design: From William Morris to Walter Gropius*, Penguin, Harmondsworth, 1986, p. 27.
2 Pevsner, *Pioneers of Modern Design*, p. 39.

Such a theory of nationalistic determinism suited Pevsner's own agenda well. However, subsequent writers have taken a rather more pluralistic approach, which attempts to address the variety of expressions of proto-Modernism and Modernism during Pevsner's 'lost period'. Tim Benton suggests that the traditional view espoused by Pevsner *et al.* was not the whole story:

> It is said that Gropius used to advise students at the Bauhaus to ignore history. Behind all the rhetoric, however, the influence of the German Classical tradition, notably of the Schinkel type, influenced every design Gropius ever made.[3]

The question of technology and the related themes of standardization, mass-production and functionalism as the exclusive preserve of Modernist theory, was outlined by Modernists as

> Mass production, the inevitable purpose for which the first power-driven machine, the modern tool was invented, today can be utilised for the production of essential elements for the millions who at the moment lack them... Mass production and prefabrication of all essential structural parts of the simplest dwellings could contribute some form of standardised architecture.[4]

As Paul Greenhalgh notes, 'Mass production and prefabrication were embraced as being the means through which Modernism could arrive on the streets.'[5] This had served as the traditional view of the development of Modernism, and is challenged by Simon Pepper and Mark Swenarton, who note,

> For a scheme [Dormanstown] of this scale, stated the Liverpool school, the mass production of standardised components was essential. Using language and argument curiously similar to that employed by Muthesius, Gropius and other Modern Movement theorists, Lionel Budden declared that in mass housing individual treatment of the elements of the house was impossible.[6]

Pevsner's assertions concerning Britain's apparent failure to advance Modernism from 1900–1930 as being based on nationalistic peculiarities of class and social structure are re-examined by Julian Holder. Holder acknowledges the ambivalent nature of Modernism's progress in Britain, but deals with the issue

---

3   T. Benton, 'The Myth of Function', in P. Greenhalgh (ed.), *Modernism in Design*, Reaktion Books, London, 1990, p. 45.
4   S. Chermayeff, 'The Architect and the World Today' (1935), quoted in R. Plunz (ed.), *Design and the Public Good*, Cambridge, MA, 1982, p. 117.
5   Greenhalgh (ed.), *Modernism in Design*, p. 10.
6   S. Pepper and M. Swenarton, 'Neo-Georgian maison-type', *Architectural Review*, Vol. 168, 1980, p. 90.

from a more complex angle than that of Pevsner:

> Modernism has had ambivalent success in Great Britain... Whatever argu-
> ments might be put forward to explain this ambivalence, lack of presentation
> cannot be maintained as one of them... Indeed, some of the official and quasi-
> official bodies which were set up in Britain to promote 'good design', ie
> Modernism, served as models for other countries... This essay explores the
> presentation of the Modernist cause in Britain... in terms which go beyond the
> generalisations of 'national temperament'.[7]

Reilly's role in these moves towards Modernism, both through the
Liverpool School of Architecture and into his retirement, needs to be
examined in the light of both the Pevsnerian model and other recent
reassessments. Alan Powers notes,

> The common view in the past has been that Reilly's lack of awareness of
> European proto-modernism in the pre-1914 period implicated him in the 30
> wasted years between the completion of Glasgow School of Art and the
> construction of the Boots D10 building by Owen Williams in 1930... This view
> identifies the future modern style and traces its gradual and inevitable
> dissemination around the world. To concentrate on America, as Reilly did so
> emphatically in the 1920s, was arguably to unbalance English architecture...[8]

Typically, this traditional view considered the intervening years as being
neatly split by the First World War, and did not recognize any sense of
continuity between the two. This affected the interpretation of Modernist
development in the 1920s. In Reilly's case, the period he spent during the war
as an inspector for the Ministry of Munitions could provide some clues to his
philosophical stance. Reilly was influenced in the matters of mass production
and standardization by the work of the ministry's head of design, Raymond
Unwin, and the government's Office of Works architects Frank Baines and
R. J. Allison, on munition workers' estates such as the 'picturesque' New Hall,
Woolwich. Certainly, the ideas regarding the standardization of building
components that characterized both the Duchy of Cornwall estates and
Dormanstown were informed by the consultative work Adshead and Ramsey
had carried out for the war effort. Contemporary commentators noted that

---

7   J. Holder, 'Design in Everyday Things, Promoting Modernism in Britain 1912–1944', in
    Greenhalgh (ed.), *Modernism in Design*, p. 122.
8   A. Powers, 'Liverpool and Architectural Education in the Early Twentieth Century', in J. Sharples
    (ed.), *Charles Reilly and the Liverpool School of Architecture 1904–1933*, Liverpool University
    Press, Liverpool, 1996, pp. 14–15.

the Neoclassical designs of Adshead and Ramsey formed part of a separate movement influenced by the New Hall estate, and were fated to be overwhelmed by it.[9] As Pepper and Swenarton point out,

> Time was to disprove this assertion. While the use of a variety of materials provided one answer to the problem of war-time shortages, there was a growing school of thought which looked to the standardization and mass production of materials and fittings to overcome this difficulty in both war and peace.[10]

Pepper and Swenarton argue that just such a continuity of approach existed in the Liverpool School during and after the war. Powers had argued that Reilly's own enthusiasm for American Beaux-Arts, which was regenerated after 1919, unbalanced the Liverpool School and led to a growing divergence in opinion between Adshead and Reilly – an examination of which is central to any investigation as to how Reilly came to his final Modernist position. While the ideas developed by the two men may have diverged after the war, what did unite them was a dislike of the Romantic and the Picturesque. The *Town Planning Review* of 1916 carried two articles by Budden and Adshead condemning these 'little coteries of Romantic enthusiasts' and calling for a 'standard cottage' which would

> depend for any attraction that it may possess, not on the toolmarks of the workman, not on its peculiarity or idiosyncrasy, nor in a word on its individuality, but on more general characteristics such as suitability to purpose and excellence of design...[11]

Reilly's own developing Modernism was evidenced in his journalism and books from this period. The general shifts in his design philosophy until his retirement from the Liverpool chair are also reflected in the work produced by staff and students throughout the period.[12] After his retirement Reilly's

---

9   See 'A Government Housing Scheme: Roe Green Village, Kingsbury', *The Builder*, Vol. CXIV, 1918, p. 5.
10   S. Pepper and M. Swenarton, 'Home Front: Garden Suburbs for Munition Workers 1915–1918', *Architectural Review*, June 1978, Vol. CLXIII, No. 976, pp. 366–75.
11   S. D. Adshead, 'The Standard Cottage', *Town Planning Review*, Vol. 6, 1916, pp. 244–49. See also L. B. Budden, 'The Standardisation of Elements of Design in Domestic Architecture', *Town Planning Review*, Vol. 6, 1916, pp. 238–43.
12   For an account of the two-way influences between Reilly and his students see J. Sharples, 'Reilly and His Students, on Merseyside and Beyond', in Sharples (ed.), *Charles Reilly and the Liverpool School of Architecture 1904–1933*, pp. 25–42.

commitment to and acceptance by the practitioners of the 'New Architecture' was demonstrated by his work on buildings such as the Peter Jones department store, London, 1935–1939, together with his honorary membership of organizations such as the MARS group in the 1940s.

The Liverpool School of Architecture 1919–1933

During the war, the school had been left in the hands of Reilly's second-in-command Lionel Budden, while Reilly worked as an inspector of munitions. The most pressing need following the war was to build the school back up to the position it had occupied previously, and there are numerous stories of Reilly's recruitment techniques, many of which do not seem to be entirely true.[13] Reilly spent time once again in Canada and the United States in the immediate post-war period, partly because of his wife's illness and also to renew his acquaintance with American contacts and revitalize his previous interest in American Beaux-Arts. The general design philosophy of the school continued in the early 1920s much as before. As Myles Wright notes, 'In the 1920s Reilly's students were rigorously drilled in the Classic Orders and in Classical designs.'[14] Certainly the work published in the *Sketch Book* of 1920 demonstrates this to be the case. While Reilly was able to continue to expound Classicism as the best style for Liverpool, developments on the continent nevertheless began to exert some influence on the work produced in the school as the 1920s progressed, albeit still interpreted through the Classical idiom. As Powers notes,

> The ethos of Liverpool in the 1920s remained Classical, although it was possible through the Beaux-Arts method to retain the principles and change the details towards a cooler or perhaps more Art Deco character…[15]

Indeed the Classical Beaux-Arts language proved to be more flexible than subsequent writers such as Pevsner were disposed to admit. *The Book of the Liverpool School of Architecture* from 1932, a catalogue of the school's work up until that date, illustrates the variety of styles employed and how they were ciphered through the Classical language of the 1920s. They include the

---

13   See R. Bisson, *The Sandon Studios Society and the Arts*, Parry Books, Liverpool, 1965, pp. 130–31.
14   M. Wright, *Lord Leverhulme's Unknown Venture*, Hutchinson Banham, London, 1982, p. 63.
15   Powers, 'Liverpool and Architectural Education', p. 15.

Monumental Classicism of the Egyptian State Telegraphs and Telephones Building, Cairo, by Maurice Lyon (Fig. 21); the domestic, square Georgian of Herbert Rowse's house at Gayton; the Art Deco treatment of Rowse's Martin's Bank Pavilion, Royal Agricultural Show, Manchester; the Jazz Moderne of Harold E. and H. Hinchcliffe Davies's Clock Inn, Liverpool; and the urbane Art Deco interior of 20 Belgrave Square, London, by Gerald Wellesley and Trenwith Wills (Fig. 22).[16] The book also contained photographs and a short essay on the design for the new building for the Liverpool School of Architecture. This illustrated what Ramsey called the 'modernism with ancestry' employed by Reilly, Budden and Marshall, both here and in their veterinary hospital scheme, also for Liverpool University.

The flexibility of the Beaux-Arts style, while having certain limitations, allowed Reilly to change the teaching of the school throughout this period, and so avoid the dogmatic stance of his one-time mentor Reginald Blomfield. Ramsey, in his essay in *The Book of the Liverpool School of Architecture*, describes this process as

> He [Reilly] is at the present moment with Professor Budden and his other colleagues initiating (or perhaps I should say has initiated – I prefer to keep to terms of relativity) what purports to be a very important – and not less important because local and peculiar – contribution to 'Modern' architecture. I am here using the word 'modern' to mean the beginning of a new epoch as something distinct from the traditional – and yet... Behind these fresh and sometimes startling presentations of designs for modern buildings, is the quiet force of a traditional culture... the new modern note at Liverpool... is modern with a difference... It is, if I may so phrase it, 'Modernism with ancestry'...[17]

The ancestry Ramsey describes can be traced through the work of staff and students throughout the inter-war period, and while they are not always consistent in style or chronologically neat in progression, they share the common feature of the adaptation of Classicism – with varying degrees of success – to Modernism. The work of the Liverpool student Frederick Williamson in collaboration with Frank Emley on the University of Witwatersrand, Johannesburg (from 1922) displays the typical Liverpool manner of Monumental Classicism on a Beaux-Arts plan. Edgar Quiggin and Ernest Gee's housing scheme on Muirhead Avenue, Liverpool, draws heavily on the

16   D. Thistlewood, 'The Liverpool School of Architecture Under Charles Reilly', unpublished paper read at a study day at the Reilly exhibition, Walker Art Gallery, Liverpool, 9 November 1996.
17   S. C. Ramsey, 'Charles Herbert Reilly', in Budden (ed.), *The Book of the Liverpool School of Architecture*, Liverpool University Press, Liverpool, 1932, pp. 27–28.

designs produced by Adshead and Ramsey in their Kennington and Dormans-town estates, particularly in the use of neo-Georgian detailing – a fact that Reilly acknowledged in his 1931 book *Representative British Architects of the Present Day*.[18] Similar tendencies can be seen in Herbert Rowse's design for the Rainhill housing estate, which combines neo-Georgian proportioning with a move towards stripped Classicism in the cubist treatment of the door and window casements. Full-blown stripped Classicism is demonstrated in Charles Anthony Minoprio's and Hugh Grenville Spencely's extension to the School for the Blind, Hardman Street, Liverpool of 1931. Reilly wrote enthusiastically about the building, considering it 'strong and good and fresh and modern with interesting details – indeed with all the things one wants and so rarely finds'.[19]

Architects such as Rowse illustrate this shift in microcosm. In Liverpool, his move from the Monumental Classicism of India Buildings in the early 1920s, through the stripped Classicism of his ventilation towers for the Queensway Tunnel in the early 1930s, to the Dudokesque cubist-inspired Philharmonic Hall of 1939 illustrates his own growing awareness of Modern-ist theory, tempered by Classical considerations. Similarly, Francis Xavier Velarde's work on ecclesiastical buildings in Liverpool and beyond provides a successful fusion of Classical and Modernist theory. For example, Velarde's Church of St Gabriel, Blackburn (1932–1933) was described by Pevsner in *The Buildings of England* as 'One of the milestones in the (late) development of English church architecture towards a twentieth-century style'.[20] B. A. Miller's St Christopher's, Norris Green, Liverpool (1930–1932) demonstrates the same bold massing. As Powers notes, 'Miller… specialised in churches, being to some extent Verlarde's Anglican opposite number. St Christopher's is one of his earliest, playing on the elliptical arch theme with success.'[21]

Of the schemes designed but never built, Alwyn Sheppard Fidler's design for a skyscraper tower (1929–1930) provides evidence of Reilly's own enthusiasms for Classically dressed American Monumental architecture as expressed in his 1924 book *Some Architectural Problems of Today*.[22] The 'city of towers' theme was to become a common feature of the Modernist vocabulary,

18 Reilly, *Representative British Architects of the Present Day*, Batsford, London, 1931, pp. 25–26.
19 Letter from Reilly to C. A. Minoprio, 10 December 1931, quoted in Sharples (ed.), *Charles Reilly and the Liverpool School of Architecture 1904–1933*, p. 132.
20 N. Pevsner, *The Buildings of England: North Lancashire*, Penguin, Harmondsworth, 1969, p. 65.
21 A. Powers, 'Mersey Marvels', catalogue to the Thirties Society Liverpool Visit, 23–24 September 1988, p. 11.
22 Reilly described the experience of the New York skyscrapers at night as 'towers of light floating in the sky…' Reilly, *Some Architectural Problems of Today*, Liverpool University Press, Liverpool, 1924, p. 175.

via Le Corbusier's city plans. When in 1931 Edwin Maxwell Fry was commissioned to produce a drawing of the city of the future as part of the development of New York, he produced a hybrid design that drew heavily on his Liverpool School training, combining it with the Modernist ideas being promoted through the writings of Le Corbusier, Taut and so on. Le Corbusier's influence can also be seen in the 1932 design for a silk factory by Gordon Stephenson – Stephenson had worked with Le Corbusier in Paris in 1931–1932. On its publication in 1932 *The Book of the Liverpool School of Architecture* provided few built examples of the full-blown Modernist style – an exception is George Checkley's house at Conduit Head Road, Cambridge (Fig. 23); but had it been produced a few years later, many more Modernist designs by ex-Liverpool students could have been included. Work such as Checkley's Thurso House, Cambridge (1932) and Maxwell Fry's Sun House, Hampstead (1934–1935) were prime examples. By the end of the 1920s a number of publications, most prominently the translation of Le Corbusier's *Towards a New Architecture*, had begun to have major repercussions on architectural thinking and required a response from all commentators on architecture regardless of their previous design philosophy. For Reilly, who read the book while travelling to India with Sir Edwin Lutyens in 1927, Le Corbusier was 'that strange young man… whose first disturbing book we had with us'.[23]

Reilly's Responses to Modernism

Reilly's position vis à vis the developing Modernist movement was somewhat ambivalent by the end of the 1920s. In a series of BBC radio broadcasts under the general title 'Some Modern Buildings' from 1926 to 1927,[24] he sought to tackle the architectural problems facing 'The Office Block', 'The Small House of Today' and 'The Town of Today'. In the first of the series, 'The Modern Problem', Reilly stated that 'there is a fine modern English architecture being done today which is as expressive of our time as the Georgian was of the eighteenth century'.[25] The architecture Reilly had in mind was clearly based on a Classical Beaux-Arts model. However, when addressing the question of the full-blown Modernism of Mendelsohn and other Europeans, Reilly's position

23   Reilly, *Scaffolding in the Sky*, Routledge, London, 1938, p. 267.
24   The series is listed in the Reilly papers in Liverpool University Archives. Only one of the talks is dated, 'The Street of Today', broadcast on 25 February 1927. Reilly Papers, Box D207/27.
25   Reilly, 'The Modern Problem', Reilly Papers, Liverpool University Archive, Box D207/27, p. 2.

becomes more equivocal. In a broadcast from around the same time entitled 'The New Architecture', Reilly said,

> Erich Mendelsohn's strange concrete structures which appear to be rising in various parts of Germany and to be finding their echoes and admirers in other countries need not unduly alarm us. If we are to have them however let us hope they will be built in garden cities or in other isolated places where the new life, the new morals and the new architecture can all flourish together.[26]

The dilemma facing Reilly over European Modernism can be traced back to 1925, when he condemned it in an article in *The Architects' Journal* for 'consciously trying to create a new style out of thin air'.[27] Indeed, Ramsey's definition of 'Modernism with ancestry' informed his philosophy throughout the late 1920s and early 1930s, and was shared by a number of other British commentators and architects. Anthony Jackson states that Amyas Connell's ground-breaking – at least in British terms – house High and Over (1930) relied heavily on Connell's own Classical training. He noted that 'Even though the Y-shaped plan... is novel, its exterior spatial development is traditional... What is new for Britain is the treatment of its form...'[28] For Jackson, this is due to the fact that

> For the Classicist, modern architecture was part of a logical historical sequence but in physical design, the Classical tradition was stylistically a handicap, for a contemporary discipline was not just a matter of avoiding obsolete motifs but also of transforming the rules of composition.[29]

The conflict Jackson detects lay in the dichotomy of reality and appearances which a number of contemporary commentators believed was inherent in Modernism:

> the logic of the new architecture was more often symbolic than real. Based on a machine mythology, the aim was not just to imitate the technological process but to create a new species of modern objects. The modern architect extolled the virtues of the utilitarian engineer but copied him more in spirit than in practice. Appearances were more important than actuality.[30]

26 Reilly, 'The New Architecture', p. 3, Reilly Papers, Liverpool University Archive, Box D207/27.
27 Reilly, 'Recent American Architecture', *The Architects' Journal*, 29 April 1925, p. 648.
28 A. Jackson, *The Politics of Architecture: A History of Modern Architecture in Britain*, The Architectural Press, London, 1970, p. 22.
29 Jackson, *The Politics of Architecture*, p. 23.
30 Jackson, *The Politics of Architecture*, p. 12.

The arguments for and against Modernism, as expressed by Jackson, bear similarities to the theories put forward in Geoffrey Scott's book *The Architecture of Humanism*, as well as to the debate Reilly had engaged in about the cultural significance of the Neoclassical style in the early 1900s. Scott had argued that 'for certain purposes in architecture, fact counted for everything, and that in certain others, appearance counted for everything.'[31] This allowed, as Christopher Crouch notes, a

> reinforcement of the new set of cultural values that were attached to the new neoClassical building style... It is this acknowledgement of the ideological nature of the new Classical designs that legitimizes the assumption that Reilly was able to impose a set of cultural values on this style.[32]

At the end of the 1920s, Reilly seemed to have been unaware of the parallels between his earlier Neoclassical arguments and the current debate over the 'New Architecture', at least in terms of his publicly stated position. His wish to banish it to the periphery of British society in some 'isolated place' indicates that his mistrust of the new theories was still unresolved and that he did not consider it a suitable urban style. The possibilities of adapting his Classical preferences to accommodate Modernist theory were to remain untapped for several more years, at least until after his retirement. Around 1933 and his retirement from the Liverpool chair, he appears to have undergone something of a conversion which – if not quite the 'Pauline' one described by his former student Maxwell Fry – put him firmly on a Modernist course. Early indications of this can be detected in the design Reilly produced in collaboration with Budden and J. E. Marshall for the new Liverpool School of Architecture building in 1932–1933. This design manages to look back to the Classical preferences of the early years of the school, and forward to Modernism. Fry's conversion to Modernism, according to his own account, took place while standing in front of Devonshire House, Piccadilly, during the course of its construction in 1925 (Fig. 18). Devonshire House was designed by the New York firm of Carrere and Hastings in collaboration with Reilly. Fry states that he

> stood contemplating over the hoardings the rising volume of the new Devonshire House in Piccadilly. The steel framework had been standing there for some time in sufficient elegance, and what I saw now was a crust of

31 G. Scott, *The Architecture of Humanism*, Constable, London, 1914, p. 61.
32 C. Crouch, 'Design Initiatives in Liverpool 1881–1914', PhD thesis, Liverpool University, 1992, p. 135.

stonework… being hung and bolted and jointed on to the framework like so much scenery. Broad but flat-cut Florentine rustications… were joining in an elaborate cornice, with over it a frieze of fat cherubs… Memories of New York and the school established their provenance. I knew it all like a game played out, and in those duplicating amorini, the last of their long line, I thought to find the cherubic face of my naughty professor playing Ariel to old man Hastings in New York and turned in a gesture of moral revulsion from everything I had been taught.[33]

His actual turn towards Modernism, while absolute, appears not to have happened until around 1932 – that is, at about the same time that Reilly's own awareness of Modernism was gaining a new impetus. This apparently dramatic change of tack may not have required so great a shift in mindset as converts to Modernism like Fry would like to imply. As Jackson notes, 'The aspiring modern architect with a Beaux-Arts training, wishing to obey Le Corbusier's exhortations, had no need to change his method but only his formula.'[34]

Whatever the actual circumstances of Fry's conversion, Reilly's own seems to have been more gradual; this is borne out by an examination of his writings from the early 1930s. In *The Theory and Practice of Architecture*, he devotes the final two chapters to an examination of the Modern Movement in the United States and Europe. His allegiance to American architecture remains as strong as ever, but his earlier antipathy to European Modernism shows signs of softening. In Modernism he felt,

> it appears that the most powerful and satisfactory structures are those for some isolated factory, where the various units of the group can be seen both as individual structures and in relation to the group.[35]

Reilly states that the German and Dutch examples 'To an Englishman or an American… have… the effect of a giant prison where the individual is reduced to an inconspicuous unit.'[36] He preferred the Viennese model which 'has prevented the rigidity and mechanical appearance of the German and Dutch…,'[37] preferring their 'curved plan forms, which are certainly not dictated by function.'[38] He goes on to praise in particular the Swedish position,

33 E. Maxwell Fry, *Autobiographical Sketches*, Elek, London, 1975, p. 136.
34 Jackson, *The Politics of Architecture*, p. 20.
35 Reilly, *The Theory and Practice of Architecture*, Victor Gollancz, London, 1932, p. 132.
36 Reilly, *The Theory and Practice of Architecture*, p. 134.
37 Reilly, *The Theory and Practice of Architecture*, p. 134.
38 Reilly, *The Theory and Practice of Architecture*, p. 135.

singling out Gunnar Asplund's work and stating that Swedish designs are 'free interpretations of the Classical or Gothic motives controlled by the excellent taste and personalities of the designers'.[39] This, as I have already stated, has a familiar ring to it, being in line with Blomfield's preferences for Scandinavian Modernism as outlined in *Modernismus*.

This, by and large, was to be Reilly's position within the Modernist range, leaning more towards the Oliver Hill approach and drawing on a stylish, eclectic, debased rendition of the Modernist language – at least from a purist's perspective.[40] This shift can be judged against Reilly's earlier antipathy to the Stockholm Town Hall design of 1923 by Ostberg, which he had condemned in his 1925 article for *The Architects' Journal*. The annual articles Reilly wrote for *The Architects' Journal* during the 1930s also provide an insight into Reilly's growing acceptance of Modernism. The small but significant number of Modernist buildings appearing in the professional journals must have played a part in Reilly's move towards a Modernist stance, not least because a number of them were being produced by his former students.

If Reilly's public pronouncements on Modernism from the beginning of the 1930s indicate that he was not totally committed, a small but nevertheless interesting account from his personal life gives an indication of his developing attitude towards the movement. While staying with his old friend and colleague Augustus John at Fryern Court, Fordingbridge, during the early autumn of 1931 in order to sit for his portrait, Reilly wrote a series of letters to his wife. In one of these he states 'I have suggested his [John] building a large new studio, modern, in ferro concrete, and he likes the idea...'[41] There is no other documentary evidence to suggest that Reilly had any other hand in what eventually was built. John's chosen architect, Christopher Nicholson – younger son of the painter Sir William Nicholson – produced two designs. The first was a looser interpretation of Modernist principles, and the second and executed design was, as David Dean notes, 'built to a precise mathematical grid, the reinforced concrete frame has been raised for maximum light on stilts, in the approved Corbusian manner...'[42] John wrote back to Reilly the

39   Reilly, *The Theory and Practice of Architecture*, pp. 140–41.
40   For an account of Hill's responses to Modernism as well as his other work using his highly individual design philosophy, see A. Powers, *Oliver Hill: Architect and Lover of Life*, Mouton Publications, London, 1989.
41   Letter from Reilly to D. Reilly, 9 September 1931, Reilly Papers, Liverpool University Archive, Box D207/37/3.
42   D. Dean, *The Thirties: Recalling the English Architectural Scene*, Trefoil Books, London, 1983, p. 35.

year after the studio was completed to say that it had been a great success.[43] Such a commission fitted in with Reilly's view that the new style was suitable for those isolated places where the new morality and new life could work together. Certainly a Modernist studio must have seemed appropriately avant garde to Reilly, and as such a suitable style for his notoriously bohemian friend. It would seem, however, to be more significant as an indicator of Reilly's growing adoption of a Modernist stance when placed in the context of his subsequent statements with regard to the new architecture.

As the decade progressed the position adopted by Reilly and a number of his contemporaries was marked by a sharp divide between those who chose to adapt to the 'New Architecture', and those who sought to remain with their original philosophical and stylistic position. Howard Robertson at the Architectural Association adopted a similar approach to Reilly. As Powers notes, he

> felt able to normalize it [Modernism] as an extension of their previous teaching but left to his successors the difficult resolution of Modernism's more demanding agenda of research-based design study in collaborative groups.[44]

A resolution which, as I have already stated, Budden managed to achieve through his lecture programme following Reilly's retirement in 1933.

Others, such as Albert Richardson at the Bartlett School, resisted Modernism. Sir Reginald Blomfield sought to attack the alien style which he saw as 'spread[ing] like a plague to this country...' Writing in *The Listener*, Blomfield stated 'As an Englishman and proud of his country I despise and detest cosmopolitanism.'[45] In a broadcast debate with Amyas Connell, Blomfield said 'whether it is communism or not, modernismus is a vicious movement which threatens the literature and art which is our last refuge from a world that is becoming more and more mechanized every day'.[46] Connell was astute in stressing the traditional aspects of Modernism – a parallel of Reilly's 'Modernism with ancestry'. In an attempt to defuse Blomfield's objections he said,

43 Letter from A. John to Reilly, 15 February 1935, Reilly Papers, Liverpool University Archive, Box D207/40/56.
44 Powers, 'Liverpool and Architectural Education', pp. 17–19.
45 R. Blomfield, *The Listener*, 26 July 1933.
46 'For and Against Modern Architecture', BBC broadcast debate, *The Listener*, 28 November 1934.

modern architecture is in the highest sense traditional... from its understanding of the spirit of the past it is able to create, not superficial imitations in this or that style, but living successors in the true line of descent.[47]

Such a stance, delivered from a sincere Modernist standpoint, was also used as a justification by those who were unwilling as yet to accept Modernism as a totally new style.[48] As Benton notes,

On the whole... the English tradition in the thirties was to contrast the supposedly rational and organic Georgian architecture with the eclectic and 'superficial' Victorian. A good example is the frontispiece of Yorke's book *The Modern House in England*, which juxtaposes Gropius's house in Church Street, Kensington, with a Georgian terrace row.[49]

The *Modernismus* debate divided commentators and must have played a central role in clarifying Reilly's position. In fact a number of the views expressed by Blomfield were close to Reilly's own position around this time. For example, Blomfield's opinion that

modern Swedish architecture [is] in some ways the most advanced of that of any country. In Sweden and Denmark, modern architecture has developed on different and very much sounder lines, and in England the best of our modern architecture follows, in the main, traditional lines...[50]

It is this emphasis on tradition, which Blomfield is careful to differentiate from revivalism, that distinguishes what he terms 'good Modernism' from 'bad Modernism'. Despite strong similarities in their opinions, Reilly gradually moved away from Blomfield's version of Modernism, based on tradition and national character, towards a purer and more mainstream Modernist stance.

By 1938 with the publication of his autobiography, Reilly was firmly in the Modernist camp and sought to make this clear when writing about his former mentor:

---

47   'For and Against Modern Architecture'.
48   For example, F. R. S. Yorke and Colin Penn in their 1939 book, *A Key to Modern Architecture*, said, 'To build in accordance with tradition is not to imitate in one period the obsolete work of a former time. It is to do as the architects of those periods did: to build for contemporary needs, getting the best out of the materials to hand. It is traditional to look forward, not to look back', p. 108. This was easily adapted by those who wished to justify Modernism in historical terms.
49   Benton, 'The Myth of Function', p. 46.
50   R. Blomfield, *Modernismus*, Macmillan, London, 1934, p. 61.

In those days Blomfield was very friendly to, and a great supporter of, the schools of Architecture in general and of Liverpool, I like to think in particular… Now I fear he thinks the schools are all Bolshevik institutions badly bitten with 'Modernismus' as he calls modern design, and that I am too tainted. I hope I am, for I like still to be alive.[51]

The previous year Reilly had ventured further into the Modernist debate over the planning and building regulations that hampered the erection of many Modernist buildings. In an article in *Building* from 1937 concerning the appeal over Serge Chermayeff's house at Bentley Wood, Sussex, Reilly attacked in mocking tones both the xenophobic stance of the likes of Blomfield, and the petty official attitude adopted by many local authorities towards modern building techniques:

Bungalows we have heard of, suburban villas we know and indeed have passed by the hundred, but what is this? Something foreign and therefore unpleasant in spite of its whiteness. Indeed one may be pretty sure of that. Our surveyor, that excellent authority on drains and road surfaces, says the building is un-English. What more do you want? So the blind lead the blind and naturally they lead to the ditch.[52]

It would seem that Reilly's earlier wish to see Modernism contained to some 'isolated place' had been replaced by a zealous campaign with a familiar theme, waged against those non-architects who in Reilly's opinion were attempting to restrict and encroach on the creative rights of the profession.

The increasing amount of literature in journals such as the *Architectural Review*, together with the publication of books such as Anthony Bertram's *The House, a Machine for Living In* in 1935 and F. R. S. Yorke's *The Modern House in England* in 1937, had led to a sea change in architectural thought in Britain. By the end of the 1930s Reilly's move towards Modernism was virtually complete. In an article for *The Listener*, Reilly wrote glowingly of Modernism:

very exciting… producing strange-looking, and even to some people alarming-looking, buildings. To others these buildings are already the symbol of a new and better way of life because they are a simpler, franker and more truthful expression of what they stand for and of their construction. They are no longer decked out in the fancy dress of long-past styles.[53]

51 Reilly, *Scaffolding in the Sky*, pp. 214–15.
52 Reilly, *Building*, April 1937, p. 136.
53 Reilly, 'Modern Movements in Architecture', *The Listener*, 29 March 1941, pp. 399–401.

Nevertheless, despite his growing appreciation of Modernism, he still felt it necessary to provide some historical justification and context. The article was illustrated with photographs by Modernists such as Gropius and Alto, together with Charles Rennie Mackintosh, Frank Lloyd Wright and Herbert Rowse, in order presumably to underline American and British sources. If a part of his conversion can be traced to the influence of former students teaching their 'old' professor a few new tricks, Reilly's continued association with the likes of Maxwell Fry would enable him to gain entry to the inner circle of British Modernist thought. In 1944 it was Fry who proposed Reilly as an honorary member of the influential Modern Architectural Research (MARS) group.

The Modern Architectural Research Group (MARS)

The formation of the MARS group came out of an approach in 1933 by Sigfried Giedion – the Swiss secretary of the Congres Internationaux d'Architecture Moderne (CIAM) – to Morton Shand, to form a group to represent England at future congresses. The founding members of MARS represented the nucleus of Modernist thought in Britain and consisted of Wells Coates as chairman, Maxwell Fry as vice-chairman, F. R. S. Yorke as secretary, together with Modernist pioneers such as Connell, Ward and Lucas. However, the criteria for membership was strict, if not always consistent. As John Summerson notes, 'MARS was nothing if not exclusive. Architects with an established reputation for mild versions of modernity, like Oliver Hill and Gray Warnum, were considered not to be doctrinally sound...'[54] Even prominent figures from the architectural community such as Howard Robertson, who had been an early promoter of the Modernist cause, were denied entry to the group. On the other hand one of the main innovations of the group was to bring in non-architects such as John Gloag and John Betjeman,[55]

54   J. Summerson, 'Architecture', in B. Ford (ed.), *Early Twentieth Century Britain: The Cambridge Cultural History*, Cambridge University Press, Cambridge, 1992, p. 240.
55   Like Reilly, Betjeman might seem at first to be an unlikely member of the MARS group and apologist for the Modernist cause. A tribute to Sir John Betjeman written shortly after his death shows the two men to have a number of similarities. The writer noted that 'The enemy... was not Modern Architecture but the knighted traditionalists – Baker, Blomfield and Co. Betjeman was a friend of Frederick Etchells, the translator of Le Corbusier, and of P. Morton Shand, who first made the *Architectural Review* go Modern. He was even a member of the MARS group, although it is unlikely that he took his colleagues' pretensions very seriously.' 'Sir John Betjeman', *The Thirties Society Journal*, No. 4, 1984, p. 1.

who had both contributed to the pace-setting journal *Architectural Review*. The main remit of the group was to undertake research into the problems of modern architecture and to move towards a solution. One of its early members, Ove Arup, recalled that the aims of the group were not always clear:

> While I was a member of the executive committee of MARS, we spent a whole year discussing what Modern architecture really meant, and what MARS really stood for. It was supposed to mean 'Modern Architectural Research group', but what kind of research? Apparently, it was supposed to be into heat and sound insulation of walls, acoustics, light angles and so on. I pointed out that this is engineering or building research and that we, as a group predominantly of architects, were neither competent or equipped to undertake it. We should do architectural research: planning research. Lubetkin maintained that no two architects would be able to agree on architectural questions – that was Art, a personal matter – and that architectural research was nonsense.[56]

The group spent a good deal of its time arguing over dogmatic points of architectural theory, with few unanimous conclusions being reached. Its various committees examined matters related to legislation, schools propaganda, lectures, housing and building costs. The period before the outbreak of the Second World War was arguably the group's most productive phase. By the time of MARS's 'New Architecture' exhibition at the New Burlington Galleries in 1938, which sought to celebrate the group's progress in synthesizing building needs and contemporary techniques through Modernism, 'The peak... had already been passed',[57] and by the end of the 1930s, 'it was the MARS group itself that had lost its reforming zeal'.[58]

It is perhaps because the group's ideals had been relaxed following the pre-war high point that a figure such as Reilly could be proposed as an honorary member in 1944 when others had earlier been refused or reprimanded by MARS for alleged contraventions of the strict ideals of Modernism.[59] The group's discussions had formed part of a debate that taken place in Britain

---

56 O. Arup, 'Art and Architecture, The Architect–Engineer Relationship', *RIBA Journal*, Vol. LXXIII, 1966, p. 354.

57 Jackson, *The Politics of Architecture*, p. 60.

58 Jackson, *The Politics of Architecture*, p. 75.

59 For example, when Connell, Ward and Lucas entered a Neoclassical design for the Newport Civic Buildings competition in 1936, they were called before a meeting of the MARS group to explain their actions in abandoning Modernism. As Jackson notes, for the members of MARS 'changing one's style to meet the situation suggested a superficiality of artistic involvement that was unacceptable...', Jackson, *The Politics of Architecture*, p. 69. This attitude was quite obviously to change in the coming years, when stylistic pragmatists such as Reilly were accepted into the group.

throughout the 1930s around the promotion of Modernism and the education of the public's taste for an appreciation of Modern design. Many of the participants were ambivalent as to how this might be achieved, and while articles in *The Listener* and talks on the BBC were felt to carry sufficient intellectual gravitas, other channels that might arguably have allowed more direct access to the man in the street were considered too populist to be appropriate to the aims of the group. The members of MARS were typical of a broader paternalistic attitude that existed in the British establishment with regard to mass design education. In the case of MARS, it led to considerable conflict in their approach to spreading the Modernist word, with one faction pushing for a greater mass market approach. As David Dean notes, 'MARS was not merely an inward looking collection of theoreticians. They had a keen sense of public relations...'[60] However, as Maxwell Fry recalled,

> we, as a group, and I always insisted very strongly on this, had nothing to do with the general press, with the general media, because the ideas were too difficult to bridge the gap between ourselves and the *Daily Mail*, or even with television when it came. We had to go through another stage to spread our ideas. We had first to present our ideas to the talkative intellectuals of the age.[61]

Perhaps sensing that the Modernist message was not making as much headway as they would have liked, and realizing that the war would create a new climate, the members of MARS needed a different approach to publicity. Reilly fitted well the role of the 'talkative intellectual', while his connections with Fry and the work he had recently undertaken on the Peter Jones store gave him enough Modernist credentials to enter the group without it appearing to have compromised its principles too much. It is interesting to speculate how Reilly's more populist style of journalism – which he continued to write throughout this period – was viewed by the remaining hardline members of the group.

Reilly's first involvement with the group appears to have been to chair a meeting held in December of 1944, in which the topic for discussion was appropriately enough 'What is Modern Architecture?' The meeting was reported in *The Builder*, where the writer noted that

> A bad London fog did not prevent the meeting of the MARS group... but an intellectual fog seemed to affect those who took part in the proceedings. More

60   Dean, *The Thirties*, p. 113.
61   E. Maxwell Fry, 'How Modern Architecture Came to England', Pidgeon Audio–Visual PAV 3/800, no date.

than one speaker complained that the discussion did little to answer the question, 'What is Modern Architecture?'[62]

It was attended by a number of Reilly's former students, among them William Holford, Anthony Minoprio and Peter Shepheard, who seemed to share the opinion that 'architecture was not an affair of personalities'. This perhaps reflected the ethos Reilly had promoted for so long at Liverpool during their student days. However, the general tone of the discussion was fractious, resulting in few useful conclusions being reached. Interestingly, one speaker identified a problem that would plague Modernist architecture and help to discredit it in the post-war period: the level of finish and quality of materials used. For example, Anthony Chitty was reported to have commented that

> modern architecture could be improved in finish, colour and texture. As to finish too many details were skimmed over… With regard to colour, our buildings had been dull and the choice of materials meagre. If we look at buildings that had been up 10 years we saw cracked and crazing concrete, dirty and blotched rendering, faded colours etc.

It was not a new concern and had been raised some 10 years earlier in *Modernismus*, but had been lost among the more sensational nationalistic language Blomfield had employed. The discussion generally underlined the fact that the group had indeed passed, as Jackson noted, its 'white hot' revolutionary phase and abandoned its initial aim to undertake research; it had become a mere talking shop. Reilly concluded the meeting by drawing on the philosophy he had himself promoted at Liverpool concerning the eradication of individualism from architectural practice. In doing so, he adapted his stance from his previously preferred Neoclassical context, and applied it to the Modern condition. He is reported to have said that

> the new architecture was humanism in the new age which the war and everything else was bringing. It must be grand to be young today, looking ahead to an architecture that would rank with the Greek and other things of the past, when the individual would be content to work with the group and sink his personality. The evil time we had been going through was due to the emphasis that the individual architect, the individual commercial man and the advertising person had laid on his own individuality. So long as that existed no great work could be done.

62 'What is Modern Architecture? MARS Discussion at RIBA', *The Builder*, 29 December 1944, p. 510.

The reports of the meeting in publications as diverse as *The Illustrated Carpenter and Builder* and the *Evening Standard* all concentrated on the modern and youthful outlook Reilly had adopted in his definition of modern architecture. *The Illustrated Carpenter and Builder* noted that

> The principle discussion of the meeting of the 'Mars' group was 'What is Modern Architecture?' And what it seemed to be was the subject of much deliberation on the part of hundreds of young architects. Sir Charles, however, out-youthed the youngest of them by his definition: 'A new conquest of space with the help of new materials.'[63]

From such accounts a casual observer might well have believed Reilly to have represented the radical edge of a movement that was, not least by his own efforts, increasingly filtering into the consciousness of the public via the popular media.[64]

Modernism Revisited

A questioning of the whole basis of Reilly's former associations with Classicism is evident in a number of his statements, both public and private, from the early 1940s onwards. In a letter to Giles Gilbert Scott from 1942, Reilly states, in what is an astonishing *volte face*,

> The Liverpool fellows in my time did all go through the discipline of Classical architecture. Except for the precision of its rules I wish now it had been Gothic, for Gothic with its constructional basis is much nearer modern stuff with its steel and ferro concrete basis. I wish you had been born 10 years later though you would have missed your Liverpool Cathedral. You would have been the ideal person to lead the Modern Movement out of its crudities and find some form of decorative expression for its products which it has not found yet.[65]

During a series of monthly discussions during 1946 and 1947, Reilly continued to maintain that he belonged firmly within the Modernist camp. He was prepared even to express regret for his hand in the earlier promotion of

63 'Calling All Readers, Martians Sound a Martial Note', *The Illustrated Carpenter and Builder*, 12 January 1945, p. 29.
64 For a full account of the media promotion of Modernism throughout the 1930s and 1940s, see J. Holder, 'Promoting Modernism in Britain 1912–1944', in Greenhalgh (ed.), *Modernism in Design*, pp. 123–43.
65 Letter from Reilly to Gilbert Scott, quoted in A. Powers, 'Architectural Education in Britain 1880–1914', PhD thesis, Cambridge University, 1982, pp. 269–70.

Classicism. In a discussion from October 1946 with, among others, Alfred Bossom MP, Clough Williams-Ellis and Philip Hepworth concerning the role of assessors in architectural competitions, Reilly's statements provide an interesting indication of just how far down the Modernist road he had travelled:

> *Reilly:* I feel there has been a tremendous revolution in architecture in the past 20 years. I assessed long ago a competition under the old idea, one in Liverpool that was won by a Classical design. But the real thing that won it was that it gave twice the accommodation for a set of offices by using modern steelwork and then hiding it. It solved the modern problem with a Classical facade, and all the steel that did the work was hidden. But it will be on my conscience until I die.
> *Hepworth:* Why on your conscience?
> *Reilly:* I feel the main thing that settled the award was the solving of the problem of getting a tremendous amount of extra floor space by a certain form of steel construction. But the steel was all hidden, and there was no indication of it inside or out, yet this had been a new and at the time extraordinary use of steel.
> *Hepworth:* But why on your conscience if it was a good plan and satisfying to the clients? Did anybody give more space by other means?
> *Reilly:* I would have liked an architecture that was truthful.
> *Tripe: Did* any other competitor give more space by other means?
> *Williams-Ellis:* Don't you think if the Greeks had had that same steel they would have done the same thing?
> *Reilly:* They would have let you know the steel was there.[66]

By the time of his death in 1948, if statements such as those above are to be believed, Reilly was a complete convert to Modernism. His conversion had been less than wholehearted to begin with, and with characteristic enthusiasm he may well towards the end of his life have overstated his reservations regarding his previous enthusiasm for Classicism. His retreat from Neo-classicism and Beaux-Arts was more a pragmatic acknowledgement on his part that his position had become untenable than any idealistic conversion. It was certainly Reilly's pragmatic nature that stopped him from following Blomfield's line and painting himself into a nationalistic corner.[67]

Other factors also worked in Reilly's favour in maintaining at least the appearance of a relatively smooth transition from Classicism to Modernism. First, the timing of Reilly's early retirement from the Liverpool School meant

66   'Dinner for Six', *The Builder*, October 1946, p. 301.
67   The relationship between Reilly and Blomfield is interesting. Blomfield wrote to Reilly in 1912 congratulating him on his papers on Monumentalism and hoping that Reilly would continue to hammer at the 'idiotic' modernism of modern architecture.

that he was free from the restraints of teaching and the maintenance of an ethos associated with the Liverpool School, at around the same time that Modernism was gaining ground in the philosophical debate. This allowed him a clean sheet on which to develop a new position through his writing and architectural work. Secondly, the fact that a number of his former students – notably Checkley and Fry – were in the vanguard of British Modernism and had developed links with those European Modernists who temporarily settled in Britain gave Reilly a certain Modernist credibility. While Reilly did not have a monopoly on former students working in a Modernist idiom, his natural publicity skills gave him the advantage over his contemporaries when it came to promoting his own opinions. Thirdly, despite his later reservations regarding the validity of Classicism, much of the Classical philosophy Reilly had espoused at Liverpool was adaptable to the new Modernist rhetoric, requiring only a shift in emphasis in order to make a logical case. In an examination of Modernist philosophy in the introduction to *Modernism in Design*, Paul Greenhalgh identifies a list of theoretical features that characterized the movement. These included social morality, truth, technology, function, internationalism/universality, and the transformation of consciousness, among others. Many of these features share elements of Reilly's earlier vision of Beaux-Arts Classicism. Social morality and the transformation of consciousness were central to the ethos of the Department of Civic Design as espoused in the pages of the *Town Planning Review*. Reilly's emphasis on the role of technology in his early promotion of Classicism and its role as the preferred teaching method within university schools of architecture is echoed in the Modernist philosophy. However, it is perhaps the internationalist/universal nature of Modernism that has most in common with Reilly's vision of an international Beaux-Arts, and allowed him to adapt to Modernism with relative ease. Internationalism appealed to Reilly both from a political point of view – being central to his socialist outlook – and also architecturally since it avoided the 'national style' debate that continued to occupy parts of the architectural community and prevented other Classicists such as Blomfield adopting Modernism in the 1920s and 30s.

While it is possible to judge the degree to which Reilly moved towards a Modernist position by reference to his writings and other activities, just how convincing his conversion was is debatable. For some commentators such as Myles Wright, the omnipotent influence of his former professor can be detected in the 'New Architecture'. Writing in 1937 Wright said,

I have always felt privately that Mr Fry was one of the few British architects who are completely masters of this treacherous modern business. I now suspect that Liverpool has something to do with it: even that Professor Reilly may be behind it all.[68]

For later commentators the whole question of Classicism versus Modernism was less relevant. For James Stirling, studying in the 1950s under the system that had largely been shaped by Reilly, neither philosophy was wholly satisfactory, and he considered that both 'are for us now equally unfortunate. There surely must be another way driving down between them.'[69] This position is reiterated by the likes of Mark Crinson and Jules Lubbock, for whom Beaux-Arts is the precursor of the outdated and discredited 'Modernist Academy'. For Crinson and Lubbock, the methods pursued by Reilly and his successors at Liverpool had led to a Modernism which – based as it was on Classical methods – was ultimately ill-suited to modern architectural practice and educational needs:

> With Liverpool, as at the AA, there is an important distinction to be made between work produced in a Modernist mode and distinctively Modernist educational techniques. By and large the second of these were absent in British schools.[70]

Perhaps the success of Reilly's Modernist conversion is best summed up by his successor as Roscoe Professor, the scholarly Lionel Budden, a man not noted for his overstatement. Writing an appreciation for the *RIBA Journal* following Reilly's death in 1948, Budden noted,

> In the latter years of his direction of the Liverpool school his sympathies were engaged by work that was contemporary in spirit and technique and he became and remained an ardent champion of the virtues and possibilities of the new international architecture... he reached his ultimate aesthetic position by a route that had much to commend it, even if towards the end he found himself in the company of a somewhat odd assortment of fellow-travellers... whatever inconsistencies may have characterised his teaching it had one over-riding virtue: it presented architecture never as a dull, prosaic business but always as an affair of high adventure.[71]

68   H. Myles Wright, 'The Work of the Liverpool School', *The Architects' Journal*, 29 May 1937, p. 848.

69   J. Stirling, 'Reflections on the Beaux-Arts', *Architectural Design*, Vol. XLVIII, Nos 11–12, p. 88.

70   M. Crinson and J. Lubbock, *Architecture, Art or Profession?*, Manchester University Press, Manchester, 1994, p. 108.

71   L. B. Budden, 'Charles Reilly, An Appreciation by Professor L. B. Budden', *RIBA Journal*, March 1948, Vol. 55, No. 5, pp. 212–13.

9 Later Architectural Work: 1918–1939

Following the end of the First World War, Reilly and the School of Architecture found themselves in a very much less advantageous position than they had enjoyed before 1914. The disputes over the Blue Coat building, and the university's decision to accept Lever's offer to pay for a new building for the school on the main university campus, meant that their temporary accommodation consisted of cramped conditions in the old Lock Hospital in Ashton Street (the building was dubbed 'Reilly's Cowsheds'). Reilly recalls in his autobiography that the school now consisted of

> a poor little shrunken thing, in half of one of the two wards of the old disused Lock Hospital in Ashton Street, where the university library now stands. The school ward was shared with the Professor of Pathology, who kept animals for experimental purposes behind a partition. It was a miserable show. Not only were there poor squeaking animals, but in the basement below there were rats, which from the history of the place we took to be syphilitic. After our beautiful old Blue Coat Hospital, with its ranges of ample rooms and its lovely courtyard, I could not stand it. Something had to be done to 'burst' it up. We must, at any rate, get hold of the whole of the building for ourselves.[1]

This he achieved by going on a recruitment drive, increasing student numbers to such an extent that the university authorities were forced to allocate the whole of the building to the School of Architecture. The offer of a new building was, for various reasons, delayed for a number of years and while Reilly played a role in its design, his early retirement meant that he did not get to enjoy the benefit of a purpose-built building. In a series of letters between Reilly and the university treasurer from 1922, Reilly complained of the fact that the school still occupied the Lock Hospital premises, rather than the new building they had been promised:

1 C. H. Reilly, *Scaffolding in the Sky*, Routledge, London, 1938, p. 203. It is interesting to note here an example of Reilly's inconsistencies in his 1938 autobiography. He had earlier described the Lock Hospital building as 'a little low Georgian building… very insignificant at first glance, but with a certain reticence and character… there is no struggle anywhere for effect: everything is of the right size and at the right level, even to the door handles.' Reilly, *Some Liverpool Streets and Buildings in 1921*, Liverpool Daily Post and Mercury, 1921, p. 67.

In the agreement between the then Mr W. H. Lever and the university of the 4th of April 1910 Lord Leverhulme promises to pay for a new building together with a site for it for the School of Architecture... The excellent site was bought in 1914 and a design made by me for the new building which was approved by the university... The result... is that through a series of misfortunes for which it was in no way responsible, the School of Architecture has lost both its old and new home, either of which would more worthily have expressed the leading position the Liverpool school holds than the present hospital building.[2]

Ironically, despite the unfavourable conditions in which the school was housed throughout the 1920s, this period proved to be the most productive in terms of Reilly's promotional activity. This would eventually provide the Liverpool School of Architecture with the highest profile of all the university schools in the country.

If the pre-war years had been short of architectural commissions for Reilly, the 1920s were to be equally lean; although he acted as an assessor for the new Liverpool Martin's Bank headquarters building and the Heswall Golf Clubhouse competitions – both won by the former Liverpool student Herbert Rowse – he built relatively little. The commissions Reilly did receive in the early years after the war consisted mainly of memorial work, both designing and acting as an assessor for various competitions around Britain and abroad. In 1920 Reilly visited Canada twice, as a jury member for the Canadian Battlefields Memorials competition,[3] while his designs for the Accrington War Memorial of 1922[4] and the County War Memorial, Durham, of 1928 were both produced in collaboration with Herbert Tyson Smith. The latter design is modelled on the Romanesque piers of Durham Cathedral using a similar incised patterning on the column. Reilly also acted as an assessor for the Dewsbury War Memorial competition of 1923–1924, which was won by William Naseby Adams and Eric Ross Arthur with Tyson Smith as sculptor. In addition he assessed the Liverpool Cenotaph competition in 1926, which attracted a number of entries from the university,[5] including that of the

---

2 Letter from Reilly to H. Rathbone, 17 January 1922, Vice-Chancellor's Papers, Liverpool University Archive, Box P4A/3/5.

3 See Reilly, *Scaffolding in the Sky*, pp. 223–24 and p. 237.

4 'The Accrington War Memorial', *The Builder*, 22 October 1920.

5 Reilly wrote to Sir Archibald Salvidge that 'I have carefully considered the position of the proposed Cenotaph on St George's Hall Plateau... There is... only one place for the Cenotaph... between the statues of Queen Victoria and Prince Albert centrally on the transverse axis of the Hall. The Cenotaph... should be a long low monument lying parallel to the Hall.' Proposed Cenotaph, Report of Professor C. H. Reilly to Council, 22 February 1926. See also Cenotaph (Special) Committee, Reports to Council: 2 December 1925, 27 February 1926, 3 March 1926, 7 July 1926, 27 October 1926. Liverpool Record Office, Liverpool Central Library, Box H325 COU. See also T. Cavanagh, *Public Sculpture of Liverpool*, Liverpool University Press, Liverpool, 1997, pp. 98–102.

winner Lionel Budden with sculpture again provided by Tyson Smith.[6] The design produced by Budden, as published in *The Builder*,[7] was altered slightly in accordance with requirements written into the rules by Reilly, although the relief panels on the side of the cenotaph appear to have remained unchanged. Aside from this work, the first half of the 1920s appears to have been a fallow period for Reilly in terms of major architectural commissions with one exception, Devonshire House.

Devonshire House, Piccadilly, London

Reilly's resentment over his perceived ill-treatment by the university authorities continued to occupy him after the end of the war. While the great building programme of the pre-war years had ceased, Reilly turned to his journalistic work both to promote the school on a national and international level and also as a means to compensate for the lack of architectural work on offer. It was through his journalism that the major piece of work Reilly undertook in the 1920s came his way. In his autobiography he states that

> I had written a picturesque sort of article for *Country Life* suggesting that the new buildings for London university should be on the river… It was never published… Edward Hudson, the editor of *Country Life*, handed the proof over to his friend J. B. Stevenson, the managing director of the great firm of Messrs Holland and Hannen and Cubitts… I received a telegram one day… asking me to meet him at the Adelphi Hotel… He greeted me with 'It is not about the site for the university… but about Devonshire House, Piccadilly… We think the right thing to do is build an American apartment house on it… It is very important that we get the right American architect for the job. You, I believe, know them all… ' Finally I mentioned Thomas Hastings… That appeared to settle it. He called for a cable form and wrote out a message… 'Would you design with Professor Reilly as joint architect a million pound apartment house on the site of Devonshire House, Piccadilly?' All I could do was to stutter out a suggestion he should add: 'British scale of charges.'[8]

Reilly travelled to New York to work on the scheme on the understanding that a number of his students should be engaged to work on a variety of the interiors.[9] In the event the designs Reilly produced in 1924 were quite radically altered,

6   The winners were announced on 15 October 1926 and published in the Report to Council dated 27 October 1926. Liverpool Record Office, Liverpool Central Library, Box H325 COU.
7   'Liverpool Cenotaph', *The Builder*, 22 October 1926.
8   Reilly, *Scaffolding in the Sky*, pp. 226–28.
9   For an account of one of Reilly's student's experiences in the New York office of Carrere and Hastings during this period see E. Maxwell Fry, *Autobiographical Sketches*, Elek, London, 1975, pp. 95–98.

and due to an overestimation of the viability of the size of the project the scheme was dramatically reduced.[10] As Reilly recalled,

> It was too big for its time. Finally two-thirds of the site was sold off... Stevenson went back to America to get a new scheme, which was the one actually built. That had little to do with me therefore except that by some strange luck my outline of the masses to Piccadilly survived throughout.[11]

Despite being a fine and rare example of Monumental American Beaux-Arts produced by a leading American architect in London,[12] the final scheme, when completed in 1927, was already seen by a number of commentators as out of date (Fig. 18). Between its original conception in 1924 and its realization in 1927, both Reilly's and the broader architectural community's taste had started to retreat from this form of American Classicism in favour of the developments coming out of Europe. For long-standing enemies of Reilly such as Charles Rennie Mackintosh, the building provided the ammunition with which to criticize him as 'a 23rd rater'.[13] For former students of Reilly such as Christian Barman, the setting-back of the upper stories of the building in the American style was illogical and unnecessary, conforming as it did to an American planning regulation that did not apply in London.[14] Maxwell Fry cited the building's heavy decoration in the form of Renaissance cherubs and so on as the turning point in his adoption of a full-blown Modernism.[15] Reilly also had reservations over the use of decoration on the building; his nephew Sir Patrick Reilly recalled that '[Hastings] insisted on the rather fussy decoration on the exterior of the building which Uncle Charles disliked heartily.'[16]

---

10 The building was mentioned in a review of recent architecture: 'British Architecture in 1926', *The Architect and Building News*, Vol. CXVII, January 1927, p. 54.

11 Reilly, *Scaffolding in the Sky*, p. 230.

12 Reilly and Hastings read a paper on the Devonshire House scheme to RIBA in 1927. See *Architect and Building News*, Vol. CXVII, 3 June 1927, p. 937.

13 Quoted in T. Neat, *Part Seen: Part Imagined*, Canongate Press, Edinburgh, 1994, p. 174. See also letter from C. Rennie Mackintosh to his wife, 1 June 1927, Mackintosh Archive, Hunterian Museum and Art Gallery, University of Glasgow.

14 C. Barman, *Balbus, or the Future of Architecture*, London, 1926, pp. 50–51.

15 Fry's account that his conversion to Modernism was almost Pauline in its suddenness is disputed by Alan Powers who states in the entry he wrote on Fry for the *Dictionary of National Biography* that 'Fry's conversion to Modernism was gradual, and came principally through his membership of the Design and Industries Association, which introduced him to modern German housing... The conversion is evident at Sassoon House in Peckham (1934)...' A. Powers in C. S. Nicholls (ed.), *Dictionary of National Biography 1986–1990*, Oxford University Press, Oxford, 1990, pp. 146–47.

16 Quoted in J. Sharples (ed.), *Charles Reilly and the Liverpool School of Architecture 1904–1933*, Liverpool University Press, Liverpool, 1996, p. 94.

The Devonshire House scheme is one of the last physical manifestations of Reilly's allegiance to Monumental Beaux-Arts. From the late 1920s he would, with varying degrees of enthusiasm, turn his attentions to Modernism. However, despite the apparent declarations of Modernity, much of what Reilly subsequently said and designed would not stray far from his earlier Classical preferences.

The Leverhulme Building, Liverpool

The new building for the School of Architecture that had been promised by Lever before the First World War was finally realized in the early years of the 1930s. The design Reilly had produced in 1914 was unsuitable by 1930 due to the expansion of the school in the intervening years, and a new design was developed on a new site behind a group of houses on Abercromby Square, one of the city's early nineteenth-century squares that had recently been acquired by the university (Fig. 25). The design for the building was previewed by Budden in *The Book of the Liverpool School of Architecture* in 1932, in which he stated that

> In the planning and general treatments of the buildings, work on which is now in progress, two objects have been principally sought – an efficient architectural arrangement of the various elements comprised in the scheme and the adaptation of the four houses to their new functions without sacrificing the qualities which characterise them both internally and externally. Modifications in the existing fabric have been as few as possible. For the new two-storey structure containing the main studio accommodation design in the simplest terms has been thought to be most appropriate. Externally, brick is being used as the facing material of the broad surfaces, as the facades of the existing houses are of brick. The walls of the central court are being finished with a cream stucco to ensure adequate light in the adjacent portions of the building. For the rest the internal walls of the studios are to be of unplastered light grey brick, these studios being conceived as workshops in which a more elaborate treatment would be out of place.[17]

The attention to architectural good manners in the external treatment of the building followed Ramsey's description of Reilly's new style as 'Modernism with ancestry', and as if to underline the Classical origins of this new architec-

17   L. B. Budden, 'The New School Buildings', *The Book of the Liverpool School of Architecture*, Liverpool University Press, Liverpool, 1932, p. 68.

ture, in the central courtyard of the building – arguably the most successfully Modern section of the design – it was planned to place a Greek doric column 'as a symbol of architecture and of permanent architectural values' (Fig. 26).[18]

The building was opened on 21 July 1933 by Viscountess Leverhulme,[19] and reviewed by *The Builder* in which the correspondent noted that

> The new Leverhulme building is planned simply round an attractively paved courtyard, with its main axis parallel to Bedford Street. It is two stories in height, and it has on the ground floor two immense studios, a materials bureau, and a large lecture theatre: on the first floor it has three large studios, a lecture room, and a large 'crit room,' specially arranged for the hanging of drawings. In planning, construction and design the whole building is intensely reasonable. It is quite free from any stylistic affectations, and has been built with the greatest of economy... It will be noticed that the studios on the ground floor are side-lit by the large expanses of glass in the external wall. Here, quite logically, the largest amount of light is needed... In architectural design this building... goes to the very heart of its subject without any confusion, obscurantism, or weak-kneed compromises with what the ordinary person regards as architecture. The purpose of a school of architecture is to provide well lighted studios in which students may work and an atmosphere in which they may think clearly, unprejudiced by stylish features of some passing phase: an atmosphere also which will remind the student of that cool reasoning which is the basis of his art.[20]

The anonymous correspondent, who may well have been Ramsey himself given the similarities in tone with his own earlier preview, constantly stresses those elements of the building – efficiency, functionalism, logic and freedom from 'stylistic affectation' – which gave it a Modernist credibility. Yet the writer is also careful to link these elements to a deeper and more enduring tradition from which Reilly, Budden and Marshall are said to have drawn inspiration. This is demonstrated by their successful marriage of the new school building with the older section that consisted of 'solid Georgian houses... reconditioned to their former Georgian elegance...'[21] A reviewer for the *Manchester Guardian* saw the building as 'a good example of "functionalism" at its sanest and best'.[22] The combination of the old and new is also picked out by later

---

18 Budden, 'The New School Buildings'. The column was to have come from the recently demolished chapel of the Liverpool School for the Blind on Hardman Street.

19 *Liverpool Daily Post and Mercury*, 22 July 1933.

20 'The Liverpool School of Architecture', *The Builder*, 28 July 1933, pp. 141–47.

21 'The Liverpool School of Architecture', p. 141.

22 *Manchester Guardian*, quoted in *The Builder*, 28 July 1933, pp. 74–78; Reilly Papers, Liverpool University Archive, Box D207/3/1.

commentators such as Pevsner, who noted that 'The extension... obviously endeavours to harmonise with the square and yet be modern of a kind still rare in England by 1932.'[23]

Reilly, Budden and Marshall designed two other schemes in a similar style to the Leverhulme building: the Veterinary Hospital at Liverpool University (1926–1928, Fig. 24), and an extension to Reilly's 1909–1914 students' union building of 1935. Pevsner describes the latter building as an 'indifferent, tentatively modern brick extension...'[24] Perhaps the reason for the failure of this scheme can be found in the application of architectural good manners, and the fundamentals of the 'Modernism with ancestry' theory. Whereas the Leverhulme building had harmonized with the early nineteenth-century town houses of Abercromby Square and their strict Classical composition, the union building extension attempts to address itself to Reilly's hybrid neo-Grec/Beaux-Arts design. The quality of Reilly's interpretation of Modernism was dependent – at least in these extension schemes – on the purity of the Classicism to which it was attempting to address itself. A better example of Reilly's variations on the Modernist theme can be found in his contributions to the Peter Jones department store in Sloane Square, London (1935–1939), conceived and built as a single unit.

Peter Jones Department Store, Sloane Square, London

The origins of William Crabtree's involvement in the design for the Sloane Square store date from 1929, when he produced a design for a department store in Oxford Street for his final year thesis at Liverpool. Reilly sent photographs of the design, which had recently been published in *The Architect and Building News*, to his friend Spendan Lewis, chairman of the John Lewis Partnership. The design was heavily Art Deco-influenced and was described by the reviewer as showing 'aptness for good arrangement. The internal alley, which provides extra display space is ingenious, although this must be very dark when the front cases are filled with goods.'[25] Lewis engaged Crabtree as a research assistant on the proposed rebuilding of the Peter Jones store in Sloane Square (Fig. 27). This entailed travel to Holland and Germany to view work

23   N. Pevsner, *The Buildings of England: South Lancashire*, Penguin, Harmondsworth, 1969, p. 201.
24   Pevsner, *South Lancashire*, p. 200.
25   'Design for a Department Store on Oxford Street by William Crabtree', *Architect and Building News*, 26 July 1929, pp. 114–15.

produced by leading Modernist designers, such as Mendelsohn's Columbus House. After a short delay, work commenced on the new store, and Reilly was engaged as consultant architect, while John Slater and Arthur Moberly were appointed as joint architects, together with Crabtree. As Crabtree noted,

> the Chairman invited Slater and Moberly, a firm of architects which had recently built a large store for Bourne and Hollingsworth, to join with Reilly and myself in designing and building Peter Jones. Reilly and I were to be responsible for design and appearance, and Slater and Moberly for the working drawings and contractual matters. Of course there was some friction as we were all opinionated people, and rival schemes were argued over at the building committee. Reilly did the talking on our side while I produced the drawings, and I think we persuaded Slater and Moberly that we were not such crackpots as they first thought. What soon became evident was that in the early 1930s money was just not available for the heavy masonry kind of buildings prevalent and that modern steel buildings demanded a different approach.[26]

The early section of the building was reviewed in *Building* in 1935, in which the writer described it as

> colourful, gay, and vivacious. The tall mullions are fronted with bright metal, the side returns of which are faced with red glazed faience tiles: the corner member is also covered with faience of a rich green tint. The railing at the top is painted an Indian red, and the casement frames are coloured dull green-grey. At the ends and around the entrance door the walls are faced in polished marble of a colour and figuring resembling Lunel. The marquise is painted a glossy cream: the shop fronts are in antique bronze, and the entrance doors are of bright metal with a diagonal square panelled motif. Some of the panels are glazed, others are painted red.[27]

The Art Deco colouring of the earlier section of the building was modified in the subsequent section and replaced with a stricter, almost monochrome Modernist scheme. The reviewer in *Building* stated that

> Some modifications in the facing materials and general colour scheme have been made in the new building: the red glazed tiled returns to the mullions have gone, also the green tiles to the crowning cornice. White stucco replaces

---

26 W. Crabtree, quoted in Sharples (ed.), *Charles Reilly and the Liverpool School of Architecture 1904–1933*, pp. 151–52. For further accounts by Crabtree of his involvement in the store's design see *The Architects' Journal*, 5 March 1969, p. 615, and 11 March 1970, pp. 596–97. For a full account of Crabtree's unpublished memoirs see J. Bhoyroo, 'The Rebuilding of the Peter Jones Department Store by William Crabtree', BA dissertation, University of Newcastle, 1995.

27 J. R. Leathart, 'Current Architecture', *Building*, May 1935, p. 188.

the marble wall finishings – where there are portions of solid in this great array of void – to the upper floors. The metal balustrade surmounting the main wallhead is no longer coloured red: this restraint has the effect of robbing the design of a great deal of its original vivacity.[28]

The modifications to the later sections were thought detrimental by other contemporary commentators.[29] Reilly noted in a letter to Lewis from 1946 that

Giedion the Swiss-American architect, author of the fine book, 'Time, Space and Architecture', told me how he preferred the colouring on the small Cadogan Gardens front where the little red tiled strips remain beside the metal mullions.[30]

Crabtree's reference to 'friction' between the parties involved in the design team is interesting in the light of a series of letters between Reilly and Lewis in the 1940s. In his autobiography – published during the course of the building's construction – Reilly gives much of the credit for the building's design to Crabtree, saying,

it should be remembered as regards its [the Peter Jones store's] external expression I am but a small, if entirely consenting, partner. The real author of it is my dear old student William Crabtree. I stand behind agreeing and approving, and making an occasional suggestion. That however, is enough to make clear where I am architecturally today.[31]

Letters between Reilly and Lewis, written some five or six years after the completion of the building, paint a different picture. In a letter to Reilly in October 1945, Lewis expresses his own opinion about where the credit for the building should rest:

In the case of Peter Jones he [Crabtree] has got I believe, a great deal of credit that did not belong to him. If the building had been left entirely to him, its appearance would have been very far different and one of the features, that is, I understand, particularly admired by professional opinion and that really was his doing, was gained at the cost of a sacrifice of part of the site. The sacrifice

28 'New London Store', *Building*, July 1936, pp. 278–83.
29 The building was quite widely written about in the first few years after its erection. In a letter to Reilly from 23 November 1946, Lewis provides a list of references and illustrations from the RIBA library. Reilly Papers, Liverpool University Archive, Box D207/4/2.
30 Letter from Reilly to S. Lewis, 23 November 1946, Reilly Papers, Liverpool University Archive, Box D207/4/2.
31 Reilly, *Scaffolding in the Sky*, p. 287.

was slight and may have been well worth while but to achieve good effects by sacrificing the economic functions of the site is obviously a little like winning a game by breaking the rules.[32]

Lewis continues by saying

The trouble with William is that his temperament is so arrogant and domineering that he is really disqualified for team-work unless perhaps in circumstances that we are not able to give him… I have always been bitterly sorry that, when we asked your help in finding an architect, you recommended William instead of Holford.[33]

Reilly appears to have defended Crabtree throughout, but Lewis points out an inconsistency with Reilly's earlier estimation of Crabtree's ability as a designer (such inconsistencies were not uncommon with Reilly):

I notice that you say in your present letter that in your opinion William is 'the best young architect extant to-day'. But you may remember that, when we were in Liverpool, you told me that you would not consider that he was by any means the best of those who had been through your school and that, when I asked you whom you would rank above him, you answered, 'well, for one, Holford'. Obviously it is perfectly clear that you may have had since then ample reason for changing your mind but, when you write that you 'think his work at Peter Jones proves this', you are, to my mind, quite certainly mistaken, for I know for a fact that his work at Peter Jones was far less important to the general character of the building. That was due largely to the fact that it was not designed in the ordinary way, from the outside inward, but from the inside outward and it was further due largely to the preservation of a general effect of vertical lines and to a successful use of unusual colour. With all these three things William had no more to do than the man in the moon… Without having nearly your own extreme modesty of mind, magnanimity and gener-osity of temper, William might quite easily have held his place in our boat. The whole trouble is that his capacity to consider open-mindedly, good-humouredly and receptively ideas other than his own is so limited that for work of this particular kind he is for us an impossible colleague… as a team-worker we have carried to the limit our efforts to adjust ourselves to him.[34]

The crux of the dispute – and the resulting termination of Crabtree's contract with the John Lewis Partnership – centred on a clash of personality between

32 Letter from Lewis to Reilly, 13 October 1945, Reilly Papers, Liverpool University Archive, Box D207/4/2.
33 Letter from Lewis to Reilly, 13 October 1945.
34 Letter from Lewis to Reilly, 13 October 1945.

Crabtree and the partnership's Director of Building, Michael Allen. In his defence of Crabtree, Reilly appears to have stated that Allen had 'a deep prejudice against Crabtree', and that Lewis had in an earlier letter implied that it had been Allen who had designed Peter Jones. In a letter to Reilly, Lewis sought to deny the charges and once again placed the blame for the breakdown of relations squarely on Crabtree's temperament.[35]

This serves to illustrate that the public image of the Peter Jones store as having been designed by a team in which there were inevitable but amicably resolved creative disputes – an image promoted by both Reilly and Crabtree – was false. Further, Reilly's assertion that he had had little input to the final design of the building is also questionable. For Lewis, it was Reilly and not Crabtree who was the driving force behind the building's Modernist design. In Lewis's opinion Reilly had, due to his own sense of modesty, been unwilling to take the credit: 'I am very glad that the considerable share that William really had in the Peter Jones building, and the much larger share, that thanks, I believe, mainly to your own unselfish kindliness he is supposed to have had, have been so advantageous to him...'[36] While this can be accounted for as mere flattery between old friends, it is nevertheless an interesting indication of Reilly's role in this building in particular.

In a series of articles published in *Building* from 1946–1947, Reilly seems to have dispensed with his former rule that members of the design team should not break ranks, and should 'stand up for them [the designs] afterwards. We

35   Letter from Lewis to Reilly, 1 November 1945, Reilly Papers, Liverpool University Archive, Box D207/4/2. Allen finally resigned from his position of Director of Building. The incident is an indicator of Reilly's methods and the lengths to which he was prepared to go in the defence of a former student, as well as his habit of indiscretion, which on a number of occasions nearly ended in litigation. In a letter to Reilly dated 20 September 1946, Lewis says, 'Many thanks in the meantime for your letter. But I infer from it that Allen is not wholly mistaken in supposing that you are to some extent responsible for these rumours that he left us because of our dissatisfaction with certain procedures of his. In his opinion these rumours are likely to prevent his getting a valuable appointment that he might probably have got otherwise. They are completely false, for he left us wholly and solely of his own accord, quite against our intention and expectation... I could not attempt to deny that there have been... signs of very definite personal ill-will between Allen and yourself... due to the very strong paternal kindness that you show so conspicuously for your students... I should hope that there is no possibility of litigation... I can well believe that I had given you the facts as I know them and that I still feel no doubt whatever that I was perfectly justified in doing so... I should not have dreamed of doing so if I had thought that you would disclose them to anyone else without getting first of all my absolutely clear consent.' Reilly Papers, Liverpool University Archive, Box D207/4/2.
36   Letter from Lewis to Reilly, 23 January 1946, Reilly Papers, Liverpool University Archive, Box D207/4/2.

must not have folk ratting…'[37] Reilly contradicts his earlier modest claims to the building when he states in answer to the question 'Had you to "rank" (as they do tennis stars) famous foreign architects of recent date, what would be your first three choices and why?':

> *Reilly:* August Perret I would put first: and I rather think Asplund of Sweden… second: and Eric Mendelsohn who started a new type of store which I copied – Peter Jones – third.
> *Chairman:* Did Mendelsohn inspire it?
> *Reilly:* Yes.[38]

This is an interesting insight into Reilly's architectural ethos at the very end of his life, as well as confirmation of the striking similarities between the Peter Jones design and that of Mendelsohn's work, such as his Schocken department store. Mendelsohn's influence is also evident in student work at Liverpool; S. A. Marshall's fifth-year thesis design for a department store in Lime Street, Liverpool,[39] produced in 1935, demonstrates the continuing and growing influence of European Modernism on the school's ethos in the years following Reilly's retirement. Crabtree was also to acknowledge Reilly's role in the Peter Jones design in a letter to *The Observer* from 1959, in which he said 'that the building turned out as well as it did was remarkable and in great measure due to Reilly's enthusiasm and pertinacity'.[40]

Later commentators have usually described Reilly's contribution as a general guiding hand in the project.[41] Sir Edwin Lutyens described Reilly's contributions to both Devonshire House and the Peter Jones store in somewhat vitriolic terms:

> Professor Reilly, when not teaching architecture and architects, has shared authorship of two conspicuous 'modern' London buildings – conspicuous by virtue of their size and sites: the new Devonshire House, which is decorated with a replica of the Versailles frieze hung on a girder, and that curiously

---

37 Letter from Reilly to M. Allen, 22 December 1943, Reilly Papers, Liverpool University Archive, Box D207/4/2.
38 'Dinner for Six', *Building*, May 1947, pp. 152–55.
39 'A Department Store, Lime Street, Liverpool, by S. A. Marshall', *The Builder*, 19 July 1935, p. 113.
40 Letter from Crabtree to *The Observer*, 13 March 1959, quoted in Sharples (ed.), *Charles Reilly and the Liverpool School of Architecture*, p. 152.
41 See, for example, M. Effendowicz, 'The Modern Peter Jones: An Unusual Store', *The Gazette*, 11 October 1986, pp. 866–67; M. Scott, 'The Rebuilding of Peter Jones', *The Gazette*, 4 April 1992, pp. 243–45; E. Johnston, 'Sloane Leader', *Architectural Review*, Vol. CLXXXVII, No. 1115, January 1990, pp. 75–79; Bhoyroo, 'The Rebuilding of the Peter Jones Department Store by William Crabtree'.

rhomboid shop, Peter Jones. They are both 'modern' – or aren't they? Therefore, one can only conclude that the word, as indicating contemporary
architectural style, is entirely devoid of meaning.[42]

David Dean notes that the light-reflecting curved ceilings of the display
windows were a particular contribution from Reilly.[43] Reilly himself commented on this feature in a letter to Lewis from November 1946; while he does
not mention his part in the design, he does note that – along with a number of
other details from the original scheme – it was abandoned, and that the final
result was not as had been originally intended:

> Another innovation… was the provision of a continuous shop window with no
> division inside or out except for necessary doorways with a curved plaster
> background like that of the modern theatre so that, with appropriate lighting,
> the window dressing could appear as a continuous design standing out in
> infinite space, as in the built up scenery of the modern stage for an outdoor set.
> This too was abandoned…[44]

For William Curtis, the Peter Jones building ranks alongside Owen Williams's
Boots factory (1930–1932) as 'Two of the most remarkable buildings of the
Modern movement in Britain'; he notes the 'elegantly proportioned mullions
and urbanity of Peter Jones'.[45] Indeed, the proportions of the mullions are
basically Georgian,[46] which – according to Lewis – was due to his insistence. In
a letter to Reilly from 1945 Lewis said

> when our architects produced their first design for Peter Jones – a design
> reminiscent of the Pavilion [Mendelsohn and Chermayeff's De La Warr
> Pavilion, 1933–1935] that you like so much at Bexhill – I turned it down at
> once and absolutely insisted on a radical alteration of its general character, so
> that the impression made on the eye should be of perpendicular and not of

---

42 Letter from E. L. Lutyens to *Evening Standard*, 20 October 1942. Reilly Papers, Liverpool
    University Archives, Box D207/3/8. This attack was in reply to Reilly's own criticism of Lutyens's
    work on the 'Academy Plan' for the rebuilding of London after the war.

43 D. Dean, *The Thirties: Recalling the English Architectural Scene*, Trefoil Books, London, 1983, p.
    97. Dean notes that this information was given to him by Crabtree.

44 Letter from Reilly to Lewis, 23 November 1946. Reilly Papers, Liverpool University Archive, Box
    D207/4/2. Given Reilly's long-standing interest in theatre design his references to stage design
    add weight to the attribution of this particular feature to him, as Crabtree observed to David
    Dean.

45 W. J. R. Curtis, *Modern Architecture Since 1900*, Phaidon Press, London, 1996, pp. 335–36.

46 This point was made in a paper entitled 'A Dance to the Music of Time: Reilly, Regency and
    Modernism' read by Alan Powers to a study day for the exhibition 'Charles Reilly and the
    Liverpool School of Architecture', Walker Art Gallery, Liverpool, 9 November 1996.

horizontal lines and so that the building should not have the appearance, that, for example, the (to me) dreadful John Barnes building has, of a series of trays threaded on supporting uprights.[47]

The muted Classicism of the design must have appealed to Reilly's own 'Modernism with ancestry' philosophy, and may well have accounted for the building's almost instant appeal to both the general public and professional commentators alike.[48] A proposed scheme for a John Lewis department store for Oxford Street in London was also prepared by Reilly and Crabtree in 1937. However, this scheme was never built, as the ground landlord Howard de Walden preferred an alternative design by Moberly to the 'glassy bay-windowed proposal'[49] submitted by Reilly and Crabtree.

Anthony Jackson, while acknowledging the Peter Jones store's significance, places it in the context of what he considers to be a blind alley in the development of British Modernism:

few buildings were built in Britain and these were not part of any progressive development. The modulated glass facade of the Peter Jones store was designed by architects of no further consequence: Fry's Sun House, at Hampstead in London, with its eloquent balconies and canopies exquisitely balanced against an immaculately fenestrated facade, came between his slow struggle against a neo-Georgian training and his occupation with an indifferent Modernism.[50]

For Jonathan Glancey, the major achievement of the building was that the designers were able to convince the British public that 'Modern architecture was not some dangerous foreign perversion…'[51]

47 Letter from Lewis to Reilly, 1 November 1945, Reilly Papers, Liverpool University Archive, Box D207/4/2.
48 Reilly noted in a letter to Lewis that 'The best public appreciation of the Peter Jones building, in my opinion, is that which is summarised in the *Gazette* of which Crabtree says you have a file at Longstock. The BBC was asked at a *Brains Trust* one day which were the six best modern buildings, and that set *The Architects' Journal* trying to find out by a survey of educated public opinion. They got a jury of 60 (I think) together under the chairmanship of Lord Derwent, the President of the Georgian Society, which included the editors of the leading London papers and people of that sort. They published from week to week the voting, and though Battersea Power Station, the Liverpool Cathedral and lots of well-known buildings got votes, Peter Jones came out top. That is the most striking thing I can recall.' Letter from Reilly to Lewis, 23 November 1946. Reilly Papers, Liverpool University Archive, Box D207/4/2. See 'Scoreboard', *The Architects' Journal*, 25 May 1939, pp. 851–52.
49 Crabtree, quoted in Sharples (ed.), *Charles Reilly and the Liverpool School of Architecture 1904–1933*, p. 153.
50 Jackson, *The Politics of Architecture*, p. 54.
51 J. Glancey, *Twentieth Century Architecture: The Structures that Shaped the Century*, Carlton Books, London, 1998, p. 177.

Jackson's estimation of Reilly *et al.*, and their significance in the development of a British Modernism, is questionable. Certainly it contrasts sharply with one contemporary commentator's estimation of Reilly's transition to an appreciation of Modernism. In *The Architects' Journal* of 1937, this transition is described as follows:

> It can be said of him [Reilly] that there has been no one in this century who in his building and in his teaching has done so much to influence the course of English architecture: and no other single member of his generation who has reacted to post-war developments in so creative a way. The chasm between Devonshire House and Peter Jones is a big one... for many of our friends and neighbours a bottomless pit... but it is typical of Professor Reilly that he has leapt it, or perhaps it would be truer to say that he has waved the chasm aside with a noble gesture and, behold, there is no longer a chasm.[52]

This serves more as an insight into Reilly's rather imperious personal manner than as an accurate account of his handling of the move towards a Modernist stance. Reilly's adoption of Modernism can be described as having been 'managed... skillfully and productively'.[53] This was due to a combination of Reilly's own stylistic pragmatism and his growing realization of the 'inevitable development'[54] of Modernism, rather than being in any sense a leap of faith on his part. Reilly's real move towards Modernism was achieved not by a giant leap, and certainly not by any imperious waving aside of a chasm, but rather through a series of small and often meandering steps. These led along a path to, as Powers puts it, a largely 'unrealised future style'.[55]

---

52 'Editor's Note', *The Architects' Journal*, 21 October 1937, p. 609.
53 A. Powers, 'Liverpool and Architectural Education', in Sharples (ed.), *Charles Reilly and the Liverpool School*, p. 17.
54 Powers, 'Liverpool and Architectural Education', p. 17.
55 Powers, 'Liverpool and Architectural Education', p. 17.

10 The Reilly Plan

From the time of his retirement until his death in 1948 Reilly's concern with town planning issues was to find new impetus, further increased during the latter years of the Second World War when it became apparent that many of Britain's towns and cities would need massive rebuilding following wartime bomb damage. Reilly's credentials as a commentator on such matters were impeccable: he was one of the founding fathers of urban planning; he had had a leading role in the establishment of the world's first university department of civic design; and he had close associations with such planning luminaries as Adshead, Abercrombie, and his former student William Holford, who was a rising star. Reilly was every newspaper editor's first choice when they required an authoritative commentator on contentious planning issues.[1] Myles Wright considered that Reilly's stance on planning ideology changed little from 1909 onwards, when he had helped William Lever to set up the Department of Civic Design at Liverpool University. This is both right and wrong, for although Reilly remained committed to 'civic' (essentially urban) planning, his ideas were inevitably modified both by the influence of dedicated planners such as Abercrombie, and his own gradual shift in stylistic allegiance from the grandiose Beaux-Arts vistas of his earlier conceptions, to the Modernist, 'organic' community planning of his Reilly Greens.[2]

The origins of Reilly's reassessments of town planning theory can be traced back to a number of possible sources. Following the Wall Street Crash of 1929 the Liverpool School of Architecture found it increasingly difficult to place the same number of students in American practices as had been the case throughout the 1920s. Alternative sources of practical training were sought, and a number of his most able students took work placements in municipal authorities and government departments around the country. Although less

1 See, for example, Reilly's review of C. H. James and S. Rowland Pierce's *City of Norwich Plan* (Norwich Corporation, 1945) in *Tribune*, 15 June 1945, Reilly Papers, Liverpool University Archive, Box D207/10/2; or Reilly, 'London – When the Lights Go Up', *Daily Mail*, 15 December 1943, Reilly Papers, Box D207/13/7.
2 Reilly was still following an American model here, favouring an American organic plan as outlined by the likes of Clarence Perry over European rectilinear models.

glamorous than a New York placement, such work experience exposed students to the new developments in social housing taking place in a number of local authority architecture departments at that time, not least in Liverpool where the Corporation Director of Housing, Lancelot Keay, was overseeing a major public housing programme. A number of Reilly's students from this period helped in the new housing developments within Liverpool, among them Gordon Stephenson,[3] John Hughes and Leonard Berger, who worked on vast Dudok-inspired tenement blocks such as St Andrew's Gardens,[4] as well as large estates built on what were then the fringes of the city at Dovecot and Norris Green.

Later commentators have credited the Liverpool School for its pioneering efforts during this period in the development and encouragement of social architectural policy.[5] Joseph Sharples notes that

> it is true that the existence of the Department of Civic Design within the school made students think about the broader social and environmental setting of their work. But any wholehearted conversion of the school to 'social architecture', such as Walter Gropius described in 1936, seems to have come right at the end of Reilly's professorship and to have developed further after his departure.[6]

Sharples goes on to quote one of Reilly's students from this period, Bruce Allsopp, who felt that his fellow students were 'not much concerned with putting the world to rights', believing that 'an architect's job was to produce beautiful buildings'.[7] This may well have been the case for the majority of the students, but although Reilly's teaching to date had not primarily been directed to social issues, his part in the establishment of the Department of Civic Design, together with his own well-documented and long-standing socialism, indicate that his eventual embrace of social architecture was not mere bandwagon-jumping. The long-term outcome of Reilly's student

3   See G. Stephenson and C. Demarco (eds), *On a Human Scale: A Life in City Design*, Freemantle Arts Centre Press, South Freemantle, 1992. Professor Stephenson was Lever Professor of Civic Design at Liverpool University, 1948–1953. For further information see Stephenson Papers, Liverpool University Archive, Boxes D112–D307.
4   See F. Newbery, 'Flats in Liverpool 1919–1939', BArch thesis, Liverpool University, 1980.
5   See A. Saint, *Towards a Social Architecture: The Role of School Building in Post-War England*, Yale University Press, New Haven, 1987, and also A. Jackson, *The Politics of Architecture: A History of Modern Architecture in Britain*, The Architectural Press, London, 1970.
6   J. Sharples, 'Reilly and his Students on Merseyside and Beyond', in Sharples (ed.), *Charles Reilly and the Liverpool School of Architecture 1904–1933*, Liverpool University Press, Liverpool, 1996, pp. 34–35.
7   Quoted in Sharples, 'Reilly and His Students', p. 35.

placement policy was that, following the war, Liverpool-trained architects and planners had a virtual stranglehold on major public appointments in Britain; the city architects of Birmingham, Manchester and Newcastle were all 'Liverpool men'.[8] In the short term, the ideas that were current in the social housing sphere began – albeit slowly – to have an effect on Reilly's teaching. By the time of his retirement, we can detect the influence of social architectural policy informed by Modernist theory in much of Reilly's writing and in his lectures.

In key articles such as 'Citizen or Peasant'[9] and 'Architecture and the Community'[10] from the early 1940s, Reilly reinforced his position in the urban, rather than the quasi-rural, school of planning. He constantly stressed the importance of community and neighbourliness, and in lectures such as 'A New Type of Suburb'[11] he focused on the evils of the speculatively built suburbs of the inter-war period, along with their implicit promotion of an isolationist lifestyle.[12] These ideas had found re-expression in his 1934 valedictory Roscoe Lecture 'The Body of the Town'.

The Body of the Town

Reilly outlined his position in the Roscoe Lecture at an important transitional point for him, shortly after his retirement from the Roscoe Chair. He condemned the vision of Le Corbusier (whom he describes as the 'most destructive critic of our present towns')[13] for future urban development, together with the ribbon developments which were then, as now, prevalent along the main arterial roads leading out of British towns and cities.[14] He cited as his

8   In the 1940s and 1950s the city architects of Birmingham, Manchester, Newcastle and Southampton were, respectively, A. G. Sheppard Fidler (BArch 1932), Leonard Howitt (CertArch 1922, BArch 1925), George Kenyon (DipArch 1930) and Leon Berger. See Sharples, 'Reilly and His Students', pp. 34–36.
9   Reilly, 'Citizen or Peasant?', The Architects' Journal, 4 November 1943, pp. 344–46.
10 Reilly, 'Architecture and the Community', Reilly Papers, Liverpool University Archive, Box D207/4/16.
11 Reilly, 'A New Type of Suburb', Reilly Papers, Liverpool University Archive, Box D207/23/1.
12 Reilly had been a long-standing campaigner against the development of speculative suburbs and garden suburbs by the Arts and Crafts fraternity. His friendships with Clough Williams-Ellis and Arthur Trystan Edwards, and the papers they published in the Town Planning Review, is evidence of this.
13 Reilly, 'The Body of the Town', the Roscoe Lecture delivered at the Royal Institution, 12 March 1934, quoted in Reilly, Scaffolding in the Sky, Routledge, London, 1938, appendix 1, p. 321.
14 Clough Williams-Ellis described such developments as consisting of 'Blasphemous Bungalows': C. Williams-Ellis, England and the Octopus, Bles, London, 1928, p. 66. See also T. W. Sharp, English Panorama, Dent, London, 1936.

preferred model the Viennese approach to slum clearance, which led to the development of large areas of green spaces within the city, freed up by rings of tenement blocks that had been built to replace the terraced slum housing. By adopting such an approach, Reilly claimed that

> Liverpool might become, if its inhabitants had the energy and determination of the poverty-stricken war-beaten workmen of Vienna, not a garden city with all that that implies in pettiness and snobbishness and the village outlook, but what I think is a far finer conception, *a city planted in a park*...[15]

The model of belts of tenement blocks ringing the city has faint echoes of the grand Beaux-Arts vistas that Reilly had envisaged for the city 20 years earlier,[16] modified by the development of Modernism in the intervening years. For Reilly in 1938, at the time of the publication of *Scaffolding in the Sky*, the lecture represented

> some more definite indication of my architectural creed... although what I wrote in 1934 is not necessarily all that I feel in 1938. On that point I can truthfully say, however, that my conviction that we live today in a new world requiring a new architecture, and that we have the new materials for it at hand, has grown stronger since then, not less.[17]

The realization that a new world had dawned would find expression in projects such as the Peter Jones store, and in the books and articles that Reilly produced in the 1920s and 1930s. However, it was not until the 1940s that

15　Reilly, 'The Body of the Town', p. 333.
16　It is also interesting to note the similarity in the language used by Reilly and that of Le Corbusier in his book *Urbanisme* of 1925 (translated as *The City of Tomorrow* by Etchells and published in Britain in 1929), although Reilly meant something rather different from Le Corbusier by the phrase 'a city planted in a park'. Despite the strong Beaux-Arts elements to Le Corbusier's proposals in the book and parallells that can be drawn between the two men's views on standardization and uniformity in town planning, Reilly nevertheless challenges Le Corbusier's thoroughgoing Modernism. 'Le Corbusier... begins his book, *Urbanisme*, by a chapter headed, "The Pack-Donkey's Way and Man's Way" – "Man," he says, "walks in a straight line because he has a goal and knows where he is going. The pack donkey meanders along... he takes the line of least resistance... The pack donkey's way is responsible for the plan of every European city." This, of course, like other brilliant things, does not reflect quite truly the state of affairs.' 'The Body of the Town', pp. 321–22. Reilly then goes on to provide a series of historical precedents to disprove Le Corbusier's assertion and ends up by proposing a compromise solution which takes elements of Beaux-Arts and Modernist theory, as illustrated for him by the Viennese and Antwerp solutions. This would be Reilly's preferred approach to town planning from now on, and represented a major re-evaluation of his theories on planning in the light of Modernist developments.
17　Reilly, *Scaffolding in the Sky*, p. 287.

another aspect of Reilly's Modernist re-evaluation found an outlet in the reassessment and development of his planning philosophy. In the early years of the Second World War, Reilly was already turning his attention to the problems the country would face in rebuilding its towns and cities. In articles such as 'Architecture After the War', Reilly saw the conflict as a catalyst in the use of Modernist technologies: 'In one particular it may well hasten on what is already happening. Ferro-concrete will come still more into its own.'[18] In 1941 Reilly wrote an article entitled 'The Suburbs We Should Build', in which he outlined his concept of future large-scale housing development; here we can detect the ideas that would be developed in the Reilly Greens. Reilly states that new developments must

> be architecturally related not only to one another but to all the other buildings in the town of their own epoch... To obtain this cousinly relationship they must be rigorously truthful to the general needs and aspirations of our time as well as to their own construction... If steel is increasingly used, as is highly probable after the experience we have been through, we must glory in its lightness and the sunniness it permits and not bury it behind brick and stone... The size and arrangements of the individual houses and flats will clearly follow the sort of social life which the war leaves behind it... We may hope that, as in the eighteenth century, the squares, terraces and closes – whatever forms the new lay-out leads to – will be designed as wholes however many individual homes they contain. Perhaps we shall rise to the continuous gardens in front and around the blocks...[19]

The germ of the Reilly Green idea is clearly identifiable in this vision of a unified community. This article is also a clear indication of Reilly's firm commitment to Modernism as the appropriate style for a post-war society. His vision was clearly identified with both Modernist styling and its attendant technologies, and was allied to his long-stated belief that the city was the ideal model for modern living. These ideas would be further expressed in the debates about the plans for redevelopment after the war.

---

18   Reilly, 'Architecture After the War', *Manchester Guardian*, 18 October 1940. See also Reilly, 'A Plan by Which to Build', *Manchester Guardian*, 9 December 1940; 'Parade Streets in Our Towns', *Manchester Guardian*, 4 February 1941.
19   Reilly, 'The Suburbs We Should Build', *Manchester Guardian*, 14 February 1941.

Rebuilding London: The Academy and Abercrombie Plans

Reilly was to become involved in controversy surrounding the proposals for the rebuilding of London, in particular the Academy Plan[20] produced by the Royal Academy Planning Committee under the chairmanship of Sir Edwin Lutyens. This was severely criticized by a number of commentators, including Reilly, who considered that

> There is not a single drawing of a modern building in the whole plan, a modern building in the sense of expressing the life of today... Sir Edwin Lutyens... belongs to a dying school of art which will have no successors. The plan's chief merit is that it made the rebuilding of London the subject of public and private discussion. But the plan itself will never be carried out. It is all Monumental planning, fine sites and still finer palaces regardless of the life of poorer people! Nor does it tackle successfully modern traffic problems.[21]

This dismissal on the grounds of Monumental planning – given his earlier predilection for Beaux-Arts planning on a Monumental scale – seems to indicate just how far he had come from his 1909 position. Reilly's criticisms of the plan also led to some ill-feeling between himself and his former ideological ally, Sir Edwin Lutyens.[22]

The debate over the appropriate way to plan London continued to rage in the professional and general press throughout the latter part of 1942 and into early 1943. Reilly took a leading part through a series of articles he published in national papers. In an article for the *Evening Standard* in October 1942, Reilly claimed that the Academy Plan's drawings

---

20 Royal Academy Planning Committee Interim Report, 'London Replanned', *Country Life*, 1942.
21 Quoted in 'Reilly's Commandoes', *News Review*, 31 December 1942, p. 18.
22 Reilly's attacks on 'The Academy Plan' led Lutyens to write a stinging attack on Reilly, in which he states: 'Professor Reilly, whose past academic status may lead your readers to mistake his amiable prejudices (to which his practising colleagues have been long indulgent) for the pronouncement of authority... Professor Reilly would have wished the style of the new London to be clearly indicated... he claims... that the buildings... reveal a "period" affinity... he wants a "modern" city... Does he perhaps mean contemporary? If Professor Reilly really means and hopes that our London heritage will be restored by good young architects then why not say so, instead of seeking to borrow credit by untimely and ill-considered criticism of other men's work.' Letter from E. L. Lutyens to the *Evening Standard*, 20 October 1942; Reilly Papers, Liverpool University Archive, Box D207/3/8. There is also a reply to Lutyens from the paper's editor: 'Professor Reilly was expressing his own opinions... in our view his services to British architecture are sufficiently great to permit him to express his opinions as he wishes', 29 October 1942, Box D207/3/8.

take no notice of the new architecture which has grown up all over the world during the last 30 years, an architecture which belongs by its very nature to the age of the motorcar, the airplane and a thousand other modern things.[23]

Reilly continued to attack the ideas behind the Academy Plan, contrasting them with a city plan that he now believed must be dictated by the motor car. In dismissing what had been essentially his own vision of urban life in the pre-war period, he claimed that the Academy Plan

> with its widened streets… wide parade streets for slow traffic imply vistas and balanced facades, and in the end… the whole paraphernalia of the Renaissance town as developed by Hausmann and the Ecole des Beaux-Arts in Paris.[24]

An alternative plan for the capital devised by John Henry Forshaw, Chief London County Council Architect, and Professor Abercrombie was announced in July 1943.[25] It was immediately applauded by Reilly as representing

> the real plan for London, real not only in the sense that it is the official plan for the London County Council area, but real because it goes to the heart of the problem… it is a plan to give Londoners a better life… The motive of the planning is the village green, its essence neighbourliness, even if some of the buildings are blocks of flats or tenements of workshops. The tyranny of the street is largely abolished… The desert of London is gradually to disappear… To live near one's work, in touch with one's neighbours, in sight of grass and trees, and by quick transport to be in touch with every other centre… and so to own the whole town; that is the ideal of this plan and it is a great one.[26]

The ideas behind Abercrombie's plan can be traced back as far as 1912, when he wrote an article for the *Town Planning Review* in which he argued for the replacement of piecemeal planning with a unified plan for Greater London.[27] The County Plan was followed by a larger Greater London Plan,[28] prepared by Abercrombie in 1944 and published in 1945. The plans were hailed at the time

23 Reilly, 'This London of the Future is Already Out of Date', *Evening Standard*, 26 October 1942. See also Reilly, 'Replanning of Central London: A Royal Academy Exhibition', *Manchester Guardian*, 13 October 1942.
24 Reilly, 'Rebuilding the Big Towns', *Manchester Guardian*, 25 May 1943. Reilly resigned from the Town and Country Planning Association over its opposition to the replanning of London, believing it to 'want London to be a hundred Welwyn Garden Cities…', *Liverpool Echo*, 24 November 1943. See also debate between Reilly and F. J. Osborn: Reilly, 'Tall Flats and no Fires'; Osborn 'Real Family Homes', both in *Manchester Evening News*, 17 December 1943.
25 J. H. Forshaw and L. P. Abercrombie, *County of London Plan*, Macmillan, London, 1943.
26 Reilly, 'Brave New London', *Evening Standard*, 9 July 1943.
27 L. P. Abercrombie, 'Town Planning in Greater London', *Town Planning Review*, Vol. II, 1912, p. 262.
28 L. P. Abercrombie, *Greater London Plan 1944*, HMSO, London, 1945.

as 'the town planning classic for which the time is ripe, and the world has been waiting'.[29] However, they were not implemented as Abercrombie had envisaged, and the eventual rebuilding failed to take up the unified and comprehensive nature of his schemes.[30]

A number of the features outlined by Abercrombie in both plans were to have a great deal of influence on contemporary and post-war planning theory, not least on Reilly's 1944 scheme for Birkenhead. The County Plan's theory of an organic London made up of a series of smaller towns and villages, but planned on a unified scale (or, as Reilly put it, a 'village green') was evident in Reilly's own scheme for Birkenhead.[31] The individual village communities of London are scaled down to small groups of houses clustered around an open space, fitting together in the overall plan in the manner of flower petals. This idea formed the basis of the Reilly Greens, and indeed of Reilly's ethos for the new age, as outlined in Lawrence Wolfe's *The Reilly Plan: A New Way of Life* (Figs 28–32). When it was published in 1945 this book drew heavily on the ideas Reilly had been developing, and allied them to Wolfe's own sociological, economic and psychological theories concerning the appropriate living patterns for an ideal post-war society.[32]

A New Way of Life: The Reilly Plan as Paradigm

In the introduction to Wolfe's book, Reilly states that

> A book with the title, *The Reilly Plan*, I think, certainly needs an introduction by the author of the housing layout designated by the title to explain how this

29 Osborn, 'A Great Future for a Great City', *Observer*, 17 December 1944.
30 For a history of the post-war rebuilding of the city of London see D. Foley, *Controlling London's Growth: Planning the Great Wen 1940–1960*, University of California Press, Berkeley and Los Angeles, 1963.
31 Reilly may well have been thinking along the same lines as Steen Eiler Rasmussen, who outlined his theory on the city's development in *London: The Unique City*, Jonathan Cape, London, 1947. Although the book was not published in Britain until 1947, it drew on established ideas about London's development from Roman times onwards. Rasmussen notes that 'Some say: Paris is a fortified city whose space was restricted by its fortifications, while London is an open city, which enabled it to spread freely in all directions... It is, however, not due to one single and particular reason that London has become the type of the spreading city. It is due to the co-operation of many circumstances', p. 24. Rasmussen then goes on to outline in some detail the various social, economic and political factors that had led to the London plan which Abercrombie was then seeking to address.
32 Wolfe was a child psychologist who saw many possibilities in Reilly's ideas for a better organized post-war society.

layout came to be produced. What I cannot attempt to explain, much as I appreciate it and am flattered by it, is the enthusiasm of Lawrence Wolfe for the many implications he has found in the plan which, I confess, I did not fully see when I drew it.[33]

The extent to which Reilly foresaw the implications of his plan is uncertain. Wolfe outlines a number of principles informing the Reilly Plan, including neighbourhood planning and the principle of housing. Out of these principles and their attendant implications Wolfe developed 'The Reilly Plan', which he expanded into an integrated theory that he believed would solve the nation's housing and planning needs. Wolfe is careful to note that

> I am not reading these principles into the Reilly Plan as a preacher might read all sorts of things into a biblical text. I formulated them long before the Reilly Plan came into existence, as a result of years of investigation and thought, propagating them whenever and wherever I could, in print as well as by word of mouth. The Reilly Plan constitutes the practical expression of these principles and is therefore, in my conviction, the 'blue-print' of a New Britain.[34]

The origins of the plan, as described by Reilly, lay in his chance observation of a scheme within the Birkenhead County Borough's Engineering Department:

> Not liking very much the look of this layout, which was on ordinary garden suburb lines, with what Wolfe calls isolationist houses, mostly looking away from one another on curving roads... I suggested to the borough engineer that we should make a new layout plan together... They were pleased with the idea and, chiefly wanting to get a semi-new planning principle adopted, that of houses [a]round greens... and the greens themselves arranged like the petals of a flower round a community building...[35]

Under the plan, a larger community may be formed by the linkage of each green and community centre in a unified scheme, with a central 'civic community centre'. Wolfe describes this in the following terms:

> in addition to the local community centres, those of each Reilly Unit, there is also a Civic Community Centre for the town or district as a whole, which may have a total population of 10,000 or more. The civic community centre compares with the 'locals' somewhat as the county council compares with the

33   Reilly, 'The Reilly Plan: Introduction', in L. Wolfe, *The Reilly Plan: A New Way of Life*, Nicholson and Watson, London, 1945, p. 9.
34   Wolfe, *The Reilly Plan*, p. 39.
35   Wolfe, *The Reilly Plan*, p. 10.

rural councils or, in military terms, as the division compares with the battalion. The family does not go to the civic community centre direct from the house home, but via the local community centres. That is, it first makes friends with its own immediate community: then, through sports and other joint events, it gets acquainted with the residents of adjacent Reilly Units: so that by the time it reaches the civic community centre, it is already more or less well acquainted with a great many other families and individuals who go there, and is of that community.[36]

The highly organized nature of Wolfe's planned society, with its emphasis on the group at the expense of the individual in the manner of military or public school theories of organization, may have drawn some of its inspiration from the community spirit fostered by wartime. Wolfe was in tune with the mood of the time, although his plan was an extreme form of the one that was eventually adopted by the government. This mood would give rise to the welfare state, in which the citizen would – in theory at least – be provided for 'from the cradle to the grave'. The ideas in Wolfe's book also owe something to the paternalism that Reilly was familiar with from Lever's Port Sunlight community, with its emphasis on family values and community-based educational activities that could be channelled towards the greater good of the company. However, the book now seems hopelessly naive and prescriptive, given our present-day perspectives and the fragmented, multifarious nature of family and community life. For example, Wolfe's theories on matrimony ran thus:

> Ordinarily the young couple do not take a whole house, but one of the kitchenless 'bridal suites' provided in the village green, and they either feed at the community centre or have their meals delivered in an insulated container. This means that both husband and wife can go to work or continue their studies… just as if they were unmarried, until the sixth or seventh month of the first pregnancy, which may occur within about two years of the marriage.[37]

It is hard to imagine when, if ever, such a compliant and coherent social order had existed.

The idea of a degree of communal living, and of a community bound together by a common employer, was certainly not new. Service flats had long provided a restaurant and cleaning service to residents, albeit at a price; Modernist ventures such as the Lawn Road Flats in Hampstead, London, had

36 Wolfe, *The Reilly Plan*, p. 97.
37 Wolfe, *The Reilly Plan*, p. 124.

experimented with a community bar for residents in the 1930s, in order to foster a sense of common purpose.[38] As James King notes,

> Coates' boldly modern building… had 'minimum' flats but compactness was offset by services: bed-making, shoe-cleaning, laundry collection, window cleaning and hot meals from a central kitchen. From 1937, an 'Isobar' on the ground floor even provided snacks.[39]

However, such schemes were exclusively for small-scale middle-class housing, and did not involve the all-embracing social theory that Wolfe and Reilly were proposing.

The basic structure of the Reilly Plan can also be seen to represent, in a scaled-down form, the idealized urban life that Reilly had promoted in his earlier Beaux-Arts model, with its emphasis on a civic centre to which its citizens looked for enlightenment and cultural guidance. What had changed from this earlier model was the architectural style that was to be adopted. Gone were the Monumental vistas, replaced by a village green borrowed from an older rural planning tradition, transplanted into the town and built around by regularly spaced Modernist houses and flats. Abercrombie's London plan, with its emphasis on a decentralized city rather than enlarged suburbs, would provide another model for Reilly's 10,000-resident communities.

Population density within the existing towns and cities had long been a matter for debate. The MARS group had argued for a high-density solution for London in their Master Plan for London; proponents of a medium-density solution included figures such as Geoffrey Boumphrey, Thomas Sharp, Professor Adshead and Trystan-Edwards. Thomas Sharp was the author of a number of influential books in the 1930s and 1940s, including *Town and Countryside*,[40] *English Panorama*[41] and *Town Planning*.[42] Sharp, in common with Reilly, was a fierce opponent of the garden city principle; in *Town and Countryside* he called the street and the town the true expressions of a civilized society. Adshead and Trystan-Edwards both had close associations

---

38 The Lawn Road Flats experiment owed something to the political outlook shared by its residents, who were writers, designers and other intellectuals drawn from London's bohemian circles. Reilly's son Paul was a resident during this period. For an account of the community see J. Pritchard, *View From a Long Chair: The Memoirs of Jack Pritchard (with an Introduction by Fiona MacCarthy)*, Routledge and Kegan, London, 1984.

39 J. King, *The Last Modern: A Life of Herbert Read*, Weidenfeld and Nicolson, London, 1990, p. 140.

40 T. Sharp, *Town and Countryside*, Oxford University Press, London, 1932.

41 T. Sharp, *English Panorama*, Dent, London, 1950 (1936).

42 T. Sharp, *Town Planning*, Penguin, Harmondsworth, 1940.

with Reilly from the Liverpool days; Reilly and Adshead had produced a number of articles for the *Town Planning Review* from 1914–1918 in which many of the themes from the Reilly Plan were rehearsed. Edwards had also entered the debate during this period, with a series of articles published while he was serving in the Royal Navy during the First World War. During the middle years of the 1930s he wrote a series of articles in *The Builder*[43] in which slum clearance and the relative merits of high-density and low-rise building were discussed. Reilly's description in *The Reilly Plan* of his greens as a 'semi-new' principle was therefore an accurate admission of the debt he owed to a range of sources.

On its publication a number of contemporary commentators were enthusiastic about the potential of the Reilly Plan. Clough Williams-Ellis, while aware that Reilly and Wolfe's theory represented the communal facilities that most households already enjoyed stretched to their logical conclusions, believed that

> Of course, even now what he [Reilly] calls 'isolationist' households are already and anyhow linked up to various central services and 'co-operate', even if unconsciously, in sharing such things as roads and street lighting, posts, police, schools and so forth, as well as water supplies, gas, electricity and drainage, which are paid for more directly and which it would be difficult, if not impossible, for each house to provide for itself even at a far higher cost. Sir Charles' plan is simply an idea for a lay-out that would make it easy to extend this co-operation much further but in new and obviously sensible directions.[44]

Others were less enthusiastic about the possible merits of such a scheme and this became apparent when Reilly attempted to implement his ideas in his plans for the Woodchurch Estate, Birkenhead, in 1944–1945, as well as in his later and more wide-ranging *Outline Plan for the County Borough of Birkenhead* of 1947. Given the political implications inherent in Wolfe's assessment of the Reilly Plan, it was inevitable that its full application would split opinion along party political lines.

---

43 In a series of lectures delivered to architectural societies around the country, Edwards put forward his plans to develop 'A Hundred New Towns for Britain'. See *The Builder*, 18 October 1935, p. 690. The ideas put forward by Edwards are in line with those of Abercrombie in terms of the decentralization of the large urban areas. However, it is interesting to speculate to what extent Edwards's ideas influenced Reilly's theories in the formulation of his 'Reilly Plan', since it is known that he was much respected by Reilly.

44 C. Williams-Ellis, *The Adventure of Building*, The Architectural Press, London, 1946, p. 68.

The Reilly Plan Applied: Woodchurch Estate, Birkenhead

The origins of the plan that Reilly drew up for the development of Birkenhead (with the aid of one of his former students Naim Aslan) dated back to early 1944. Reilly notes that

> In February, 1944, I was appointed planning consultant by the City Council of Birkenhead to make a civic survey of the town and an outline plan for its development. On one of my early visits I saw lying about in the borough engineer's office a layout plan for a new satellite dormitory town on an estate of some 350 acres which the Corporation had bought... about three miles from the centre of Birkenhead...[45]

The initial plan was to develop the Woodchurch estate using the Reilly Greens concept (Fig. 34), which would involve the building of 3000

> cream painted houses with gardens and, in some cases, garages, set amid a green belt a mile-and-a-half in extent. Incorporated would be 30 village greens each of more than one acre. The suburb would have its own shopping centre, community hall, churches surrounded by trees, and inns where workmen could meet with their wives for refreshment.[46]

This scheme challenged another, slightly earlier, plan that had been prepared by the Borough Engineer and Surveyor, Mr B. Robinson (Fig. 33). The rival scheme consisted of

> a lay-out on a less ambitious scale, comprising upwards of 2500 houses with no village greens... members of the council are being issued with blue-print copies of the two plans for immediate consideration. At the next meeting of the council, early in May, the choice will be made.[47]

The *Birkenhead News* noted the points of difference in what became known as Reilly versus Robinson.[48] Regarding the need to maintain a sense of neighbourliness for a community to thrive, it made the point that

> The Reilly Plan envisages much more – a design for living... sociability for the sociably-minded is to be encouraged. And this is the height of civic wisdom and sound common sense, for the lack of neighbourliness is the root cause of many of our social ills...[49]

45 Reilly, 'Introduction', *The Reilly Plan*, pp. 9–10.
46 'Village Green Or – Birkenhead Considers Two Plans', *Liverpool Echo*, 14 April 1944.
47 'Village Green Or – Birkenhead Considers Two Plans'.
48 'Reilly v Robinson – Rate Payers are Referees', *Birkenhead News*, 29 April 1944.
49 'The Two Plans', *Birkenhead News*, 3 May 1944.

The debate over the merits of the two plans attracted national attention. *Tribune* noted that

> One Tory councillor called the plan a socialist memorial... To what do the Tories object in the Reilly plan?... is it that they are frightened of the principle of community planning? Neighbourliness has developed amongst workers, largely because of adversity. Helping each other when necessary has built up a social attitude... How well that community spirit came to the fore in the Blitz days.[50]

While the *Picture Post* ran a series of mini-interviews with residents of Birkenhead, including a railway fireman, a housewife and the editor of the *Birkenhead Daily News* – they all came out in favour of the Reilly proposal – *The Architects' Journal* ran an article entitled 'Birkenhead: Community versus Segregation'.[51]

The decision over the choice of plan had been postponed from the May meeting. A vote in July confirmed that the Conservative group on the council were solidly opposed to Reilly's proposals, which led the Labour group to announce that they would press for a poll to decide the issue.[52] By September a further plan had been submitted, this one by Reilly's former student Herbert Rowse.[53] The *Birkenhead News* in December 1944 reported that the Labour group were suggesting that the Conservatives' allegiance was switching from the Robinson to the Rowse plan, and indeed the Conservative group formally adopted the Rowse plan in March 1945.[54] It was this plan that was eventually built.

Despite reports to the contrary by contemporary commentators,[55] Rowse's scheme seems to incorporate certain elements of Reilly's village green idea (Fig. 35). However, Reilly's greens were replaced with allotments and playgrounds. The basic layout is more in keeping with a Beaux-Arts radial plan, albeit on a less formal basis, consisting as it does of three main boulevards radiating out from Holy Cross Church and its school. The central boulevard contained the main civic amenities: library, clinic, shops, swimming

---

50   H. Short, 'Where Will You Spend Eternity', *Tribune*, 16 June 1944.
51   'Planning Post-War Britain', *Picture Post*, 8 July 1944; 'Birkenhead: Community versus Segregation', *The Architects' Journal*, 3 August 1944.
52   'Labour Threatens to Break Political Truce', *Birkenhead Advertiser*, 8 July 1944.
53   'Woodchurch Plan Revised', *Birkenhead News*, 9 September 1944.
54   'Conservatives Adopt Rowse Plan', *Birkenhead News*, 10 March 1945; 'New Plan for Woodchurch', *Liverpool Daily Post*, 3 March 1945.
55   The *Birkenhead News* said 'The plan [Rowse's] does not obviously derive either from the Robinson design or Sir Charles Reilly's layout...' *Birkenhead News*, 13 January 1945.

baths and community centre. Also included were a number of nursery, primary and secondary schools, ringing the outer fringes of the estate. Rowse described his plan as having

> developed on the basis of the natural topographical features of the site… Every effort has been made in the planning of the estate to provide prospects of the rural surroundings from every possible point and to allow the maximum amount of rural character to permeate the estate by means of planted green closes, forecourts, quadrangles, recreation spaces and allotment gardens: also by means of three broad parkways converging on the hill. In contrast to the familiar monotony of bye-law streets or their suburban counterpart, the estate will present varied internal prospects of groups of houses and trees set in green spaces and having the general character of a modern version of the traditional English village scene… a central parkway, slightly more formal in character… flanked by the community buildings which provide for the social life of the estate. These community buildings for social activity, recreation and interest, provide for the fullest enjoyment of social intercourse based on the accumulated experience of social experiments carried out on housing estates during the period between the two wars.[56]

Despite having lost the battle over the planning of the Woodchurch estate, Reilly and Aslan continued with their larger plan. In their *Outline Plan for the County Borough of Birkenhead* of 1947 they used aspects of the Reilly Greens scheme, disposing of the organic nature of the greens and adapting them into a more formalized hexagon plan, which was subsequently incorporated into a general plan for the town.

The Outline Plan for the County Borough of Birkenhead

The details of Reilly and Aslan's plan were published in the *Birkenhead Advertiser* in September 1945. The plan divided the town into a series of specialized areas, including neighbourhood areas, a shopping centre, parks and sports centre, an industry centre consisting of 13 major sites, and an academic centre (Figs 36–43). The scheme required a major rethink of the road system in the centre of Birkenhead, which would have created a bypass to funnel industrial traffic away from the town centre into the specially created industrial areas on the fringe of the town. The plan provided for large areas of pedestrianized walkways in the shopping centre, and the amalgamation of a number of

56   H. Rowse, quoted in *Birkenhead News*, 13 January 1945.

existing shopping areas into one main thoroughfare along Conway Street. The parkland and open spaces of the town were also to be rethought; the existing Birkenhead Park would be complemented by an additional 100 acres of open public spaces spread throughout the town. The academic centre would link the cultural amenities of the Williamson Art Gallery with a new library and museum complex to form what was described as a 'spacious, dignified setting'.[57]

As far as housing was concerned, the plan used the Reilly Greens concept, adapted to a more formal hexagonal plan.[58] Reilly outlined the thinking behind this idea:

> The obvious method of development to give light, air and space, and yet to maintain the same number of people on the site... would be the erection of flats. The north country population generally, and especially in Birkenhead... do not take kindly to flat conditions. Experiments in them in Birkenhead have not been happy. What seems to be needed is that each residence should have its own front door at ground level with a little private patch of garden.[59]

He then goes on to list the advantages of the hexagonal scheme with its mixture of private and communal gardens, club rooms, nurseries and laundries all facing one another around an open court: 'enough to make a pleasant community, neither too big, nor too small'.

The plan was heavily criticized by the controlling Conservative group, who described Reilly's plans as 'fantastic, extravagant and impractical'.[60] Despite the criticisms, it was decided to progress with a limited publication of the plan in the press, with an accompanying exhibition at the Williamson Art

57 'What the Reilly Plan Means to You', *Birkenhead Advertiser*, 8 September 1945.

58 In the final published version of the plan Reilly and Aslan provide both the organic Reilly Greens and the hexagonal plans as complementary types of housing plan. The former, it is suggested, is more appropriate to a rural area, while the latter allows for higher urban density solutions. See C. H. Reilly and N. J. Aslan, *The Outline Plan for the County Borough of Birkenhead*, 1947, pp. 86–96.

59 'Hexagonal Site Planning: A Scheme for Birkenhead', *The National House Builder*, January 1946, pp. 13–17. The article claimed that the hexagonal site plan was here published for the first time. In fact the plan was published in a shorter form in the *Birkenhead News*, on 27 October 1945. There had been a good deal of debate at the Council meetings in October 1945 with regard to the release of plans to the press; see 'No Publication of Reilly Plan', Reilly Papers, Liverpool University Archive, Box D207/20/2. Apparently the press were having difficulty in obtaining copies throughout this period, with an article in the *Birkenhead News* apologizing for 'The Missing Map' and stating: 'Arrangements had been made to illustrate this article with one of the drawings of the hexagonal lay-out. Publication of this, however, is subject to the Town Council's approval, and although our application was sent on September 20th no permission has yet been given.' 'Sunlight Houses of the Future', *Birkenhead Advertiser*, 13 October 1945.

60 'Reilly Plan Comes Under Fire Again', *Birkenhead Advertiser*, 13 October 1945. See also 'Sir Charles Challenges Tory Leader', *Birkenhead Advertiser*, 20 October 1945.

Gallery.[61] The exhibition, held in April 1946, was opened by Lewis Silkin, Minister of Town and Country Planning. In the press release issued for the exhibition it was stated that the basis of the plan was

> to harmonise and improve where possible the relation between the individual elements of the town for the happiness and prosperity of all... There are two main aspects from which the town must be considered. They are (1) Birkenhead as an independent unit, a well balanced harmonious whole: (2) Birkenhead as an important component of the Merseyside Region and the most important centre in Wirral, perhaps one day to be 'Wirral City', the recognised capital of the peninsula.[62]

The exhibition was a mixed success, combining record attendances with requests for the provision of public lectures in order to explain the plan in greater detail to a confused general public.[63] In addition the plan received coverage in the professional and national press,[64] and a number of articles centred on Reilly's inclusion of a Modernist design for a hotel and casino on the riverfront. Designed to allow residents and visitors to take advantage of the river frontage and views of Liverpool, it was an innovative approach to what was generally considered at the time to be a dirty industrial waterway.[65] The *Manchester Guardian* said that the plan

> is based on a thorough survey of Birkenhead's site, growth and present condition... (Particularly significant is the correlation between housing densities and the incidence of tuberculosis, and between shop distribution and road accidents.) It conforms to what is now standard practice in respect of neighbourhood units, ring roads, and the rest of 'the Abercrombie stuff', as Professor Reilly calls it. But it is distinguished at every point by an imaginative treatment of details, and even more by an acute sense of the human need for gaiety.[66]

The plan was published in its full form in 1947, including a detailed account of all aspects of the replanning of the town, and illustrated with numerous colour maps, drawings, photographs, diagrams and charts. The scheme,

61 'Fantastic Plan', *Birkenhead News*, 13 October 1945. The reporter noted that 'The Labour Party were in favour of a full publication of the report and maps, but this was opposed by the Conservatives on the grounds of additional costs.'
62 Press release to the *Birkenhead Plan Exhibition* at the Williamson Art Gallery, April 1946. Reilly Papers, Liverpool University Archive, Box D207/20/7.
63 'Birkenhead is Puzzled by Reilly Plan', *Birkenhead Advertiser*, 27 April 1946.
64 See 'Birkenhead: A New Plan by Sir Charles Reilly and N. J. Aslan', *The Architects' Journal*, 9 May 1946, pp. 359–62; and 'Plan for Birkenhead', *The Builder*, 19 April 1946, pp. 376–80.
65 'Birkenhead in 1986: A Capital City of Glass and Steel', *Birkenhead Advertiser*, 10 April 1946.
66 'The Birkenhead Housing Scheme', *Manchester Guardian*, 9 April 1946.

however, was finally rejected and although there are faint echoes of some of Reilly's ideas for the town in present-day Birkenhead – most notably in the form of pedestrianized shopping areas – they were substantially ignored.

The Reilly Plan in Action: Bilston and Dudley

Despite its rejection by Birkenhead, the Reilly plan was implemented in the towns of Bilston in Staffordshire and Dudley in Worcestershire. In addition, Reilly was involved in a private scheme devised by the Miles Aircraft Company of Reading, in partnership with its workforce, to develop a site using his Reilly Greens idea (Figs 44 and 45).[67]

The scheme for Bilston had its origins in Bilston Borough Council's 1945 invitation to Otto Neurath – former President of the Central Office of Planning in Munich, founder of a research institute for social planning, and General Secretary of the Garden City Association in Vienna – to examine the problem of rehousing the slum dwellers of the area. As Derek Wragge Morley noted,

> With his help, the council started plans for doing this. Neurath insisted, as in Vienna, that no town planning is any use unless an attempt is made to approach the individual who is to be rehoused and to find out what he feels are his needs – to make him realise that the whole success of the venture depends on his taking his own part in its working. The people of Bilston must be told what conditions are already like – how many houses are good or bad: how many families have no house of their own… They must be asked for solutions to these problems and presented with possible solutions to criticise… Communal life should not be enforced, but allowed to develop naturally in those who feel the need for it… He stressed that people with ties of friendship or mutual help should be moved together, and the old and young, married and unmarried, should not be segregated. Yet individuals should not be forced to move with other individuals whom they did not like. At this point the Bilston authorities saw the plan designed for Birkenhead by Sir Charles Reilly and felt that it provided in architectural form many of the ideas they had developed largely on the basis of what Neurath had suggested.[68]

67　See Reilly Papers, Liverpool University Archive, Box D207/4/13.

68　D. W. Morley, 'Sociological Approach to Town Planning: The Bilston Experiment', *Discovery*, August 1947, pp. 250–51. The ideas put forward by Neurath, in which a pro-active citizenry help shape and inform planning policy, are interesting when compared with the social engineering solutions employed by local authorities in Britain after the war in which Neurath's ideas are turned on their heads.

Bilston was largely a product of the Industrial Revolution, although its origins go back as far as 1315 when small-scale coal mining was recorded. The social conditions in the nineteenth century had left a legacy of poor housing and widespread environmental pollution, and the council was urgently seeking a radical solution to the town's social problems. As A. M. Williams noted,

> It is hoped that Bilston, which is practically the birth place of the Industrial Revolution which led to the majority of the evils that populations have to suffer, is now to be the first place to benefit from a new type of outlook and planning which attempts to eliminate those evils and to lead to a greater individual development within the community.[69]

Reilly's solution consisted of an adaptation of his Reilly Greens principle, as outlined in the rejected Woodchurch estate plan. He first produced a quick sketch of the proposed groupings for the site, which appears to be a negotiation between his original, organic 'flower petal' scheme and the hexagonal scheme of the Birkenhead plan. William Crabtree, who undertook the project, seems to have reverted to the organic form for the final solution. Reilly said that his plans for Bilston, in which the communal aspects are stressed, had their ancient origins in the academic communities of Oxford and Cambridge:

> The Bilston greens are usually oval in shape (but not strictly elliptical, to avoid the necessity of similar and symmetrical houses on either side) and radiate like the petals of a flower from a centre where is placed the Club house. Together they form a communal unit in the town... like the buildings at King's College, Cambridge...[70]

Bilston would provide the perfect conditions for the Reilly Plan to be realized in its purest form.

> Between the scattered works at Bilston the large expanses of very broken waste land... when levelled by bulldozers and covered with soil and turf... offer ideal large billiard tables of many acres each... on which to build up these semi-enclosed communities... At Bilston I have aimed at communities varying from 500 to 1000 persons...[71]

The scheme had been planned to incorporate a telephone system linking each of the houses to the central community centre, in order that meals might be

69   A. M. Williams, 'The Details of the Problem', *Discovery*, August 1947.

70   Reilly, 'A Town Planner's Solution', *Discovery*, August 1947. Reilly often used the analogy of King's College in order to make similar points; he compared King's with the St Andrew's Gardens flats in Liverpool. See Newbery, 'Flats in Liverpool 1919–1939'.

71   Newbery, 'Flats in Liverpool 1919–1939'.

ordered from the central kitchens. This was intended to aid in the establishment of a community network, but it was eventually dropped on technical
and legal grounds.[72]

In 1946 Reilly had been approached by the Dudley Town Corporation to
prepare an outline scheme for Dudley's Old Park Farm along his 'village
greens' lines. The site was approximately 90 acres, and the plan was boosted by
the council's acquisition of special powers under the Dudley Corporation Bill
of 1947, which enabled them to develop a policy for the provision of cultural
and communal amenities in the older parts of the borough. The final scheme
was carried out by Reilly's former student Derek Bridgewater, who was
nominated to oversee the detailed work on the scheme. As Sheila Turner and
Adrian Allen noted, the plan 'provided for two-, three-, and four-bedroomed
houses and flats and incorporated, as basic essentials, a community centre or
"Club house" and nursery school, and the incorporation of district heating for
the individual houses'.[73]

In 1947 Dudley council also invited Professor T. S. Simey, Charles Booth
Professor of Social Science at Liverpool University, to advise on the social
problems it was felt would arise from the implementation of this type of
experimental community-based planning. In an article for the *Manchester
Guardian* Simey outlined that – as might be expected from a sociologist – he felt

> The social aspects of the Reilly Plan are... in the long run, of greater
> importance than its architectural features, or the technicalities of the layout of
> the greens, shopping centres, and so on, which the town-planner has so far
> regarded as his sole concern. The plan amounts... to a most striking assertion
> of the importance of the human factor in town-planning... Social life is
> indeed, something which can no more be imposed on the inhabitants of a
> ready made housing estate than can beauty be given to a house by sticking
> ornaments on the facade... Working on such lines, town-planners are now
> attempting to develop their science as a social study and the cooperation of the
> Department of Social Science of the University of Liverpool in the
> development of the Dudley scheme is significant. The new greens must, in the
> first place, be inhabited by groups of persons, rather than by a miscellaneous
> assemblage of individuals, if they are to succeed in their primary purpose.
> Great care will, therefore, be necessary in choosing the first tenants, and a new
> policy both of selection and of resettlement will be necessary so that the
> growth of social relationships may be assisted rather than left to develop by

72 For details of the Bilston plan see Reilly Papers, Liverpool University Archive, Box D207/4/14.
73 S. Turner and A. Allen, 'The Papers of Sir Charles Reilly: A Recent Accession to the University
    Archives', *Liverpool University Recorder*, No. 81, 1979, pp. 159–62.

chance. The old practice of grouping persons together in new houses in order of their social needs resulted in the massing together of those who were out of the ordinary, united only by weak social bonds. This must be replaced by a more imaginative policy, which, while taking needs into proper account will also assess the contributions which each family is able to make to the community before any decision is arrived at as to where it will be housed. Research work will be necessary before a policy of this kind can be formulated, and this will be the task... of the Department of Social Science. The department will subsequently be given the opportunity to observe the growth of social life on the greens, and the knowledge accumulated... will be of the greatest interest to town-planners wherever the Reilly Plan has been discussed...[74]

Such a policy of highly controlled social profiling[75] became widespread in the towns and estates that developed across the country in the 1950s and 1960s. However, it was not a universally accepted policy even among radical social thinkers such as Wolfe. In a letter in response to Simey's article, he stated that

Professor Simey's article... combines a perfect summary of my book on the Reilly Plan with a perfect summary of a plan to frustrate it... To exercise 'great care... in choosing the first tenants' and to pursue 'a new policy of selection and of resettlement... so that the growth of social relationships may be assisted rather than left to develop by chance' is to destroy the whole sociological basis of the Reilly Plan. What happens in a group of hand picked people cannot be said to 'come about by a natural process' because the selection itself is not natural. Professor Simey's 'village greens' would be inhabited by guinea-pig families and, being guinea-pigs, they would be set apart from the rest of the community in a form of group isolationism.[76]

Reilly was to die before work began on a modified version of the Reilly Green idea at the Dudley estate in 1950. A year later the Liverpool University Press published the Social Science Department's study of Dudley, *Social Aspects of a Town Development Plan*.

The implementation of the Reilly Plan at Bilston and Dudley, together with general planning issues, continued to concern Reilly until his death. In articles such as 'Suburbia as We Know It Must Go'[77] Reilly pressed for his long-

74 T. S. Simey, 'The Village Green Revived: An Experiment in Planning', *Manchester Guardian*, 19 January 1948.
75 This is examined in 'A Home of Your Own', in which the 'social engineering' used to select suitable candidates for the new towns is outlined. *The New Jerusalem*, A Barraclough/Carey Production for BBC TV, 1995.
76 Letter from Wolfe to the *Manchester Guardian*, 25 January 1948.
77 Reilly, 'Suburbia as We Know It Must Go', *Liverpool Daily Post*, 23 July 1947.

standing aim of a truly urban solution to the planning problems facing post-war society. This would be the common theme of most of his writing, including 'Organisation for Culture'[78] and 'Rebuilding the Towns'[79] in which his Reilly Greens idea was repeatedly applied to contemporary problems. In a series of talks entitled 'Dinner for Six', Reilly discussed the question of efficiency versus beauty in future reconstruction schemes for towns, in conversation with A. V. Williams, Town Clerk of Dudley and former Town Clerk at Bilston. Reilly summed up that he had stood for the power of education and local government enlightenment in the quest to solve the social and architectural problems of the day – a view he had consistently promoted since his appointment to the Roscoe Chair in 1904. Regarding the contemporary problem of the state's involvement in the large-scale town planning schemes, Reilly felt that the solution lay in both the training of architects and planners, and the adoption by officials at local government level of a progressive attitude.

> Training is the basis. It must be a training where the student in his five-year course develops the relation of building to buildings and buildings to people... You must have an intelligent local authority. At Bath a few years ago I found the people on the committee that passed the plans were largely speculative builders. The local authority ought to include the most intelligent people in the community, and I should like to see the authority advised by the best artistic brains.[80]

The relationship between local authorities, speculative builders and the generation of architects that Reilly and his fellow architectural educators had trained was cited by many commentators as having contributed to a built environment which was at the root of many of the social problems that emerged in the 1970s, 80s and 90s. The hope of building what they saw as a 'New Jerusalem' would eventually be frustrated and corrupted by political and economic expedience. As a result, the faith in Modernism as a positive element in social reform suffered a fatal blow.[81]

78   Reilly, 'Organisation for Culture', *The Civic Hall Quarterly*, Wolverhampton Civic Hall Committee, 1947. Reilly Papers, Liverpool University Archive, Box D207/5/19.
79   Reilly, 'Rebuilding the Towns: Two Regional Plans', *Britain Today*, No. 115, November 1945, pp. 23–27; see also No. 116, December 1945, pp. 17–20; No. 117, January 1946, pp. 16–20.
80   'Dinner for Six', *Building*, February 1947, pp. 52–55.
81   See 'A Home of Your Own', *The New Jerusalem*.

Conclusion

The range of tributes paid to to Sir Charles Reilly by former students and colleagues following his death on 2 February 1948 is evidence of the depth of his influence on the architectural world over the best part of the first half of the twentieth century.[1] William Holford (later Lord Holford), arguably Reilly's most illustrious former student, described his former professor as having become

> an international figure, not only by reputation but by the building up of personal contacts. In the 1920s he used to recommend his students to read the life of Benvenuto Cellini: and looking back now, one can recognise certain traits common to the two men. They both believed in competition as a stimulus to effort: but they owed a greater loyalty to the art they practised than to any subdivision of it by place or group. Reilly made himself synonymous with the Liverpool School of Architecture, but acknowledged in a much more realistic way than most that art has no frontiers. He drew his students from all walks of life and from nearly all the countries of the world... Nor was his interest given only to his students... with the migration... of architects and painters and actors... who were unable to live under the changing regime in their own countries. Reilly gave them hospitality... recognised their integrity... helped them with introductions and commissions... what influence his patronage has had on the arts of our times, only time can tell... It is an achievement... at... 74, to be still in the stream of progressive movements in painting and architecture and social development... to be actively engaged in surveying recent building work and assessing the value of town planning schemes, to be able to watch the astonishing growth of seeds sown broadcast in earlier years, and at the same time to be planting new ones.[2]

Beyond the hyperbole associated with the conventions of obituary writing, we can see in Holford's assessment of Reilly the essential elements of his success:

1 Tangible evidence of the degree of acclaim Reilly achieved during his lifetime can be seen in the various awards and honours he received. In 1920 he was awarded an OBE; in 1925 he was appointed Corresponding Member of the American Institute of Architects; in 1931 he was elected Vice-President of RIBA; in 1934 he was created Emeritus Professor, Liverpool University; in 1943 he was awarded the Royal Gold Medal for Architecture, the first architectural educationalist to receive the award; and in 1944 he was knighted.
2 W. Holford, 'Sir Charles Reilly', *Architectural Review*, Vol. 103, May 1948, pp. 180–83.

a charismatic and competitive personality; a talent for publicity; a natural leaning towards internationalism; and an openness to new ideas. These qualities remained constant throughout his life. His network of former students and contacts was an important indicator of his shifting philosophies; but to take this approach to the analysis of his achievements would be to distort the context of his operational base. In many ways Reilly was fortunate, both in the period in which he operated, and in the allegiances, friendships, and professional acquaintances he made.

Reilly's appointment to the Roscoe Chair saw him inherit an important role in a city at the very height of its commercial and economic powers; Liverpool was rich enough to support the ambitious plans for expansion and experimentation that Reilly had in mind, and far enough away from London to develop an independent outlook with regard to aesthetic and cultural matters. In addition, the largely Classically primed environment meant that Reilly's penchant for Classicism would be enthusiastically received by many of the key operators in the city. His predecessor Professor Simpson, far from having taken the fledgling School of Architecture down the cul-de-sac of Arts and Crafts ideology, had in fact done a good deal of the groundwork, preparing the school for the Beaux-Arts ideas that Reilly would go on to develop. With his own natural abilities and the help of powerful friends such as William Lever, Reilly was able to establish himself relatively quickly – via projects such as the Bluecoat, the Department of Civic Design and the Repertory Theatre – in the important social and cultural circles of the city. The close-knit nature of Liverpool's architectural community enabled Reilly to disseminate his ideas effectively through his membership and subsequent presidency of the Liverpool Architectural Society.[3] However, it would be wrong to imply that Reilly – even with the help of figures such as Lever – was able to shape events entirely according to his own impulses, and many times he patently failed to achieve what he had set out to do. As Crouch notes,

> Even they [Reilly and Lever] were not able to transcend the cultural environment in which they found themselves. They were simply part of a complex inter-locking of personalities and events that is given coherence only in retrospect...[4]

3   The Liverpool Architectural Society (LAS) was founded in 1848 and was older than similar societies such as Newcastle (1858), Edinburgh (1859), Manchester (1860), Birmingham (1868), and Glasgow (1870s). Reilly was made a fellow of the LAS in 1904 and was president from 1926 to 1928. Budden was an associate by 1913, a fellow by 1925 and president from 1947 to 1949. See Liverpool Record Office, S Boxes H 720 5 ARC and H 720 6 ARC, for an incomplete run of yearbooks, minutes and annual reports.
4   C. Crouch, 'Design Initiatives in Liverpool 1881–1914', PhD thesis, Liverpool University, 1992, p. 173.

In terms of the local cultural community, Reilly's influence is difficult to quantify. His involvement with the Bluecoat and his part in the foundation of the Liverpool Repertory Theatre, while considerable, has become muddied both by his own mythologizing and by the motivations and interpretations of subsequent writers. It can safely be said that William Lever proved to be Reilly's closest and most important ally in such campaigns; without his money and social contacts, the Bluecoat's success as a precursor of the arts centre industry would not have been possible. Similarly, Reilly's moves to establish a repertory theatre relied not just on his own drive and determination, but also on a groundswell of support from a number of minor characters who were operating towards the same goal, in some cases since before Reilly's arrival in the city. His failure to achieve certain other objectives – most notably the establishment of a powerful arts faculty within the university – is evidence of his inability to operate in opposition to Liverpool's establishment, despite the fact that the project had much in its favour.

Where Reilly's influence is most apparent is in schemes such as the establishment of the Department of Civic Design. Again, while this was by no means a totally new idea on Reilly's part, tapping as it did into the town planning zeitgeist, its time had come, and this – allied to Lever's willingness to fund it – made it the success that it was, and still is. Reilly's ability to read the mood of the time and forge ahead with an idea should not be understated; but had all the other elements been missing, it might well have suffered the same fate as the 'art chair that failed'. The founding of the Department of Civic Design set in motion a train of events that would have far-reaching consequences, not only for Reilly's career, but also for figures such as Adshead, Abercrombie and Holford, all of whom would go on to be considered pioneers of the town planning movement. In Reilly's case, his insistence on an urban environment that celebrated its urbanity, rather than attempting to disguise itself as suburbia or a rural village – an idea which occupied his planning philosophy from the outset – is only now coming to be re-evaluated in the light of the current fashion in urban redevelopment.

The rediscovery of the city by modern-day planners, developers and architects recalls Reilly's vision of the ideal city. While I do not claim a direct causal link between the two, it is interesting to note statements such as the following in many of Reilly's later articles:

The elemental unit of planning... is no longer the house or the houseblock... the elemental unit is the city, because it is only in terms of this more complex social formation that any particular type of activity or building has significance.[5]

This holistic approach has been sadly missing in the intervening years in so much British planning policy. Within this elemental unit Reilly called for amenities such as parade streets[6] in the continental manner, which would enable citizens to meet, see, and be seen. Ideas such as this were no doubt considered somewhat frivolous at the time (1941), given the more pressing needs to win a war and rebuild shattered cities. However, we can now appreciate Reilly's vision of the mechanism of the urban environment, even in its seemingly more inconsequential details. Contemporary trends include features such as those outlined by Reilly in almost every large urban environment. This is a testament to his far-sighted grasp of the essential demands of civic design.

Reilly's other big planning theme – the Reilly Greens – arose out of a concern for the unity of the environment. He sought to take the most cherished elements of the village plan and adapt them to an urban setting, without falling into the trap of developing garden cities. Again, I do not claim to provide a direct link between the Reilly Plan and subsequent community planning theories, but it is interesting to note that many of the themes laid out in Wolfe's interpretation of Reilly's theories have been echoed by the promoters of the Community Architecture movement, established in Britain in the late 1970s and 1980s. Schemes such as Eldonian Village in the Vauxhall district of Liverpool provide community-based employment, housing, leisure and educational facilities along the lines envisaged by Reilly. The development of post-war planning theory can of course be traced back, at least in part, to Reilly's establishment of the Department of Civic Design, given that many of the city planners responsible for town planning policy were products of the Liverpool School. In that sense, for every example of Reilly's apparent prescience in formulating what are now fashionable urban theories, he must also be charged – at least by association – with those theories that are now judged to have been so harmful to post-war urban Britain.[7]

5   C. H. Reilly, 'Citizen or Peasant?', *Local Government Journal and Official's Gazette*, December 1943, p. 235.
6   Reilly, 'Parade Streets in Our Towns: Places for Walking, Talking, Sitting and Seeing', *Manchester Guardian*, 4 February 1941.
7   This was not always the case; A. G. Sheppard Fidler resigned from his post at Birmingham after the decision was made to reject brick build in favour of system-build blocks. See 'A Home of Your Own', *The New Jerusalem*, A Barraclough/Carey Production for BBC TV, 1995; and M. Glendinning and S. Muthesius, *Tower Block: Modern Public Housing in England, Scotland, Wales and Northern Ireland*, Yale University Press, New Haven and London, 1994, pp. 247–51.

If Reilly's legacy can be judged partially by the performance of his students, then a portion of the credit for the school that produced them must go to Lionel Budden. Budden has generally been portrayed as Reilly's lieutenant; an able administrator, scholarly and rather low-key, suffering in comparison with Reilly's flamboyant profile.[8] Certainly they were contrasting person-alities, but perhaps a better analogy would be between that of an interpreter and a transcriber; Reilly was the architectural interpreter, quick and instant in his approach; Budden was the transcriber, slower, erudite and methodical. Budden was one of a number of students from the very early years of Reilly's time at Liverpool who appears to have had a strong influence on his sub-sequent approach. Reilly considered him 'an extraordinarily mature student for his age'.[9] Certainly his scholarly interest in Classicism must have proved useful to Reilly in his quest to consolidate Liverpool's Classical teaching methods, particularly given that Reilly had no pretensions to scholarship himself. Another student, Adrian Berrington, also appears to have impressed Reilly in these early years, and as Powers notes, 'Berrington was interested in poetry and philosophy, and may have stimulated Reilly to a deeper search for unifying qualities in architecture.'[10] The exchange of ideas between Reilly and his students has generally been overlooked in favour of an assumption of a more traditional teacher–student relationship. If, as the evidence seems to indicate, Reilly was supplied with fresh ideas from his students and colleagues throughout his period as professor, it has a profound effect on our interpretation of the development of his careers both as an educationalist and as an architectural writer and theorist.[11] While Reilly may well have been

8   In his obituary for Budden Peter Shepheard noted that 'Those of us who were students in 1933, under the spell of the flamboyant and spectacular Reilly, had formed the idea that Budden was the perfect second-in-command... We were soon to learn how much of the strength of the Liverpool School depended on Budden's rational and liberal approach to architecture.' P. Shepheard, 'Obituary', *RIBA Journal*, Vol. 63, No. 11, September 1956, p. 478.

9   Letter from Reilly to Baker-Penoyre, 9 December 1909, Reilly Papers, Liverpool University Archive, Box S 3205.

10   A. Powers, 'Architectural Education in Britain 1880–1914', PhD thesis, Cambridge University, 1982, p. 143. See also Reilly's introduction to the catalogue of the *Exhibition of Etchings and Other Drawings by the Late Adrian Berrington*, Architectural Association, May 1925.

11   There are other instances of Reilly drawing inspiration for his teaching methods from people and organizations with which he was in contact. They include his employment of Slade School theories in teaching aesthetics during the early years of his professorship. Reilly's wife, Dorothy, was trained at the Slade, as was a leading figure and future friend of the Reillys in Liverpool, Augustus John. This point is made by Powers in 'Architectural Education in Britain', p. 139. Reilly also entertained Tonks and Chowne, members of the New English Art Club, at his Liverpool home; see Reilly, *Scaffolding in the Sky*, Routledge, London, 1938, pp. 131–32.

recycling ideas drawn from other sources, he undoubtedly transformed them into a successful system which produced a generation of architects who covered the British Empire with architecture in the 'Liverpool Manner'.

From a broader perspective, Reilly's theories about the appropriateness of Monumental Classicism as the preferred style for the Liverpool School, and his subsequent move towards a Modernism based largely on Classical principles, can now be seen in the context of later developments. Towards the end of his life, Reilly came to question the very basis of his faith in the validity of Classicism; and the belief in Monumentality and Classicism as approaches to architectural design was, from as early as 1946, already being reassessed by the broader architectural community.[12] Later evaluations of Monumentalism and its relationship to Modernism, such as Franco Borsi's *The Monumental Era*, have failed to acknowledge the specific role played by Reilly and the Liverpool School in the British scene. However, Borsi does concur with Ramsey's belief that much British Modernism in the 1930s exhibited an ancestry which he terms an 'aspect of the blend of traditional continuity and modern style… Neo-Georgian, international style and eclectic historicism intermix… according to typological divisions…'[13]

It is debatable how successful Reilly was in establishing a school at Liverpool modelled on the Ecole des Beaux-Arts. For Powers,

> Reilly's personality… was too impulsive and theatrical to allow for a profound understanding of the problems of reviving classical architecture… Perhaps it is unrealistic to expect that in a few years the Liverpool School could have equalled the accumulated expertise of the Ecole des Beaux-Arts…[14]

The characteristics that have been used so often to account for Reilly's success are here seen as part of the failure of the Liverpool School to achieve its Beaux-Arts aims. The failure was, as with all such things, relative; and in the mature style of ex-students such as Herbert Rowse or Harold Dod, we can see that not all of Reilly's efforts had been in vain. For Crouch, the continuity inherent in the development of the Liverpool School provides an estimation of Reilly's ultimate worth in terms of the broader sweep of architectural history: 'Just as there were conceptual links between the Arts and Crafts and the Beaux-Arts,

---

12   S. Giedion, 'The Need for a New Monumentality', *Architectural Review*, September 1948; L. Mumford, 'Monumentalism, Symbolism and Style', *Architectural Review*, April 1949, pp. 173–79.
13   F. Borsi, *The Monumental Era: European Architecture and Design 1921–1939*, Lund Humphries, London, 1987, pp. 99–100.
14   Powers, 'Architectural Education in Britain', p. 154.

so too are there links between the Beaux-Arts as practised at Liverpool and the nascent Modern Movement.'[15] Reilly's ability to negotiate the shift from Beaux-Arts Classicism to Modernism was due in part to those very qualities identified by Powers. If the attempt to revive Classicism had largely been a failure, the system Reilly had put into place was, nevertheless, to be a fertile ground for Modernism following his retirement from the school. As Crouch notes,

> The School of Architecture at Liverpool was to play an important role in the dissemination of European Modernism in the 1930s. Why was this? It can only be the case that the rationalising, technologically based view of architecture that Reilly inculcated at Liverpool was immediately receptive to the underlying ideology of Modernism.[16]

The other Reilly legacy, however, was a deep mistrust of ideology. This meant that it would only ever be able to interpret Modernism by reference to previous models. This lack of a strict Modernist consistency and an unwillingness to break cleanly with the past, which was evident in much of the Liverpool output, might explain why Reilly's successor to the Roscoe Chair was not to be Walter Gropius, as had been widely speculated at the time, but Lionel Budden. If Reilly has been largely overlooked by writers of Modernist histories, it is as a result of those very aspects of his architectural and personal ethos – pragmatism and eclecticism – which enabled him to be successful in negotiating the stylistic pitfalls which were the undoing of so many of his contemporaries.

15   Crouch, 'Design Initiatives in Liverpool', p. 172.
16   Crouch, 'Design Initiatives in Liverpool', p. 172.

Appendix

The following list of Charles Reilly's writings and broadcasts is included to give an indication of the chronological development of his work, together with a sense of its breadth. Although not comprehensive, it does include the majority of the books and articles he wrote between his appointment to the Roscoe Chair in 1904 and his death in 1948.

1905

'Some Tendencies in Modern Architecture', *British Architect*, Vol. LXIII, p. 329
'Some Tendencies in Modern Architecture', *Building News*, 12 May, pp. 673–74
'The Training of Architects', *The University Review*, Vol. 1, No. 3, p. 241
The Training of Architects, Sherrat & Hughes, London

1906

'A Beautiful Liverpool', *Daily Post and Mercury*, 29 January
The Liverpool Portfolio of Measured Drawings, Liverpool University Press, Liverpool

1907

'Urban and Suburban Planning', *The Builder*, 6 June
'Small Houses: Book by Baillie Scott', *Manchester Guardian*, 11 January

1908

'The University Teaching of Architecture', *Daily Courier*, 12 October
'The Proposed Diplomat at Cambridge', *The Times*, 18 February
The Liverpool Portfolio of Measured Drawings, Liverpool University Press, Liverpool

1910

'The Modern Renaissance in American Architecture', *RIBA Journal*, 25 June, pp. 630–35
'Town Planning Schemes in America', *Town Planning Review*, April, Vol. 1, No. 1, pp. 54–55
'The City of the Future: The Immediate Future in England', *Town Planning Review*, October, Vol. 1, No. 3, pp. 191–97
The Liverpool Architectural Sketch Book, Liverpool University Press, Liverpool

1911

'Criticism of Drawings Submitted for the Institute Prizes and Studentships 1910–1911', *RIBA Journal*, 4 February, pp. 220–26

The Liverpool Architectural Sketch Book, Liverpool University Press, Liverpool

1912

'Review of Students' Work', *The Architect*, 20 September
'On the Need for an English School of Architecture', *Architects' and Builders' Journal*,
        31 January, pp. 115–17
'The Monumental Qualities in Architecture', *Town Planning Review*, April, Vol. 3, No. 1,
        pp. 11–18

1913

The Liverpool Architectural Sketch Book, Liverpool University Press, Liverpool

1914

'Architecture as an Academic Subject', in *A Miscellany Presented to J. M. Mackay*,
        Liverpool University Press, Liverpool
Selected Etchings by Piranesi, Technical Journals, London

1920

The Liverpool University Architectural Sketch Book, Proprietors of Architectural
        Review, London

1921

'Ruined French and Belgian Streets', *Liverpool Post*, 1 January
'Crossing the Atlantic: The Return Voyage', *Liverpool Post*, 5 May
'Some Impressions of Canadian Towns I: Montreal', *Liverpool Post*, 8 July
'Some Impressions of Canadian Towns II: Ottawa', *Liverpool Post*, 15 July
'Ocean Travellers: American Types', *Liverpool Post*, 16 September
'Lure of Quebec's Romance told by a Noted Traveller', *Quebec Chronicle*, 3 September
Some Liverpool Streets and Buildings in 1921, published by the *Liverpool Daily Post and
        Mercury*, Liverpool

1922

'Fifth Avenue New York', *Country Life*, 1 April, pp. 435–36
'London Streets and Their Recent Buildings I', *Country Life*, 27 May, pp. 691–94
'London Streets and Their Recent Buildings II', *Country Life*, 10 June, pp. 777–81
'American Architecture: The Work of Mr T. Hastings', *Country Life*, 24 June, pp. 856–61
'London Streets: The Strand Western Portion', *Country Life*, 15 July, pp. 57–60
'London Streets: The Strand Eastern Portion', *Country Life*, 5 August, pp. 155–58
'London Streets: Fleet Street and Ludgate Hill', *Country Life*, 30 September, pp. 401–
        403
'The Port of London Building', *Country Life*, 14 October, pp. 461–66
'The Choice of a Small Country House I', *Country Life*, 21 October, p. 498
'The Choice of a Small Country House II', *Country Life*, 28 October, pp. 538–59
'The Choice of a Small Country House III', *Country Life*, 4 November, p. 575

'London Streets and Their Recent Buildings VI: Piccadilly', *Country Life*, 30 December, pp. 869–72

'The University of Liverpool', *Cox's Annual and Year Book*, pp. 105–13

'Architecture and the Public I: The Muddle of Our Streets', *John O'London's Weekly*, 4 April

'Architecture and the Public II: Coming Renaissance in Britain', *John O'London's Weekly*, 13 May

'American Railway Travelling: An Englishman's Impressions', *Liverpool Post*, 12 January

'Advertising with Chess', *Liverpool Post*, 24 January

'Past and Present', *Liverpool Post*, 24 January

'Weekend Visits', *Liverpool Post*, 19 April

'A Canadian Lourdes St Anne de Beaupre', *Liverpool Post*, 27 October

1923

'Old Burlington House Piccadilly', *Country Life*, 13 January, pp. 37–40

'London Streets and Their Buildings VII', *Country Life*, 14 April, pp. 495–98

'Architectural Practice in America and England', *Country Life*, 23 June, pp. 883–84

'A Note on the Architecture of Liverpool', in *Merseyside: A Handbook*, Liverpool University Press, Liverpool

1924

'The Bush Buildings: New York and London', *Architecture*, 10 April

'London Streets and Their Recent Buildings VIII: Whitehall and Parliament Street', *Country Life*, 9 February, p. 194

'London Streets and Their Buildings: Bond Street', *Country Life*, 3 May, p. 704

'Liverpool Cathedral', *Country Life*, 28 June, p. 1042

'Liverpool Cathedral', *Country Life*, 26 July, p. 123

'Modern Architecture in South Africa', *Country Life*, 15 November, p. 752

'London Streets and Their Buildings', *Country Life*, 13 December, p. 941

'Liverpool Cathedral', *John O'London's Weekly*, 7 June

'The Work of Thomas Graham Jackson', *John O'London's Weekly*, 29 November

'The Baroque Attitude to Life', *Liverpool Post*, 4 April

'Experiences in Italy: A Professor's Misadventure', *Liverpool Post*, 4 April

'A Problem in Psychology: Italy and its Churches', *Liverpool Post*, 19 April

'Byron and the Early Christians', *Liverpool Post*, 26 April

'Gestures in Rome Italian and British', *Liverpool Post*, 6 May

'Old Romance: The Hill Towns of Tuscany', *Liverpool Post*, 16 May

'The Fall of the Giants: Mantua', *Liverpool Post*, 22 May

'Books of the Day', *Liverpool Post*, 12 November

'Manchester Street Architecture I', *Manchester Guardian*, 24 May

'Manchester Street Architecture II', *Manchester Guardian*, 31 May

'Manchester Street Architecture III', *Manchester Guardian*, 7 June

'Manchester Street Architecture IV', *Manchester Guardian*, 14 June

'Manchester Street Architecture V', *Manchester Guardian*, 21 June
'Manchester Street Architecture VI', *Manchester Guardian*, 28 June
'Everyday Architecture', *The Observer*, 20 January
'Regent Street: Old and New', *The Observer*, April
McKim, Mead and White, Ernest & Benn, London
Some Architectural Problems of Today, Hodder & Stoughton, London
Some Manchester Streets and their Buildings, Liverpool University Press, Liverpool

1925

'Recent American Architecture', *The Architects' Journal*, 29 April, p. 648
'Bank Architecture', *The Banker*, January
'Some English Country Banks', *The Banker*, February
'Bank Directors and Architecture', *The Banker*, March
'Some Branches of Lloyds', *The Banker*, July
'Messrs Lazard's Messrs Shroeder's New Banks', *The Banker*, August
'New City and West End Quarters of the Westminster Bank', *The Banker*, October
'Some Further Midland Branch Banks', *The Banker*, November
'Baring's Bishopsgate Street', *The Banker*, December
'An Architectural Oasis', *Manchester Guardian*, 20 May
'Ashburn Hall', *Manchester Guardian*, 21 May
'The New Gallery's Features', *Manchester Guardian*, June
'Manchester Housing: Past and Future', *Manchester Guardian*, 12 September
'Modern Streets: Lost Unity of Design', *The Times Housing Supplement*, 7 April
'A Renaissance in the North', *The Weekly Westminster*, 30 May

1927

'Bank Architecture Alterations to Existing Premises', *The Banker*, January
'The Royal Bank of Scotland', *The Banker*, February
'Some Branches of Liverpool and Martins Bank', *The Banker*, March
'Some Branches of Barclays Bank (Dominion, Colonial and Overseas)', *The Banker*, April
'Bank Architecture at the Royal Academy', *The Banker*, June
'Bank Architecture', *The Banker*, July
'Messrs Williams Deacon's Premises', *The Banker*, August
'Some Buildings of the Bank of Scotland', *The Banker*, October
'Some of the Buildings of la Societé Generale de France', *The Banker*, November
'Some Buildings of the Banca Commerciale Italiana', *The Banker*, December
'St George's Hall, Liverpool', *Country Life*, 23 July, pp. 127–31
'The Training of Architects in the Liverpool School', *The Journal of Careers*, May
'The Human Worm', *Liverpool Post*, 31 January
'The Architect and his Opportunities', *Liverpool Post*, 5 August
'A City of Silver and Gold: An Impression of Ostend', *Liverpool Post*, 2 September
'A City of Peace: An Impression of Bruges', *Liverpool Post*, 6 September
'Brussels: French Clothes and Burgher Spirit', *Liverpool Post*, 12 September

'An Impression of Prague: A City of Baroque Gaiety', *Liverpool Post*, 23 September
'Vienna: The Old Order and the New', *Liverpool Post*, 1 October
'A Clean City: A Real Election Slogan', *Liverpool Post*, 26 October
'A Day in Belfast: An Impression', *Liverpool Post*, 14 November
'Some Liverpool Monuments', *The Liverpool Review*, Vol. 2 No. 1, February, pp. 1–5
'The Bungalow Menace', *The Times*, 5 March
'Some Liverpool Buildings', in *Impressions of Liverpool*, The Incorporated Chamber of
     Commerce, Liverpool

1928

'The New Headquarters of the Midland Bank', *The Banker*, January
'The Problem of Small Bank Branches: Some New Buildings of Martins Bank', *The
     Banker*, June
'The Imperial Bank Bombay', *The Banker*, September
'Some Branch Banks by W. Edmund Maufe for Lloyds', *The Banker*, November
'Why Visit America?', *Cunard Christmas Number*, December
'The Indian Problem', *John O'London's Weekly*, 31 March
'This Bungalow Madness', *John O'London's Weekly*, 4 August
'Going East: The P&O Train', *Liverpool Post*, 4 January
'Going East: Marseilles to Suez', *Liverpool Post*, 27 January
'Going East: The Canal', *Liverpool Post*, 6 February
'Going East: The Red Sea and the Indian Ocean', *Liverpool Post*, 21 February
'In the East: First Day in Bombay', *Liverpool Post*, 27 February
'Letters from India: H. H. The Jam of Jamnagar', *Liverpool Post*, 6 March
'Letters from the East: Delhis of all Sorts', *Liverpool Post*, 16 March
'Letters from the East: Farewell to India', *Liverpool Post*, 2 April
'Merseyside's New Era: Tunnel Ceremony Under the River', *Liverpool Post*, 4 April
'Happiness in Hospital', *Liverpool Post*, 10 April
'The Pyramids: An Impression', *Liverpool Post*, 3 May
'Liverpool First: A Causerie', *Liverpool Post*, 25 June
'Liverpool First: A Causerie', *Liverpool Post*, 3 July
'Liverpool First: A Causerie', *Liverpool Post*, 10 July
'Liverpool First: A Causerie', *Liverpool Post*, 17 July
'Liverpool First: A Causerie', *Liverpool Post*, 24 July
'Liverpool First: A Causerie', *Liverpool Post*, 31 July
'Le Touquet: Its Luxury and Extravagance', *Liverpool Post*, 7 August
'Liverpool First: A Causerie', *Liverpool Post*, 7 August
'Liverpool First: A Causerie', *Liverpool Post*, 14 August
'Liverpool First: A Causerie', *Liverpool Post*, 28 August
'Liverpool First: A Causerie', *Liverpool Post*, 4 September
'Pilots of the North Sea: The Men and Their Work', *Liverpool Post*, 27 September
'Liverpool First: A Causerie', *Liverpool Post*, 9 October
'Liverpool First: A Causerie', *Liverpool Post*, 23 October
'Liverpool First: A Causerie', *Liverpool Post*, 30 October

'Durnstein on the Danube: A Village Welcome', *Liverpool Post*, November
'Liverpool First: A Causerie', *Liverpool Post*, 6 November
'Liverpool First: A Causerie', *Liverpool Post*, 13 November
'Liverpool First: A Causerie, *Liverpool Post*, 27 November
'Liverpool First: A Causerie', *Liverpool Post*, 4 December
'Liverpool First: A Causerie', *Liverpool Post*, 11 December
'An Architect's Tour Some German Towns V: Cologne', *Manchester Guardian*, 1
    February
'London to Bombay: With the Proconsuls', *Manchester Guardian*, 15 February
'The Indian Scene I: Bombay', *Manchester Guardian*, 21 February
'The Indian Scene II: Jamnagar', *Manchester Guardian*, 23 February
'The Progress of New Delhi: A Warning', *Manchester Guardian*, March
'The Indian Scene IV: Delhis New and Old', *Manchester Guardian*, 23 March
'The Indian Scene V: A Hindu Host', *Manchester Guardian*, 30 March
'A Comfortable Sleep: Criticism of the Present Policy', *Manchester Guardian*, 21 May
'An Architect's Tour Some German Towns Today I: Hamburg', *Manchester Guardian*,
    28 October
'An Architect's Tour Some German Towns Today II: Berlin', *Manchester Guardian*, 29
    October
'An Architect's Tour Some German Towns Today III: Stuttgart', *Manchester Guardian*,
    30 October
'An Architect's Tour Some German Towns Today IV: Frankfort', *Manchester Guardian*,
    31 October
'The University of Liverpool: Coming of Age', *The Observer*, 6 May
'The Changing Face of Liverpool', in *The Book of Liverpool*, Liverpool Organisation

1929

'The National City Company Building', *The Banker*, January
'The Building of the New Midland Bank Headquarters', *The Banker*, February
'Messrs Guiness, Mahon and Company, Cornhill', *The Banker*, March
'The New Lloyd's Bank Headquarters', *The Banker*, April
'The New Headquarters of the Westminster Bank', *The Banker*, May
'Lloyds Bank "Prix de Rome" Branches', *The Banker*, June
'Martins Bank Liverpool Headquarters', *The Banker*, July
'Some Barclays Bank Interiors' *The Banker*, August
'Some Lloyds Bank Interiors', *The Banker*, September
'Some National Provincial Bank Interiors', *The Banker*, October
'Some Westminster Bank Interiors', *The Banker*, November
'Some Midland Bank Interiors', *The Banker*, December
'Sir Reginald Blomfield', *Building*, February
'Arthur J. Davis', *Building*, April
'Sir Edwin Lutyens', *Building*, May
'E. Vincent Harris', *Building*, September
'A New Liverpool', *Cox's Merseyside Annual 1929*, pp. 85–89

'Dream Streets in Our Cities', *Evening World*, 19 June
'The Cottages of England', *John O'London's Weekly*, 25 December
'Mainly About Liverpool: A Causerie VII', *Liverpool Diocesan Review*, Vol. 4, pp. 244–46
'Notes on the Bluecoat Chambers', *Liverpool Diocesan Review*, Vol. 4
'The City to Come: Poor Dirty 1929 Liverpool', *Liverpool Echo*, 28 October
'Making a New Oxford College', *Liverpool Post*, 23 July
'Oxford and Cambridge Compared', *Liverpool Post*, 3 September
'Mainly About Liverpool', *The Liverpool Review*, Vol. 4, No. 1, January
'Mainly About Liverpool', *The Liverpool Review*, Vol. 4, No. 3, March
'Mainly About Liverpool', *The Liverpool Review*, Vol. 4, No. 8, August
'Mainly About Liverpool', *The Liverpool Review*, Vol. 4, No. 10, October
'Mainly About Liverpool', *The Liverpool Review*, Vol. 4, No. 11, November
'Mainly About Liverpool', *The Liverpool Review*, Vol. 4, No. 12, December
'Power Stations in Cities', *The Times*, 6 May

1930

'Landmarks of the Year', *The Architects' Journal*, 8 January, pp. 55–62
'Barclays Bank (Dominion and Overseas)', *The Banker*, January
'Some District Bank Branches', *The Banker*, February
'The New Banks of the Month', *The Banker*, March
'Banks of the Month', *The Banker*, April
'Some Projected Banks', *The Banker*, May
'Some Continental Bank Buildings', *The Banker*, June
'Lloyds Bank New Headquarters', *The Banker*, July
'Some Recent National Provincial Banks', *The Banker*, August
'Some Martins Branches', *The Banker*, September
'Messrs Glyn Mills & Co's New Bank at Whitehall', *The Banker*, October
'The Societé Generale of Paris', *The Banker*, November
'Some Single Storey Banks', *The Banker*, December
'Sir Percy Scott Worthington', *Building*, March
'E. Berry Webber', *Building*, September
'Oliver Hill', *Building*, October
'Herbert J. Rowse', *Building*, December
'Some Younger Architects of Today', *Building*, December
'Old Tunes in a New Setting: Notes on the New City of London', *Financial News*, 24
     February
'A Free State Watering Place', *Liverpool Post*, no date
'Changed Dublin: A Clean City', *Liverpool Post*, 9 April
'Sunday on the Kiel Canal: A Beautiful Waterway', *Liverpool Post*, 15 August
'Stockholme's Crystal Palace: A Magical Exhibition', *Liverpool Post*, 26 August
'Up the Baltic in a Tramp: An Interesting Experience', *Liverpool Post*, 26 August
'Railway Centenary Street Decorations', *Liverpool Post*, 2 September
'Mainly About Liverpool: A Causerie', *The Liverpool Review*, Vol. 5
'New Architecture of the North I: Gothenburg', *Manchester Guardian*, 28 August

'New Architecture of the North II: Stockholm', *Manchester Guardian*, 29 August
'New Architecture of the North III: Copenhagen', *Manchester Guardian*, 1 September
'New Architecture of the North IV: Danzic and Gdynia', *Manchester Guardian*, 2 September
'Our Present and Future State', *Sphinx*, University of Liverpool

1931

'Landmarks of the Year', *The Architects' Journal*, 14 January, pp. 57–63
'Martins Bank New London Headquarters', *The Banker*, January
'The Midland Bank Headquarters', *The Banker*, February
'Some New Lloyds Bank Branches', *The Banker*, March
'The Emergence of the New Bank of England', *The Banker*, April
'Post-War Bank Architecture', *The Banker*, May
'Some Westminster Bank Branches', *The Banker*, June
'Some Barclays Bank Branches in the Birmingham Area', *The Banker*, July
'Messrs Higginson & Company's New Banking Premises', *The Banker*, August
'Two New City Banks: The Old Order and the New', *The Banker*, September
'Some New National Provincial Banks', *The Banker*, October
'Some Lloyds Bank Branches', *The Banker*, December
'Darcy Braddell', *Building*, January
'Percy Thomas', *Building*, February
'Edward Maufe', *Building*, May
'Gray Wornum', *Building*, July
'Joseph Emberton', *Building*, August
'Charles Holden', *Building*, September
'Thomas Smith Tait', *Building*, October
'Howard Hornby Robertson', *Building*, December
'Architecture as a Profession for Men and Women', *The Journal of Careers*, March
'A Smaller but Brighter Liverpool: The Sights of Rotterdam', *Liverpool Post*, 7 September
'The Wood Opera: A Festival at Zoppsot', *Manchester Guardian*, 6 August
'The Thames by Night: Through the Heart of London', *Manchester Guardian*, 19 August
'Liverpool and the Sea: Her Attitude of it Today', *Manchester Guardian*, 26 August
'Hamburg and the Elbe: The Second Port in Europe', *Manchester Guardian*, 4 September
'Glasgow and the Clyde: Paradise Defaced', *Manchester Guardian*, 14 September
Representative British Architects of the Present Day, B. T. Batsford, London

1932

'Lloyds Bank Church Street Liverpool', *The Architects' Journal*, 19 October, p. 497
'Some Recent Barclays Bank Branches', *The Banker*, January
'Some Westminster Branches', *The Banker*, February
'The Year's Banks', *The Banker*, June

'Some National Provincial Branches', *The Banker*, July
'Three Branches Which Have Won Distinction', *The Banker*, August
'Royal Bank of Scotland Lothbury', *The Banker*, September
'Some New Barclays Branches', *The Banker*, October
'The New Headquarters of Martins Bank at Liverpool', *The Banker*, November
'Martins Bank Headquarters: Mechanical Equipment', *The Banker*, December
'Christ Church Norris Green', *Liverpool Diocesan Review*, Vol. 7, pp. 390–92
'St Christopher's Church Norris Green', *Liverpool Diocesan Review*, Vol. 7, pp. 360–62
'St Colomba's Church Anfield', *Liverpool Diocesan Review*, Vol. 7, pp. 276–78
'Sunshine in Spain: An Impression of Visitors and Natives', *Liverpool Post*, 24 February
'Romance Real and Affected: A Visit to Granada', *Liverpool Post*, 10 April
'Stratford in Summer', *Liverpool Post*, 22 July
'Seville and Guadalquivir: An Enchanted City', *Manchester Guardian*, 26 April
'New Buildings in Manchester', *Manchester Guardian*, 16 June
'New Buildings in Manchester', *Manchester Guardian*, 21 June
The Theory and Practice of Architecture, Victor Gollancz, London

1933

'Martins Bank', *The Architects' Journal*, Vol. 77, p. 77
'Some Recent Empire Banks', *The Banker*, January
'The Liverpool Headquarters of Lloyds Bank', *The Banker*, February
'Some New Westminster Branches', *The Banker*, March
'Some Lloyds Bank Branches', *The Banker*, April
'Some District Bank Branches', *The Banker*, May
'Some National Provincial Branches', *The Banker*, June
'Some More National Provincial Branches', *The Banker*, July
'The New Bank of England', *The Banker*, August
'Glyn Mills New Headquarters in Lombard Street', *The Banker*, September
'Banks of the Month', *The Banker*, October
'Glyn Mills New Headquarters in Lombard Street II: The Interior', *The Banker*, November
'Some New Barclays Branches', *The Banker*, December
'Some Liverpool Memories', *Liverpool Post*, 8 May
'Some Liverpool Memories', *Liverpool Post*, 9 May
'Some Liverpool Memories', *Liverpool Post*, 16 May
'Some Liverpool Memories', *Liverpool Post*, 21 May
'Some Liverpool Memories', *Liverpool Post*, 29 May
'Some Liverpool Memories', *Liverpool Post*, 30 May
'Some Liverpool Memories', *Liverpool Post*, 6 June
'The City's Impressive New Buildings', *Liverpool Post*, 13 June
'Industrial Art: A Revolution in Public Taste', *Manchester Guardian*, 21 March
'British Bridges', *Manchester Guardian*, 7 November
'New Buildings in Manchester I', *Manchester Guardian*, 11 December
'New Buildings in Manchester II', *Manchester Guardian*, 12 December

'The Modern Factory', *Manchester Guardian*, 19 December

'Bath and its Environs', *The Times*, 7 October

'Building Construction: Thirty Years Change', *The Times Trade and Engineering Supplement*, 6 May

'The Cathedral and the Town', programme to mark the laying of the foundation stone of the Liverpool Metropolitan Cathedral of Christ the King, 5 June

1934

'Landmarks of the Year', *The Architects' Journal*, 11 January, pp. 65–72

'Live Furniture', *The Architects' Journal*, 2 August

'The Architectural Scene 1900–1934', *Architectural Review*, Vol. 75, pp. 170–76

'Grey Wornum and His Building', *Architectural Review*, Vol. 76, pp. 192–94

'The Birmingham Municipal Bank', *The Banker*, January

'The Colombo Branch of the Chartered Bank of India, Australia and China', *The Banker*, February

'Some Recent Westminster Branches', *The Banker*, March

'Some National Provincial Branches', *The Banker*, April

'Some Lloyds Bank Branches', *The Banker*, June

'The National Provincial Bank's New Headquarters at Liverpool', *The Banker*, July

'Some National Provincial Banks', *The Banker*, August

'Some Westminster Banks', *The Banker*, September

'Some Barclays Branches', *The Banker*, October

'Some Scottish Banks', *The Banker*, November

'Some More Scottish Banks', *The Banker*, December

'Manchester Reference Library', *Building*, February

'How Shall We Renovate Our Cities?', *Daily Mail*, 15 November

'Living a Fine Art in the New Mansion Flats', *Daily Telegraph Housing Supplement*, 26 November

'What the Architect Stands for Today', *The Listener*, 7 November

'Whitewashing the Slums', *Liverpool Diocesan Review*, Vol. 9, pp. 64–66

'The Tunnel Entrance', *Liverpool Post*, 8 August

'The Diversions of a Great Scholar', *Liverpool Post*, 1 November

'Brighton Faced With a Great Problem', *Manchester Guardian*, 15 January

'Brighton: Her Need of a Town Architect', *Manchester Guardian*, 15 January

'Whither Architecture?', *Manchester Guardian*, 26 January

'Manchester Goes Roman', *Manchester Guardian*, 13 February

'Steelwork', *Manchester Guardian*, 21 February

'The Moderns as Targets', *Manchester Guardian*, 12 March

'Architectural', *Manchester Guardian*, 26 March

'RIBA Growth of a Great Institution Today's 100th Annual Meeting', *Manchester Guardian*, 14 May

'Modern Expressions in Architecture: Cinema', *Manchester Guardian*, 20 June

'The Little New House', *Manchester Guardian*, 26 July

'Modern Expressions in Architecture: Churches', *Manchester Guardian*, 3 August

'Modern Expressions in Architecture: The Factory', *Manchester Guardian*, 17 September
'Architecture Without Tears', *Manchester Guardian*, 9 October
'The New Library at Cambridge', *Manchester Guardian*, 22 October
'Modern Expressions in Architecture: The Great Store', *Manchester Guardian*, 6 November
'The RIBA', *Manchester Guardian*, 26 November
'Architecture of Today: An International Show', *Manchester Guardian*, 1 December
'Modern Architecture', *Manchester Guardian*, 5 December
'Modern Expressions in Architecture: The Library', *Manchester Guardian*, 28 December
'Disfigurement of Signs', *Sign and Display Advertising*, 22 February
'Motor Tracks on South Downs', *The Times*, 7 February
'Illuminated Signs', *The Times*, 19 February
'Manchester's New Library', *The Yorkshire Post*, 17 July
The Body of the Town, E. A. Bryant, Liverpool

1935

'The Year's Work', *The Architects' Journal*, 10 January, pp. 69–76
'Banks', *Architectural Review*, no date
'Railway Stations', *Architectural Review*, no date
'The Modern Store', *Architectural Review*, May
'Shop Fronts', *Architectural Review*, July
'The Cinema', *Architectural Review*, August
'Some Empire Banks', *The Banker*, January
'Some More Empire Banks', *The Banker*, February
'Some National Provincial Banks', *The Banker*, March
'Some New Barclays Branches', *The Banker*, April
'Some Westminster Branches', *The Banker*, June
'Some National Provincial Banks', *The Banker*, July
'Some Martins Branches', *The Banker*, August
'The Scottish Widows' Fund New Cornhill Building', *The Banker*, September
'The Midland Bank's New Manchester Premises', *The Banker*, October
'Some Scottish Banks', *The Banker*, November
'Some New Barclays Branches', *The Banker*, December
'Professor Reilly and the New Bath Springs', *Bath Chronicle and Herald*, 9 November
'Bexhill Pavilion', *Bexhill Observer*, 4 January
'First Class Building: Manchester Envies Bexhill', *Bexhill Observer*, 21 December
'I Defend This New Architecture', *Daily Mail*, 30 December
'Bentalls at Kingston: The New Building', *Daily Telegraph*, 14 September
'The Older Brighton', *Liverpool Post*, March
'The Indian Princes', *New Statesman and Nation*, 9 March
'A School Problem', *New Statesman and Nation*, 23 March
'A School Problem', *New Statesman and Nation*, 4 May

'Modern Expressions in Architecture: The Elementary School', *Manchester Guardian*, 22 March
'Sicily in Spring: A Toylike Country', *Manchester Guardian*, 23 April
'The Epstein Statues', *Manchester Guardian*, 5 June
'Modern Buildings', *Manchester Guardian*, 6 June
'Colour in Concrete Buildings', *Manchester Guardian*, 16 June
'Modern Houses', *Manchester Guardian*, 26 June
'Shop Architecture', *Manchester Guardian*, 25 July
'Professor Gropius', *Manchester Guardian*, 1 August
'Modern Expressions in Architecture: The Modern Dwelling House', *Manchester Guardian*, 16 August
'Modern Housing', *Manchester Guardian*, 16 October
'A New Church at Heaton Chapel', *Manchester Guardian*, 22 October
'Bexhill Pavilion', *Manchester Guardian*, 13 December
'New Worlds for Old', *The Oak*, no date
'Rebuilding Terminal Stations', *The Times*, 22 June
'Preserving the Countryside', *The Times*, 2 August
'Bank Architecture', *The Times Trade and Engineering Supplement*, July

1936

'The Year's Work at Home', *The Architects' Journal*, 16 January, pp. 109–20
'The Hong Kong and Shanghai Banking Corporation's New Headquarters', *The Banker*, January
'The First Modern Bank Building: The Philadelphia Saving Fund Society's New Offices', *The Banker*, February
'Some Midland Bank Branches', *The Banker*, March
'Some Lloyds Banks', *The Banker*, April
'Some Westminster Branches', *The Banker*, May
'A Bank Takes a Step Forward', *The Banker*, June
'Some National Provincial Branches', *The Banker*, July
'Some Recent Martins Branches', *The Banker*, August
'Some Branches of the Australian Banks', *The Banker*, September
'Headquarters Buildings of Australian Banks', *The Banker*, October
'Some New Scottish Banks', *The Banker*, November
'Williams Deacon's Bank London Headquarters', *The Banker*, December
'Architectural Crooning', *Daily Mail*, 4 February
'A Suggestion for a Liverpool Memorial to His Late Majesty King George V', *Liverpool Diocesan Review*, Vol. 11, pp. 127–29
'A Village College', *New Statesman and Nation*, 23 April
'Gateway to the West', *News Chronicle*, 21 May
'The Title of the House ', *Manchester Guardian*, 7 January
'The English Abbey', *Manchester Guardian*, 20 January
'The New Architectural Sculpture', *Manchester Guardian*, 26 January
'Old and New Morocco I: Marrakesh', *Manchester Guardian*, 22 February

'Old and New Morocco II: Rabat Modern French Architecture', *Manchester Guardian*, 25 February
'Old and New Morocco III: City of Fez Back to the Middle Ages', *Manchester Guardian*, 27 February
'Architecture', *Manchester Guardian*, 2 June
'Manchester Revisited', *Manchester Guardian*, 15 June
'Manchester Revisited', *Manchester Guardian*, 17 June
'Garden Ornament', *Manchester Guardian*, 22 September
'An English Architect', *Manchester Guardian*, 2 October
'The Lesson of Japanese Architecture', *Manchester Guardian*, 23 October
'Modern Cinemas', *Manchester Guardian*, 29 December
'New Cathedral at Guildford', *The Times*, 22 April
'The Training of Architects', *The Times*, 3 August
'Architecture at Cambridge', *The Times*, 31 October

1937

'The Year's Work at Home', *The Architects' Journal*, 14 January, pp. 91–103
'The National Theatre: Two Views', *The Architects' Journal*, 16 September
'Professor Reilly Speaking', *The Architects' Journal*, 21 October
'Professor Reilly Speaking', *The Architects' Journal*, 25 November
'Some Recent Canadian Banks', *The Banker*, January
'Some Westminster Branches', *The Banker*, March
'Some New Midland Bank Branches', *The Banker*, April
'The New Paris Office of the Westminster Foreign Bank', *The Banker*, May
'Some More National Provincial Banks', *The Banker*, June
'Some Recent Lloyds Branches', *The Banker*, July
'The Tivoli Corner of the Bank of England: Then and Now', *The Banker*, August
'Some Recent Australian Branch Banks', *The Banker*, September
'Some New Barclays Branches', *The Banker*, October
'Some New Scottish Banks', *The Banker*, November
'Some New Midland Bank Branches', *The Banker*, December
'Facade: A Commentary on Various Matters', *Building*, April
'Facade: A Commentary on Various Matters', *Building*, June
'Facade: A Commentary on Various Matters', *Building*, August
'Allerton Tower', *Liverpool Post*, 15 February
'British Architecture: The RA Winter Exhibition', *Manchester Guardian*, 9 January
'Art and the Machine', *Manchester Guardian*, 26 February
'Housing Compared', *Manchester Guardian*, 19 March
'Modern English Architecture', *Manchester Guardian*, 23 April
'Liverpool in London: RIBA Exhibition', *Manchester Guardian*, 30 April
'Architecture at the RA: Sir Edwin Lutyens's New Hyde Park Corner', *Manchester Guardian*, 5 May
'Our Great Houses', *Manchester Guardian*, 21 May
'Franciscan Architecture in England', *Manchester Guardian*, 28 May

'Small Houses', *Manchester Guardian*, 13 July
'Seaside Homes', *Manchester Guardian*, 17 August
'A Study in Contrasts: Three Seaports, Plymouth, Havre and Amsterdam', *Manchester Guardian*, 24 September
'Sea Cities: Oslo, Copenhagen, Stockholm', *Manchester Guardian*, 25 September
'New Buildings Near Paris: Modern Schools Decoration and Colour', *Manchester Guardian*, 23 October
'The New Hotel at Leeds', *Manchester Guardian*, 13 November
'Recent Building Schemes in Two Cities', *Manchester Guardian*, 4 December
'Some Recent Manchester Buildings', *Manchester Guardian*, 6 December
'Whitewashing the Slums', *Manchester Guardian*, 21 December
'Flats', *Manchester Guardian*, 24 December
'Model House', *News Chronicle*, February
'It Was a Great Win', *News Chronicle*, 19 March
'What These Young Men Have Taught Us', *News Chronicle*, 22 March
'Old Hastings', *The Times*, 16 February
'The Brighton Pavilion', *The Times*, 20 July
'A National Theatre', *The Times*, 14 September

1938

'The Year's Work at Home', *The Architects' Journal*, 13 January, p. 87
'Professor Reilly Speaking', *The Architects' Journal*, 26 May
'Rood Screen at Shackelwell', *The Architects' Journal*, Vol. 87, p. 194
'Note by Professor Reilly', *Art Notes*, January/February, p. 34
'Glass Yesterday and Today', *Country Life Supplement*, 26 February
'Metropolitan Architectural Changes', *Financial Times*, 14 February
'Painted Ceiling at the Sandon', *Liverpool Post*, no date
'Painting Architectural Stonework', *Liverpool Post*, 6 August
'A Fine Modern Building', *Manchester Guardian*, 10 January
'New Architecture: Forms and Materials of the Future', *Manchester Guardian*, 12 January
'The Uses of Glass', *Manchester Guardian*, 14 January
'Modern Building', *Manchester Guardian*, 14 March
'The Rehousing of Europe', *Manchester Guardian*, 10 May
'Manchester Town Hall: Old and New', *Manchester Guardian*, 21 June
'The Glasgow Exhibition: Second Thoughts', *Manchester Guardian*, 22 June
'Sir John Vanbrugh', *Manchester Guardian*, 29 July
'Manchester's Complexion', *Manchester Guardian*, August
'Interiors', *Manchester Guardian*, 16 September
'The New School', *Manchester Guardian*, 4 October
'Finsbury's New Health Centre', *Manchester Guardian*, 26 October
'A Miniature History of the English House', *Manchester Guardian*, 29 November
'The Art of Architecture', *Manchester Guardian*, 20 December
'Cottages', *Manchester Guardian*, 23 December
'Your Home and Mine', *Manchester Guardian*, 30 December

'Parish Churches', *The Times*, 23 April
Scaffolding in the Sky, Routledge, London

1939

'The Year's Work at Home', *The Architects' Journal*, 19 January, pp. 133–46
'Royal Night Club: Royal Pavilion', *Manchester Guardian*, 7 February
'West Indian Towns', *Manchester Guardian*, 26 May
'The Spanish Main', *Manchester Guardian*, 27 May
'Modern Building', *Manchester Guardian*, 14 July
'The Late Sir Percy Worthington', *Manchester Guardian*, 18 July
'The Changing Aspects of the English House', *Manchester Guardian*, 4 August
'Better Architecture', *Manchester Guardian*, 5 August
'Nazis at Home', *News Chronicle*, 31 October
'The Architects' Plight', *The Times*, 30 October
'Beyond the Silver Sands and Palm Trees', *Tribune*, 26 May

1940

'Oxford's Buildings Surveyed', *Manchester Guardian*, 5 February
'An Idealist', *Manchester Guardian*, 13 February
'Eric Mendelsohn: Architect of Light', *Manchester Guardian*, 8 April
'Architecture After the War', *Manchester Guardian*, 18 October
'English Furniture', *Manchester Guardian*, 19 November
'A Plan by Which to Build', *Manchester Guardian*, 9 December
'The Buildings of Oxford', *Manchester Guardian Weekly*, 16 February
'How Shall We Rebuild London?', *News Chronicle*, 8 October
'Building the Britain of Tomorrow', *Telegraph and Independent*, 28 November
'How Can We Plan a New and Beautiful Britain?', *Telegraph and Independent*, 16
    December
'Town Planning', *Tribune*, 9 August

1941

'Organization of Town Planning', *The Architect and Building News*, 5 September
'Anglo-Soviet Relations', *The Builder*, 5 September
'Modern Movements in Architecture', *The Listener*, 20 March, pp. 399–401
'Richard Norman Shaw', *Manchester Guardian*, 21 January
'Parade Streets in Our Towns', *Manchester Guardian*, 4 February
'The Suburbs We Should Build', *Manchester Guardian*, 14 February
'Town and Country Tomorrow', *Manchester Guardian*, 25 February
'Quiet Streets and Districts', *Manchester Guardian*, 6 March
'Wren's Difficulties and Ours', *Manchester Guardian*, 10 March
'Mechanised City of Towers', *Manchester Guardian*, 18 March
'Aims of Civic Design', *Manchester Guardian*, 1 April
'An Architectural Army to Remake Our Damaged Towns', *Manchester Guardian*, 20
    August

'Town Planning', *Manchester Guardian*, 9 September
'When We Build Again', *Manchester Guardian*, 28 October
'What Every Town Should Know', *News Chronicle*, 28 October

1942

'Towards a Settlement in India', *The Church of England Newspaper*, 23 January
'This London of the Future is Already Out of Date', *Evening Standard*, 26 October
'Town Planning After the War', *Homes and Gardens*, June
'Pre-Steel Plans', *The Irish Times*, 27 October
'Rebuilding Britain', *Manchester Guardian*, 27 January
'The Village College of Impington', *Manchester Guardian*, 18 July
'The End of an Era: To Patch or Replan?', *Manchester Guardian*, 11 September
'Replanning of Central London', *Manchester Guardian*, 13 October

1943

'Citizen or Peasant?', *The Architects' Journal*, 4 November, pp. 344–46
'Replanning London', *Art and Industry*, September
'Devastation in Liverpool', *Building*, December
'London When the Lights Go Up', *Daily Mail*, 15 December
'Let's Make London a Pleasant Place to Live In', *Evening Standard*, 12 February
'Brave New London', *Evening Standard*, 9 July
'Don't Have Another Fake at Westminster', *Evening Standard*, 1 November
'They Want London a Glorified Garden City', *Evening Standard*, 30 November
'A City Fine Arts Commission', *Liverpool Post*, 25 May
'Communal Life and Replanning', *Liverpool Post*, 10 August
'Park Like Cities of the Future', *Liverpool Post*, 29 October
'Citizen or Peasant?', *Local Government Journal and Officials' Gazette*, December, p. 235
'Leave Out The Tinsel: Build Our MPs a Plain but Modern Home', *Manchester Evening News*, 4 November
'Tall Flats and No Fires', *Manchester Evening News*, 17 December
'Sir Edwin Lutyens', *Manchester Guardian*, 13 January
'The Process of Architectural Tradition', *Manchester Guardian*, 5 February
'Planning', *Manchester Guardian*, 24 February
'Town Planning and Rebuilding', *Manchester Guardian*, 25 February
'Rebuilding the Big Towns: Two Lines of Approach', *Manchester Guardian*, 25 May
'The Plan for London', *Manchester Guardian*, 11 July
'Civic Diagnosis: An Exhibition from Hull', *Manchester Guardian*, 8 September
'House of Commons', *Manchester Guardian*, 3 November
'The City of the Future', *Municipal Journal*, 5 November
'According to the Plan', *The Observer*, 30 May
'Make London Fit to Live In', *The Star*, 20 December
'The Royal Academy Plan for Central London', *The Studio*, February
'Garden Cities', *The Times*, 5 January
'The Oxhey Estate', *The Times*, 1 December

'Citizen or Peasant?', *Town and Country Planning Association*, 28 October
'Modern Town Planning', *Tribune*, 26 February
'A Sketch for a Town Plan', *Tribune*, 5 March
'Planning London', *Tribune*, 17 September

1944

'Lutyens: The Man as I Knew Him on a Visit to India', *The Architects' Journal*, 10 February, p. 16
'Plan for Post-War Plymouth', *Building*, July, pp. 182–83
'The Village Green Comes Back', *Daily Express*, 22 November
'Four Rings for London', *Evening Standard*, 14 December
'The City Plan is Confusion; Worse Confused', *Evening Standard*, 14 December
'Stories of Lutyens', *The Listener*, 27 January
'Architecture', *Manchester Guardian*, 29 October
'The Architect', *Manchester Guardian*, 27 December
'Lord Portal's Steel Bungalows', *News Chronicle*, 26 May
'Sir Edwin Lutyens: Master Builder of His Age', *The Observer*, 2 January
'The Crystal Palace', *The Times*, 10 January
'Small Houses', *The Times*, 19 February
'Industrial Design', *The Times*, 10 December
'Cooling Towers', *The Times*, 27 December
'Royal Palaces', *Tribune*, 25 February
'Best Buildings of the Year', in *The Architects' Yearbook*, Elek, London

1945

'Cooling Towers and Waste Heat', *The Architects' Journal*, 4 January
'Sir Charles Discusses the Plan for Plymouth', *The Architects' Journal*, 13 September
'A Plan to be Thankful For', *Architectural Review*, May
'Rebuilding the Towns: Two Regional Plans', *Britain Today*, No. 115, November
'Rebuilding the Towns: Manchester Region and City', *Britain Today*, No. 116, December
'A Plan for Merseyside', *Building*, April, pp. 94–95
'The Problem of the Cooling Tower', *Country Life*, 1 June, p. 942
'Men to Plan Our Houses', *Evening Standard*, 24 May
'New London', *Evening Standard*, 17 August
'London County Council Housing Plans', *Evening Standard*, 26 November
'Threat to Durham', *Manchester Guardian*, 9 January
'Books for Export', *Manchester Guardian*, 26 January
'A Plan for Merseyside: Need for New Industries', *Manchester Guardian*, 6 March
'A New Plan for Old Norwich', *Manchester Guardian*, 30 May
'The City of Manchester Plan', *Manchester Guardian*, 31 October
'Many Mansions', *The Observer*, 27 May
'My Ideal Student', *Sphinx*, Vol. XLVI, No. 1, January, p. 10
'Regency Hove', *The Times*, 20 February
'London Housing Plans', *The Times*, 5 November

'Plan for Norwich', *Tribune*, 15 June
'Exit Brick Boxes', *Tribune*, 3 August
'Further Town Planning Reports from Big Cities', *Tribune*, 16 November

1946

'Hints from the Poles', *Architectural Review*, July
'Rebuilding the Towns: Four Provincial Plans', *Britain Today*, No. 117, January
'National Amenities Council', *The Builder*, 14 June
'The RIBA Report on Education', *Building*, July, pp. 202–203
'Hexagonal Site Planning: A Scheme for Birkenhead', *The National House Builder*, January, pp. 13–17
'Bilston Communities', *New Statesman*, 23 November
'Plea for Architects', *News Chronicle*, 14 May
'Wooden Houses', *Official Architect*, February, pp. 80–82
'A National Theatre', *The Times*, 7 January
'The Thames at Kingston', *The Times*, 1 March
'National Amenities Council', *The Times*, 13 May
'The 1951 Exhibition', *The Times*, 15 June
'About Houses', *Tribune*, 23 August
'Introduction', in H. Feibusch, *Mural Painting*, London
'Foreword', in G. Hemm, *Selected Drawings of Liverpool Cathedral*, Littlebury Bros, Liverpool

1947

'Kingston School of Architecture', *Builder*, 18 July
'Mendelsohn in America', *Building*, November, pp. 345–51
'Bilston: Its Problems and Its Way of Tackling Them', *Discovery*, August
'Architects in Arms Against the LCC', *Evening Standard*, 26 November
'Suburbia As We Know It Must Go', *Liverpool Post*, 23 July
'Bankside Power Station', *The Times*, 30 April
'Planning in Malta', *The Times*, 31 December
The Outline Plan for the County Borough of Birkenhead, Birkenhead County Council
'Organisation for Culture', *Civic Hall Committee Wolverhampton*, p. 4

1948

'The University of Ceylon: Colombo', *Building*, February, pp. 40–42
'The Heritage of the Town', in M. L. Lightman (ed.), *The British Heritage*, Odhams Press, London

Radio Broadcasts and Undated Articles

Radio Broadcasts

For the BBC: series title *Some Modern Buildings*, typescripts in Reilly Papers, Liverpool University Archive, Box D207/27:
'The Modern Problem', no date
'The Office Block', no date
'The Church of Today', no date
'The Small House of Today', no date
'The Town of Today', no date

Other broadcast manuscripts in Box D207/27:
'The Spirit of the Architect', no date
'A Main Duty of Bankers', no date
'Bank Architecture', no date
'Good and Bad Manners in Architecture', no date
'Architecture and the Public I', no date
'Architecture and the Public II', no date
'The New Architecture', no date
'The New London', no date
'In Praise of Brick', no date
'Bricks and Brickmaking', no date
'The Orders of Architecture', no date
'Country Towns, Country Shops and Country Banks', no date
'What You Should Look for in the Design of Your Home', no date
'Building Methods, Old and New', no date
'The Street of Today', broadcast 25 February 1927

Articles

'The English Contribution to Theatre Design Since the 19th Century ', no date. Copy in Reilly Papers, Liverpool University Archive, Box D207/12/1
'The Work of Jacqueline Gloag', *Design for Textiles*, no date

Bibliography

Primary Sources

Liverpool University Archive, Sydney Jones Library

L. P. Abercrombie, Papers, Box D439
S. D. Adshead, Papers, Boxes D247/1–2
Architecture/Civic Design Committee Minutes 1910–1977, Box S3435
L. B. Budden, Papers, Box D249
Building Committee for the New Building for the School of Architecture, 1914, Box
    S280
F. E. Hyde, Papers, Boxes D116/1–3
C. H. Reilly, Papers, Boxes D207/1–42, S3205–13
Vice-Chancellors' Papers, Boxes P3/30, P4/1/23, P4/1/26, P4A/3/4, P4A/3/5, P4A/3/6,
    P6A/4, P6A/10, P6B/3/5

Local History Archives, Liverpool Central Library

L. B. Budden and M. Budden, Papers, Boxes HQ 052 721 LIV, HQ 378 09 CUT, HQ
    378 05 REC
City Beautiful Plan, Box H 711 582 ROS
City Beautiful Wayside Cafe, Box HQ 378 05 SPH
Liverpool Architectural Society, Papers, Boxes H 720 6 ARC, HQ 720 6242 ROY
Architecture of Liverpool (General), Boxes H 726 BRO, HQ 708 8 CEL, HQ 050 (72)
    LAN, H 942 7215 COX, HF 072 DAI, RQ 690 5 BUI, H 720 9 HUG, HF 380 LIV,
    RQ 720 5 ARC, HQ 942 721
Liverpool Repertory Theatre (Playhouse), Papers, Boxes HF 792 1 PLA, HQ 792 1
    PLA, HQ 792 06 LIV, HQ 052 721 LIV
C. H. Reilly, Papers, Boxes H 283 05 LIV, HF 282 1 LIV, H 027 31 ATH, H 282 1 SOL,
    HQ 711 (719) BIR, H 352 COU, H 942 721 HOL, H 942 721 IMP, H 720 REI
Sandon Studios Society (Blue Coat), Papers, Boxes H 706 5 CAT, H 708 6 BUL, H 708
    8 SAN, HQ 360 CUT

Secondary Sources

Abercrombie, L. Patrick, *Greater London Plan 1944*, HMSO, London, 1945
——'The Square House', *Town Planning Review*, Vol. 4, 1914, p. 35

——*Town and Country Planning*, Thornton Butterworth, London, 1933

——'Town Planning in Greater London', *Town Planning Review*, Vol. 2, 1912, p. 262

Abercrombie, L. Patrick, with S. Kelly and A. Kelly, *The Dublin of the Future*, Hodder & Stoughton, London, 1922

Adshead, Stanley D., 'City Improvement', *Town Planning Review*, Vol. 1/3

——*The Duchy of Cornwall Estate in London*, HMSO, London, 1911

——'Liverpool: A Preliminary Survey With Some Suggestions for Remodelling its Central Area', *Town Planning Review*, Vol. 1/2

——'The New Delhi Plan', *Architects' and Builders' Journal*, Vol. LXXXVIII, 1913, p. 267

——'The Standard Cottage', *Town Planning Review*, Vol. 6, 1916, pp. 244–49

——'Style in Architectural Draughtsmanship', *RIBA Journal*, Vol. XIV, 1907, p. 485

——'Style in Architecture', *RIBA Journal*, Vol. XVI, 1909, p. 304

——'A Suggestion for the Reconstruction of St John's Gardens, St George's Hall, Liverpool', *Town Planning Review*, Vol. 1/1

——*Town Planning & Town Development*, Methuen, London, 1923

Allan, Adrian, and Ann L. Mackenzie, *Redbrick University Revisited: The University of Liverpool 1920–1952*, The University of Liverpool Art Gallery, 3 May–1 July, 1994 (catalogue)

Allan, Adrian, and Sheila Turner, 'Si Monumentum Requiris Circumspice: A Note on the Older Plans in the Custody of the Chief Engineer', *The University of Liverpool Recorder*, No. 81, 1979, pp. 162–67

——'The Papers of Sir Charles Reilly: A Recent Accession to the University Archives', *The University of Liverpool Recorder*, No. 81, 1979, pp. 159–62

Anscombe, Isabelle, *Omega and After*, Thames & Hudson, London, 1981

Architect & Building News, 'Design for a Department Store in Oxford Street by William Crabtree', 26 July, 1929, pp. 114–15

——'Dining Room of Sir Charles H. Reilly', 25 March 1927, p. 515

——'Liverpool University Architectural Exhibition 1929', 26 July, 1929, pp. 114–15

——'Sir Charles Reilly: An Appreciation', 13 February, 1948, p. 131

Architects' Journal, 'Birkenhead: A New Plan by Sir Charles Reilly and N. J. Aslan', 9 May, 1946, pp. 359–62

——'Birkenhead Community versus Segregation', 3 August, 1944

——'Editor's Note', 21 October, 1937

——'Scoreboard', 25 May, 1939, pp. 851–52

Arts and Crafts Exhibition Society, *Arts and Crafts: Essays by Members of the Arts and Crafts Exhibition Society*, Rivington, Percival & Co, London, 1893

Arts Council of Great Britain, *Thirties: British Art and Design Before the War*, Hayward Gallery, London, 25 October, 1979–13 January, 1980 (catalogue)

Arup, Ove, 'Art and Architecture, The Architect–Engineer Relationship', *RIBA Journal*, Vol. LXXIII, 1966, p. 354

Banham, Reyner, *Theory and Design in the First Machine Age*, Architectural Press, London, 1960

Barman, Christian, *Balbus: Or the Future of Architecture*, London, 1926

Belcher, John, *Essentials in Architecture*, Batsford, London, 1907

Belcher, John, and Mervyn Macartney, *Later Renaissance Architecture in England*, London, 1898–1901

Bell, N. Martin, *Fifty Years of Merseyside Art*, Bluecoat Chambers, Liverpool, 22 July– 12 August, 1951 (catalogue)

Bennett, Mary, *The Art Sheds 1894–1905*, Walker Art Gallery, Liverpool, 1981 (catalogue)

Benton, C., T. Benton and A. Scarf, *The History of Architecture and Design*, Open University Press, Milton Keynes, 1975

Betjeman, John, *First and Last Loves*, Murray, London, 1952

Bhoyroo, Jane, 'The Rebuilding of the Peter Jones Department Store by William Crabtree', BA dissertation, Newcastle University, 1995

Bisson, Roderick, *The Sandon Studios Society and the Arts*, Parry Books, Liverpool, 1965

Blomfield, Reginald, *Architectural Drawing and Draughtsmen*, Cassells, London, 1912

——*A History of French Architecture 1494–1661*, George Bell & Sons, London, 1911

——*A History of French Architecture 1661–1774*, George Bell & Sons, London, 1921

——'Is Modern Architecture on the Right Track?', *RIBA Journal*, 26 July, 1933

——*Memoirs of an Architect*, Macmillan, London, 1932

——*Richard Norman Shaw*, Batsford, London, 1940

——*Six Architects*, Macmillan, London, 1935

——*Studies in Architecture*, Macmillan, London, 1905

——*The History of Renaissance Architecture in England 1500–1800*, George Bell & Sons, London, 1897

——*The Mistress Art*, Edward Arnold, London, 1908

——*The Touchstone of Architecture*, Clarendon Press, Oxford, 1925

——*Modernismus: A Study*, Macmillan, London, 1934

Bluecoat Society of Arts, *An Exhibition of the Art and Architecture of Liverpool at the Turn of the Century*, Bluecoat Chambers, Liverpool, 1960 (catalogue)

Borsi, Franco, *The Monumental Era: European Architecture and Design 1921–39*, Lund Humphries, London, 1987

Briggs, Martin S., *Everyman's Concise Encyclopaedia of Architecture*, Dent & Sons, London, 1959

Broadbent, R. J., *The Annals of the Liverpool Stage*, Edward Howell, Liverpool, 1908

Browning, Philip, *Liverpool Heritage Walks*, Liverpool City Planning Department, 1989

Budden, Lionel, 'Architectural Education and the New Charter', *Architects' and Builders' Journal*, Vol. XXXIX, 1914, p. 56

——'Charles Reilly: An Appreciation', *RIBA Journal*, March, 1948, pp. 212–13

——'The Liverpool School of Architecture', *The Liverpolitan*, November, 1951, pp. 9–11

——'Report of the Special Committee on Architectural Education', *Royal Institute of British Architects*, 1939

——'The Standardization of Elements of Design in Domestic Architecture', *Town Planning Review*, Vol. 6, 1916, pp. 238–43

Budden, Lionel (ed.), *The Book of the Liverpool School of Architecture*, Liverpool University Press, Liverpool, 1932

The Builder, 'The Accrington War Memorial', 22 October, 1920, p. 456

——'Architectural Education at the Liverpool University', Vol. XCV, 1908, p. 341

——'Architectural Schools' Section: Liverpool', Vol. CVII, 1914, p. 297

——'Charles H. Reilly: Gold Medallist', Vol. CLXIV, 1943, p. 40

——'A Department Store Lime Street Liverpool by S. A. Marshall', 19 July, 1935, p. 113

——'A Government Housing Scheme: Roe Green Village, Kingsbury', Vol. CXIV, 1918, p. 5

——'A Hundred New Towns for Britain', 18 October, 1935, p. 690

——'The Ideal of a Modern Cathedral', 26 October, 1901, pp. 350–51

——'The Liverpool Cathedral Question', 21 December, 1901

——'Liverpool Cenotaph', 22 October, 1926, pp. 649–50

——'The Liverpool School of Architecture', 16 July, 1910, pp. 63–65

——'The Liverpool School of Architecture', 28 July, 1933, pp. 141–42

——'Obituary: Sir Charles Reilly OBE, DLitt, MA, FRIBA', 6 February, 1948, p. 161

——'Opening of New School of Architecture Liverpool', 28 July, 1933, pp. 141–47

——'Plan for Birkenhead', 19 April, 1946, pp. 376–80

——'The Repertory Theatre Liverpool', 16 August, 1912, pp. 202–03

——'What is Modern Architecture?', 29 December, 1944, p. 510

Builders' Journal, 'An Architects' Qualifications: What Liverpool is Doing', Vol. I, 1895, p. 61

Builders' Journal and Architectural Record, 'University of Liverpool School of Architecture', Vol. XXX, 1909, p. 85

Building, 'Dinner for Six', February, 1947, pp. 52–55

——'Dinner for Six', May, 1947, pp. 152–55

——'New London Store', July, 1936, pp. 278–83

Building News, 'The Grand Manner in Architecture', 13 October, 1908

——'Students' Union Building Liverpool University', 9 September, 1907

——'Students' Union Building Liverpool University', 29 October, 1909, p. 641

——'Students' Union Building Liverpool University', 8 July, 1910

Campbell, Louise, 'A Call to Order: The Rome Prize and Early Twentieth Century British Architecture', *Architectural History*, Vol. 32, 1989, pp. 131–51

Carrington, N. (ed.), *Mark Gertler: Selected Letters* (introduction by Quentin Bell), London, 1965

Carter, E. J., 'C. H. Reilly', *Journal of the Association of Building Technicians*, March, 1948, p. 61

Cavanagh, Terry, *Public Sculpture in Liverpool*, Liverpool University Press, Liverpool, 1997

Chandler, George, *William Roscoe of Liverpool 1753–1831*, Batsford, London, 1953

Cherry, Gordon E., *Pioneers in British Planning*, The Architectural Press, London, 1981

Cherry, Gordon E., and Penny Leith, *Holford: a study in architecture, planning and civic design*, Mansell, London, 1986

Compton, Ann, *Edward Halliday: Art for Life 1925–1939*, Liverpool University Press, Liverpool, 1999

Compton, Ann (ed.), *Edward Carter Preston 1885–1965: Sculptor, Painter, Medalist*, University of Liverpool Art Gallery, 19 March–16 July, 1999 (catalogue)

Cornforth, John, 'Christopher Hussey and Modern Architecture', *Country Life*, 22 and 29 October, 1981, pp. 1366–8 and 1468–70

—— 'The Husseys and the Picturesque', *Country Life*, 10 and 17 May, 1979

—— *The Search for a Style: Country Life and Architecture 1897–1935*, W.W. Norton, New York and London, 1988

Cotton, Vere E., *The Book of Liverpool Cathedral*, Liverpool University Press, Liverpool, 1964

Crabtree, William, 'Peter Jones Shop', *The Architects' Journal*, 5 March, 1969, p. 615

Creese, Walter L., *The Search for Environment: The Garden City Before and After*, Yale University Press, New Haven, CT, 1966

Cret, Paul, 'The Ecole des Beaux-Arts: Its Teaching and its Influence on American Architecture', *Builders' Journal and Architectural Record*, Vol. XXX, 1909, p. 106

Crinson, Mark, and Jules Lubbock, *Architecture, Art or Profession?*, Manchester University Press, Manchester, 1994

Crouch, Christopher, 'Design Initiatives in Liverpool 1881–1914', PhD thesis, Liverpool University, 1992

Cunningham, Valentine, *British Writers of the Thirties*, Oxford University Press, Oxford, 1989

Curtis, Penelope, *Sculpture on Merseyside*, Tate Gallery, Liverpool, 1988

Curtis, Penelope (ed.), *Patronage and Practice: Sculpture on Merseyside*, Tate Gallery, Liverpool, 1989

Curtis, W. J. R., *Modern Architecture Since 1900*, Phaidon Press, London, 1996

Darley, G., *Villages of Vision*, The Architectural Press, London, 1975

Darwin, B., *Fifty Years of Country Life*, London, 1947

Dean, Basil, *Seven Ages: An Autobiography 1888–1927*, Hutchinson, London, 1970

Dean, David, *The Thirties: Recalling the English Architectural Scene*, Trefoil Books, London, 1983

Department of the Environment, *List of Buildings of Special Architectural and Historic Interest*, Liverpool, 1975

Dix, Gerald, 'Little Plans and Noble Diagrams', *Town Planning Review*, Vol. XLIX, 1978, p. 331

Dod, Harold A., 'Liverpool School of Architecture', *The Builder*, 8 July, 1932, pp. 48–49

Drexler, A., *The Architecture of the Ecole des Beaux Arts*, Secker & Warburg, London, 1977

Duggan, H., 'The Function of a Playgoers' Society', *The Playgoers' Society*, No. 5, March, 1913

Eaton, Leonard, *American Architecture Comes of Age: European Reaction to H. H. Richardson and Louis Sullivan*, MIT Press, Cambridge, MA, 1972

Edwards, Arthur Trystan, *Architectural Style*, Faber & Gwyer, London, 1926

—— 'A Criticism of the Garden City Movement', *Town Planning Review*, Vol. 4/2

——'The Duchy of Cornwall Estate', *Architects' and Builders' Journal*, 1914, p. 151

——'A Further Criticism of the Garden City Movement', *Town Planning Review*, Vol. 4/4

——*Good and Bad Manners in Architecture*, Philip Allan & Co, London, 1944

——*The Things Which are Seen: A Revaluation of the Visual Arts*, London, 1921

Effendowicz, M., 'The Modern Peter Jones: An Unusual Store', *The Gazette*, 11 October, 1986, pp. 866–67

Elias, F., *John Lea, Citizen and Art Lover*, Philip Son and Nephew, Liverpool, 1928

Esher, L., *A Broken Wave: The Rebuilding of England 1940–1980*, Allen Lane, London, 1981

Farey, C., and A. T. Edwards, *Architectural Drawing, Perspectives and Rendering*, Batsford, London, 1931

Fleetwood-Hesketh, Peter, *Murray's Lancashire Architectural Guide*, John Murray, London, 1955

——'Recollections of the Twenties and Thirties', *Thirties Society Journal*, No. 1, 1980, p. 13

Foley, D., *Controlling London's Growth: Planning the Great Wen 1940–1960*, University of California Press, Berkeley and Los Angeles, 1963

Ford, Boris (ed.), *Early Twentieth Century Britain: The Cambridge Cultural History*, Cambridge University Press, Cambridge, 1992

Forshaw, J. H., and L. P. Abercrombie, *County of London Plan*, Macmillan, London, 1943

Fry, E. Maxwell, *Maxwell Fry: Autobiographical Sketches*, Elek, London, 1975

Geddes, Patrick, *Cities in Evolution* (with introduction by Percy Johnson-Marshall), Ernest & Benn, London, 1968

Geidion, Sigfried, *Mechanization Takes Command: a contribution to anonymous history*, Oxford University Press, Oxford, 1955

——'The Need for a New Monumentality', *Architectural Review*, September, 1948

——*Space, Time and Architecture*, Oxford University Press, Oxford, 1941

George, W. L., *Labour and Housing at Port Sunlight*, 1909

Gill, Eric, *Autobiography*, Jonathan Cape, London, 1940

Glancey, Jonathan, *Twentieth Century Architecture: The Structures that Shaped the Century*, Carlton Books, London, 1998

Glendinning, M., and S. Muthesius, *Tower Block: Modern Public Housing in England, Scotland, Wales and Northern Ireland*, Yale University Press, New Haven, CT, 1994

Goldie, Grace Wyndham, *The Liverpool Repertory Theatre 1911–1934*, Liverpool University Press, Liverpool, 1935

Goodhart-Rendell, H. S., 'Architectural Memories 1905–1955', *The Builder*, Vol. CLXXXIX, 1952, p. 1044

Gould, W., and A. Hodgkiss, *The Resources of Merseyside*, Liverpool University Press, Liverpool, 1982

Gowan, J. (ed.), *A Continuing Experiment: Learning and Teaching at the Architectural Association*, Architectural Press, London, 1975

Gray, A. Stuart, *Edwardian Architecture: A Biographical Dictionary*, Gerald Duckworth, London, 1985

Greenhalgh, Paul (ed.), *Modernism in Design*, Reaktion Books, London, 1990

Hawkes, D., and N. Taylor, *Barry Parker and Raymond Unwin*, Architectural Association, London, 1980

Hearnshaw, F. J. C., *The Centenary History of King's College London 1828–1928*, London, 1928

Hemm, Gordon, *Selected Drawings of Liverpool Cathedral* (with an introduction by Charles Reilly), Littlebury Bros, Liverpool, 1946

Hewitt-Jones, Robin, 'The Background, Origins and Development of the Blue Coat School of Liverpool and Chester 1700–1834', MA thesis, Liverpool University, 1974

Hill, Oliver, 'Architect's Autobiography No. 10', *Building*, 1949, p. 406

Hitchcock, H. Russell, *Architecture: Nineteenth and Twentieth Centuries*, Penguin, Harmondsworth, 1958

Hobsbawm, E. J., *Industry and Empire*, Penguin, Harmondsworth, 1969

Holford, William G., 'Sir Charles Reilly: An Appreciation', *The Listener*, 15 July, 1948, pp. 93–94

——'Sir Charles Reilly: Obituary', *Architectural Review*, Vol. 103, 1948, pp. 180–83

Holroyd, Michael, *Augustus John: A Biography. Vol. I. The Years of Innocence*, Heinemann, London, 1974

Hone, J., *The Life of Henry Tonks*, London, 1939

Houfe, S., *Sir Albert Richardson: The Professor*, White Crescent Press, Luton, 1980

Howard, E., and F. J. Osborn (eds), *Garden Cities of Tomorrow*, Faber & Faber, London, 1946

Hubbard, Edward, and Michael Shippobottom, *A Guide to Port Sunlight Village*, Liverpool University Press, Liverpool, 1988

Hughes, J. Quentin, 'Before the Bauhaus: The Experiment at the Liverpool School of Architecture and Applied Arts', *Architectural History*, Vol. 25, 1982, p. 102

——'Dock Warehouses at Liverpool', *Architectural History*, Vol. IV, 1961

——'Education and the Architectural Profession in Britain at the Turn of the Century', *Journal of Art and Design Education*, Vol. I, No. 1, 1982, p. 135

——'Harvey Lonsdale Elmes and St George's Hall, Liverpool', *Architecture North West*, Vol. 24, August–September, 1967

——*Liverpool*, Studio Vista, London, 1969

——*Liverpool: City of Architecture*, Bluecoat Press, Liverpool, 1999

——*Seaport: Architecture and Townscape in Liverpool*, Bluecoat Press, Liverpool, repr. 1993

Hughes, J. Quentin, and Simon Pepper, 'Liverpool', *Thirties Society*, February, 1982

Hussey, Christopher, *The Picturesque: Studies in a Point of View*, Frank Cass, London, 1967 [1927]

Illustrated Carpenter and Builder, 'Calling All Readers: Martians Sound a Martial Note', 12 January, 1945, p. 29

Jackson, Anthony, *The Politics of Architecture*, The Architectural Press, London, 1970

Jackson, T. G., 'The Training of Architects to the Pursuit of Architecture', *The Builder*, Vol. LXI, 1891, p. 460

Jencks, Charles, *The Language of Post-Modern Architecture*, Academy Editions, London, 1987

——*Le Corbusier and the Tragic View of Architecture*, Penguin, Harmondsworth, 1987

——*Modern Movements in Architecture*, Penguin, Harmondsworth, 1973

Jencks, Charles, and George Baird, *Meaning in Architecture*, Barrie and Jenckins, London, 1970

John, Augustus, *Chiaroscuro*, Jonathan Cape, London, 1952

Johnson, Paul, *The Birth of the Modern: World Society 1815–1830*, Weidenfeld & Nicolson, London, 1991

Johnstone, E., 'Sloane Leader', *Architectural Review*, Vol. CLXXXVII, No. 1115, January, 1990, pp. 75–79

Jolly, W. P., *Lord Leverhulme: A Biography*, Constable, London, 1976

Jones, Ronald P., 'The Life and Work of Harvey Lonsdale Elmes', *Architectural Review*, Vol. 15, No. 91, June 1904

Journal of Education, 'Art', June, 1945

Kaplan, Wendy (ed.), *Charles Rennie Mackintosh*, McLennan Galleries, Glasgow Museum, 25 May–30 September, 1996 (catalogue)

Kaye, B., *The Development of the Architectural Profession in Britain*, George Allen & Unwin, London, 1960

Kelly, Thomas, *For the Advancement of Learning: The University of Liverpool 1881–1981*, Liverpool University Press, Liverpool, 1981

Kennerley, Peter, *The Building of Liverpool Cathedral*, Carnegie Publishing, Preston, 1991

King, James, *The Last Modern: A Life of Herbert Read*, Weidenfeld & Nicolson, London, 1990

Knowles, Lorraine, *St George's Hall, Liverpool*, National Museums and Galleries on Merseyside, Liverpool, 1988

Lanchester, H. V., *The Art of A. E. Rickards*, Technical Journals, London, 1920

——*The Art of Town Planning*, Chapman & Hall, London, 1925

——'Park Systems for Great Cities', *The Builder*, 3 October, 1908

Lane, Tony, *Liverpool: Gateway of Empire*, Lawrence & Wishart, London, 1987

Leathart, J. R., 'The Peter Jones Department Store', *Building*, 1935

Lefkowitz-Horowitz, Helen, *Culture and the City: Cultural Philanthropy in Chicago from the 1880s to 1917*, Chicago University Press, Chicago, 1976

Lethaby, William, *Architecture, Mysticism and Myth*, Architectural Press, London, 1974

Lever, Jill (ed.), *Catalogue of the Drawings Collection of the Royal Institute of British Architects O–R*, Gregs International, Farnborough, 1976

Lightman, M. L. (ed.), *The British Heritage*, Odhams Press, London, 1948

The Listener, 'For and Against Modern Architecture', 28 November, 1934

Liverpool Heritage Bureau, *Buildings of Liverpool*, Liverpool City Council, Liverpool, 1978

——*Liverpool Conservation Areas*, Liverpool, 1982

Lloyd-Jones, Thomas, *101 Views of Edwardian Liverpool and New Brighton*, Gallery Press, Liverpool, 1972

MacCunn, W. S., *Bluecoat Chambers: The Origins and Development of an Arts Centre*, Liverpool University Press, Liverpool, 1956

MacKenzie, Ann, and Adrian Allan (eds), *Redbrick University Revisited: The Autobiography of 'Bruce Truscot'*, Liverpool University Press, Liverpool, 1996

MacLeod, Robert, *Style and Society: Architectural Ideology in Britain 1835–1914*, RIBA Publications, London, 1971

McMahon, Pelham, and Pam Brooks, *An Actor's Place*, Bluecoat Press, Liverpool, 2000

Manchester Guardian, 'The Birkenhead Housing Scheme', 9 April, 1946

——'Post Impressionists at Liverpool', 20 April, 1912

——'Sir Charles Reilly: Obituary', 3 February, 1948

March Philips, L., 'Liverpool and its Architecture', *Morning Post*, 9 June, 1913

Marx, Karl, *Capital* (first published as *Das Kapital* in 1867), Penguin, Harmondsworth, 1976

Mayer, J., *Early Exhibitions of Art in Liverpool*, Spottiswood, London, 1876

Middleton, R., *The Beaux Arts*, Academy Editions, London, 1978

Miller, A., *Poverty Deserved*, Liverpress, Liverpool, 1988

Montague, C. E., 'A City that has a Theatre', *Manchester Guardian*, 18 September, 1922

Morley, D. W., 'Sociological Approach to Town Planning: The Bilston Experiment', *Discovery*, August, 1947

Morris, Edward, and Emma Roberts, *The Liverpool Academy and Other Exhibitions of Contemporary Art in Liverpool 1774–1867: A History and Index of Artists and Works Exhibited*, Liverpool University Press / National Museums and Galleries on Merseyside, Liverpool, 1998

Muir, R., and C. H. Reilly, 'The University Teaching of Architecture', *Daily Courier*, 12 October, 1907

Mumford, Lewis, 'Monumentalism, Symbolism and Style', *Architectural Review*, April, 1949, pp. 178–80

Nairn, Ian, *Nairn's London*, Penguin, Harmondsworth, 1988

National House Builder, 'Hexagonal Site Planning: A Scheme for Birkenhead', January, 1946

News Review, 'Reilly's Commandoes', 21 December, 1942, p. 18

Neat, Timothy, *Part Seen, Part Imagined*, Canongate Press, Edinburgh, 1994

Newbery, Frank, 'Liverpool's Flats 1919–1939: Policy and Design of Central Area Redevelopment by the Liverpool Housing Department', BArch thesis, Liverpool University, 1980

Osborn, F. J., 'Great Future for a Great City', *The Observer*, 17 December, 1944

——'Real Family Homes', *Manchester Evening News*, 17 December, 1943

Papadakis, Andreas, and Harriet Watson (eds), *New Classicism*, Rizzoli, New York, 1990

Pepper, Simon, and Mark Swenarton, 'Home Front: Garden Suburbs for Munition Workers 1915–1918', *Architectural Review*, Vol. CLXIII, No. 976, June, 1978, pp. 366–75

——'Neo-Georgian Maison-type', *Architectural Review*, Vol. 168, 1980, pp. 87–92

Pepper, Simon (ed.), 'The Garden City Legacy', *Architectural Review*, Vol. CLXIII, No. 976, June, 1978, pp. 321–77

Pevsner, Nikolaus, *The Buildings of England: North Lancashire*, Penguin, Harmondsworth, 1969

——*The Buildings of England: South Lancashire*, Penguin, Harmondsworth, 1969

——*Pioneers of Modern Design: From William Morris to Walter Gropius*, Penguin, Harmondsworth, 1975

Picton, James A., *Architectural History of Liverpool*, Liverpool, 1858

——*Views in Modern Liverpool*, Liverpool, 1864

Picture Post, 'Planning Post-War Britain', 8 July, 1944

Plunz, R. (ed.), *Design and the Public Good: Selected Writing 1930–80 by Serge Chermayeff*, MIT Press, Cambridge, MA, 1982

Poole, Susan Joy, 'A Critical Analysis of the Work of Herbert Tyson Smith: Sculptor and Designer', PhD thesis, Liverpool University, 1994

Powers, Alan, '"Architects I Have Known": The Architectural Career of S. D. Adshead', *Architectural History*, Vol. 24, 1981, pp. 103–23

——'Architectural Education in Britain 1880–1914', PhD thesis, Cambridge University, 1982

——'Fry (Edwin) Maxwell', in C.S. Nicholls (ed.), *Dictionary of National Biography 1986–1990*, Oxford University Press, Oxford, 1996

——'Mersey Marvels', Thirties Society Pamphlet to Liverpool Tour, *The Thirties Society Journal*, 1988

——*Oliver Hill: Architect and Lover of Life*, Mouton Publications, London, 1989

Pritchard, Jack, *View From a Long Chair*, Routledge and Kegan, London, 1984

Ramsey, Stanley C., 'The Work of McKim, Mead and White', *RIBA Journal*, Vol. 25, 1917, pp. 25–29

Rasmussen, Steen Eiler, *London: The Unique City* (introduction by James Bone), Jonathan Cape, London, 1947

Rathbone, Edmund F., 'Current Architecture: The Church of Humanity, Liverpool', *Architectural Review*, March, 1911, pp. 148–50

——*William Rathbone: A Memoir*, Macmillan, London, 1905

Readings, Bill, *Introducing Lyotard: Art and Politics*, Routledge, London, 1991

Reeve, A., 'The Beloved Prof. ', *Leader Magazine*, 22 September, 1945, p. 15

Reilly, Charles Herbert, 'Architects in Arms Against the LCC', *Evening Standard*, 26 November, 1947

——'The Architectural Scene 1900–1934', *Architectural Review*, Vol. 75, 1934, pp. 170–76

——'Architecture After the War', *Manchester Guardian*, 18 October, 1940

——'Architecture as an Academic Subject', in Reilly (ed.), *A Miscellany Presented to John Macdonald Mackay*, pp. 9–13

——'Architecture as a Profession for Men and Women', *The Journal of Careers*, March, 1931

——'The Body of the Town', Roscoe Lecture delivered at Royal Institute, Liverpool, 12 March

——'Brave New London', *Evening Standard*, 9 July, 1943
——'Building the Britain of Tomorrow', *Telegraph and Independent*, 16 December, 1940
——'Christ Church, Norris Green', *The Liverpool Review*, Vol. VII, 1932, pp. 390–92
——'Citizen or Peasant?' *Local Government Journal & Official's Gazette*, December, 1943, p. 235
——'The City of Manchester Plan', *Manchester Guardian*, 31 October, 1945
——'The City of the Future', *Town Planning Review*, Vol. 1, No. 3, 1910, pp. 191–97
——'The City Plan is Confusion Worse Confused', *Evening Standard*, 23 August, 1945
——'Criticism of Drawings Submitted for the Institute Prizes and Studentships 1910–11', *RIBA Journal*, 4 February, 1911, pp. 220–26
——'Hexagonal Site Planning: A Scheme for Birkenhead', *The National House Builder*, January, 1946, pp. 13–17
——'Let's Make London a Pleasant Place to Live In', *Evening Standard*, 12 February, 1943
——'The Little New House', *Manchester Guardian*, 26 July, 1934
——'Lloyds Bank, Church Street, Liverpool', *The Architects' Journal*, 19 October, 1932, p. 497
——'This London of the Future is Already Out of Date', *Evening Standard*, 26 October, 1942, p. 6
——'London When the Lights Go Up', *Daily Mail*, 15 December, 1943
——'Lutyens: The Man I Knew on a Visit to India', *The Architects' Journal*, 10 February, 1944, p. 16
——'Make London Fit to Live In', *The Star*, 20 December, 1943
——'Martins Bank', *The Architects' Journal*, Vol. 77, 1933, p. 77
——'Master Builder of His Age', *The Observer*, 2 January, 1944
——*McKim, Mead and White*, Ernest and Benn, London, 1924
——'Men to Plan Our Houses', *Evening Standard*, 24 May, 1945
——'Mendelsohn in America', *Building*, November, 1947, pp. 345–51
——'Modern Houses', *Manchester Guardian*, 26 June, 1935
——'Modern Movements in Architecture', *The Listener*, 20 March, 1941, pp. 399–401
——'The Modern Renaissance in American Architecture', *RIBA Journal*, 25 June, 1910, pp. 630–35
——'The Moderns as Targets', *Manchester Guardian*, 12 March, 1934
——'The Monumental Qualities in Architecture', *Town Planning Review*, Vol. 3, No. 1, 1911, pp. 11–18
——'A New Liverpool', *Cox's Merseyside Annual 1929*, pp. 85–89
——'New London', *Evening Standard*, August 1945
——'A Note on the Architecture of Liverpool', *Merseyside: A Handbook to Liverpool*, 1923
——'Notes by Professor Reilly', *Art Notes*, January/February, 1938, p. 34
——'On the Need for an English School of Architecture', *Architects' and Builders' Journal*, 1912, p. 11
——'Organization for Culture', *The Civic Hall Quarterly*, 1947, p. 4
——'Parade Streets in Our Towns', *Manchester Guardian*, 4 February, 1941

——'A Plan by Which to Build', *Manchester Guardian*, 9 December, 1940

——'The Plan for London', *Manchester Guardian*, 10 July, 1943

——'A Plan for Merseyside', *Building*, April, 1945, pp. 94–95

——'A Plan for Merseyside: Need for New Industries', *Manchester Guardian*, 6 March, 1945

——'Plan for Post-War Plymouth', *Building*, July, 1944, pp. 182–83

——'Planning London', *Tribune*, 17 September, 1943

——'Professor Gropius', *Manchester Guardian*, 1 August, 1935

——'Rebuilding the Big Towns: Two Lines of Approach', *Manchester Guardian*, 25 May, 1943

——'Rebuilding the Towns: Four Provincial Plans', *Britain Today*, No. 117, January, 1946, pp. 16–20

——'Rebuilding the Towns: Manchester Region and City', *Britain Today*, No. 116, December, 1945, pp. 17–20

——'Rebuilding the Towns: Two Regional Plans', *Britain Today*, No. 115, November, 1945, pp. 22–27

——'Recent American Architecture', *The Architects' Journal*, 29 April, 1925, p. 648

——'Replanning of Central London: A Royal Academy Exhibition', *Manchester Guardian*, 13 October, 1942

——*Representative British Architects of the Present Day*, Batsford, London, 1931

——'Review of Students' Work', *The Architect*, 20 September, 1912

——'Rood Screen at Shackelwell', *The Architects' Journal*, Vol. 87, 1938, p. 194

——*Scaffolding in the Sky*, Routledge, London, 1938

——*Selected Etchings by Piranesi*, Technical Journals, London, 1914

——'A Sketch for a Town Plan', *Tribune*, 5 March, 1943

——*Some Architectural Problems of Today*, Liverpool University Press, Liverpool, 1924

——'Some Liverpool Buildings', *Impressions of Liverpool*, 1927

——'Some Liverpool Memories, School of Architecture and the Late Lord Leverhulme', *Liverpool Post & Mercury*, 16 May, 1933

——'Some Liverpool Monuments', *The Liverpool Review*, Vol. II, No. 1, February, 1927, pp. 1–5

——*Some Liverpool Streets and Buildings in 1921*, Liverpool Daily Post and Mercury, 1921

——'Some Tendencies in Modern Architecture', *British Architect*, Vol. LXIII, 1905, p. 329

——'Some Tendencies in Modern Architecture', *Building News*, 12 May, 1905, pp. 673–74

——'Some Younger Architects of Today', *Building*, December, 1930, pp. 524–29

——'St Christopher's Church, Norris Green', *Liverpool Diocesan Review*, Vol. 7, 1932, pp. 360–62

——'St Christopher's Norris Green', *The Liverpool Review*, Vol. III, 1932, pp. 360–62

——'St Columba's Church Anfield', *The Liverpool Review*, Vol. III, 1932, pp. 276–78

——'Suburbia as We Know It Must Go', *Liverpool Daily Post*, 23 July, 1947

——'A Suggestion for a Liverpool Memorial to His Late Majesty King George V', *Liverpool Diocesan Review*, Vol. XI, 1936, pp. 127–29

——'They Want London a Glorified Garden City', *Evening Standard*, 30 November, 1943

——'The RIBA Report on Education', *Building*, July, 1946, pp. 202–03

——'The Suburbs We Should Build', *Manchester Guardian*, 14 February, 1941

——'Tall Flats and No Fires', *Manchester Evening News*, 17 December, 1943

——*The Theory and Practice of Architecture*, Victor Gollancz, London, 1932

——'The Training of Architects in the Liverpool School', *The Journal of Careers*, May, 1927

——'The Training of Architects', *The University Review*, Vol. I, No. 3, July, 1905, pp. 241–56

——*The Training of Architects*, Sherrat & Hughes, London, 1905

——'A Town Planner's Solution', *Discovery*, August, 1947, p. 253

——'Town Planning Schemes in America', *Town Planning Review*, Vol. 1, No. 1, p. 54

——'Urban and Suburban Planning', *The Builder*, 6 June, 1907

——'Urban and Suburban Planning', *Architectural Review*, Vol. XXII, 1907, p. 102

——'The University of Liverpool', *Cox's Annual and Year Book*, 1922, pp. 105–13

——'Whitewashing the Slums', *The Liverpool Review*, Vol. IX, 1934, pp. 64–66

——'Wooden Houses', *Official Architect*, February, 1946, pp. 80–82

Reilly, Charles Herbert (ed.), *A Miscellany: Presented to John Macdonald Mackay*, Liverpool University Press, Liverpool, 1914

——*The Liverpool Architectural Sketch Book*, Liverpool University Press, Liverpool, 1910, 1911 and 1913

——*The Liverpool University Architectural Sketch Book*, Architectural Review, London, 1920

——*The Liverpool Portfolio of Measured Drawings*, Liverpool University Press, Liverpool, 1906 and 1908

Reilly, Charles Herbert, and Naim J. Aslan, *The Outline Plan for the County Borough of Birkenhead*, Birkenhead County Council, Liverpool, 1947

Reilly, Paul, *An Eye on Design*, Reinhardt, London, 1987

——*An Introduction to Regency Architecture*, Art and Technics, London, 1948

RIBA Journal, 'Review of Scaffolding in the Sky', 5 December, 1938, pp. 144–45

——'Sir Rennell Rodd on the British School at Rome', 26 November, 1910, p. 61

Richards, J. M., *An Introduction to Modern Architecture*, Pelican, London, 1940

Richardson, Albert E., 'Liverpool School Exhibition', *RIBA Journal*, Vol. 19, 1912, p. 222

——'The Liverpool School Annual', *RIBA Journal*, 27 January, 1912, pp. 222–23

——*Monumental Classical Architecture in Great Britain and Ireland During the Eighteenth and Nineteenth Centuries*, Batsford, London, 1914

Richmond, Peter, 'Rebuilding the Temple: The Inter-War Architecture of Herbert J. Rowse', MDes dissertation, Liverpool University, 1992

Ritchie-Noakes, Nancy, *Jesse Hartley: Dock Engineer to the Port of Liverpool 1824–1860*, Merseyside County Council/Merseyside County Museums, Liverpool, 1980

——*Liverpool's Historic Waterfront*, HMSO, London, 1984

Robertson, Howard, *Architecture Explained*, Ernest and Benn, London, 1927

——*Modern Architectural Design*, The Architectural Press, London, 1932

Robinson, C. H., *The Improvement of Towns and Cities or the Practical Basis of Civic Aesthetics*, Putman, London, 1901

Rohdenburg, T. K., *A History of the School of Architecture, Columbia University*, Columbia University Press, New York, 1954

Roth, Leland M., *McKim, Mead and White, Architects*, Thames & Hudson, London, 1984

Rothenstein, William, 'Art and the Municipality', in C.W. Sharpe, *The Sport of Civic Life, or Art and the Municipality*, Chas. Sharpe, Liverpool, 1909, pp. 5–9

Royal Academy, *Lord Leverhulme*, Royal Academy Galleries, London, 1980 (catalogue)

R.R.P., 'Current Architecture: Mission Church of St Barnabas, Shacklewell, London', *Architectural Review*, September, 1910

Saint, Andrew, *Towards a Social Architecture: The Role of Social Building in Post War England*, London, 1987

Sandon Studios Society, *Sandon Society of Artists Exhibition of Modern Art*, Blue Coat School, Liverpool, 2 May–30 May, 1908 (catalogue)

Schroeder, Jim, *The Life and Times of Wavertree Parish Church of the Holy Trinity 1794–1994*, 1994

Schuyler, M., 'Last Words About the World's Fair', *Architectural Record*, Jan/March, 1894

Scott, Geoffrey, *The Architecture of Humanism*, The Architectural Press, London, 1980

Scott, M., 'The Rebuilding of Peter Jones', *The Gazette*, 4 April, 1992, pp. 243–45

Service, Alastair, *Edwardian Architecture: A Handbook to Building Design in Britain 1890–1914*, Thames & Hudson, London, 1977

——*Edwardian Architecture and Its Origins*, The Architectural Press, London, 1975

——*London 1900*, Crosby Lockwood Staples, London, 1979

Sharp, D., and P. Wylde, 'Anglo-American Connections: Alfred Bossom and the American Skyscraper', *Architectural Association Quarterly*, Vol. 13, No. 2/3, 1982, p. 22

Sharp, Thomas, *English Panorama*, Dent, London, 1950

——*Town and Countryside*, Oxford University Press, London, 1932

——*Town Planning*, Penguin, Harmondsworth, 1940

Sharpe, C. W., *The Sport of Civic Life, or Art and the Municipality*, Chas. Sharpe, Liverpool, 1909

Sharples, Joseph (ed.), *Charles Reilly and The Liverpool School of Architecture 1904–1933*, Walker Art Gallery, Liverpool, 25 October, 1996–2 February, 1997, Liverpool University Press, Liverpool, 1996 (catalogue)

Shepheard, Peter, 'Lionel Budden Obituary', *RIBA Journal*, Vol. 63, No. 11, September, 1956, p. 478

Short, H., 'Where Will You Spend Eternity?', *Tribune*, 16 June, 1944

Simey, Margaret, *Charity Rediscovered: A Study of Philanthropic Efforts in Nineteenth Century Liverpool*, Liverpool University Press, Liverpool, 1951

Simey, T. S., 'The Village Green Revived', *Manchester Guardian*, 19 January, 1948

Simpson, Frederick M., 'Architectural Education and a School of Architecture', *The Builder*, Vol. LXXI, 1896, p. 539

——'Architectural Education No IV: University College Liverpool', *Architectural Review*, Vol. XIV, 1903, p. 87

——'Impressions in Architecture', *Architectural Association Notes*, VI, 1891, p. 21

——'The New Cathedral for Liverpool', *Architectural Review*, Vol. X, October, 1901, pp. 138–46

——'On the Need for an English School of Architecture', *The Architects' and Builders' News*, 21 February, 1912

——*The Scheme of Architectural Education Started at University College Liverpool in Connection with the City of Liverpool School of Architecture and Applied Art*, Marples, Liverpool, 1895

Spalding, Frances, *British Art Since 1900*, Thames & Hudson, London, 1986

Sphinx, 'City of Liverpool School of Architecture and Applied Arts', 1894, p. 3

——'Students' Union Building', Vol. XIII, No. 16, 1906, pp. 259–61

Sparke, Penelope, *An Introduction to Design and Culture in the Twentieth Century*, Allen & Unwin, London, 1986

Spiers, R. Phené, 'The French Diplome d'Architecture and the German System of Architectural Education', *RIBA Transactions*, Vol. XXXIV, 1884, p. 124

Stamp, Gavin, *The Great Perspectivists*, Trefoil Books, London, 1982

——*London 1900*, Academy Editions, London, 1978

——*Temples of Power*, Cygnet Press, Burford, 1979

Stamp, Gavin (ed.), *Britain in the Thirties*, Academy Editions, London, 1979

Stephenson, G., and C. Demarco (eds), *On a Human Scale: A Life in City Design*, Freemantle Arts Centre Press, Freemantle, 1992

Stirling, James, 'Reflections on the Beaux-Arts', *Architectural Design*, Vol. XLVIII, Nos 11–12, p. 88

Summerson, John, 'Architecture', in B. Ford (ed.), *Early Twentieth Century Britain: The Cambridge Cultural History*, Cambridge University Press, Cambridge, 1992

——'British Contemporaries of Frank Lloyd Wright', in Millard Weiss (ed.), *Studies in Western Art*, IV, Acts of the XX International Congress of the History of Art, Princeton University Press, Princeton, NJ, 1963

——*The Turn of the Century: Architecture in Britain around 1900*, Glasgow University Press, Glasgow, 1975

Sutcliffe, Anthony, *The Rise of Modern Urban Planning 1888–1914*, London, 1980

——*Towards the Planned City*, Basil Blackwell, London, 1981

Swenarton, Mark, 'The Role of History in Architectural Training', *Architectural History*, Vol. 30, 1987, pp. 201–15

Taylor, Nicholas, *The Village in the City*, Temple Smith, London, 1973

Thicknesse, Philip, 'The School of Architecture, Liverpool University', *RIBA Journal*, 28 August, 1909, pp. 639–94

Thirties Society Journal, 'Sir John Betjeman', No. 4, 1984, p. 1

Thistlewood, David, 'Modernism With Ancestry', Liverpool School of Architecture Centenary Review, *The Architects' Journal*, 11 May, 1995, pp. 60–65

Thomas, J., 'The Style Shall be Gothic', *The Architectural Review*, September 1975

Town Planning Review, 'Review of *Some Liverpool Streets and Buildings in Liverpool 1921* by C. H. Reilly', Vol. 9, December 1921, p. 184

University of Liverpool, *Redbrick University: A Portrait of University College and Liverpool University 1881–1981*, Senate House, Liverpool University, 11 May–3 July, 1981 (catalogue)

The University of Liverpool Recorder, 'Lionel Bailey Budden: Obituary', No. 12, October, 1956, p. 5

Waller, P. J., *Democracy and Sectarianism: A Political and Social History of Liverpool 1868–1939*, Liverpool University Press, Liverpool, 1981

Ware, William, *Address Before the Alumni Association of Columbia College on the twelfth of June 1888*, New York, 1888

Waterhouse, Paul, 'American Architecture', *RIBA Journal*, Vol. 3, Series 3, 1895

Watkin, David, *The Rise of Architectural History*, Architectural Press, London, 1980

Weaver, L., 'The Duchy of Cornwall Estate', *Country Life*, June, 1915, pp. 2–8

Whitefield, George, 'Liverpool Artists No IV: Professor Reilly', *The Liverpool Review*, Vol. III, 1928, pp. 22–25

Whiteley, Nigel, 'Modern Architecture Heritage and Englishness', *Architectural History*, Vol. 38, 1995, pp. 220–37

Willett, John, *Art in a City*, Methuen, London, 1967

Williams, A. M., 'The Details of the Problem', *Discovery*, August, 1947

Williams, Raymond, *Culture and Society: 1780–1950*, Chatto & Windus, London, 1958

Williams-Ellis, Clough, *The Adventure of Building*, The Architectural Press, London, 1946

——*The Architect*, Bles, London, 1929

——*England and the Octopus*, Bles, London, 1928

Wolfe, Lawrence, *The Reilly Plan: A New Way of Life*, Nicholson & Watson, London, 1945

Woodham, Jonathan, 'Design and Empire: British Design in the 1920s', *Art History*, Vol. 3, No. 2, June, 1980

Wright, Myles, *Lord Leverhulme's Unknown Venture*, Hutchinson Banham, London, 1982

——'The Work of the Liverpool School', *The Architects' Journal*, 20 May, 1937, pp. 847–48

Yerbury, F. R., 'Some AA Reminiscences', *The Builder*, Vol. CLXXIII, 1947, p. 697

Yorke, F. R. S., and C. Penn, *The Key to Modern Architecture*, London, 1939

Audio-Visual Material

'A Home of Your Own', *The New Jerusalem*, Barraclough/Carey Production for BBC TV, 1995

'A New Style of Architecture', *The Long Summer*, Uden Associate Production for
    Channel 4, 1993
Fry, E. Maxwell, *How Modern Architecture Came to England*, Pidgeon Audio Visual
    PAV 3/800, no date

Index

'n' following a page number denotes a reference in a footnote